How We Became Human

Studies in Violence, Mimesis, and Culture

SERIES EDITOR
William A. Johnsen

The Studies in Violence, Mimesis, and Culture Series examines issues related to the nexus of violence and religion in the genesis and maintenance of culture. It furthers the agenda of the Colloquium on Violence and Religion, an international association that draws inspiration from René Girard's mimetic hypothesis on the relationship between violence and religion, elaborated in a stunning series of books he has written over the last forty years. Readers interested in this area of research can also look to the association's journal, *Contagion: Journal of Violence, Mimesis, and Culture.*

How We Became Human

MIMETIC THEORY AND THE SCIENCE OF EVOLUTIONARY ORIGINS

Edited by Pierpaolo Antonello *and* Paul Gifford

Michigan State University Press · *East Lansing*

♾ The paper used in this publication meets the minimum requirements of ANSI/NISO Z39.48-1992 (R 1997) (Permanence of Paper).

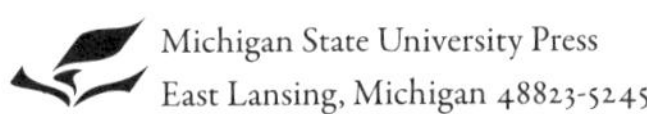
Michigan State University Press
East Lansing, Michigan 48823-5245

Printed and bound in the United States of America.

21 20 19 18 17 16 15 1 2 3 4 5 6 7 8 9 10

LIBRARY OF CONGRESS CONTROL NUMBER: 2015930572
ISBN: 978-1-61186-173-0 (pbk.)
ISBN: 978-1-60917-461-3 (ebook: PDF)
ISBN: 978-1-62895-233-9 (ebook: ePub)
ISBN: 978-1-62896-233-8 (ebook: Kindle)

Book design by Charlie Sharp, Sharp Des!gns, Lansing, Michigan
Cover design and original back cover art by David Drummond, Salamander Design, www.salamanderhill.com. Front cover image of pillars at the temple of Göbekli Tepe (Anatolia, Turkey) is by Vincent J. Musi, National Geographic Creative, and is used with permission.

green press INITIATIVE Michigan State University Press is a member of the Green Press Initiative and is committed to developing and encouraging ecologically responsible publishing practices. For more information about the Green Press Initiative and the use of recycled paper in book publishing, please visit *www.greenpressinitiative.org*.

Visit Michigan State University Press at *www.msupress.org*

Contents

PART FIVE. THE EVOLUTIONARY HERMENEUTICS OF *HOMO RELIGIOSUS*

Acknowledgments

This book originated in a series of conferences held between 2009 and 2011 at St John's College, Cambridge and Stanford University. Our most grateful thanks go to the Girardian foundation Imitatio, a project of the Thiel Foundation, and in particular to Lindy Fishburne, for the outstanding financial support, which made all our endeavors possible. Our thanks are also due to the Master and the Fellows of St John's College for invaluable logistical provision and financial support. Jean-Pierre Dupuy gave us much appreciated advice and help with the organization of the Stanford event; and we are indebted to Noah Burbank, Jimmy Kaltreider, and Christopher Woods for their contribution in successfully resolving organizational and logistical difficulties on both sides of the pond. Our warmest gratitude goes to René and Martha Girard for their help, friendship, hospitality, and kind encouragement throughout.

We are most grateful to Ian Hodder, Jason Quinlan, and Yildiz Dirmit for their help in acquiring the Çatalhöyük images featured in the chapters "Interpreting Archaeological Data: Mimetic Readings of Çatalhöyük and Göbekli Tepe" and "Self-transcendence and Tangled Hierarchies in Çatalhöyük"; also to Jens Notroff and the DAI, Oriental Department for the

Göbekli Tepe images included in the chapter "Rethinking the Neolithic Revolution: Symbolism and Sacrifice at Göbekli Tepe."

The cover image for this volume, featuring a detail of the T-pillar at the Neolithic temple of Göbekli Tepe, was most generously provided by National Geographic.

This book is dedicated to the memory of Bob Hamerton-Kelly, whose energy, enthusiasm, and inspiration were instrumental in the realization of this project.

Introduction

According to the American philosopher Elliot Sober, "Biologists interested in culture are often struck by the absence of viable general theories in the social sciences. All of biology is united by the theory of biological evolution. Perhaps progress in the social sciences is impeded because there is no general theory of cultural evolution" (Sober 1994, 486). Likewise, anthropologists, historians, sociologists, or natural scientists who start off in search of social theories compatible with scientific premises, and capable of explaining how "culture" or "religion" emerged, eventually end up reverting to Émile Durkheim's theorizations—or else find themselves going away empty-handed. For this reason, twentieth-century theorization has progressively expelled any consideration of the origins and the genesis of human culture and institutions, considered as a totally unattainable moment of human proto-history—a "lost Object" to be vigorously "put out of mind," as decreed by the late-twentieth-century ideological turn against all "grand narratives."

From his groundbreaking *Violence and the Sacred* (1972), René Girard's mimetic theory is presented, notwithstanding, as elucidating "the origins of culture." More radically, in *Things Hidden since the Foundation of the World*

(1978), Girard sketched a hypothesis of hominization based on anthropological, ethnological, and ethological premises in an effort—certainly under-refined at the methodological and expository levels, but courageous and supercharged with fruitful insights—to define a possible scenario of the developmental emergence of culture. He claims that the theory is capable of illuminating in a decisive new way the hidden and momentous things that Darwin saw when he hinted in the closing pages of *On the Origin of Species* that "much light will be thrown on the origin of man and his history" (Darwin [1859] 1958, 449). Girard goes where Darwin feared to tread. Girard claims to explain the emergence of culture among hominids, and to provide the missing explanatory links connecting the animal to the human, while simultaneously accounting for the differential emergence of humanity from animal antecedents. This is a bold move, coming from a new direction. Girard's theory is one of the very few anthropological hypotheses that tries to explain social and cultural events in generative terms—while viewing human origins from a vantage point in evolved human complexity, at which level they are visible still in contemporary echoes and traces of origin (there are, in Darwinian terms, always "fossils," though in this case, with a vigorous, subterranean "phylogenetic" afterlife).

In general, and more philosophically, this approach engages the whole sense and significance of what Darwin also calls "the descent of Man": that is, the provenance and strange exceptionality of *Homo sapiens* within the natural world. Darwin himself—though he, of course, reveals and makes plausible the momentous fact of human derivation from animal antecedents—cannot really explain the articulation of nature to culture, or comprehend in any full and proper sense how the transition from animal to human is accomplished, still less say to what effect and with what meaning this momentous transition has occurred. Indeed, the way he, in his time and by his lights, conceived the "descent of man" placed him under an inhibiting shadow of reductionism and polemic that made him shrink from examining these matters too closely, even had he possessed the tools to do so.

The proposed enterprise of the present volume is, in some sense, to follow Girard—better equipped and with all the advantages of hindsight—in going where Darwin feared to tread. We shall be attempting to justify the claim already entered by the French philosopher of science Michel Serres—that Girard's work provides a Darwinian theory of culture, because it "proposes a dynamic, shows an evolution and gives a universal explanation" of culture (Serres 1994, 219–20).

Girard's mimetic theory—as it came to be labeled because of the foundational role played by imitation—indeed offers to account for the emergence, for endogenous ecological reasons, of a specifically human culture: these reasons being not purely and simply related to the physical evolution of specific individuals within a given species, but rather to the emergence of systemic group behavior, which eventually and gradually shaped the coevolution of both the physical and the sociocultural potentials of this one particular species.

It provides a mechanism and a model of social interaction based on instinctual structures and patterns observable in animal behavior, such as imitation, redirected aggression, ritualization, and cultural reinforcement. Developing through "catastrophic" or "critical" events, these potentials bring about new forms of social organization that can only be described as "cultural," since they provoke the emergence of "proto-institutions," and these in turn become the regulatory principles that stabilize and reinforce the cohesion of the social group—something no longer based on instinctual and proto-cultural patterns (hierarchical systems of social organization in animals, submission rituals, etc.), but now on symbolic codes and fully ritual practices.

Recognizing Mimetic Theory

What makes Girard's theory of the origins of culture an original and promising approach-track to the key evolutionary problem of "hominization"? At first sight, and to the uninitiated glance, little or nothing. Here, to all seeming, is a very broad, deductively cogent, but still highly speculative anthropology, which, in point of academic practice, has little direct currency in the social sciences—though it has certainly caught the attention of the more curious anthropologists, and of many eminent scholars working today in the humanities.

In the research profiles of anthropology departments, however, at least in English-speaking universities, Girard does not feature prominently (if at all). Yet hundreds of books and articles have been devoted to his theory;

conferences and workshops are periodically organized worldwide in disciplines as diverse as political science and international relations, theology and literary studies. The reasons for this patchy and selective reception may be situated in the particular history of how the theory emerged, and the particular academic context that helped to shape it. Girard is a curious anomaly: an exponent of a certain variant type of "French theory" speaking within, from, and to an unlikely—initially unscientific, humanities-dominated—environment, on the "wrong" side of the Atlantic in relation to his native France. He is, of course, well-known in literature departments and among Continental philosophers for a series of books he published in the 1960s and 1970s, in particular *Deceit, Desire, and the Novel* (1961), *Violence and the Sacred* (1972), and *Things Hidden since the Foundation of the World* (1978). He came to be widely discussed within theological circles starting from the late 1980s, particularly with reference to his theory of the violent origins of religion and the conforming-yet-exceptionalist role of the Judeo-Christian tradition within this general history. The key texts for this further understanding are *The Scapegoat* (1982), *Job* (1985), and *I See Satan Falling Like Lightning* (1999).

Girard has been defined as an "untimely thinker" (to pick up Nietzsche's expression), in the sense that he has always been out of tune with the ideological and theoretical trends of his late-twentieth-century (postmodern) culture-context. In the case of his first book, for instance, while traditional literary scholars would typically look for the uniqueness of a work of art, and for the distinctive differences carried by these enduring classics, and while postmodern ones would discuss their representational codes and signs to the exclusion of any underlying relation to the real world, Girard thinks in terms of the exceptional insights offered by these works, when questioned comparatively, into the structural patterns and functioning of a real human "universal" (i.e., desire). This comparative method, together with a recurring emphasis on the structural patterns it can display and bring to our cognizance, returns in later books, such as in *Violence and the Sacred* and *Things Hidden*, with Girard's analysis of ancient and classical myths, as well as key anthropological and ethnological studies on the role of religion and sacrificial practices in different cultural contexts—both these sources being viewed as forms of writing capable of acting as stepping stones back to the valid hearing of lost origins.

By the late 1960s and 1970s, Girard had indeed begun to constitute himself as a self-taught, unsystematic anthropologist, of a type inspired by the tradition of the early twentieth-century English anthropological school (James George Frazer, Bronisław Malinowski, William Robertson Smith, Alfred Radcliffe-Brown, among others). Although he claimed he was never influenced by Émile Durkheim in the elaboration of his theory, Girard also shares the Durkheimian view that it is impossible to understand the evolution of culture if we discount the emergence and development of religion as a distinctively human phenomenon (Durkheim [1915] 1995). For Girard, as for Durkheim, religion is the great matrix of all things cultural: initially, in its first beginnings, culture is not distinct from religion, since it is "religion," or rather the "sacred," that originally generates and informs all cultural, social, and political acts, beliefs, and practices in archaic societies. Girard would actually claim that the matrix of the archaic sacred represents still today the secretly surviving generative logic from which stem many of the acts, attitudes, and practices of the most technologically advanced and secularized societies. In evolutionary terms, therefore, his mimetic theory asserts that man is first and fundamentally "the religious animal." In so doing, it addresses the question posed by Pascal Boyer (and others), based on an epidemiological account of cultural evolution: why are religions, and "religious concepts . . . so 'catching' that we find them in many different cultural settings, whilst other concepts of (seemingly) equal potential use or cognitive effect are very rare" (Boyer 2001, 94)? To put it simply: because it is generative of all human culture; it is the principle of its origination and development.

Girard's work of this period invokes parallel work by a number of historians of religion who have studied the intrinsic logic of sacrifice and its diffusion in Indo-European cultures, such as Georges Dumézil, Mircea Eliade, or more recently Bruce Lincoln. However, in this company Girard lacks systematicity, since his theory is primarily interpretative in nature, and never aimed to produce any form of classificatory mapping. What he leaves us, therefore, are the fruits of a superior and talented art of interpretation, pursued—albeit with a tenacious underlying logic of vision and enquiry—according to the many particular tasks of textual analysis he set himself. We can "take him wrong" in two ways, therefore: on the one hand, by expecting him to proceed discursively like Hegel, or methodologically like Darwin; and, on the other, by failing to recognize that he bears, deep in the "flesh of the mind" (Paul Valéry's expression), the imprint of a Cartesian culture, and its immense and searching consequentiality of rational understanding.

For all his cherry-picking particularism, Girard's theoretical move into evolutionary anthropology implied a more boldly strategic approach than was native to his predecessors. As he came to recognize (Girard, Antonello, and de Castro Rocha 2007), his theory of hominization is compatible and continuous with Darwin's, perhaps even to the extent of forming a parallel construction in the domain of human cultural development. More specifically, Girard's theory addresses with cogency and insight the recent growth of interest in using evolutionary approaches to attempt to explain many of the distinctive and uniquely human attributes that constitute religious traditions, as these are understood in a broadly comparatist sense. The perspective instanced by Girard's mimetic theory may also act as a bridge between the long tradition in anthropology and folklore studies that attempts to organize the world religious traditions essentially from a descriptive standpoint, according to various categorical systems, in order to demonstrate diversity and commonalities in their major features (e.g., classic theories by Tylor 1873; Frazer 1922; Durkheim 1915; Evans-Pritchard 1965; Eliade 1958), and the recent interest in utilizing evolutionary analyses, in explanatory and causal terms, to develop hypotheses concerning the most common shared attributes of religious traditions (e.g., Boyer 2001; Wilson 2002; see Pals 1996 and Preus 2000 for an overview of some classic evolutionary approaches).

However, major claims for his theory have remained deliberately understated by Girard himself and have never been systematically pursued by scholars working on his theory. With the exception of one section in Girard's conversation with Pierpaolo Antonello and João Cezar de Castro Rocha (Girard, Antonello, and de Castro Rocha 2007), and the volume *Mimesis and Science*, edited by Scott Garrels (2011), there has, indeed, been very little work done that has consciously espoused this perspective. Likely reasons for this deficit are the intrinsic difficulty of the transdisciplinary thinking required, and especially the problem of a common terminology, aggravated by and aggravating the poverty of existing interdisciplinary communication.

Opening Questions of Methodology, Epistemology, and Hermeneutics

Even if we recognize the specificity of Girard's approach and perceive its complementarity in relation to Darwin's, there remain formidable problems of methodology and hermeneutics in bringing together the biological and the cultural dimensions of evolution.

To make a pioneering foray into the uncharted but potentially rich territory of the interface between Darwin's theory of evolution and Girard's theory of cultural origins is, first and fundamentally, to raise certain key questions.

What are the challenges mimetic theory poses to evolutionary thinking? How well does it account for both the continuities and the "quantum leap" involved in hominization? How do we assess the offer of a new intelligibility that mimetic theory brings to evolutionary thinking? How possible—and how fruitful—is it to review evolutionary theory, and in particular theories of cultural evolution, in continuity with, and by the light of, Girard's theory? And, if this theory can be construed as illuminating the emergence of culture from nature, hence also the transition from animal to human, in which respects, then, will it produce a wider vision of evolution, differing from the "big picture" Darwin himself saw and shrank from—the picture that still often sets the agenda of evolutionary thinking today?

Has Girard's theory, in principle, the potential to become for the human and social sciences something akin to the integrating framework of theory that the biological sciences received from Darwin's evolutionary hypothesis? Finally, what is the part of religion in this discussion, and how does the central role given by mimetic theory to the sacred as the matrix of all things cultural refashion, in a cumulatively fundamental way, the parameters within which the relationship between evolution and religion are discussed?

It will be clear enough from this agenda that there can be no hope of closure in the vast matter of "how we became human." The thickness, range, and complexity of the issues raised exclude this outcome, and, if this point were in any doubt, the nature of the contributions to be discovered in this volume—heterogeneous and eclectic both in terms of disciplinary approaches included and the play of hermeneutical viewpoints espoused—would already provide testimony enough. They form an index of complexity, and this in turn gives fair warning that what follows is just the beginning of an expanding research program that, far from being exhausted within the scope of this volume (and its companion), finds in them, rather, an interrogative and pathfinding first foray.

One of the most formidable methodological challenges, posed immediately by any such enterprise as that envisaged here, is to know whether it is possible to have any sort of fruitful exchange between the humanities (which consciously and consistently assume human difference) and the social and exact sciences (which view human difference as continuous with, and therefore reducible to, the "natural world"). Can a theory that was formulated in a very specific, "idiosyncratic" language and with a set of conceptual parameters borrowed from history, literary criticism, cultural anthropology, philosophy, and biblical studies migrate profitably into a different domain like evolutionary culture theory? Is the Girardian hypothesis of origins, to change the metaphor, translatable?

This challenge—the first of many that Girard's theory poses to our various disciplinary comfort zones—is the one we most attempted to take on board in a series of conferences organized at Cambridge University and at Stanford (2009–12). The present volume, along with its companion, is a distillation of these exploratory reflections.[1]

It is not, it should be stated clearly, that mimetic theory needs to fit into the discursive and theoretical parameters of fields such as evolutionary anthropology, neo-evolutionism, sociobiology, evolutionary culture theory, or archaeology. The point is rather one of knowing, on the one hand, how to corroborate Girard's claims in evidential terms, in the light of the paradigmatic convergence of many scientific disciplines (sometimes at odds with the premises of Girardian theory); on the other, it is to isolate a series of convergent issues engaging mimetic theory and other relatable disciplines, using a terminology that allows a certain degree of discursive translatability, hence also enabling an imaginative "hearing" of the "other." This is where we need to be if we are to prompt the required encounters-in-dialogue, bringing mutually profitable cross-fertilization of ideas. In this sense, one aim of the present volume is to provide an opening friendly to diverse backgrounds of method, and to various orientations of interpretation and theory.

At a basic level, we would like to try to re-present mimetic theory in such a way that it would make a good deal of sense for scholars outside the humanities. This is to be done by highlighting key issues explored by Girard's theory; by showing relevant links to conundrums at the core of much thinking in many social and empirical sciences; and by touching on the points where the scientific analysis of cultural evolution grinds to a halt for want of a more encompassing perspective to frame and direct the proposed analysis.

Conversely, because mimetic theory has been presented by Girard in very broad and often speculative terms, it certainly needs much greater theoretical refinement, so as to provide maximum applicability at various levels of complexity (biological, neurocognitive, ethological, anthropological, cultural), thus helping scholars prepared to engage with mimetic theory to have a better grasp of what is at stake, and to see how a shared common-core enquiry can be fruitfully articulated and pursued. On the other side of the spectrum, our book would also aim to enter into the sustained dialogue between social and natural sciences and theologians in the common definition of the *vexata quaestio* of the relationship between evolutionary thinking and religion, proposing a theory that posits religion and the sacred as the most fundamental matrix of cultural development in humans.

Mimetic Theory and Evolutionary Theory

Inserting, reshaping, and rephrasing mimetic theory within the parameters of evolutionary theory, particularly as applied to human culture, is by no means an easy feat. There is a wall of preconceived refusal that is called upon to disappear. For Girard has often been dismissed peremptorily, at a glance, as evidence-light, speculative, highly suspect, and implausible.

Yet, as this volume will show, at many levels of its explanatory structure, mimetic theory does rely a very great deal on most carefully sifted evidence: at least, for all the basic elements of genetic elucidation that are structurally crucial to the Girardian scenario of human origins. These may be immediately specified and tested in this volume: the ubiquity and effects of imitation or mimesis (amply surveyed by Garrels both in his chapter, "Convergence between Mimetic Theory and Imitation Research," and in Garrels 2011); the ethology of redirected aggression and emissary victimization (see David P. Barash's chapter, "The Three Rs: Retaliation, Revenge, and (Especially) Redirected Aggression," and Girard, Antonello, and de Castro Rocha 2007);

the foundational role of violence (discussed by Melvin Konner and Zoey Reeve in this volume); the historical presence of ritual, and in particular ritualistic sacrifice, as the matrix for religion and culture (eloquently evoked by Durham in his chapter, "Coevolution and Mimesis," and illustrated, both by Girard himself and by others, in crucial archaeological case studies in part 4); the link between ritualization and the emergence of the symbolic activity (as discussed by Antonello in his chapter, "Maladaptation, Counterintuitiveness, and Symbolism," with reference to the work of Terrence Deacon).

Inversely, and in a complementary dimension of dialogue, mimetic theory may be used as a sort of elucidating frame of reference that would help evolutionary theorists to focus and redynamize large parts of their attempt to draw together perspectives on the origins and evolution of religion-and-culture already available. Such attempts are often challenged by difficulties and conundrums, as well as beset by a certain spirit of evasiveness and other inadequacies of theory.

The first strategic problem in the dialogue between mimetic theory and evolutionary thinking is the limited view, which prevails not infrequently among scientists, of what "culture" and "religion" are. There are, indeed, frequent difficulties in dealing with the symbolic order as such from a scientific standpoint. Ernest Gellner wryly comments that "if a native says something sensible it is primitive technology, but if it sounds very odd then it is symbolic" (Gellner 1987, 163). There is indeed an interesting ambivalence in current evolutionary accounts of the process of hominization: on the one hand, researchers assume proto-humans to be rational and consciously intentional agents (with reference, for instance, to hunting, tool-making, foraging); but then, on the other, they assume that religious practices, despite being so ubiquitous and widespread, are merely "superstitious," i.e., are forms of arbitrary and fundamentally "irrational" behavior.[2] Moreover, scientists (unlike Darwin himself) tend to see cultural evolution as a secondary matter, to be often explained as "the product of choices made in the marketplace of cultural possibilities" (Durham 1991, 332). They are looking at culture as if it were merely an optional, accessory, and sometimes almost "decorative" adjunct of biologically evolved humanity, whereas the core of Girard's concern is to recognize that matters of religion and culture are, on the contrary, realities of structuring and transformational significance in both cultural and biological terms. In relation to the origins of religion,

Terrence Deacon and Tyrone Cashman have also argued against the various evolutionary approaches to religious phenomena that are simply framed in functional terms:

> [They] are reductive accounts that largely treat the content of religious reflections and spiritual experiences as mere incidental artifacts of more fundamental mechanisms, and not possessing intrinsic meaning or value beyond these instrumental ends. As a result, they offer impoverished accounts of what might be described as the transformational experiences and ultimate meaning that religious ideas and practices provide to their believers. If religious traditions were merely epiphenomenal, they would likely not be ubiquitously present and they would probably be far more diverse in content. If they were merely cultural adaptations or parasitic memes it would be difficult to explain the powerful social functions they serve and the apparent psychological value they provide. Moreover, the first thing to explain is why essentially all societies of humans have some form of spiritual tradition while the other species of social animals do not, at least as religion is conventionally understood (i.e. as having to do with perceptions and beliefs related to spiritual beings or forces). They offer no explanation or place for any contribution to the creation of novel *meanings or values* derived from spiritual practices, beliefs, or experiences. In this respect, reductionist explanations ignore the role of religious experiences in expanding the human perspective beyond the personal and the mundane. (Deacon and Cashman 2009)

There is in fact nothing mundane in a primitive society, since everything emerges from ritualistic religious and sacred practice. Religion is embedded in the social and it is an expression of it. The British archaeologist Ian Hodder underscores, for instance, how in the Pre-Pottery Neolithic B (PPNB) site of Çatalhöyük, as in other nearby coeval villages, "many (if not all) daily acts seem to have been embedded in ritual." Daily practice was formalized by division of space and activity. Food is laid out in a ritual manner, "various doorways depend on social positions," the rooms of each house "incorporated into one building all the differentiated functions that we would expect to see in the different parts of a modern town—residential, industrial, religious, burial. . . . In the house, symbolic and practical aspects of daily life are thoroughly integrated" (Hodder 2006, 110–12). Religion, rituals, and the sacred are the sources of all cultural and symbolic meaning for the first humans because they organize semantically and symbolically in a "hierarchical structure of meaning," as Giuseppe Fornari puts it in his chapter in this volume, the natural and the societal world, which before the emergence of religion was overtly unreflexive.

The Emergence of Culture

A second point of contention in the potential dialogue between mimetic theory and evolutionary thinking relates to the problem of origins (of culture and religion). In most of the current accounts on the evolutionary emergence of culture, we do not have any "origin," but mainly the progressive accumulation of genetic and physical traits judged likely to bring about at some point the expected—indeed, already covertly supplied—"emergence." Culture, morality, religion, the symbolic order: all are explained as a function of encephalization and the growing of the neocortex. Or else they are referred, by way of explanation, to the transformation of the larynx and the vocal apparatus (which seems at best one enabling condition). For the post-Saussurean twentieth century, the sudden appearance of language, as genetically preprogrammed and neurologically wired in our brain, is invoked as "decisive"; while rituals and taboos are very often accounted for (but in fact discounted) via the platitudes of a reductive cultural materialism.

Characteristically, the emergence and evolution of culture are seen as linear and progressive, a form of "phyletic gradualism," involving no "punctuated equilibria," or "quantum leaps." At which point, the notion of "culture" can operate as an unobserved deus ex machina precisely because it is mistaken for a sufficiently explained "given."[3] The problem in this "phyletic" understanding of culture may be due to the fact that the analysis of cultural evolution has borrowed the genetic model of Neo-Darwinism, while overlooking the particularity of cultural phenomena—which are always socially mediated constructions. Culture is generally reckoned to be difficult to analyze in evolutionary terms unless it is broken down into manageable units. Yet, cultural processes are not transmitted, and cannot be understood, as a series of discrete parts; they are and must be grasped as holistic process.

For Sperber (1996), Atran (2001), and Boyer (1999), among others, cultural transmission does not involve the accurate replication of discrete, gene-like entities (for a general discussion of this point, see Henrich, Boyd, and Richerson 2008). This remark is even more true of Girard's theory, since religion and culture are emergent phenomena and their emergence is structured by means of ritualization, giving a continuous stream of behavior irreducible to single steps. In this sense Girard's theory, in spite of cognate labeling, cannot be associated at any level with Richard Dawkins's highly problematic "memetics" (Dawkins 1976; Atran 2001).

Rather than an accountancy of the genetic accumulation of physical traits, Girard's theory is relational and systemic. It is not a sociobiological theory *stricto sensu*, i.e., it does not posit that culture could be explained solely and sufficiently via genetic determinism, or merely as an accumulation of artifacts or mentifacts. Just as the biological cannot be reduced to the chemical or the physical, the cultural, though it can be approached through the biological or the neurocognitive processes it presupposes, cannot be simply reduced to them, since it expresses a new level of systemic complexity—an emergence of novelty. Mimetic theory is a "strong emergence" theory, in which the emergent property is irreducible to the sum of its prior individual constituents (for this, see Dupuy and Varela 1992; Kauffmann 1992, 2007; Goodenough and Deacon 2008).

Mimetic theory also envisages the cultural coevolution of the human. Culture emerged and was initially shaped by biological structures and instinctual patterns; but as it progressively became itself endogenous, and an increasingly complex and autonomous shaping "force," it altered biological processes in response to cultural change. As William H. Durham states in his opening chapter of this volume, "Coevolution and Mimesis," Girard provides in fact a cogent scenario in which the first moral and social "impositions" (i.e., forms of coercion or social binding) structured those "secondary values" (socially transmitted cultural standards), which began to shape "primary values" (hardwired and programmed into the human organism) in a coevolution of genetics and culture.

Violent Origins

Another point of contention may relate to the fact that mimetic theory moves decisively against a surreptitious Rousseau-ism that tints or taints the ideological premises of much thinking in evolutionary theory—i.e., the assumption that human beings are in general naturally cooperative and "good spirited," and, consequently, that institutions are contractualistic in nature. Girard claims that they are "rational," certainly, in his realist-functional sense, but he firmly excludes the possibility that they could be, at the dawn of hominization, any form of social contract between rational agents—Paul Dumouchel writes in his chapter, "Genes and Mimesis," that, like Darwin's theory, "Girard's theory is radically non-agential."

However, this is one of the problems with the current paradigm in the human and social sciences (maybe expected from scholars in the humanities, but surprising when it comes from natural scientists): despite the evidence, there is a reluctance to see the pervasive and foundational role of violence in the building of our societies. Both Barash and Konner in their chapters speak at length about the structural, ethological, and anthropological underpinnings of human violent behavior, and there is a good deal of evidence in this respect from the literature in the field. Moreover, we could argue that cooperation and altruistic behavior are evident in animals as well as in humans (Shermer 2004),[4] and thus they should be regarded in general as "unproblematic" from an evolutionary standpoint: they are a theoretical concern for evolutionary theorists who need to overcome the stumbling block of the dominant paradigm of individual selection, to solve the theoretical conundrum of selflessness and group behavior.

This is not the place to discuss competing theories of the emergence of altruistic behavior in humans—whether based on kin selection, reciprocal altruism, or costly signaling (for a general discussion see Nowak 2006); for mimetic theory, it is only tangentially relevant. Two general and framing points are, however, worth making here. Firstly, there is no question in mimetic theory of an either/or as applied to altruism and violence. The hallmark of the human is that it is exceptionally violent in proportion to its capability for highly developed altruism: these are reciprocal, if inverse, effects of one single, mimetically supercharged process of transformation (the phenomenon of "parochial altruism," discussed by Reeve in "Mechanisms of Internal Cohesion," is one of the many examples). Secondly, because it treats mimetically engendered, systemic, and violent group behavior, mimetic theory always requires us to think at the social and group level, rather than at the genetically programmed and individual one. Boyd and Richerson (1985) have particularly argued for the possibility of group selection at the cultural level. A well-known treatment of altruism, *Unto Others*, by Elliot Sober and D. S. Wilson (1998), has also emphasized the need to think in terms of "multilevel selection": groups that cooperate better may have out-reproduced those that did not. In their view, the more internally cooperative cultures may have been more likely qua cultures to survive and reproduce, in spite of the depressed genetic fitness of particularly norm-observing individuals. The key point for Girard, however, is not only enhanced cooperation per se, but cooperation having as a perpetual shadow its other face of violence—in particular intraspecific violence. The Darwinian—and Girardian—point is that groups that were able to find means to regulate and control internally generated violence and infighting must have out-reproduced and outlived those that did not. This two-sided potential was shaped by the development of norms, taboos, and ritualistic practices; and these were later structured and organized in the form of institutions, all stemming from the evolutionary traction provided by what Girard calls the "emissary mechanism."

According to this same account, "religion" does not figure as a byproduct of the evolution of mental and conceptual tools, but of the Darwinian need to survive and adapt. Mimetic theory does not share this nineteenth-century positivistic take on the role of religion in human cultural development. It sees that religious practices were, on the contrary, the "safest" way to deal with structural violence, with the fear and danger of mob phenomena: they were, in this functional sense, highly rational. Not that they were devised "intentionally," but they are, as Darwin shows all evolutionary adaptation to be, "advantageous" in the sense of fit-for-purpose. Equally, mimetic theory observes that adaptation has been structured here by basic cognitive and ethological mechanisms still visible today, under specific social conditions, in animals and humans. Religion, as we shall see more fully in a number of contributions, is the environmental (societal) form of binding and bonding that channels, but also enables and drives, cognitive development. If religion is in any way cognitively "natural" to children (as the cognitive "science of religion" has frequently suggested), it has become so because religion itself, way back in our evolutionary past, formed the culture-world within which infants underwent a self-organizing process of formation.

Myths of Origins

Can we articulate freshly a thesis already overfamiliar to many working on mimetic theory, while appearing still novel and seemingly simplistic to those coming to it for the first time, and from a variety of other disciplinary horizons? Perhaps we can, if we take seriously the deductive-inductive nature of a theory that, starting from a strategic understanding of the role of imitation in structuring individual and social psychology in the contemporary world, moves regressively backwards towards a projected hypothesis of human origins.[5] Such a projection highlights elements of the problem of hominization not previously given due weight, or, at least, not thought out consequentially. Let us specify these: the key role of imitation (or mimesis, in Girard's vocabulary) in supercharging group intelligence in the higher primates; the axis of developmental adjustment provided by the perils of specifically human violence, growing exponentially in tandem with the differentiating superiority of cooperative group intelligence in the hominid line; the neglected (but inescapable) problem of controlling and managing the threat of social implosion though intra- and intergroup violence; the failure of hardwired mechanisms sufficient for controlling animal rivalries and conflict; the need for symbolic-ritual controls on violent disorder in humans; the self-organizing "invention" or "discovery" of the victimary mechanism, which, as it fulfills the required saving function of social lightning conductor, simultaneously provides the elements of all specifically human cultural institutions, thus founding "human culture" as such. Readers wishing to get to know this account, or preparing to reappraise it in company with our contributors, may like to read the first section of *Things Hidden since the Foundation of the World* devoted to "hominization" (Girard 1987b, 3–140) and the further discussions on related matters in *Evolution and Conversion* (Girard, Antonello, and de Castro Rocha 2007).

As a preliminary formulation that may help to clarify some argumentative and theoretical steps in the understanding of mimetic theory, we should underscore the fact that the theory takes shape as narrative of origins, deductively essentialized. This should not come as a surprise, considering that a narrative formulation is consistent with the structuring role and developmental emergence of human culture. The anthropologist Terrence Deacon, for instance, claims that, at a deep anthropological and cognitive level, humans present a "tendency to create a symbolic narrative" of group or tribal identity and world provenance, with all that this entails, in function "of the way symbolic communication reorganizes the otherwise orthogonally functioning mnemonic systems of the mammalian brain" (Deacon and Cashman 2009, 5). Narratives are the forms through which common knowledge and cultural understanding are organized and transmitted through generations. In the same vein, Merlin Donald in *Origins of the Modern Mind* (1991) argues that "myth is the prototypal and fundamental, integrative mind-tool," which "integrate[s] a variety of events in a temporal and causal framework":

> The pre-eminence of myth in early human society is testimony to the fact that humans were using language for a totally new kind of integrative thought. Therefore, the possibility must be entertained that the primary human adaptation wasn't language qua language, but rather integrative, initially mythical, thought. Modern humans developed language in response to pressure to improve their conceptual apparatus, not vice versa. (215)

Girard's formulation resonates with, and actually derives from, those artifacts that account for our "lost" origins: myths and rituals, seen as vestigial remnants of a slow process of cultural elaboration and revisitation of the originary generative matrix. Our archaeological data and interpretation, Girard seems to suggest, should not rely only on physical and material remnants but also on cultural ones. We cannot understand the origin of religion and culture if we do not take into account the primordial cultural forms at our disposal: myths and religious texts alike. The Girardian articulation of the notion of mythical origin narratives was made possible by a comparative reading of archaic myths and rituals, as well as of Greek tragedy (which registers an undoubted "memory of origins"); but also of religious texts, in particular the Bible and the Vedic scriptures (Girard 2011), all of which are regarded as expressing a common anthropological insight in relation to ritual sacrifice, sacrificial mechanisms, scapegoating, and mob phenomena generally. This is one of the greatest challenges that Girard presents to less imaginative or less supple theories of cultural evolution. Mimetic theory takes myths and rituals seriously, in the sense that these things are seen to express a referential concern for actual events, while yet supposing that these accounts of real events were then gradually transfigured in the telling, as also in the highly symbolic institutional forms that enacted their useful functionality.

However, there are obvious difficulties in constructing an evidential argument based on myths, since more than physical objects (fossils), cultural products generally (myths, rituals, pictorial representations, artifacts, etc.), by their very nature, are themselves subject to interpretation, requiring also a context-referred, historically and culturally situated understanding of their meaning. This difficulty is compounded by a protracted ideological resistance to any methodically useful comparative approach to anthropology and religion (Golsan 1993, 107–24). At this point, it would appear that a careful and systematic procedure of comparing the structures, motifs, and functioning of myths in most widely different ethnic and religious traditions could help substantiate Girard's hypothesis.

Imitation and Violence

An interesting and quite fruitful counterexample to the general hostility to comparative anthropological analysis is Bruce Lincoln's work (1975, 1981). By building on the approach of Georges Dumézil and what has been called the "genetic model" of Indo-European mythology (see also Littleton 1973; Larson, Littleton, and Puhvel 1974), Lincoln documents an impressive array of correspondences among myths about the origins and peopling of the world. As Durham explains recapitulatively in his opening chapter, Lincoln uses these correspondences, structural as well as linguistic, to reconstruct the outline of the ancestral "Proto-Indo-European" creation myth. That myth centers around what he calls the first or primordial sacrifice—a sacrifice that both created the world and serves as the mythical prototype of all sacrifice in traditional Indo-European religion; indeed, it served as prototype of all creative action.

A similar narrative of genesis, derived from these sources, is also formulated by Girard, who finds an essentialized image in this defining proto-event that stands at the beginning of humanity's historical career-in-culture—a scenario of origin to be regarded as "originating" for the emergence of both symbolicity and proto-institutions. This proto-event could be defined as an episode of "spontaneous scapegoating," though it later becomes ritualized in a concerted way, developing then in the forms of human and/or animal sacrifice. This represents an intraspecific, systemic, endogenously triggered mechanism operating to "control" internal violence within a given group of hominids or humans.

The use of the term "scapegoating," though handy, is somewhat anachronistic from a historical standpoint. It is also potentially misleading—for this concept, in its fully modern sense (i.e., on a level with the understanding of our contemporaries and readers), is actually a much later acquisition, traced by Girard, via the precocious part-recognition it finds in the biblical Book of Leviticus, to a first set of occurrences in seventeenth-century Europe (for a general discussion see Dawson 2013). For the sake of clarity in the context of transdisciplinary academic discussion of human origins, it has been largely replaced in this volume by the other terms—"emissary victimization" or "arbitrary persecution"—that Girard also uses.

Social structures, social order, so Girard argues, emerge out of a primordial disorder of rivalry, conflict, and violence: they arise through an exasperation of the mimetic emulation and struggle that, for natural or systemic reasons (famine, disease, climate change, factors of internal or external competition, and feuds), periodically emerged within primitive societies, above all when the number of individuals composing human groupings increased above a certain critical level, altering and disrupting the stability of groups based on kin and social recognition (possibly related to the "Dunbar's number" [Dunbar 1992]).[6]

However, this is not the full story, for the stability of human social groups is also threatened by the same neurocognitive mechanism at the base of their biological and evolutionary success: imitation. As its name suggests, the very basis of Girard's mimetic theory is imitation, in particular the imitation of other people's intentionality, in respect of desires, preferences, and goals. In the past fifteen years, the discovery of so-called "mirror neurons" has become the neurocognitive basis for a new understanding of human behavior that confirms the centrality of imitation in the cognitive and relational makeup of the human mind and human behavior (Garrels 2005–6, 2011). One of the corroborating elements that comes from this research was addressed by Girard in his work a few decades before: mimesis or imitation is prelinguistic and preconscious, and therefore it works at the level of "reflex" reactions, rather than that of conscious and willed intentionality; it is also partially blind to itself (Gallese 2009, 2010).[7] We learn by imitating others, pre-reflexively; our preferences, correspondingly, are also shaped within a social context and inspired or triggered by interactions with our peers. We eventually compete for the same limited resources, or even for "transcending" benefits like self-image, social prestige, or political power (these are "metaphysical" in the sense that they generate an enhanced sense of self-identity, of being as such).

How much, then, did the increasing mimetic capacity in humans affect social behavior and social structuring, beyond the simple fostering of learning capabilities, empathy, or understanding other people's intentions? Mimetic theory assumes that encephalization and increasing imitative capacity in humans could act—and often, catastrophically, did act—as a disruption of social structuring. Conflict and disorder are in fact magnified by the strength of human imitative capacity. Imitation in humans, according to Girard, accounts, certainly, for the positive aspects of group intelligence, cultural transmission, and cooperation. Yet it is responsible also and conversely, in equal measure, for the "negative" ones.[8] It triggers negative forms of reciprocity between humans, such as envy, competition, and rivalry (in the form of reciprocal violence, retribution, retaliation, vengeance)—in sum, it multiplies those potentials of human group intelligence that are infinitely more dynamic, contagious, and prone to escalate disproportionately in our species, considered in relation to other primates.[9]

Negative mimetic reciprocity between humans triggers serial conflicts, instituting cycles of social disorder and of return to order—in each of which, mimetically supercharged violence overcomes the instinctual controls that in the higher primates, set a limit to the destructive effects of intraspecific conflict. Whereas cooperation and altruism, sympathy and empathy, direct and indirect reciprocity, conflict resolution and peacemaking, are present also in the animal realm, hatred, resentment, retaliation are emotional structures, near-exclusively, specific to humans,[10] because they are based on mirror-like relational reciprocities.

A recent study published by anthropologists Douglas Fry and Patrik Söderberg, examining data on deadly violence within twenty-one mobile foraging societies observed by ethnographers throughout the planet, discovered that only two out of 148 killings stemmed from a fight over "resources" (such as a hunting ground, water hole, or fruit tree). Most of the killings stemmed from what Fry and Söderberg categorize as "miscellaneous personal disputes," involving jealousy, theft, insults, and so on (Fry and Söderberg 2013, 270). The most common specific cause of deadly violence—involving either single or multiple perpetrators—was revenge for a previous attack. All of the cases cited point to the mimetic, i.e., reciprocal, structuring of intraspecific human violence.[11]

Emissary Victimization and the Emergence of the Sacred

Arguing about a specific behavioral ecology in humans,[12] Girard's theory maintains that mimetism is also basic to phenomena of "emotional contagion" in social groups, not only in respect of the "viral" transmission of content-based communication, but also regarding paroxystic collective behavior, like mass hysteria, movements of panic, lynching, arbitrary collective persecution of individuals or groups—all phenomena that have occurred throughout human history, and that we can assume were also very common in prehistorical times, the more so since institutional controls were not present. Girard speaks of these events as "crises of undifferentiation," in which individuals, in a contagious fever of imitation, mirror unreflexively each other, leading to an escalation of violence.[13] When social crises erupt, that is to say, the mimetic contagion of reciprocal violence gets very rapidly out of control and imperils the whole group, unless it is restrained by means of cultural (i.e., socio-symbolic), mechanisms. Crises of undifferentiation develop into the most dangerous events imaginable for proto-social groups, because they could easily, and very likely did, end up in a collective and indiscriminate rage of "all against all"—prelude to a frenzied rampage of killing. The group is then literally "possessed" by a force that it cannot rationalize or control. In such circumstances, a band of hominids would be doomed to disappear through mutual extermination of its members—and this will be the predictable outcome of the crisis—unless "some self-regulating mechanism is found *within the violence* that threatens them," as Paul Dumouchel phrased it; Girard's theory in fact "postulates a self-regulating mechanism of violence, in which the social order emerges from the self-regulation of violence" (Dumouchel 1992, 78).

That self-regulatory mechanism—both a systemic event and a blind process (there is no scope for any form of contractualism in primordial times)—takes the form of a sudden externalization of internal violence, in the shape of the killing of one or more random victims perceived as external agents or forces (for the groups of proto-humans have mostly experienced threats and dangers from outside the pack). Much as, in any episode of panic, the collective in disarray finds (or rather "produces," as a bootstrapping mechanism, through blind convergence-in-imitation) an endogenous fixed point on which to converge, an "attractor" in the language of dynamic systems (see Dupuy 2003): one randomly selected element of the social group, who is expelled and/or killed. When that fixed point is found and the entire horde discharges its fury upon that single emissary victim the collective rage of the mob abates and disappears. This "point of fixation" is normally a member (or a few members) of the group that may present elements of "externality" (he/she/they look slightly different, or display nonstandard features differentiating him/her from the majority of the group; he/she comes from outside the herd/group). "The killing of the scapegoat ends the [internal] crisis, since the transference against it is mimetically unanimous. Here is the importance of the scapegoat mechanism: it channels the collective violence against one arbitrarily chosen member of the community, and this victim becomes the common enemy of the entire community, *which is reconciled as a result*" (Girard, Antonello, and de Castro Rocha 2007). In short, the collective murder represents a "pharmacological" action or transaction; it is a limiting and "homeopathic" use of violence itself against a part of the social body, which allows the group to operate an unreflexive, systemic "operational closure" (Varela 1984).

Of course the mob never see this individual, who serves involuntarily as strike-point or lighting conductor for what he/she actually is—i.e., a random victim. They fail to do so not least because, by this killing, peace is suddenly restored. Causal agency is then projected onto the victim retroactively, making the victim responsible for the violence thus terminated. If by killing this victim, social peace is regained, it is crudely but sufficiently evident that the emissary victim "caused" it in the first place.[14] Girard assumes in fact that there was no sharp cognitive distinction between what was endogenous and what was exogenous, between violence coming from outside (predators, calamities) and from inside the group (infighting, mob phenomena). This phenomenon can be conceptualized in terms of a "cognitive externalization of causality." If, as we have seen, mimetic theory posits a lack of self-reflexivity in group behavior, it is easier—already in relation to individuals, but most especially in the case of groups—to assume an external cause for the emergence of social disorder. It is a near-universal human attitude, perfectly observable in the contemporary world, to "blame" external agents, forces, events for crises and problems that are endogenously produced (see Barash's chapter in this regard). To account for this phenomenon too, Heider (1958) introduced the concept of "perceived locus of causality," while Buss (1978) has pointed out that many studies of self-perception confuse the issues of the causes and the reasons related to action. Actors, he argued, typically provide reasons rather than causes when explaining their actions.

The exceptional capacity for mimesis in humans deeply affects the texture of social interactions: their intensity, the mechanism of identification, of transference, along with all sorts of cognitive "slippage" between "self" and "other." This is the origin and basis of the disjunction between actual events and their cognitive understanding and representation in collective memory—something that, eventually, helped in producing symbolicity, since the symbolic imagination works between terms that are incoercibly associated, but whose relation is logically obscure and of a metonymic or allusive order (see Antonello's chapter in this regard).

The transfiguring sacralization of the victim for Girard is even more complex in origin than this. Given the lack of causal understanding, the very same act of killing of a victim is perceived (not unreasonably, since the effect is real enough) as beneficial, and the very act of victimization produces a sudden collective experience of purgation, relief, and communal bonding. This is based on purely ethological, biologically grounded reasons, which, however, the proto-community or group can only perceive as the action of an external positive "force."[15] The whole process is overwhelmingly perceived as possessing some sort of "healing" power, while there is inevitably an intense and deep focalization on the victim, who becomes the focal point through which the group "negotiates" the "meaning" of the event: the emissary victim is first seen as the culprit who brought the disorder into the community, but once the killing and its effects have intervened, he/she is progressively transmuted into the one who liberates the community from the disorder into which it was plunged. This accounts for the radical ambivalence that we find in archaic deities that frequently represent principles of both good and evil: the Latin *deus*, god, in fact originates from the Old Persian *daiva*, "demon," and the Greek and Hindu deities are powerful examples of this. It also accounts for a similar ambivalence in the Ancient Greek concept of *pharmakos* (originally designating a sacrificial victim, and with the meaning of both "poison" and "medicine"), and is found again in the etymology of "sacred" (both holy and accursed), and again in the fact that words for both "oath" and "curse" are regularly, in all natural languages, words of binding. This typical antinomic or ambivalent structure of the sacred has been noticed by many anthropologists and historians of religion (see, for instance, Eliade 1958), but it is only mimetic theory that is able to provide an intelligible genetic explanation for this consistent and pervasive cultural occurrence. The victim is sacralized, in fact, both because of his/her alleged terrible potency in bringing disruption, violence, panic, crisis, and because emissary expulsion or immolation has brought a positive resolution to the crisis and a reestablishment of viable social order. However, the social group can only conceptualize this fortunate event through a form of collective projection that invests the emissary victim with transcendental power.

The ritualistic structuring of this form of social "pharmacology" is the beginning of religion and of culture (through ritual sacrifice). This systemic outcome is taken up, ritualized, and used as a "fail-safe" or "default" mechanism, i.e., it is interiorized culturally by the self-programming social psyche as a process that has the capacity to ward off the ever-threatening recurrence of conflict and crisis. This trial-and-error mode of cultural invention, protecting humankind from its own violent shadow, is the beginning of the socio-symbolic ritual system of bonding-and-binding, based on sacrificial practices, that we call "religion" (though we should, in the light of the development of Girard's theory, always recall that what is meant here is "archaic" or "natural" religion—the religion of the human sacred).

In this scheme of understanding human origins phenomenologically, deities, spirits, gods are nothing more nor less than the transfiguration of the "metaphysical" power that emanated from sacrificial victims in their killing, producing the sudden abatement of collective rage and a new reconciliation of the community. In this moment, there is, in Girard's words, a collective "divinizing transference" that credits the god or gods, i.e., the victim as transfigured and sacralized by the potent and obscurely "transcendent" effects experienced. The victim/culprit must be a god—for who else could effect the saving reversal of transcending life-energies from a negative to a positive valency? The transcendental element in this scenario is the totalizing, unanimous experience that acted as the "pull" that allowed the genus *Homo* to go beyond its biological limitations. It is the *ex-static* (literally, "going outside oneself," as Fornari argues in "A Mediatory Theory of Hominization") moment, that "forced" the first anatomically capable humans to leap outside their biological niche to become the modern *Homo sapiens*, and to be literally "created" by the sacred and by religion. Girard summarizes it in a very straightforward way: "The formula 'self-domestication' has been used quite often in reference to the human being: man is a 'self-domesticated' animal." No—Girard says—he is not a self-domesticated animal in any unmediated or automatic sense: "*it is religion, it is sacrifice that domesticated him*" (Girard, Antonello, and de Castro Rocha 2007; italics in the text). This is the genetic moment (the moment of coming-to-be, as in Genesis) in which religion or God(s)[16] literally created the human.[17]

The proto-event itself (the founding scapegoat murder, subsequently ritualized in the form of blood sacrifice) should not, of course, be considered as a unique historical occurrence (Girard criticizes Freud's conception of a single slaying of one historical Father in *Totem and Taboo* [Girard 1977, ch. 8]). Rather, the event and its ritual elaboration are thought of as being enacted in any number of "incidents," no doubt repeated over time before the pattern was actually perceived as compelling, necessary, and repeatable in respect of its socially pacifying and organizing effects. The structurally common, ritualistic behavior that later ensued among ancient humans was selected for its reconciling and protective potency. This coincides with the beginning of religion, in its ritualized form.

Prohibitions and Rituals

In this primordial scenario, what emerge are two interconnected phases that contributed powerfully to structuring the symbolic order. The first is related to the emergence of prohibitions:

> If people are threatened, they withdraw from specific acts; otherwise chaotic appropriation will dominate and violence will always increase. Prohibition is the first condition for social ties, hence one of the first elements of cultural programming as well. Fear is essentially fear of mimetic violence; prohibition is *protection* from mimetic escalation. (Girard, Antonello, and de Castro Rocha 2007, 109–10)

Religion developed out of the most basic feelings and passions of proto-humans: fear, and in particular, fear of violence. The most dangerous type, as argued, is internally generated violence, since the mimetic escalation within the confines of the group conduces more swiftly and surely to implosion and complete annihilation. The fact that the religion of the sacred is always implicated in ritualistic and symbolic violence is testimony of the kind of negotiation that is at the core of prehistoric religious practice—while also justifying evidentially the fear of supernatural punishment, as an intrinsic expression of sacred divinities and their relationship with the humans.

The second phase is related to the structuring of rituals. Ritualization still lies at the threshold between cultural phenomena and their biological preconditioning. Forms of ritualized behavior are in fact instinctively activated in animals during moments of crisis, and the same phenomenon is also visible in humans. Locomotion along relatively fixed paths displaying specific motor rituals is ingrained in the behavior of normal animals in the wild. Rituals in animals are actions designed to improve communication during encounters that could bring conflict: hierarchy, mating, feeding, and territory ("turf").

The link between animal behavior and abnormally repetitive performance was made apparent by Lorenz (Lorenz 1966, 160). Motor rituals in the context of animals in the wild, in captivity, in normal humans, as well as in obsessive compulsive disorder (OCD) patients, share an analogous form.

This point had already been discussed by Freud in *Totem and Taboo*, and has been more recently investigated, among others, by anthropologists such as Alan Fiske, who, comparing hundreds of religious ritual sequences with clinical descriptions of OCD cases, showed that the same themes recur over and over again in both domains (Fiske and Haslam 1985, 211–22; Boyer 2001).[18] Indeed, studies of human compulsions frequently describe the abundant rate of performance of behavioral patterns using terms borrowed from ethology, such as "displacement activity" and "stereotypy" (Insel 1988), or "ritualized behavior" (Rappaport 1989).

These behavioral structures are more easily activated or magnified when the community is under conditions of severe stress, as for instance in a moment of crisis, when some action must be taken to cope with the crisis (Lazarus 1966; Siegrist and Cullen, 1984). According to Girard, coping with a new mimetic crisis (with its contagion of danger, fear, panic) might well activate mechanisms of repetition of acts and gestures already experienced by the group, and which have, in analogous circumstances, resolved a critical event of the same type. Religious sacrificial rituals in fact constantly stage a form of collective "psychodrama," which mimics the original "crisis of undifferentiation" (with ritualized dance, noise, and all manner of suddenly permitted transgressions of taboo). This staged replay of anarchy and gathering mimetic crisis ends with some sort of resolution: normally, the sacrifice of a surrogate victim. This is a first building block of the sacrificial ritual constitutive of archaic religion. As an antidote to these moments of dreadful crisis, proto-societies felt compelled to repeat that *ur*-event that saved them from self-destruction: scapegoating—ritually reprised as "sacrifice," in which a two-phase dialectic is distinctly observable: (1) an initial moment of undifferentiation, of disorder, mimicking the archetypical mimetic crisis; and (2) the subsequent sacrificial expulsion of a "surrogate" victim who brings back social order, producing what we define as the sacred, always held by the earliest humans to be the origin of the entire panoply of the myths, rites, institutions, traditions, practices, and laws that, developing over time and very variously in different spaces and places, came to make up what we call "culture."

Sacrificial rituals then stem from the repetition of this systemic proto-event, which is seen to be required once more in particular moments when a new cycle of regression into social disorder and mimetic crisis threatens.

Their intention is to call down the same curative and salutary pharmacology by immolating another surrogate victim ritually. Ritualization also provides the kind of redundancy and attention-grabbing effects that are fundamental building blocks for the cultural and symbolic activity of humans to emerge and become culturally programmed by the community. Rituals, then, through sheer repetition, act as a mechanism of pedagogical reinforcement and, through time, allow the normative crystallization of procedures, acts, materials, and people involved:

> Ritual in this way becomes like a form of schooling because it repeats the same scapegoat murder over and over, albeit using substitute victims. And since ritual is the resolution of a crisis, ritual always intervenes at points of crisis; and it will always be there at the same point of the mimetic crisis. This means that ritual will, in some or other developed form, provide the institution regulating any sort of crisis: so for instance, the crisis of adolescence, calling for rites of passage; or the crisis of death, which generates funeral rituals; or the crisis of disease, which generates ritual medicine. Whether the crisis is real or imaginary makes very little difference, because an imaginary crisis may cause a real catastrophe." (Girard, Antonello, and de Castro Rocha 2007)[19]

This is the critical threshold that both connects and separates the biological and the cultural, by which culture starts to be the most relevant evolutionary force for the development of our species. It is from ritualistic sacrificial practices expressed over many millennia that human symbolic activity and its ritual potentials took shape (for more, see Antonello's chapter).

Naturally enough, this developmental process also involves the historical emergence of contingent variations of procedure and of culturally determined specific emphases within the common core of rituals and myths in different world populations. This phenomenon is illustrated by Durham's chapter—showing how such variations nonetheless maintain visibly their originary sacrificial imprint.

Ground Plan of a Problematizing Volume

The present volume and its companion, *Can We Survive Our Origins?*, are designed to retrace and examine the various aspects of the Girardian "figure of sense" concerning human origins that we have just outlined. We may conveniently sketch its ground plan by making a further foray into the more strategic evidential and hermeneutical problems in which our enterprise is embedded. For the identification of these problems, together with the way in which they are understood, reframed, and/or resolved in particular cases of application, entirely accounts for the value of each contribution and its position within the architecture of the volume as a whole. It also points the way towards further interdisciplinary research—the way ahead for interactive study of questions of hominization.

The two great concerns of this volume are, indeed, on the one hand, evidence and, on the other, the reflective and methodic art—raised, insofar as may be, to the level of an interdisciplinary science—of interpretation.

As discussed in *Evolution and Conversion*, the question of evidence has been one of the main preoccupations in Girard's writing ever since his first anthropological book, *Violence and the Sacred* (Girard, Antonello, and de Castro Rocha 2007, ch. 5). In many respects, mimetic theory, if it is to stand as a hypothesis regarding the process of hominization and the origins of culture, will need to develop the substantial corroboration that, as will have been already observed in passing, it is entirely capable of receiving. The present volume, in the areas already specified, makes a considerable advance on this front.

However, an overarching epistemological caveat is in order. Much like Darwin's evolutionary theory itself, mimetic theory is not to be simply dismissed by any simple procedure of falsification in the Popperian sense. True or false, it requires first to be developed as an explanatory hypothesis, open to progressive empirical corroboration. This will happen as bits of evidence, wherever they do fit, are inserted in order to complete the jigsaw picture to be tested, and any genuine inconsistencies or anomalies of fact noted. But for this very purpose, the hypothesis itself has to be envisaged, assumed, and maintained as a plausible and cogent premise of research—just as Darwin's theory itself has been so maintained, becoming in time largely vindicated, albeit with corrections, additions, and reinforcements, to this day. Theories of change in culture or in nature cannot be independently verified experimentally—in any event, not quickly or simply—so that we must perforce agree to consider potentially "true" simply what seems to read the picture of the jigsaw puzzle best, and to best fit its bits together into a cogent explanatory matrix, which increasingly is seen to "fit" the facts and to "work" as a framing and integrating theory. An illuminating parallel to Girard's situation and status in this respect is provided by the British anthropologist Arthur Maurice Hocart, speaking of Darwin's theory of the animal descent of humans:

> The first Gibraltar skull was discovered in 1848: it passed quite unnoticed. The *Origin of Species* appeared in 1859. It wasn't till men had become thoroughly used to the idea of man's descent from an ape-like creature that the skull was brought out of its obscurity, in order to become a link in the evidence. It was not the direct evidence of a man-ape that converted biologists. Rather, having been converted by [the] comparative evidence, they set out to find direct evidential corroboration of their deductions, so as to complete the confusion of evolution-deniers. *It took thirty-five years of* 'The Origin of Species' *to set them really looking* [our italics]. At which point, Dubois went out to find the ape-like fossil and found it. Since then, discovery has succeeded discovery, and the illusion of direct evidence has taken possession of the minds of anthropologists. (Hocart 1936, 13)

There may be a salutary parable here: a parable of patience and persistence, of the importance of distinguishing between the heuristic order (the order of things passing into knowledge) and their prior ordering in reality. The first things in the real order (the order of being) may well be the very last things we come to discover (in the order of knowing)—and this for the simple but all-powerful reason that our knowing very much supposes ourselves as agents, we who are part of the order of reality without always (sufficiently, appropriately, or at all) recognizing this invisible but fundamental possibility condition. In Hocart's account, Victorian biologists themselves, in the image of their culture-time, were in hock to ideological presupposition until the sheer weight of comparative evidence began to tip the scales. Once the persuasion of plausibility was present, the clinching evidence for Darwin's hypothesis became first visible, then obvious to all. Which is one way of saying that there is never, strictly speaking, any such thing as evidence without interpretation; hence also, no anthropology that is not also—always and ultimately—a painstaking, difficult, and ever-incomplete hermeneutics of the human condition.

Can we, however, identify precisely the issues and problems that mimetic theory faces in evidential and hermeneutical terms? If so, they will help us declare the outline and architecture of the present volume, while beginning also to chart the possible lines of enquiry that lie ahead for researchers.

The first section attempts to engage mimetic theory at both a theoretical and evidential level by placing it within the conceptual parameters of evolutionary thinking, arguing for the specific aspects brought into question by the perspective instantiated by Girard's hypothesis. Coevolution, group selection, and cultural adaptation at the social level are some of the aspects discussed by Durham, Dumouchel, and Antonello in their chapters, which help to reframe mimetic theory within some of the theoretical parameters used by cultural evolutionists, arguing for the positive contribution of the theory in respect to current scientific debates.

As Durham has argued cogently (Durham 1991), variability in human behavior and society may be interpreted more exactly and fruitfully as resulting from interactions between genetic and cultural processes. Cultural mediation is particularly important from the point of view of mimetic theory, where culture drives genetic change; Durham gives us the interesting example of variable adult lactose absorption in environmentally diverse populations that consume dairy products, as conditioned both by biological and cultural pressures. As we have pointed out, according to Girard, it is the emergence of ritualistic practices, and the more and more complex symbolic apparatus of the sacred, that enabled-and-enforced the evolutionary refinement of cognitive capabilities in humans, as well as shaping their biological makeup, through a process of progressive "domestication." As Dumouchel argues in his chapter, it becomes clear that culture, and religion in particular, "de-Darwinize" the human. On this score, there is a wide convergence of theorists maintaining that in the last twenty-five thousand to forty thousand years (roughly) following the "symbolic explosion," the dominant mode of human evolution has been exclusively cultural, building a niche that has progressively separated the further career of *Homo sapiens* from its macroevolutionary course, in order to embrace entirely the path of cultural evolution.

In this same sense, Antonello's chapter discusses the necessary discontinuity that we ought to take into account when discussing cultural evolution and argues for a redesign of the conceptual mappings of cultural phenomena as approached within an evolutionary perspective, particularly with reference to key terms such as "maladaptation," "counterintuitiveness," "conceptual fluidity," and the emergence of the "symbolic."

The second section of the volume is more tightly devoted to the evidential corroboration of three conceptual cornerstones of mimetic thinking: imitation, desire, and redirected aggression. In his chapter, Garrels extends his work on "mimesis and science" by reviewing the current scientific literature (in particular, developmental psychology and cognitive neuroscience) on the key role played by imitation in cultural learning, mental representation, empathy, language, and the entire range of intersubjective experience. The crucial addendum in this perspective, normally ignored by scientific researchers, is the acquisitive role of imitation—a key element in the Girardian theory of social dynamics—which increases the internal instability of any group, feeding a structure of negative reciprocity, one of the main causes of violence in primitive and modern societies.

In his chapter, "The Deepest Principle of Life," William B. Hurlbut then engages with the neurobiology and the psychology of desire, adding a broader philosophical introduction to his more evidential discussion of the connections between desire and reward and their role in development and behavior as discussed by current neurobiological research. He unpacks—for instance with the distinction between "liking" and "wanting"—the broad category of "mimetic desire" introduced by Girard in his work, grounding in a "tangible neural substrate" the human idealizing imagination expanded by the imitative nature of desire. He then ventures to discuss the neurohormonal foundations of sociality, particularly the role played by oxytocin in setting the relational foundations for broader dimensions of human sociality. However, much as in the case of Garrels's discussion, Hurlbut also interrogates the negative side of this phenomenon, pointing at the potentiating and intensifying effect of oxytocin in conflictual situations.

The idea that human culture could be a product of endemic violence is, as we have already suggested, deeply unpalatable. This may be the reason why many of the current theoretical discussions on the evolution of sociability and culture concentrate on cooperation and the emergence of morality—whereas it is sufficiently clear that there would be no need for morality, social norms, and taboos if more basic elements, such as intraspecific rivalry, conflict, and violence, did not require regulation in the first place. Addressing one of the problems in current evolutionary theorization in respect to the emergence of human culture and sociality, the central place of violence both in animals and humans is explored and discussed in this volume, starting from its ethological underpinnings. Providing a fitting bridge between section 2 and section 3 of this volume, Barash's chapter illustrates how retaliation, revenge, and redirected aggression tint our social behavior. Redirected aggression in particular (i.e., a form of behavior pre-tracing the core anthropological reality of emissary victimization) "is a very important and typically unrecognized cause of violence, something that is so natural that most people take it for granted and typically don't give it the attention it deserves." Here we begin to see very concretely how hominization begins in and continues in the animal world—albeit at the psychic, symbolic, and cooperative level—and why our interpretations of origin, however unwelcome this discovery, dare not neglect the implications of this most basic fact of origin.

For both evidential reasons and in the interests of deflecting ideologically motivated mistrust, our third section gives close attention to a revisiting of "violent origins." This is still a matter of examining Girard on the evidence, as is clear from the exposition of Konner in his chapter, "Violent Origins." Konner follows patterns of mimetically driven violence across the interface between animals and humans—and on, in admirably Girardian mode, to the searching reflections-in-culture they find in Shakespeare's theater. In "Mechanisms of Internal Cohesion," Reeve, meanwhile, examines how scapegoating attests to, and in turn conditions, human group behavior commonly discussed under the evolutionary category of "parochial altruism," finding a cogent and interesting convergence between these two theoretical perspectives.

The third section finds an overarching philosophic reflection in Fornari's chapter, whose long-term project, anticipated here in curtain-raising mode, is a phenomenologically inspired theory of cultural evolution, mediating not only between nature and culture, but, syncretically, between insights into human origins offered by the great voices of nineteenth- and twentieth-century fundamental anthropology: Nietzsche, Freud, and Girard. Along with the stimulus of fruitful dissent, this original overview offers a series of rich insights into the hermeneutics of origins, with particular reference to the emergence of proto-symbolic activity in proto-humans with the invention of the tomb and the domestication of fire, which would project our original developmental phase back to about one hundred thousand years ago.[20]

This is indeed one of the overarching puzzles in the decipherment of "lost origins": the question of the timeline in respect of the emergence of distinctively human culture, and religion in particular, and of its implications for future research in this area. Chronological dating and proto-historical periodization in respect of the emergence of cultural and religious practices are a far from exact science; they give rise to considerable speculation. Largely for this reason, Girard has never tried to assert any clear time frame in the discussion of his hypothesis, knowing that new findings are constantly reshaping our understanding of the evolution of all cultural forms.

Among many others, Walter Burkert, with whom Girard developed a constructive dialogue in *Violent Origins* (1988), traces the emergence of human religious behavior to the beginning of behavioral modernity in the Upper Paleolithic, coinciding with the "symbolic explosion" or "Upper Paleolithic Revolution," which occurred some forty thousand years ago. This idea of a symbolic "big bang" would be compatible with the premises of mimetic theory, since the discovery and ritualization of sacrifice is, for Girard, an initiating vehicle of symbolic awareness, and an explosive and expansive source of cultural invention. This is a further reason why the present volume tries, in section 4, to bring mimetic theory to the test of some key archaeological sites, whose recent discovery has substantially modified the way in which archaeologists think of the cultural evolution of humanity.

René Girard himself heads this series of essays devoted to the archaeological finds in Turkey, which come as close in time as humanity has yet gotten to a direct and decisive encounter with its own cultural origins. He provides a compelling reading of the mural drawings found at the nine-thousand-year-old Neolithic site of Çatalhöyük in central Anatolia, and his interpretation has attracted the attention and the serious consideration of Ian Hodder, the Stanford-based director of the Turkish excavations. Jean-Pierre Dupuy then, in his characteristically formalist excursion into matters evolutionary, takes on board Girard's suggestions and Ian Hodder's own speculation on the subject, by reframing their analyses into a wider theoretical perspective of morphogenetic principles of the emergence of rituals and religion.

The puzzle that the recent discovery of the early Stone Age temple of Göbekli Tepe has posed to archaeologists and paleoanthropologists finally receives, out of the resources of mimetic theory, an offer of Girardian decipherment, attempted in the chapter "Rethinking the Neolithic Revolution" by Paul Gifford and Pierpaolo Antonello. At this site, which is increasingly perceived by anthropologists as requiring a near-total rethink of the Neolithic Revolution (the development that led hunter-gathers into settlement, agriculture, the domestication of animals—and hence to the rise of "civilization"), Girard's theory seems to offer, consistently with this rethinking, keys to the enigmatic iconographic symbolism of this ritual site, and to discern the likely practice of animal and human sacrifice—something that no one has so far suggested proceeded there. One of the undeclarable problems mimetic theory faces in deciphering these findings is the fact that reactions to it are often tainted by ideological bias and taboo. Alongside the intellectual and moral discomfort that the idea of human sacrifice consistently produces, we might instance the even heavier proscription striking at discussion of cannibalism—a ritual practice intimately connected with sacrifice, and which figures at the core of much discussion in Girard's theory. Forensic analysis provides compelling evidence on how much ritualistic cannibalism was practiced in primitive cultures, but this entire discursive zone has been contentious and delicate for decades, and any study on this historical phenomenon has been often dismissed as ethnocentric, if not actually racist.

A similar problem of ideological prevention exists, albeit more patchily and less acutely, in relation to many of the wider issues at stake in the elucidation of human origins. This is why the closing section of this volume is devoted to the most distinctive, and for many Darwinians the most unreceivable, of these—something to which contemporary readings of the Neolithic Revolution, however, increasingly point—namely, the formative and matricial role in human origins of religion.

The account of *Homo religiosus* as recognized by Girard is opened under the sign of the consistent and enlightening hermeneutical reflections of Warren Brown, James Van Slyke, and Scott Garrels, who explore the claims of cognitivism in respect of the ambiguous entity "religion," heavily underdefined in relation to the ideological leverage often sought from it, or from the refusal of it. Their chapter, "Intrinsic or Situated Religiousness," in particular argues for the necessity of avoiding the Augustinian/Cartesian residuals of inwardness and individuality, and incorporating modern understandings of the self-organization of mental systems and environmental scaffolding of most human higher mental capacities. This move would avoid the presupposition that, because religiousness is universal in humankind, it must therefore be a genetically endowed evolutionary outcome involving physical brain systems specific to religion, or that religion came about as a byproduct of the cognitive tendencies of individual persons that evolved for other reasons.

In "*Homo religiosus* in Mimetic Perspective," Gifford concludes this closing section of the book with an essay exploring comparatively, by setting them in dialogue, the cognitivist and Girardian approaches to the key topic that most marks out Girardian difference: that of *Homo religiosus*. Girard, it transpires, asks us to consider that "religion" might have, to pick up Henri Bergson's key insight, "two sources" rather than one; that these distinct origins, made fully visible in evolutionary perspective, explain cogently why there is disagreement around this vast, ramifying, and strangely persistent human phenomenon; and why religion can be seen, at one and the same time, as the best *and* the worst of things human.

Notes

1. "From Animal to Human: Exploring the Evolutionary Interface. A Celebration of Darwin and Girard," St John's and Christ's College, Cambridge, November 16–17, 2009; "Thinking the Human: Fundamental Questions of Evolutionary Theory in Mimetic Perspective," Stanford University, Stanford, CA, November 15–16, 2010; "Surviving Our Origins: Violence and the Sacred in Evolutionary and Historical Time," St John's College, Cambridge, May 27–28, 2011.

2. The reader is referred, by way of illustration, to Stephen Pinker's cluelessness in writing on the subject of human sacrifices, in his book *The Better Angels of Our Nature* (2011).

3. According to the evolutionary psychologists John Tooby and Leda Cosmides, "most social scientists believe they are invoking a powerful explanatory principle when they claim that a behaviour is 'learned' or 'cultural.'" However, "as hypotheses to account for mental or behavioural phenomena, these terms are remarkably devoid of meaning. At this point in the study of human behaviour, learning and culture are phenomena to be explained, and not explanations in themselves" (Tooby and Cosmides 1989, 46).

4. According to Michael Shermer, the following characteristics are shared by humans and other social animals, particularly the great apes: attachment and bonding, cooperation and mutual aid, sympathy and empathy, direct and indirect reciprocity, altruism and reciprocal altruism, conflict resolution and peacemaking, deception and deception detection, community concern and caring about what others think about you, and awareness of and response to the social rules of the group (Shermer 2004, 16).

5. Girard's hypothesis also requires us to think in broader and more complex historical terms.

Mimetic theory entails a historical perspective that encompasses both history and prehistory, and needs us to move in both directions across the interface between them. This requirement runs counter to a widespread persuasion that "genetic" explanation must proceed one way only, from the *before* and the *below* of things, in the same direction as the timeline—rather than also reaching steadily backwards in time, by a movement of reflective and regressive comprehension, from a higher platform of deductive intelligibility and interpretation situated in today's evolved complexity.

6. According to the British anthropologist Robin Dunbar, there is a cognitive limit to the number of people with whom one can maintain stable social relationships. This limit is a direct function of relative neocortex size, and this in turn limits group size. It has been proposed to lie between 100 and 230, with a commonly used value of 150. Dunbar asserts that numbers larger than this generally require more restrictive rules, laws, and enforced norms to maintain a stable, cohesive group (Dunbar 1992).

7. As Vittorio Gallese writes in relation to imitation mechanisms: "The observed behavior is pre-reflexively understood because it is constituted as a goal-directed motor act in virtue of the activation in the observer's brain of the neurons presiding over the motor accomplishment of similar goals" (Gallese 2009). Paul Dumouchel also explains that we do not "feel" imitation, so often are we unaware of its action, and the extent of its action, in our own attitudes and behavior: "*Stricto sensu* there is no experience of mimesis. You may surprise yourself imitating your hated rival or your friend, but when that happens, which I think is rarely, what you experience is perhaps surprise at this discovery, but not imitation itself which does not feel like anything. Unlike emotions, mimesis is not an object of direct first person perception" (Dumouchel 2011).

8. An interesting finding in current primatological studies is the fact that skills, cognitive attention, and the ability to understand others' behavior as intentional are enhanced in competitive situations, rather than in cooperative ones (Hare, Call, Agnetta, and Tomasello 2000; Hare and Tomasello 2004; Tomasello, Carpenter, Call, Behne, and Moll 2005).

9. See the discussion by Paul Dumouchel of human violence in relation to chimpanzee violence in Antonello and Gifford, *Can We Survive Our Origins?*, 3–24.

10. This point is discussed by Paul Dumouchel in the companion volume, Antonello and Gifford, *Can We Survive Our Origins?*, 3–24.

11. We may argue that reciprocal imitation is a multiplier or a magnifier of many (if not all) behavioral mechanisms, favoring on the one hand collective convergences of intentions and actions, and on the other, structural inertia in acquiring and maintaining habits, customs, beliefs, etc.

12. In a survey article on "The Origins of Symbolic Culture," and the various competing theories that, more or less successfully, have tried to account for the emergence of symbolism in humans, Chris Knight argues that "We need a theory of the evolution of *Homo sapiens* faithful to the methods of behavioural ecology which have proved so successful elsewhere in the living world. . . . If we were looking for hypotheses which are (a) based on behavioural ecology (b) focused on the emergence of symbolism and (c) testable in the light of relevant archaeological data, the range of suggestions is limited" (Knight 2010, 197). We argue that Girard's theory of hominization complies with these three criteria and offers itself as one of the most remarkable hypotheses to account for the genesis of culture, to be equated with the genesis of religion, or rather the "sacred."

13. In their anthropological work *Witchcraft, Sorcery, Rumors and Gossip*, Pamela J. Stewart and Andrew Strathern recognize the analogous potency of rumors and gossip, virally spreading

and reinforced in a snowballing effect. These are "often crucially involved in overt violence in communal settings" (Stewart and Strathern 2007).

14. Girard's interpretation of the Oedipus myth operates on this same basis (Girard 2004).

15. On the link between redirected aggression and bonding, see Lorenz 1966; Girard, Antonello, and de Castro Rocha 2007; Barash and Lipton 2011.

16. In the Hebrew Bible, the first epithet in Genesis used to define God is "Elohim," which is the plural form of *eloah*, which may be a vestige of the historical transition from polytheism to a monotheistic religion, like Judaism.

17. In the frenzy of collective rage and scapegoating fury, the victim may be torn apart, dismembered, eaten up, as Fornari will remind us in his chapter. The Dionysiac rites in ancient Greece offer a paradigm case: in the *diasparagmos*, the tearing apart of a live animal was celebrated as a solemn rite. A goat or other sacrificial victim was ceremonially hunted down, pulled limb from limb, and eaten raw by the communicants. The slain animal was regarded as a symbol of incarnation of the god, who had in myth likewise been dismembered and eaten—and afterwards resurrected. Given this account, it is not surprising that sacrificial and ritualistic cannibalism—the ubiquity of which in prehistory and its mythological transfigurations are well documented facts—would appear to stem from these origins. Fornari in this volume offers an inverse variation on this theme in suggesting, persuasively, that *diasparagmos* may in fact have come first, as the earliest, pilot form of "scapegoating" violence, only sharing in the divinizations involved by its later forms. On the widespread practice of ritual cannibalism, see for instance White 2001; Stoneking 2003; and Antonello's chapter in this volume.

18. "Fiske's list of common themes in rituals could be used as a clinical description of the common obsessions in these patients. In both situations, people are concerned with purity and pollution; pollution can be averted by performing particular actions; . . . the actions consist in repetitive gestures; there is a sense that great dangers lie in not performing these routines, or deviating from the usual script; finally, there is often no obvious connection between the actions performed and their usual significance" (Boyer 2001, 273).

19. Luc-Laurent Salvador presents the link between imitation and repetition as a form of psychological and cognitive reinforcement through the idea of "cycle assimilateur" (Salvador 1996, 23–32).

20. As Fornari contends, there is clear evidence of symbolic activity predating the Upper Paleolithic Revolution. The earliest undisputed human burial discovered so far, in fact, dates back one hundred thirty thousand years. Pieces of ochre engraved with abstract designs have been found at the site of the Blombos Cave in South Africa, dated to around seventy-five thousand years ago. Fornari goes even further by discussing the domestication of fire as an early form of very primordial religious ritual, "dating back to the remote times of *Erectus* and *Ergaster* (about one-and-a-half million years ago)." This would suggest a slightly different, but highly compatible overall scenario. Girard's original hypothesis would then describe a further crystallization: the institutionalized and symbolically codified form of an earlier, proto-symbolic activity, something not yet fully ritualized, but attesting to a more gradual evolution in human symbolic behavior. However, the available archaeological data seems to point to a quite radical "quantum leap" in human cultural development. The use of some pigment can hardly be compared to the construction of a ritual temple like Göbekli Tepe, and the social organization it required.

Works Cited

Antonello, Pierpaolo, and Paul Gifford. 2015. *Can We Survive Our Origins? Readings in René Girard's Theory of Violence and the Sacred.* East Lansing: Michigan State University Press.

Atran, S. 2001. "The Trouble with Memes: Inference versus Imitation in Cultural Creation." *Human Nature* 12: 351–81.

Barash, D. P., and J. E. Lipton. 2011. *Payback: Why We Retaliate, Redirect Aggression and Seek Revenge.* New York: Oxford University Press.

Boyd, R., and P. J. Richerson. 1985. *Culture and the Evolutionary Process.* Chicago: University of Chicago Press.

———. 2005. *Not by Genes Alone: How Culture Transformed Human Evolution.* Chicago: University of Chicago Press.

Boyer, P. 1999. "Cognitive Tracks of Cultural Inheritance: How Evolved Intuitive Ontology Governs Cultural Transmission." *American Anthropologist* 100: 876–89.

———. 2001. *Religion Explained: The Evolutionary Origins of Religious Thought.* New York: Basic Books.

Burkert, W., R. Girard, and J. Z. Smith. 1988. *Violent Origins: Walter Burkert, René Girard, and Jonathan Z. Smith on Ritual Killing and Cultural Formation.* Edited by R. Hamerton-Kelly. Stanford, CA: Stanford University Press.

Buss, A. R. 1978. "A Conceptual Critique of Attribution Theory." *Journal of Personality and Social Psychology* 36: 1311–21.

Darwin, C. [1859] 1958. *On the Origin of Species.* New York: Modern Library.

Dawkins, R. 1976. *The Selfish Gene.* New York: Oxford University Press.

Dawson, D. 2013. *Flesh Becomes Word: A Lexicography of the Scapegoat or, the History of an Idea.* East Lansing: Michigan State University Press.

Deacon, T. W. 1997. *The Symbolic Species: The Co-Evolution of Language and the Brain.* New York: W.W. Norton & Co.

Deacon T. W., and T. Cashman. 2009. "The Role of Symbolic Capacity in the Origins of Religion." *Journal for the Study of Religion, Nature and Culture* 3, no. 4. doi:10.1558/jsrnc.v3i4.00.

Donald, M. 1991. *Origins of the Modern Mind: Three Stages in the Evolution of Culture and Cognition.* Cambridge, MA: Harvard University Press.

Dumouchel, P. 1992. "A Morphogenetic Hypothesis on the Closure of Post Structuralism." In *Understanding Origins*, ed. J. P. Dupuy and F. Varela, 77–90. Netherlands: Springer.

———. 2011. "Emotions and Mimesis." In *Mimesis and Science: Empirical Research on Imitation and the Mimetic Theory of Culture and Religion*, ed. S. Garrels. East Lansing: Michigan State University Press.

Dunbar, R. I. M. 1990. "Ecological Modelling in an Evolutionary Context." *Folia Primatologica* 53: 235–46.

———. 1992. "Neocortex Size as a Constraint on Group Size in Primates." *Journal of Human Evolution* 22, no. 6: 469–93.

Dunbar, R. 2004. *The Human Story.* London: Faber & Faber.

Dupuy, J. P. 2003. *Le panique*. Paris: Les Empêcheurs de Penser en Rond.

Dupuy, J. P., and F. J. Varela, eds. 1992. *Understanding Origins: Contemporary Views on the Origin of Life, Mind and Society*. Dordrecht: Kluwer Academic Publishers.

Durham, W. H. 1991. *Coevolution: Genes, Culture, and Human Diversity*. Stanford, CA: Stanford University Press.

Durkheim, E. [1915] 1995. *The Elementary Forms of Religious Life*. New York: Free Press.

Eliade, M. 1958. *Patterns in Comparative Religion*. London: Sheed & Ward.

———. 1963. *Myth and Reality*. New York: Harper & Row.

———. 1976. *Myths, Rites, Symbols: A Mircea Eliade Reader*. Vol. 2. Edited by W. C. Beane and W. G. Doty. New York: Harper & Row.

Evans-Pritchard, E. E. 1965. *Theories of Primitive Religion*. Oxford: Clarendon Press.

Fiske, A. P., and N. Haslam. 1985. "Is Obsessive-compulsive Disorder a Pathology of the Human Disposition to Perform Socially Meaningful Rituals? Evidence of Similar Content." *Journal of Nervous and Mental Disease* 4: 211–22.

Fracchia, J., and R. C. Lewontin. 2005. "The Price of Metaphor." *History and Theory* 44, no. 1: 14–29. doi:10.1111/j.1468-2303.2005.00305.

Frazer, J. 1922. *The Golden Bough: A Study in Magic and Religion*. Abridged ed. Edited by T. H. Gaster. New York: MacMillan.

Freud, S. 1913. "Totem and Taboo." *The Standard Edition of the Complete Psychological Works of Sigmund Freud*. Vol. 13 (1913–1914), *Totem and Taboo and Other Works*. Translated by J. Strachey, xii–162. London: Hogarth Press.

Fry, D. P., and P. Söderberg. 2013. "Lethal Aggression in Mobile Forager Bands and Implications for the Origins of War." *Science* 341, no. 6143: 270–73. doi:10.1126/science.1235675.

Gallese, V. 2009. "The Two Sides of Mimesis: Girard's Mimetic Theory, Embodied Simulation and Social Identification." *Journal of Consciousness Studies* 16: 21–44.

———. 2010. "Embodied Simulation and its Role in Intersubjectivity." In *The Embodied Self. Dimensions, Coherence and Disorders*, ed. T. Fuchs, H. C. Sattel, P. Henningsen, 78–92. Stuttgart: Schattauer.

Garrels, S., ed. 2011. *Mimesis and Science: Empirical Research on Imitation and the Mimetic Theory of Culture and Religion*. East Lansing: Michigan State University Press.

Garrels, S. R. 2005–6. "Imitation, Mirror Neurons, and Mimetic Desire: Convergence between the Mimetic Theory of René Girard and Empirical Research on Imitation." *Contagion* 12–13: 47–86.

Gellner, E. 1987. *Culture, Identity and Politics*. Cambridge: Cambridge University Press.

Girard, R. 1965. *Deceit, Desire, and the Novel: Self and Other in Literary Structure*. Baltimore: Johns Hopkins University Press.

———. 1977. *Violence and the Sacred*. Baltimore: Johns Hopkins University Press.

———. 1986. *The Scapegoat*. Baltimore: Johns Hopkins University Press.

———. 1987a. *Job: The Victim of His People*. Translated by Y. Freccero. Stanford, CA: Stanford University Press.

———. 1987b. *Things Hidden since the Foundation of the World.* Stanford, CA: Stanford University Press.

———. 1992. "Origins: A View from Literature." In *Understanding Origins: Contemporary Views on the Origins of Life, Mind and Society*, ed. J. P. Dupuy and F. J. Varela, 27–42. Dordrecht: Kluwer Academic Publishers.

———. 2001. *I See Satan Fall Like Lightning.* Maryknoll, NY: Orbis Books.

———. 2004. *Oedipus Unbound: Selected Writings on Rivalry and Desire.* Edited with an introduction by M. R. Anspach. Stanford, CA: Stanford University Press.

———. 2011. *Sacrifice.* Translated by M. Pattillo and D. Dawson. East Lansing: Michigan State University Press.

Girard, R., P. Antonello, and J. C. de Castro Rocha. 2007. *Evolution and Conversion: Dialogues on the Origins of Culture.* New York: Continuum.

Golsan, R. J., ed. 1993. *René Girard and Myth: An Introduction.* New York: Garland Publishing.

Goodenough, U., and T. Deacon. 2003. "From Biology to Consciousness to Morality." *Zygon* 38: 801–19.

———. 2008. "The Sacred Emergence of Nature." In *The Oxford Handbook of Religion and Science*, ed. Philip Clayton, 862–63. Oxford: Oxford University Press.

Hare, B., J. Call, B. Agnetta, and M. Tomasello. 2000. "Chimpanzees Know What Conspecifics Do and Do Not See. *Animal Behaviour* 59:771–85.

Hare, B., J. Call, and M. Tomasello. 2001. "Do Chimpanzees Know What Conspecifics Know?" *Animal Behaviour* 61, no. 1: 139–51.

Hare, B., and M. Tomasello. 2004. "Chimpanzees Are More Skillful in Competitive Than in Co-operative Cognitive Tasks." *Animal Behaviour* 68: 571–81.

Header, F. 1958. *The Psychology of Interpersonal Relations.* New York: Wiley.

Henrich, J., R. Boyd, and P. J. Richerson. 2008. "Five Misunderstandings about Cultural Evolution." *Human Nature* 19: 119–37. doi:10.1007/s12110-008-9037-1.

Hocart, M. 1936. *Kings and Councillors: An Essay in the Comparative Anatomy of Human Society.* Chicago: University of Chicago Press, 1970.

Hodder, I. 2006. *The Leopard's Tale: Revealing the Mysteries of Çatalhöyük.* London: Thames & Hudson.

Insel, T. 1988. "Obsessive-compulsive Disorder: New Models." *Psychopharmacology Bulletin* 24: 365–69.

Kauffman, S. 2007. "Beyond Reductionism: Reinventing the Sacred." *Zygon: Journal of Religion and Science* 42: 903–14.

Kauffman, S. A. 1992. "Origins of Order in Evolution: Self-Organization and Selection." In *Understanding Origins: Contemporary Views on the Origins of Life, Mind and Society*, ed. J. P. Dupuy and F. J. Varela. Dordrecht: Kluwer Academic Publishers.

Knight, C. 2010. "The Origins of Symbolic Culture." In *Homo Novus: A Human without Illusions*, ed. U. J. Frey, C. Störmer, and K. P. Willführ, 193–211. Berlin: Springer-Verlag.

Larson, G. J., C. Scott Littleton, and Jaan Puhvel, eds. 1974. *Myth in Indo-European Antiquity.* Berkeley: University of California Press.

Lazarus, R. S. 1966. *Psychological Stress and the Coping Process*. New York: McGraw-Hill.

Lincoln, B. 1975. "The Indo-European Myth of Creation." *History of Religions* 15: 121–45.

———. 1981. *Priests, Warriors, and Cattle: A Study in the Ecology of Religions*. Berkeley: University of California Press.

Littleton, C. S. 1973. *The New Comparative Mythology: An Anthropological Assessment of the Theories of Georges Dumézil*. Berkeley: University of California Press.

Livingston, P. 1992. "Girard and the Origin of Culture." In *Understanding Origins: Contemporary Views on the Origins of Life, Mind and Society*, ed. J. P. Dupuy and F. J. Varela. Dordrecht: Kluwer Academic Publishers.

Lorenz, K. 1966. *On Aggression*. New York: MJF Books.

Monat, A., and R. S. Lazarus, eds. 1985. *Stress and Coping*. New York: Columbia University Press.

Murphy, R. F. 1957. "Intergroup Hostility and Social Cohesion." *American Anthropologist* 59, no. 6: 1018–35.

Nowak, M. A. 2006. "Five Rules for the Evolution of Cooperation." *Science* 314, no. 8: 1560–63.

Pals, D. L. 1996. *Seven Theories of Religion*. New York: Oxford University Press.

Pinker, S. 2011. *The Better Angels of Our Nature: Why Violence Has Declined*. New York: Viking.

Preus, J. S. 2000. *Explaining Religion: Criticism and Theory from Bodin to Freud*. New York: Oxford University Press.

Rappaport, J. L. 1989. "The Biology of Obsessions and Compulsions." *Scientific American* 260: 83–89.

Reed, G. F. 1985. *Obsessional Experience and Compulsive Behaviour: A Cognitive-Structural Approach*. Toronto: Academic Press.

Salvador, L.-L. 1996. "Imitation et attribution de causalité: La genèse mimétique du soi, la genèse mimétique du réel. Applications à la 'psychose naissante' et à l'autisme." PhD diss., Université René Descartes (Paris V).

Serres, M. 1994. *Atlas*. Paris: Julliard.

Shermer, M. 2004. *The Science of Good and Evil*. New York: Times Books.

Siegrist, J., and H. Cullen, eds. 1984. *Breakdown in Human Adaptation to Stress*. Boston: Martinus Nijhoff.

Sober, E. 1994. "Models of Cultural Evolution." In *Conceptual Issues in Evolutionary Biology*, ed. E. Sober. Cambridge, MA: MIT Press.

Sober, E., and D. S. Wilson. 1998. *Unto Others: The Evolution and Psychology of Unselfish Behavior*. Cambridge, MA: Harvard University Press.

Sperber, D. 1996. *Explaining Culture: A Naturalistic Approach*. Oxford: Blackwell Publishers.

Stewart, P. J., and A. Strathern. 2007. *Witchcraft, Sorcery, Rumors and Gossip*. Cambridge: Cambridge University Press.

Stoneking, M. 2003. "Widespread Prehistoric Human Cannibalism: Easier to Swallow?" *Trends in Ecology and Evolution* 18, no. 10: 489–90.

Tomasello, M., M. Carpenter, J. Call, T. Behne, and H. Moll. 2005. "Understanding and Sharing Intentions: The Origins of Cultural Cognition." *Behavioural and Brain Science* 28: 675–735.

Tooby, J., and L. Cosmides. 1989. "Evolutionary Psychology and the Generation of Culture: Part 1, Theoretical Considerations." *Ethology and Sociobiology* 10: 29–49.

Tylor, E. B. 1958. *The Origins of Culture* and *Religion in Primitive Culture* (vols. 1 and 2 of the 1873 edition of *Primitive Culture*). New York: Harper & Brothers.

Varela, F. 1984. "Two Principles for Self-Organization." In *Self-Organization and Management of Social Systems: Insights, Promises, Doubts, and Questions*, ed. H. Ulrich and G. J. B. Probst, 25–32. Berlin: Springer-Verlag.

White, T. D. 2001. "Once We Were Cannibals." *Scientific American* 285: 58–65.

Wilson, D. S. 2002. *Darwin's Cathedral: Evolution, Religion, and the Nature of Society*. Chicago: University of Chicago Press.

PART ONE

Questions of Methodology and Hermeneutics: Mimetic Theory, Darwinism, and Cultural Evolution

Coevolution and Mimesis

William H. Durham

Recent years have brought major advances in evolutionary culture theory (ECT), a general framework for understanding cultural change over time in human societies as a kind of evolutionary process. The main idea is that cultural systems change via a special cultural form of variational evolution—that is, via the nonrandom persistence of cultural variation, caused by some variants outlasting others as they are socially transmitted—rather than via transformational evolution, which refers to sequential change in a given form across time. The general framework of ECT draws inspiration from Darwinian theory in biology, which is the best-known example of variational evolution. But when adapted to the cultural realm—that is, to the realm of ideational phenomena like ideas, beliefs, and values—it takes on different properties. Logically, it has to be different: the nonrandom persistence of cultural phenomena in human populations takes place through differential social transmission, not through the differential reproduction of genetic material as in organic evolution. In evolutionary culture theory, then, change results from the differential persistence of ideational phenomena in a given human population or populations. Cultural systems change, or not, through the selective retention over time of alternative ideas, values, and beliefs (see Durham 1991).

What sorts of processes acting on cultural variation cause this differential persistence of alternative forms? A full review of the topic, including many diverse schools of thought, is beyond the scope of this chapter (see, for example, Laland and Brown 2011). But there is an emerging, loose consensus among analysts on the importance of human decision making in cultural persistence—that is, on the role of choice (also known as individually "biased transmission") in the differential persistence of cultural forms. A key hypothesis is that cultural change over time is largely, but not exclusively, a product of people picking and choosing among existing options (within social as well as ideological constraints) what to accept for themselves and/or what to convey socially to others. "Selection by choice" sounds simple enough, but complications quickly arise. They arise from the complexities of who and what have shaped or limited the variations available for choice, who and what have shaped the values in place for comparing options, and who gets to choose what and for whom. In other words, cultural change is an intrinsically political process, inevitably shaped by social structure and power, which themselves are changeable phenomena in time (see Durham 1991). On this view, cultural evolution is an inherently political form of variational evolution, which is one reason that social analysts are so fond of asking of cultural phenomena, "who benefits and who pays the costs?," for they are often not the same people.

It is here, in this political aspect, that current evolutionary culture theory finds potentially interesting and productive common ground with René Girard's mimetic theory. Girard proposed his own uniquely generative process of cultural evolution that links ordinary desires and mimicry in a given society to a growing crisis of threatened internal violence. The threat of rampant violence is resolved, says Girard, by a political process of victimization, in which a scapegoat is held responsible for the crisis and sacrificed. "In an effort to prevent frequent and unpredictable episodes of mimetic violence, acts of planned, controlled, mediated, periodical, ritualized surrogate violence were put in place," and ritualized sacrifice becomes the social regulator of mimetic crisis thereafter (Girard, Antonello, and de Castro Rocha 2007, 71–72) and forms the basis for subsequent cultural elaboration, including religion, institutions, and prohibition, says Girard.

Girard's theory can be linked to the broader development of evolutionary culture theory. The key link is the way that "social regulator of mimetic crisis" offered a political solution to the recurrent threat to the social order. The political solution, in turn, related to some complexities I had explored in my own variational theory of cultural evolution, *Coevolution* (Durham 1991).

Cultural Selection

In my own work in evolutionary culture theory, I have found it helpful to distinguish cultural selection—that is, cultural change resulting from the value-guided decision-making of human beings (which can also be called "preservation by preference")—from natural selection, or evolutionary change by survival and reproduction advantage (Darwin's "main motor" of organic evolution). Natural selection can and does operate in cultural evolution, much in the way it does in organic evolution, but it probably governs cultural outcomes only in special cases where the success of variants is closely tied to the reproduction of their carriers.

My own hypothesis was that diverse forms of human decision-making have been far more common and consequential than natural selection during the diversification of cultures in the last dozen or so millennia. I have found it particularly helpful to distinguish two of them: choice (preservation by one's own free and uncoerced preference, according to one's own values) and imposition (preservation of someone else's choice as a result of their power and influence in the given social context, including acceptance of their values rather than one's own). Choice and imposition guide the selective retention of cultural evolution in different directions, the latter favoring ideas, values, and beliefs—and the behaviors they encourage—of advantage to those in power.

These simple mechanisms of variational evolution are capable of working in an almost infinite variety of social situations in human societies. In a situation where a set of cultural variants (designated simply as A, B, C, and so forth) are vying for representation in a largely egalitarian society (for example, favored variants will be those chosen freely by a majority of individuals in the society), a process occurs that may reasonably be called "democratic choice." By contrast, in a situation where the variants (A, B, C, and so forth) are subject to differential transmission in a hierarchical society with powerful individuals or groups, favored variants will be those imposed by powerful people (as when certain variants are eliminated from the running by the ruling elite). These mechanisms also make it easy to imagine feedback relations between ideas, values, beliefs, and power. Via imposition, powerful elites can readily propagate knowledge and beliefs that may further refine or strengthen their power to impose still more variants in the course of cultural evolution.

The integration of these mechanisms into one theoretical framework is called "coevolution" for three reasons: first, to highlight the fact that two tracks or channels of informational inheritance (genes and culture) serve as co-partners in the generation of human diversity; second, to draw attention to the symmetry of their influence on human diversity, particularly behaviors (see on this point Durham 1991, ch. 4); and third, to suggest that the two may indeed work in parallel ways in the many circumstances where selection by choice operates, each track thus operating to increase the frequency of its existing variants that enhance the ability of human beings to survive and reproduce. While the two tracks may indeed also be at odds, especially with pervasive imposition (a condition called "opposition" in Durham 1991), the word "coevolution" reinforces a theoretical expectation that natural selection and cultural selection by choice are likely to cooperate in their influence on human diversity.

Darwin Meets Girard: Is a Reconciliation Possible?

Without taking too many liberties, one can use the preceding mechanisms of cultural selection to recast or reinterpret René Girard's mimetic theory, and thus propose a reconciliation of their arguments. In Girard's view, mimetic theory offers a general model of how diverse cultures began, how they function, and how they change over time, drawing on supporting evidence from religion, myth, and ritual.

There are features of Girard's theory that are quite compelling: most particularly, the ubiquity and efficacy of imitation in humans; the power of acquisitive desire in individuals; and the "double bind" of mimetic reciprocity, which supercharges rivalries and singularly ratchets up the effects of intra- and intergroup conflict and violence—all key elements in Girard's theory. Also compelling is the notion of a "mimetic crisis," which could be catastrophic and terminal were it not disarmed by the saving mechanism, the deflection of group violence onto a surrogate victim, later ritualized in the form of sacrifice.

Viewed in terms of coevolution, what Girard provides is a theory for the imposition of a particular ideology of origin. Its two very clever features are first, how to generate hierarchy from a fairly egalitarian set of mimetic rivals who each desire the same simple things, and second, how that hierarchy goes on to protect itself and its control over individual behaviors through victimization, which deflects competitive aggression onto a surrogate victim and then uses its power to promote a ritualized account of that "sacrifice." While this "Darwinian reinterpretation" of Girard is currently only a bare outline, it does suggest that Girard's theory can be reconciled with a variational model of cultural evolution.

My general aim here is neither to confirm nor critique Girard's theory as a whole, but to flag what I think is an interesting parallel to be explored between our two trajectories of thought. Although I am certainly not alone in the search for a variational theory of cultural evolution, I find it regrettable that the ideas of scholars such as René Girard and me have had so little impact on mainstream social science. There is, throughout the social sciences today, a definite resistance to evolutionary theories of culture, even though social science might well be strengthened by attention to this "missing" dimension. Scholars like Girard and me find ourselves battling a real social-science phobia directed against evolutionary arguments, because of past mistakes at interpreting what evolution means, and because of some "racist" premises that came out of earlier transformational theories of cultural evolution. There is no room for racism in evolutionary culture theory, where the baseline assumption has always been pan-human equality in the capacity for culture. Accordingly, cultural differences are viewed as the product of accumulated effects of the differential persistence of ideational variation in different populations, environments, and social circumstances.

Tupi Warfare

In order to illustrate the congruence between my theory and Girard's, I wish to start by exploring the example of warfare among Tupian speakers in South America and its ritual modality of headhunting. Independently of Girard, to whom the example of the Tupinamba is also important (Girard 1977, ch. 11), I dedicated a good part of my early career to establishing patterns of traditional warfare among the more than thirty extant populations of Tupian speakers. Both fieldwork and comparative ethnographic analysis confirm, in relation to Girard, a parallel and largely complementary way of interpreting cultural variation, a setting for understanding it, and even a plausible scenario for its origins. My own analysis refers to Tupian speakers throughout South America, not simply the Tupinamba. On the basis of linguistic and archaeological evidence (see Noelli 2008), Proto-Tupian emerged as a language at least five thousand years ago, somewhere in the center of the Amazon basin. We speak of it as "Macro Tupi" because it is regarded as the common source language for the wider linguistic stock that differentiated from this start. Archaeologists have also pieced together the "Tupi Expansion" across South America from several kinds of pottery shards (reviewed in Noelli 2008).

What also identifies the diverse societies of the Tupian stock is a common ancestral pattern of headhunting, which appears to form a distinctive and very successful cultural adaptation to the Amazon region. So successful was Tupian headhunting that it appears to have driven all other peoples (for example, Gê-speakers and Carib-speakers) out of the way. In his influential ethnography, *Headhunter's Heritage*, the anthropologist Robert F. Murphy referred in particular to the Tupian group Mundurukú of the Amazon basin when he wrote:

> In the Amazon valley, a region where ferociousness was the mode, the Mundurucú [*sic*] Indians enjoyed a reputation for unalloyed, untempered savagery until the turn of the century. Their war parties ranged outward almost every year, striking indiscriminately at tribes anywhere within a radius of five hundred miles, burning the villages, kidnapping children, and taking heads of adults as trophies of their exploits. They did not indulge in cannibalism, as so many of their neighbors, but the terror they inspired was so great that they themselves were seldom preyed upon and eaten. Their homeland on the upper Tapajós River, south of the Amazon, was rarely attacked, and though they no longer go to war their reputation still protects them from the hostile tribes of the region. (Murphy 1960, 1)

This very effective adaptation occasioned periodic interethnic village warfare. The Mundurukú would launch surprise raids at dawn against an enemy village. The shaman would blow a special sleep trance over the enemy and wait for the call of a bird that signals the approach of dawn. Warriors then lighted firebrands and shot them at the rooftops of the enemy huts, attempting to set them afire, causing tremendous mayhem (raids occurred almost always in the dry season). As villagers ran out in a panic, the raiders swooped in, dropping their bows and arrows in favor of head axes made out of very heavy wood. Indeed, the central object of the raid was the taking of heads: "Adult males and females were killed and decapitated, and prepubescent children of both sexes were captured by the attackers." The Mundurukú then retreated by forced march "until they had reached a safe distance from the enemy" (Murphy 1957, 1023). On the way home, the captives were escorted by their captors, and trophy heads were treated and preserved according to a strict protocol. Upon return to the village, the trophies were then put on display in the men's house and were used periodically in ritual observances. The captured children were kept and cared for until they were employed in subsequent rituals.

An interesting and significant feature is that the practice of headhunting is closely linked to the religious beliefs of the group—something particularly relevant for Girard, who sees archaic religion as the generative matrix of all culture. The trophy heads had a special relationship with supernatural "spirit protectors," the most important deities who were believed to take care of game animals in their Amazon homelands. Trophy heads were said to exert a powerful charm over these spirit protectors, who would then increase the supply of game to Mundurukú. The trophy head itself would appease the protector and cause the spirit to release more game for local hunters—and in turn, the trophy's "magical" virtue contributed to the prestige and the symbolic significance of the trophy takers. That prestige would certainly have contributed to the Girardian mimetic rivalry that compelled young men to want to hunt for trophy heads in the first place. The primary game animals prized in the hunt for food were white-lipped peccaries, which travel in enormous herds, two hundred to four hundred strong, moving through the rain forest almost like a bulldozer, covering vast areas. The successful trophy taker had the highest social status in the village, and was referred to as *Dajeboiši*. This means, literally, "mother of the peccaries." This paradoxical gender connotation derives from the power of the trophy heads to cause a numerical increase in the game hunted—the *Dajeboiši* was so titled because of his fertility-promoting function. Symbolically, that is, the headhunter "fulfilled a female role" in increasing the peccaries (Murphy 1957, 1024). The *Dajeboiši* would also have been endowed with a sacred aura, and would enter a particular "liminal" status by which he was basically isolated from normal relations with his fellow Mundurukú. He was also prohibited from sexual intercourse (Murphy 1957, 1025). In Girardian terms, this would point to the *Dajeboiši*'s near-sacred nature and, consequently, to the sacrificial nature of headhunting, which could be seen as a derivative form harking back to ritualized human sacrifice, the function of which it perpetuated. Some heads were in fact taken on the spot, but captives were also brought back and, at some later time, ritually sacrificed.

This whole pattern would be seen by Girard as a form of "surrogate victimization," and as a further form of internal violence deflection. The ritual would assure everybody that the spirit mother was appeased, that the forest game would increase, and that all the mimetic tensions within the social group, including the agonistic pressures exercised by the females to get the males out hunting, fell into an overarching pattern or structure, thus achieving the desirable goals of social harmony, sacred order, and food supply. The mimetic crisis, ritually reprised and reenacted each time by the mayhem of the headhunters' attacks on other villages, would be resolved and exorcised by this particular variant form of ritualized scapegoating. What is interesting, also, is the cultural continuity of headhunting customs among the greater pool of related populations that are Tupian speakers. For example, the axes used in the different populations had the same shape and cognatic names; the trophy taker was always given a special name and celebratory status in the different populations, and male celebrants generally wore similar feathered headdresses—such elements pointing to highly codified and evidently ancient ritual practice.

In my own analysis, I favored a two-part interpretation of the Tupian pattern of warfare, including these examples of unity within the diversity of its local manifestations. First, it looked to me as if Tupian warfare might have evolved by cultural selection way back in time, under conditions of competition for scarce game in the ancestral homelands of the Tupian language stock. Killing off enemy competitors as trophies, and scaring the survivors into relocating further away from the Tupi expansion, could well have increased the game supply for Tupi speakers through reduced intervillage competition that looked like a trophy head's "magical power" to appease the spirit protector. On this view, the captured prepubescent children can also be understood as the exception that tests the rule. Why would they be captured and then fed and cared for, increasing the mouths to feed, if game were truly scarce? Linguistically labeled as "game," not children, and cared for until times of great privation, when killed and eaten like game, they may have been the Amazon Basin's closest equivalent of "domesticated animals," as frightening as that thought may be to us today (no other species was commonly domesticated). Second, if this unconscious (but effective) competitive strategy emerged early in the Tupi diversification, the branching pattern of descent from a common ancestor would result in many sustained cultural homologs among the various branches. Indeed, the danger that similar Tupian populations would pose to each other would enforce their isolation, increasing the likelihood of a treelike cultural pattern of descent (with little cross-branch diffusion). And this is exactly the pattern we find today.

Interestingly, the Tupian violence-within-warfare fits the pattern we should also expect from Girard's theory of originary sacrifice and functional ritualization. The course of mimetic rivalry over status within the villages could well have promoted and rewarded violence redirected towards outsiders (especially if truly rewarded by additional game). Raids and scapegoat victimization would have worked to increase the supply of large game, with the deities favoring those who provided trophy heads. Until very recently, the Mundurukú believed in the transcendental nature of gift-giving by the spirit protector, whose generosity in increasing game was linked to their own "ritual" reenactment of "sacrifice" of warriors and captives (especially if the ritual did actually increase the supply of scarce game and of children regarded as game).

My findings pointed also to a pattern of divergence according to local environment, thus presenting a variational aspect not specifically envisaged by Girard, something perhaps overlooked and less theoretically interesting to him. Victims of Tupian warfare in Peru, to take a single, telling instance, were not taken as captives and eaten in ritualized meals; rather, they were kept as slaves. Why this variation? On the western end of the Amazon basin, on the flatlands at the base of the Andes, the meandering Amazon generates myriad oxbow lakes teeming with fish. Simply put, it appears to have been more beneficial to the headhunting groups to make their captives into slaves for sustained fishing, rather than ritually cooking and eating them—that way, they surely obtained more animal biomass, which meant less cannibalism. This type of variation was clearly important in shaping the way sacrifice and sacrificial rituals took shape—such as, for instance, the number of people that were actually killed, and the mechanisms by which human sacrifice were here abandoned, due to specific ecological conditions, rather than on any grounds of moral objection.

It is clearly in the deductive and Cartesian nature of Girard's theory to stress the paradigm to which all variations refer—whereas variation is an expected outcome and useful data in the study of cultural evolution and divergence from a common ancestor. The most significant conclusion to be reached, therefore, is that differences between the two theories may well be mutually confirming, and that the two approaches are, in relation to each other, rather complementary.

Milk-Drinking Practices in Indo-European Culture and Myth

The second example I would like to discuss is an Indo-European one, and has to do with bovines, milk-drinking practices, and the genetic evolution of adult lactose absorption (sometimes called "adult lactose tolerance"). As more fully explored in Durham (1991, ch. 5), two processes guided the historical emergence of milk-drinking traditions in Indo-European societies: natural selection sorting among genes for milk-sugar digestion, and cultural selection sorting among attitudes towards milk and milk-drinking practices. The prevalence of adult lactose absorption covaries, in fact, with latitude in a pattern that symmetrically inverts that of incident UV-B radiation.

Using data from forty-seven samples of human populations in Europe, Greenland, western Asia, and Africa, I showed (Durham 1991, ch. 5) that the prevalence of adult lactose absorption has evolved to high frequencies in populations that have a longstanding tradition of dairying, and who live in environments of low ultraviolet radiation, where vitamin D and metabolic calcium are chronically deficient. Figure 1 shows the frequency of adult

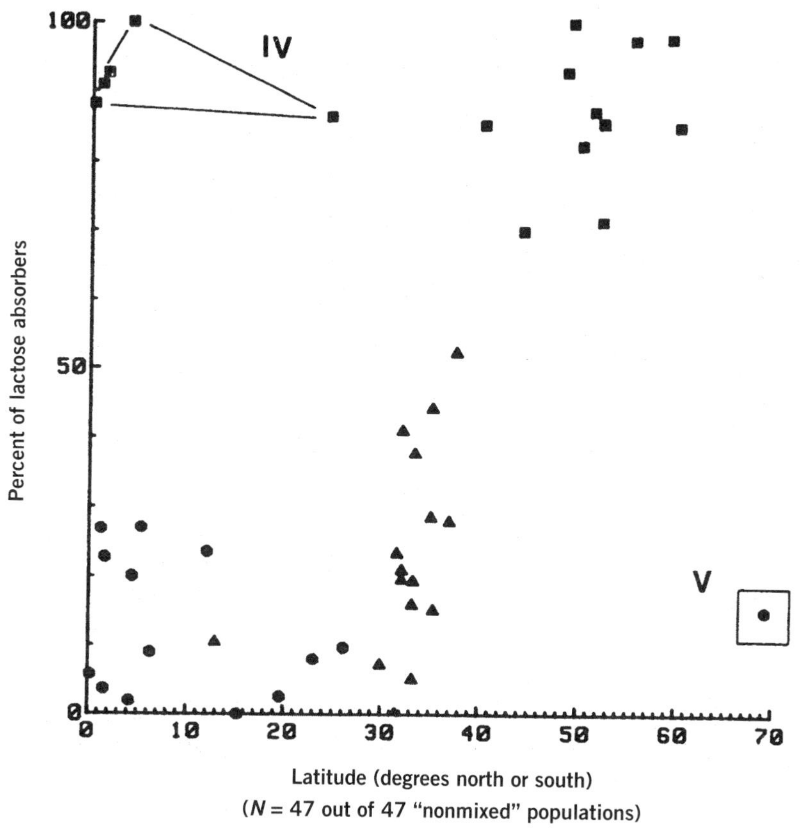

FIGURE 1. Percent of lactose absorbers/Latitude. From *Coevolution: Genes, Culture, and Human Diversity*, by William H. Durham. © 1991 by the Board of Trustees of the Leland Stanford Jr. University.

lactose absorbers in those forty-seven samples of the populations as a function of their homeland latitudes. With some important exceptions, there is a central tendency towards very low percentages of lactose absorbers in an equatorial plateau up to latitude 25 or 30 degrees north.

The reason for the equatorial plateau is that, on planet Earth, because of tropical cloud cover and the symmetry of the sphere, there is a broad latitudinal zone with high levels of ultraviolet radiation. We now realize that vitamin D is photosynthesized in the human skin; hence the problem

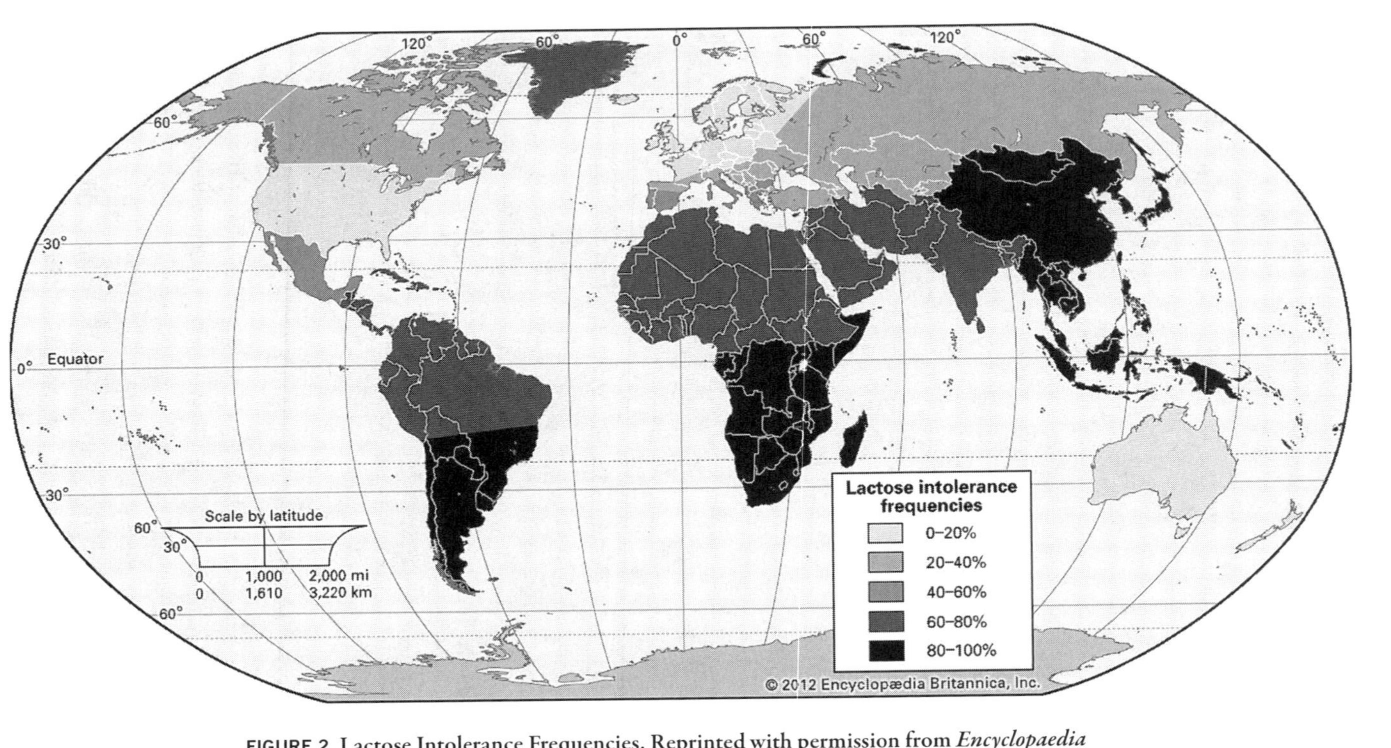

FIGURE 2. Lactose Intolerance Frequencies. Reprinted with permission from *Encyclopaedia Britannica*. © 2012 by Encyclopeadia Britannica, Inc.

of vitamin D deficiency increases consistently above 25 degrees north or south. Within that equatorial plateau there is little selection pressure for vitamin D–enhanced calcium absorption. As one moves towards the poles, there is a more-or-less steady increase in selection pressure favoring the gene for persistent lactase activity, the activity of the enzyme that breaks up milk sugar (lactose).

Adult lactose absorption is thus an instructive case where genes and culture are both implicated in human adaptation. It offers convincing evidence for a cultural change in human populations (dairying and milk production) contributing to the evolution of specific genes that are adaptive in the context of that cultural change. But the adaptive value of the genes also depends on a geographic condition: the global distribution of ultraviolet B radiation on the planet.

While, as one goes north, there is a very clear definitional tendency, there are two kinds of very obvious exceptions: (1) high levels of lactose absorption at the equator, where that trait is relatively rare, and (2) little or no lactose absorption at very high latitudes, where indeed that is rare compared to most other populations (see figure 2). The first of the two exceptions, designated Cluster IV in figure 1, are milk-dependent pastoralists from East Africa and Saudi Arabia for whom vitamin D is not an issue, but probably water and electrolytes are. The gene frequencies of adult lactose absorption have evolved to levels rivaling those at high latitude, but apparently for a very different reason—for the advantage of drinking milk for its water and electrolytes.

The second exception refers to a population that lacks dairying and fresh milk consumption, but lives at high latitude in an environment with low ultraviolet radiation: the Inuit (Eskimos) of the Arctic, who were traditionally quite healthy, with low levels of adult lactose absorption. This circumstance is explained by the fact that their diet is rich in both vitamin D and calcium, which together circumvent the problems of calcium scarcity (rickets and osteomalacia) at that latitude. Effectively shielded from UV-B by latitude and seawater, some species of marine fish contain vitamin D concentrations that range from a low of some 44 international units per 100 grams—equivalent to the amount in two egg yolks, for example—to as high as 1,500 units. Moreover, the raw livers of such fish and of the seals who feed upon them, traditionally considered a delicacy by the Inuit, may contain many times these levels. Here again, culture plays a key role in human adaptation.

Did Cultural Differences Help Shape the Adaptation?

There is, however, the important dimension of time, which remains to be considered. Because natural selection is an intergenerational process, the genes for adult lactose absorption would only have evolved to high levels if, over great expanses of time, cultural beliefs also promoted milk-drinking at high latitudes. Do cultural beliefs promote milk-drinking at high latitudes today, and did they in ages past?

In order to test this hypothesis, I undertook a statistical analysis of contemporary milk-use patterns using the best source then available: 1978 FAO data. The analysis was based on two assumptions. First, I assumed that variations in milk-use behavior (that is, in actual patterns of milk consumption and processing) reflect underlying cultural differences in the values and beliefs that people attach to milk. In other words, I assumed that a population that actively consumes a high proportion of its total milk production as fresh milk has an actual cultural preference for dairy production in that form. My second assumption is that the general trends revealed by this study of 1978 data are not entirely of recent origin.

Given these assumptions, it is possible to test for several indications of latitudinal variation in cultural preferences regarding milk use. First, the number of cows per thousand people—a measure of dairying effort—increases sharply starting at about 25 degrees north or south latitude. As shown in figure 3, the central tendency rises from an average baseline of some twenty to thirty cows per one thousand inhabitants in populations near the equator to as much as seven times that number in European populations, the highest point corresponding to population no. 36 (Danes).

Similar confirmation is found using total per capita consumption of milk, as shown in figure 4. Fresh milk consumption increases from a baseline of almost 10 liters per person per year at low latitude to the high Danish figure of 1,033—almost three liters of milk per person per day. There can be little doubt that milk consumption patterns covary with latitude.

Figure 5 confirms that the pattern of milk consumption in the subsample

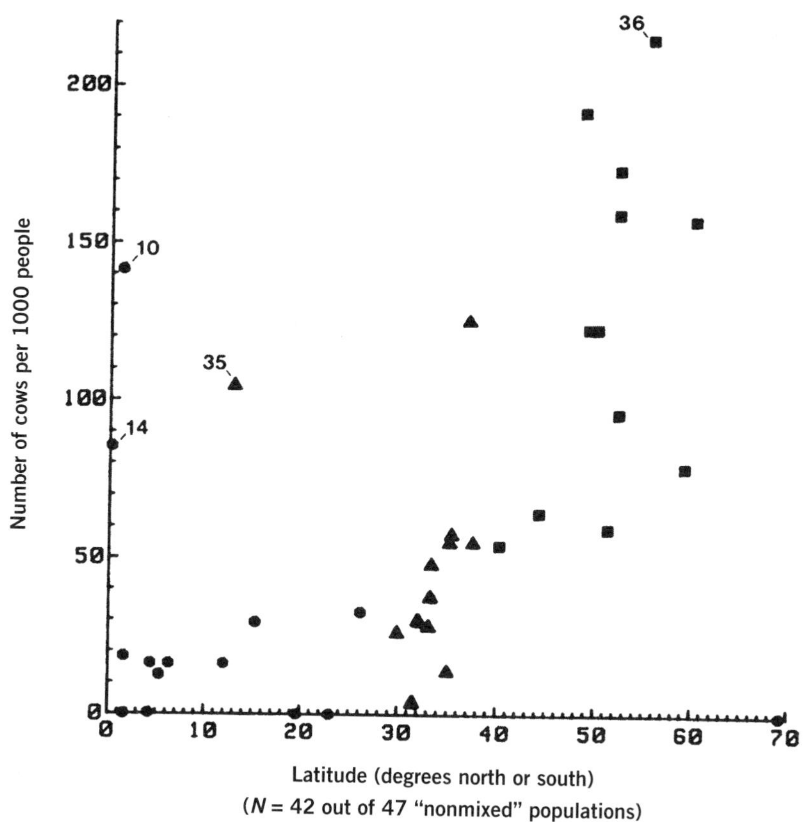

FIGURE 3. Number of cows per 1,000 people/Latitude. From *Coevolution: Genes, Culture, and Human Diversity*, by William H. Durham. © 1991 by the Board of Trustees of the Leland Stanford Jr. University.

reflects actual preference for fresh milk over the processed forms favored at higher latitudes. Since curd-based cheese solves the problem of lactose digestion (because lactose is water soluble and is drained off in the whey), one would expect a higher conversion of milk to cheese at low latitudes. In fact, except for the milk-dependent pastoralists, figure 5 shows an overall decline with latitude in the percentage of milk converted to cheese.

With few exceptions, cheese-making decreases from a high of 30 to 60 percent of milk in North Africa and southern Europe to lows on the order of 10 to 20 percent in central and Northern Europe. But we can say more than

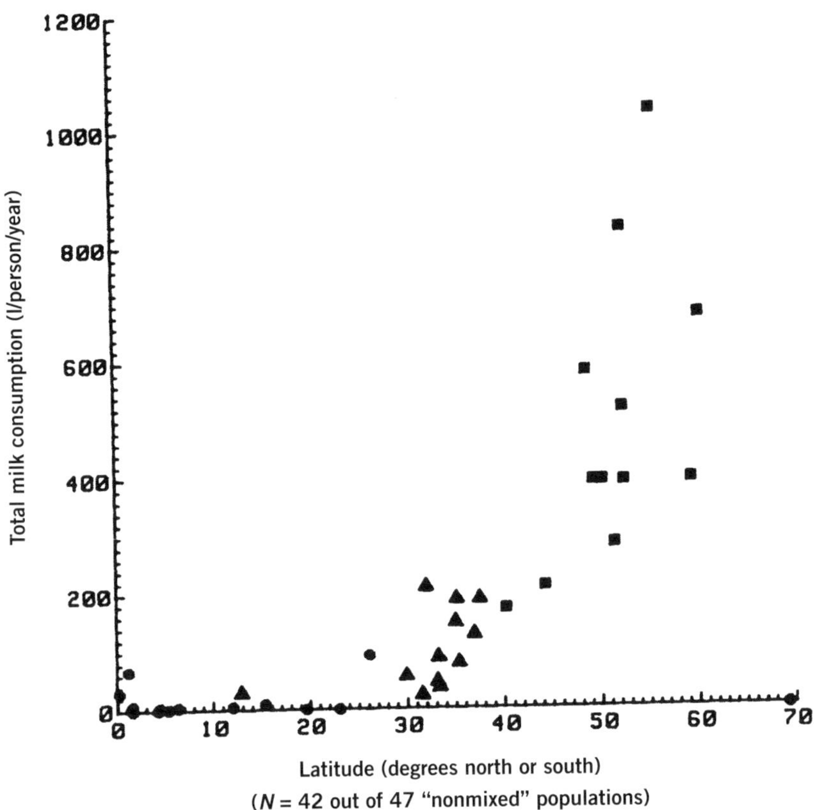

FIGURE 4. Total milk consumption/Latitude. From *Coevolution: Genes, Culture, and Human Diversity*, by William H. Durham. © 1991 by the Board of Trustees of the Leland Stanford Jr. University.

that: the cheeses produced at high-latitude locations, such as the notoriously sweet Gjetöst of Norway and the Mysöst of Sweden (made respectively from goat's-milk and cow's-milk whey), involve concentrating the lactose content so that these cheeses contain as much as 36 percent pure lactose. Again, we have another cultural solution to the problem, "how can one offset the calcium deficiency characteristic of high latitudes?" Answer: pile on the lactose by drinking fresh milk, and pile it on by eating lactose-concentrated cheese. Here is another most interesting case of the interaction of genes and culture.

But what about the role of milking in deep time? This is where Girard's theory becomes relevant to mine. I realized at an early stage that, by

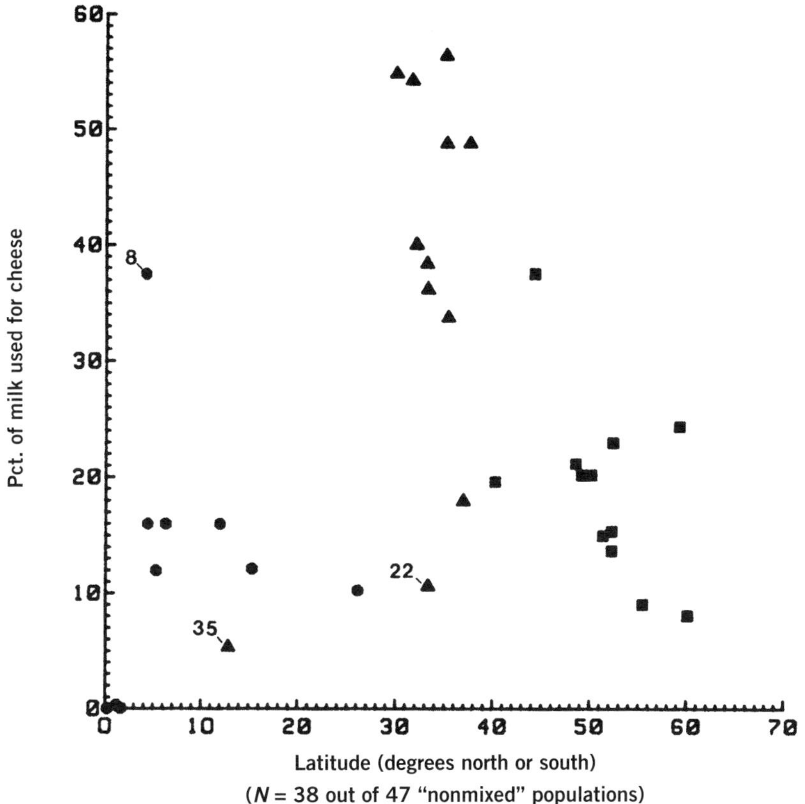

FIGURE 5. Percent of milk used for cheese/Latitude. From *Coevolution: Genes, Culture, and Human Diversity*, by William H. Durham. © 1991 by the Board of Trustees of the Leland Stanford Jr. University.

coincidence, a number of my study populations—about half of the sample—were of Indo-European origins. Indo-European is a large family of related languages, like the Tupian family in South America, and equally diverse, covering a landmass stretching all the way from India up to Iceland and across Scandinavia.

Anthropologists are still arguing about the probable place of origin of this family, but for the sake of our argument, let us assume Anatolia as the homeland of Indo-European cultures dating back some five thousand years.[1] Over the millennia, these populations dispersed across Europe and Asia, taking their languages and beliefs with them as they went, and they differentiated to fit new circumstances. But there remains a deep common pattern among them, stemming from their historical descent from a common origin located in relatively low latitudes.

As these populations traveled and carried their languages with them, so they also carried values, ideas, and even myths. In my research, I then decided to assess the role of milking as theme and motif in the traditional mythology of populations of Indo-European descent. A search through the literature revealed that common bovine themes pervade Indo-European mythologies. Moreover, we know the variants to be related by descent to the common ancestral stock, and thus they qualify as true cultural homologs. The question is: do they show appropriate variation by latitude in milking-related themes?

My thinking about this case of "cultural descent with modification" was greatly aided by an important synthesis of Indo-European myth in the work of the anthropologist Bruce Lincoln (1975, 1981), a work that complements and adds evidential depth to Girard's views of the sacrificial origins of culture. Much like Girard's, Lincoln's interpretation, based on the comparative study of Indo-European creation myths, provides both additional mythological material related to dairying, and a general cultural evolutionary framework with which to tie together some otherwise disparate observations. Building on the approach of Georges Dumézil and what has been called the "genetic model" of Indo-European mythology (see also Littleton 1973; Larson, Littleton, and Puhvel 1974), Lincoln documents an impressive array of correspondences among the set of myths describing the origins and peopling of the world. He uses these correspondences, structural as well as linguistic, to reconstruct the outline of the ancestral "Proto-Indo-European" creation myth. That myth centers around what he calls the first or primordial sacrifice—a sacrifice that both created the world and serves as the mythical prototype of all sacrifice in traditional Indo-European religion; indeed, one might regard it as a prototype of all creative action.

Lincoln's myth resonates deeply with Girard's theory of cultural origins, and of the primordial sacrifice he postulates as the inception of religious, cultural, and ritualistic practices. Echoing Girard's perspective on the original crisis of "undifferentiation" and the emergence of mythical twins as mimetic rivals (including Odin and his brothers, and Romulus and Remus [Girard 1986, 89; 1987, 38–39]), Lincoln writes that in the original myth, "the world begins with a pair of [anthropomorphic] twins: *Manu, 'man,' and *Yemo, 'twin.' *Yemo is the first king and *Manu is the first priest, and in the course of the myth, *Manu kills his brother, thus performing the first sacrifice. As a result of this act, the world is created and *Manu fashions the earth and the heavens as well as the three social classes [priests, warriors, and commoners] from his brother's body" (Lincoln 1981, 87). Also offered in the first sacrifice with *Yemo (the asterisk denotes a reconstructed form) is the "first bovine," which Lincoln believes from comparative study to have been an ox.

The basic elements of this myth—a first priest, a first king, a first bovine, a first sacrifice, and then creation—are found by Lincoln throughout his survey of ancient texts from locations as diverse as India, Iran, Rome, Ireland, and Scandinavia. But the different versions show systematic latitudinal variation in the nature and role of the first bovine, and corresponding variation in reference to milk and milk-drinking. Table 1 summarizes the major features of this variation as organized by source mythology and arranged in latitudinal order from north to south.

To the correspondences described by Lincoln, I have added two further entries from my own reading of Greek and Gaelic mythology. To begin with, the table shows that a recognizable version of the "myth of the first sacrifice," complete with corresponding personages and structurally similar roles, can be found in all six Indo-European mythologies studied. In each case a *Manu (first priest) slays a *Yemo (first king figure) who is either a twin or another close genealogical relative. The link between sacred kingship and sacrifice has been discussed extensively by Girard in *Things Hidden* (Girard 1987, 51–57). A bovine is also a part of each of the myths, a detail that is particularly relevant for my argument, although the sex of the bovine and its mythical role vary as shown in the compilation. From the first sacrifice, involving either the *Yemo figure alone or *Yemo and first bovine together, are created various aspects of the world and its human population.

Table 1 indicates that the roles of bovines and milk-drinking in Indo-European creation myths do vary with latitude in a pattern notably consistent with the pattern of adult lactose absorption. In the northernmost examples, Old Norse and Gaelic, the first animals or first bovines are female; they produce milk in great quantity. Milk is consumed directly and fresh by anthropomorphic figures. Although those figures, whether giants or gods, are clearly adult, milk for them is the most basic staple or even the sole source of food; this diet of milk is associated with their great size, strength, and

TABLE 1. Cultural Evolution of Indo-European Mythology: Correspondences in the Myth of First Sacrifice

SOURCE MYTHOLOGY	FIRST PRIEST (*MANU)	FIRST KING (*YEMO)	FIRST BOVINE	FRESH MILK PRODUCTION	FRESH MILK CONSUMPTION	FIRST SACRIFICE	CREATION
Old Norse	Odin (god)	Ýmir (giant)	Auðhumla (female)	Yes (abundant)	Adults (gods and giants)	Giant	Earth, mountains, sea, and waters
Gaelic	Lugh/Ioldanach (god)	Balor (giant)	Gray cow (female)	Yes (abundant)	Adults (gods and giants)	Giant	Mountains, lakes, and rivers
Roman	Romulus (man)	Remus (man)	She-wolf (female)	Yes	Infants	Man	City of Rome
Greek	Zeus (god)	Cronos (titan)	Amalthea (female goat)	Yes	Infants	Giant	Humanity
Iranian	Ahriman (demon)	Gayōmart (man)	"Sole-created ox" (male)	No	No	Man and ox	Plants, animals, humanity, and metals
Indic	Gods	Puruṣa (man/bull)	Puruṣa (male)	No (processed)	No	Man/bull	Animals, social classes, earth, and sky

Source: Data for Old Norse, Roman, Iranian, and Indic myths are from Lincoln 1981; for the Gaelic myth, from Squire 1905; and for the Greek myth, from Hamilton 1940 and Graves 1960. From *Coevolution: Genes, Culture, and Human Diversity*, by William H. Durham.

FIGURE 6. Print edition of Snorri Sturluson's *Prose Edda* (1666). The Royal Library, Copenhagen, NKS 1867 4°: Ólafur Brynjúlfsson: Sæmundar og Snorra Edda, 1760, f. 95r.

physical stamina. The first bovine is not sacrificed in the act of creation, but continues in a nurturing capacity thereafter. As we can read, for instance, in *Gylfaginning*, a part of Snorri Sturluson's *Prose Edda* written in Old Norse, the first king is Ýmir, a primeval "frost giant" and the ancestor of all *jötnar*, or giants. As in Lincoln's reconstructed myth, Odin and his brothers sacrifice Ýmir and make the earth from his flesh, while from the brains come clouds, from the blood come oceans, and from the bones come the rocks and mountains. Ýmir is described as a super-gigantic figure who feeds on rivers of fresh milk from a first bovine who is herself a giant cow, Auðhumla (figure 6). In a painting by Nicolai Abildgaard (1790), we can see how Ýmir suckles from the cow Auðhumla, while she licks Buri, the first god of Norse mythology, from a rock of salty ice (figure 7).

FIGURE 7. Nicolai Abildgaard: *Ymir Suckling the Cow Audhumla*. Ca. 1777, National Gallery of Denmark, Copenhagen. Danish National Gallery. © SMK Photo.

The themes of the southernmost variants of this myth stand in striking contrast. In the Iranian version, for instance, the first king, Gayōmart, slays a male bovine, a huge bull, with the help of a scorpion that attacks the testicles of the bull (figure 8). The bovines are male (bulls and oxen); they are part of the first sacrifice; and there is no mention of milk production or consumption. Rather than continuing on into the creation in a nurturing capacity, the dismembered bovines are converted, at the point of sacrifice, into other plants, animals, and varied resources. The only mention of milk at all in the creation tale is a reference to a processed byproduct, "curdled butter."

In the Mediterranean variants, one finds a version that is intermediate between these extremes. The "bovines" are neither prolific cows nor powerful bulls, but she-wolves and goats; their role is clearly nutritive, but the milk is consumed conspicuously by infants. In Greek versions, for instance, the first bovine is female, a lactating cow, who provides milk, not just meat. The milk

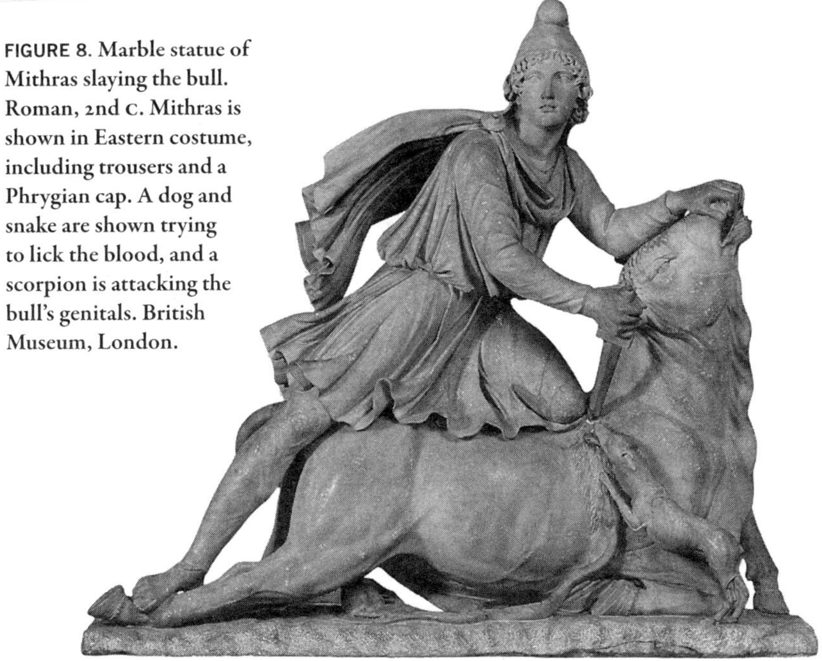

FIGURE 8. Marble statue of Mithras slaying the bull. Roman, 2nd c. Mithras is shown in Eastern costume, including trousers and a Phrygian cap. A dog and snake are shown trying to lick the blood, and a scorpion is attacking the bull's genitals. British Museum, London.

is reserved for the infant Zeus, the most important deity—as one can see, for instance, in Nicolas Poussin's depiction of this myth, where Zeus is drinking from a goat named Amalthea (figure 9). Lincoln also argues that Romulus and Remus are inflections of *Yemo and *Manu, and that the she-wolf came to substitute for the cow because the latter was not a fitting symbol for the founding of the militaristic Roman Empire. In spite of being more feisty and aggressive, the she-wolf is still lactating and feeding young culture heroes, as infants, directly from her udder.

These differences suggest an early evolutionary divergence in the mythology of the proto-Indo-Europeans, giving rise to two distinct ancestral stocks. One became Indo-European mythology, founded upon a creation myth that features female bovines in a nurturing role, and a sacrificial battle between god and giants. The other became Indo-Iranian mythology, founded upon a creation myth in which both a man-giant and a male bovine are offered together as the first sacrifice. Lincoln noted these differences, and proposed that they "may be easier to understand when we recall that the Europeans

FIGURE 9. Nicolas Poussin, *The Childhood of Zeus*. Ca. 1638. Dulwich Picture Gallery, London.

were an agricultural society for whom the chief value of cattle was the milk-giving ability of the cow. The pastoral Indo-Iranians, however, esteemed their animals in a much broader sense and described their productive value in the mythical image of the primordial ox from whose body numerous goods stream forth" (Lincoln 1981, 87). Further diversification resulted in appropriate refinements. In the case of the Mediterranean tradition, the refinements were appropriate to dairying populations that had not evolved (and would not evolve) high levels of adult lactose absorption. But more importantly for the arguments here, the northernmost refinements were appropriate, I submit, to an environment of chronic vitamin D deficiency.

From the perspective of evolutionary culture theory, these findings have two important implications. First, they imply that some force or forces of nonrandom selectivity guided the cultural evolution of Indo-European mythology. We can infer both that there were sources of variation in the content of myths and, more importantly, that the variants were subject to some systematic process of differential transmission within regional populations, such that what lasted and "stuck" was also locally appropriate. Larson states that "myth articulates the basic self-understanding of a people and thereby operates as a kind of charter for the total cultural life" (Larson, Littleton, and Puhvel 1974, 1). It is therefore likely that different forms had, in conjunction with other beliefs and values related to dairying, different consequences for people, depending upon their social and ecological setting. Those consequences would have provided various kinds of positive or negative feedback, such as better or worse food supply, calcium sufficiency, and better or worse health and survival. If people's belief in mythic variants were influenced by that feedback, cultural selection could then have favored variants that were adaptive for those who perpetuated them. The simple process of value-driven decision making is sufficient to explain the latitudinal pattern of table 1.

Mimetic Theory and Coevolution

Judging from these examples, it is clear to me that there is an interesting convergence between Girard's theory of mimetic hominization and my own work on coevolution. The cases I have presented all support and confirm basic aspects of Girard's mimetic theory. The common theme of sacrifice in Indo-European myths, for example, offers evidentiary support for mimetic rivalry, victimization, sacrificial resolution, and sacralization.

What I most appreciate about Girardian theory, however, is that it predicts a regular form of social structure, in which a group regularly forms with particular interests and needs. Mimetic rivalry sets up a crisis, which empowers the group to undertake a powerful case of cultural selection, favoring an ideology of victimization and sacrifice for the good of the group. Viewed this way, Girard adds to evolutionary culture theory a particular pattern of cultural selection by imposition: an ideology of sacrifice of one or more individuals (the "scapegoat resolution") is perpetrated for the good of a majority. Group survival is also very important, and cultural selection by imposition within groups could have been joined by natural selection between groups, reducing or eliminating those who did not prevent mimetic crisis through the victimization mechanism.

In any event, Girard's theory posits a mechanism and a social context (mimetic crisis) that drives the selective retention of victimization and sacrifice, as forced compliance with someone else's choice. I would be willing to nominate Girard's theory as a valid early mechanism for imposition (Girard would probably say "*the* original imposition"). Put differently, Girard gives us a special mode of cultural selection by imposition, and argues for its systematic influence in the course of cultural evolution.

In all the case studies I have discussed here and elsewhere (Durham 1991), we can also discern supplementary processes at work. Tupi warfare shows adaptive variations, and so do attitudes and motifs in Indo-European myths. My analysis of Indo-European mythology suggests that an ancient, prototypical "myth of first sacrifice" underwent variational evolution that resulted in a latitudinal pattern. In the north, a symbolism of heavy emphasis on cows, milk, and nurturance replaced the earlier southerly themes of male bovines, slaughter, and sacrifice. In other words, the myth changed in appropriate ways, reinforcing the drinking of milk in the north. Some process caused the differential persistence of forms that were (and are) more suitable for those northern latitude areas—forms in which the bovines are female, where the milk is produced in quantity, and where cultural heroes drink it with gusto, encouraging average people to drink milk as befits their health and adaptation.

The theory of coevolution can be seen as my attempt to understand how cultural evolution is capable of promoting both adaptation and maladaptation in human societies. A key idea is that we humans have two distinct but interacting systems of inheritance: the genetic and the cultural. They are separate, well-defined, and capable of their own mechanisms of change. In a nutshell, we could say that the causes of genetic change are well worked out in Darwinian theory—including Darwin's main means of modification, natural selection, but also mutation, migration, and chance effects. Similarly, culture can change by repeated innovation or invention; by diffusion, or "cross-lineage" borrowing; and by various transmission forces arising from the social nature of transmission. However, the main means of modification in the cultural track is value-guided decision making, or cultural selection.

It is interesting to reflect on the fact that Darwin coined the term "natural selection" to mark a similarity between his process of natural culling and the familiar case of human choice exercised by plant and animal breeders. Natural selection is thus a consciously chosen metaphor: it is a "blind," natural version of something consciously pursued by human choice. But there comes a point in evolutionary theorization when it is appropriate to reverse the direction of the metaphor and draw attention back to the role of human selection and choice as they shape evolution in the cultural track. We have to play the metaphor backwards today, so to speak, to mirror the changing nature of our understanding of coevolutionary processes.

So playing the metaphor backwards, cultural selection in its various forms is the main force of cultural evolution. In some social and environmental circumstances, cultural selection proceeds by a relatively unfettered choice of options, which will be vetted and compared to local values in place (some of which are themselves earlier products of cultural evolution—see Durham 1991, ch. 4), often with results that enhance human adaptation. In other circumstances, especially in the case of structured social inequalities, cultural selection takes the form of imposition. It is still a process of value-guided decision making, but the choices available and/or the values to judge them may be foisted on people by powerful agents. In this instance, the results will probably enhance only the survival and reproduction of the imposers. This context is where Girard's theory is so valuable, since it elucidates an originating process by which there emerges a structured regulation of collective life, creating and sustaining a force for cultural evolutionary change by imposition.

Note

1. A recent article by a team headed by Quentin D. Atkinson offers novel quantitative evidence for the Anatolian hypothesis for the Indo-European homeland, as opposed to the older Kurgan theory for a homeland in the Pontic-Caspian steppes of southern Russia and eastern Ukraine (Atkinson et al. 2012).

Works Cited

Atkinson, Q. D., et al. 2012. "Mapping the Origins and Expansion of the Indo-European Language Family." *Science* 337, no. 6097: 957–60.

Durham, W. H. 1991. *Coevolution: Genes, Culture, and Human Diversity*. Stanford, CA: Stanford University Press.

Girard, R. 1977. *Violence and the Sacred*. Baltimore: Johns Hopkins University Press.

———. 1986. *The Scapegoat*. Baltimore: Johns Hopkins University Press.

———. 1987. *Things Hidden since the Foundation of the World*. Stanford, CA: Stanford University Press.

Girard, R., P. Antonello, and J. C. de Castro Rocha. 2007. *Evolution and Conversion: Dialogues on the Origins of Culture*. New York: Continuum.

Graves, R. 1960. *The Greek Myths*. 2 vols. New York. Rev. ed. of work first published in 1955.

Hamilton, E. 1940. *Mythology*. Boston: Little, Brown.

Laland, K. N., and G. Brown. 2011. *Sense and Nonsense: Evolutionary Perspectives on Human Behaviour*. Oxford: Oxford University Press.

Larson, G. J., C. S. Littleton, and J. Puhvel, eds. 1974. *Myth in Indo-European Antiquity*. Berkeley: University of California Press.

Lincoln, B. 1975. "The Indo-European Myth of Creation." *History of Religions* 15: 121–45.

———. 1981. *Priests, Warriors, and Cattle: A Study in the Ecology of Religions*. Berkeley: University of California Press.

Littleton, C. S. 1973. *The New Comparative Mythology: An Anthropological Assessment of the Theories of Georges Dumézil*. Berkeley: University of California Press.

Murphy, Robert F. 1957. "Intergroup Hostility and Social Cohesion." *American Anthropologist* 59, no. 6: 1018–35.

———. 1960. *Headhunter's Heritage: Social and Economic Change among the Mundurucú Indians*. Berkeley: University of California Press.

Noelli, F. S. 2008. "The Tupi Expansion." In *The Handbook of South American Archaeology*, ed. H. Silverman and W. H. Isbell, 659–70. New York: Springer.

Squire, C. 1905. *Celtic Myth and Legend, Poetry and Romance*. London: Gresham Publishing.

Genes and Mimesis

Structural Patterns in Darwinism and Mimetic Theory

Paul Dumouchel

This essay constitutes an attempt at Darwinizing Girard. This attempt should be viewed as an incursion, as a first exploration into an uncharted domain, rather than as an essay in proving, for example, that the two theories are incompatible, or to determine which one provides a better understanding of human life and culture. It defends two main theses. The first is that a central resemblance between Girard's explanation of culture and Darwin's account of adaptation in terms of natural selection is that both theories provide radically non-agential explanations. The second is that based on a population understanding of natural selection, the sacrificial crisis, the victimary mechanism, and culture to which it gives rise, according to Girard, can be viewed as a mechanism that "de-Darwinizes" culture. The conclusion is that rather than try to Darwinize culture directly, we should understand the relationship between culture and natural selection somewhat like the relation between natural selection and the organizational principles of complex organisms.

Any attempt to relate large and encompassing theories like Girard's and Darwin's faces many problems. One particular set of difficulties simply springs from the passage of time. *The Origin of Species* was published in 1859. Though the original reception of the book was mostly hostile, Darwin's evolutionary theory constitutes today the overarching paradigm of all biological sciences. In consequence, given that different biological disciplines have made different discoveries thanks to Darwin, each tends to have a somewhat different Darwin. Furthermore, recently Darwinian thinking has penetrated many domains that traditionally invoked different explanatory principles, such as psychology, cognitive science, neurology, epistemology, anthropology, ethics, or economics (Barkow, Cosmides, and Tooby 1992; Allen and Bekoff 1997; Edelman 1987; Callebaut and Pinxten 1987; Boyd and Richerson 1985; Rachels 1991; Nelson and Winter 1982). It also gave rise to a new study of culture, memetics (Blackmore 1999), and the philosopher Daniel Dennett compared "Darwin's dangerous idea" to a "universal acid" destined to dissolve all traditional forms of thinking concerning society and culture (Dennett 1995). Such claims are often viewed as forms of Darwinian or of biological imperialism. The truth, however, is that the invaders disagree on the nature of the tidings that they are bringing to what they see as underdeveloped disciplines. The question therefore arises, which Darwin should we use when we want to relate Darwinian explanations to a theory in social science?[1] I will not try to rediscover the "original" Darwin. I will to a large extent rest my understanding of Darwin on the interpretation of evolution and natural selection defended by Peter Godfrey-Smith in a recent book, *Darwinian Populations and Natural Selection* (2009). It is impossible to adequately justify here the choice of this particular interpretation. However, apart from the quality and rigor of his analysis, two specific reasons can be given. First, Godfrey-Smith insists that, though evolution by natural selection requires a certain type of heritability between ancestors and descendants, natural selection, so he argues, does not require (or favor) any specific mechanism of heredity—for example, genetic inheritance. It immediately follows that Darwinian explanations (i.e., explanations invoking the principle of natural selection) can, in principle, be readily applied outside the field of biology proper, something that seems desirable in this comparative context. The second reason is that Godfrey-Smith stresses the non-agential dimension of explanations by natural selection. A fundamental aspect of Darwin's discovery is to show how complexity and organization can arise without having to postulate an agent that is responsible for the diversity of life and the adaptation of organisms. As we will see later on, these two aspects of Darwinism are closely related. I will argue that Girard's mimetic explanation similarly is a non-agential explanation of social and cultural phenomena, and in particular of natural religion or the sacred.

Darwin and Population Thinking

As the title of Godfrey-Smith's book suggests, at the heart of Darwin's thought is what Ernst Mayr called "population thinking" (Mayr 1976). What evolve are populations of individuals, and the essential prerequisites of evolution and natural selection are defined at the population level. Whether or not a population is subject to natural selection and does evolve depends on the relations that exist between the individuals or entities that make up that population. Godfrey-Smith names "Darwinian population" any population where natural selection and evolution take place. In a minimal sense, he defines a Darwinian population as "a collection of causally connected individual things in which there is variation in character, which leads to difference in reproductive output (difference in how much and how quickly individuals reproduce), and which is inherited to some extent. Inheritance is understood as similarity between parent and offspring, due to the causal role of the parent" (Godfrey-Smith 2009, 39). This minimal concept of a Darwinian population imposes some basic constraints on the type of collections in which natural selection and evolution may occur, some of which are not explicitly stated—for example, that the individual things that make up the population can reproduce, and that there be some kind of parent/offspring relation between them. Godfrey-Smith then identifies five parameters or conditions that a population must satisfy in order for natural selection and evolution to occur.

The Model

In Godfrey-Smith's model of natural selection, the first parameter, which is labeled H, is the fidelity of heredity. Offspring must be like their parents to some extent; they must inherit the characteristics that made them more successful or adapted. H is a measure of the extent to which the inheritance of characteristics is reliable. The second condition is represented by V; it corresponds to the abundance of variation among individuals. If all the members of a population are carbon copies of each other, if the population does not contain (generate and maintain) a sufficient amount of variation relevant to the differential fitness of individuals, natural selection cannot take place. The next parameter, *a*, competitive interaction with respect to reproduction, represents the extent to which the reproductive success of one individual influences the reproductive success of another. It can take values between zero and one, where zero corresponds to a complete absence of interaction, while one indicates that the addition of one offspring to one individual reduces by an equivalent amount the reproductive success of another.[2] This parameter, according to Godfrey-Smith, can be understood as a modern rendering of Darwin's "struggle for existence," and as an interpretation of the expression "causally connected," which occurs in his definition of a minimal Darwinian population: "a collection of *causally connected* individual things." Parameter *a* measures a particularly important way, though not the only way, in which individuals can be bound together in a Darwinian population. The next measure, S, represents the dependence of fitness differences on intrinsic characters of individuals. If fitness differences were completely independent of intrinsic characteristics of individuals, and only varied by reason of features of the environment, then changes in the rates of certain traits could not lead to adaptation. There could be natural selection and evolution, but not in any interesting way leading to complex adaptations. Continuity, or C, is the last parameter. "An evolving population exhibits continuity," writes Godfrey-Smith, "when small changes to an organism's phenotype lead to small changes in its fitness" (Godfrey-Smith 2009, 57). Continuity captures the idea that adaptations result from the accumulation of small changes, and that chaotic variation in fitness as a result of minor phenotypic variations would make adaptation impossible.

According to Godfrey-Smith, nothing else is necessary for evolution through natural selection to happen. In any population where these conditions are satisfied, natural selection and evolution will take place. No particular force or agency is required. Whenever and wherever the conditions are right, a population will experience natural selection and evolution. Understood in this way, Darwin's theory of evolution by natural selection is a radically non-agential explanation. No special agency is responsible for the evolution of life on earth—in a sense not even "natural selection," for natural selection is not a mysterious force or special kind of agent, but only a set of conditions operating on populations of entities. This very abstract explanation of natural selection also constitutes what we call a distal rather than a proximal explanation of evolution. All that it can tell us is that if these conditions are satisfied, natural selection will occur and evolution will follow. By itself it cannot explain how or why this, rather than that, adaptation evolves. In order to answer such questions, proximal explanations of particular evolutionary episodes are necessary. They require a large quantity of historical and environmental information, and often hypotheses concerning the mechanisms that are locally responsible for development and/or the generation of variation. However, explanations by natural selection, just as they do not need to make any hypothesis about the underlying mechanism of inheritance, are not intrinsically linked to specific ways in which different adaptations arise.

A second fundamental aspect of this model of natural selection and evolution is that it represents the five necessary conditions as parameters that can take different values. It follows that being a Darwinian population is a question of degree; it is not something that is all or nothing. Depending on the values of the five parameters—values that can change, and that often will change as a result of past natural selection—different collections of individuals will be Darwinian populations more or less subject to natural selection. Thus there will be paradigmatic Darwinian populations, but also minimal, marginal, or even trivial ones. Not all of them will be subject to natural selection in the same way and to the same extent.

De-Darwinization

An important consequence of this understanding of evolution and natural selection is that we can see how, by tinkering with these parameters, it is possible to de-Darwinize a given population, to reduce the effect of natural selection and in a sense to freeze or radically slow down its evolution. Godfrey-Smith gives one important example of this process of de-Darwinization. Take any multicellular organism like any one of us; it can be viewed as an integrated biological system. It can also be viewed as a population, or rather as a collection of populations, of cells.

> If a cell arises that has a feature that makes it able to divide faster than others, and the feature is reliably passed on in reproduction, we expect

> that feature to proliferate, whether or not that feature does any good for the whole organism. So how do collectives like ourselves remain viable? Sometimes, of course, we do not. Cancer is one consequence of cell level Darwinian processes. (Godfrey-Smith 2009, 101)

In fact, multicellular organisms take measures to protect themselves from natural selection processes occurring at cell level. Some of these protections are systemic—for example, the action of immune cells that recognize and destroy abnormal cells before they can proliferate; others rest on controlling the parameters that define a population as Darwinian. Many of these de-Darwinizing mechanisms are related to the way in which higher-level entities, multicellular organisms reproduce. For example, the reproductive cycle of multicellular organisms generally limits the number of cells from the parent organism that can participate in the generation of offspring. This reproductive bottleneck takes an extreme form in many species where the new organism begins as a single cell. In consequence, all the variations accumulated in the different cell lineages of the parent organism are lost. This reduces dramatically the value of V, the amount of variation present in the new cell population. Similarly, in many organisms, germ cells, which alone are responsible for the birth of a new organism, are segregated shortly after conception. This means that the fitness of members of the population of cells that constitute such a multicellular organism does not depend on any of their intrinsic characteristics, but on an accidental feature of their environment: where they happen to be located within the organism. Segregation of the germ line reduces the value of S; it makes the fitness of individuals independent of their intrinsic characteristics. The reproduction of multicellular organisms de-Darwinizes the cell populations they are made of and reduces the extent to which evolution and natural selection can take place at that lower level.

Systemic requirements of higher-level entities also impose limits on cellular-level evolution, and therefore on the extent to which cell populations can be subject to natural selection, for a system is more than a mere collection of populations, Darwinian or otherwise. In order for a system to exist, there must be stable relations between subunits that can only be maintained if these lower-level entities are not allowed to spontaneously disappear or radically change. In consequence, natural selection and evolution among cell populations must be curtailed and contained. As a result, multicellular organisms have managed to bottle the universal acid, keeping it in stock for local use when necessary, as in the reactions of the immune system. More generally, natural selection at a higher level of organization requires that at the lower level, natural selection be kept on a relatively short leash. It may be objected, of course, that de-Darwinization at the cell population level is itself the result of natural selection at a higher level. This observation is certainly correct, but it is irrelevant for the point being made here. At the lower level, natural selection plays a limited role, and the organizational principle characteristic at the higher level can only be maintained if natural selection and evolution of cell populations remain limited.

A Morphogenetic Hypothesis

Many years ago, Jean-Pierre Dupuy described René Girard's theory as a morphogenetic theory, a dynamic model of interaction that explains the generation of forms (Dupuy 1988, 75). The same may be said of natural selection; it produces forms and explains the generation of these forms. Individuals in a Darwinian population change; they become adapted to their environment, and this process has given rise to complex adaptations and to the whole diversity of life. Of course, as mentioned earlier, exactly which forms will appear in a particular selection process depends on contingent empirical factors, on the history of the evolving system, on the nature of the entities and the specific mechanisms responsible for reproduction and heredity. Something similar may be said of Girard's theory: which specific institutions arise out of the victimary mechanism—for example, a sacred kingship or the domestication of animals—depends on contingent historical and environmental accidents. There is, however, a fundamental difference between natural selection, the struggle for survival, and the violent victimage that ends the mimetic crisis. Girard defines his hypothesis as a self-regulating mechanism of violence. At this stage, if you can, leave violence aside; the important term is "self-regulating." Natural selection is not a self-regulating process. It simply moves forward, as the runaway growth of cancerous cells shows—the survival of the fittest, until the fittest have exhausted the resources of their environment.

Of course natural selection can give rise to self-regulating organisms—unless it is the case, as argued by Stuart Kauffman, that evolution can only occur in populations of self-organizing systems (Kauffman 1993). Be that as it may, the model described earlier does not contain any provision for self-regulation. The strength or intensity of selection will depend on the values of the five parameters, but those are determined extrinsically, from outside the model. It is true that in classical population genetic models, gene (allele) frequencies may come to an equilibrium point where evolution (changes in frequency) stops, and this could be viewed as a form of self-regulation. However, whether or not this happens depends on the value of the parameters identified earlier. Such equilibrium could only be considered as a form of self-regulation if the values of the parameters are endogenously determined—that is, as a result of the working of the system itself. This may be the case, and perhaps happens many times in nature. However, this form of circular causality is absent from Darwin's conception of natural selection, while it is precisely at the heart of Girard's mimetic explanation.

A Self-regulating Mechanism

At the beginning of *Things Hidden since the Foundation of the World*, Girard gives a succinct and very abstract rendering of the mimetic crisis and its resolution that lends itself to comparison with the model of natural selection exposed earlier (Girard 1987, 26–27). Its starting point is mimesis, a very general capacity of imitation among individuals.[3] Because it is general, mimesis also involves the imitation of acquisitive behaviors. In other words, we imitate each other not only in the way we walk or dress, but also in our attempts to acquire various kinds of objects, whether these are material goods, social positions, or the respect and affection of others. Acquisitive mimesis brings agents to converge upon the same goals, and to prefer those objects that others prefer. It constitutes a remarkable learning mechanism, but also an endless source of conflicts, at least when the desired objects can neither be shared nor divided, and many times even when they can. As rivalry proceeding from acquisitive mimesis becomes acute, argues Girard, rivals lose sight of the objects that originally occasioned the conflicts, and turn their attention towards the antagonist who blocks their road to satisfaction. This change in focus transforms acquisitive mimesis into conflictual mimesis. Agents do not anymore imitate each other's acquisitive behavior, but their mutual violence. Acquisitive mimesis and conflictual mimesis are not different forces, for the passage from one to the other simply results from the rising intensity of rivalry. This passage constitutes, however, an important threshold, for if acquisitive mimesis divides those who vie for the same object, conflictual mimesis can unite them in opposition to a common enemy. This is the heart of the mechanism. As the number of those united against a same enemy grows, the power of attraction of that rivalry also augments, leading to an even greater number of individuals closing in on that same opponent, until all the community, minus one, are united in a common antagonism. The designation of this victim is random, according to Girard, for it simply results from a slight imbalance in the rivalry that will progressively grow until it attracts everyone, for no other reason than the fact that it already attracts many. The immolation of that universal enemy brings peace back to the community, for it allows everyone to assuage their rage and violence against the same individual, who at that moment is perceived as the unique cause of all the violence, conflicts, and disorder. Because agents do not understand the blind process through which calm returns, they will tend to consider the victim itself as the origin of both the renewed order and of the violence that came before. Such, proposes Girard, is the origin of the idea of sacred being: a creature that is all-powerful for both good and bad, that can blow a wind of violence and madness upon the community and at the last minute save it from utter destruction.

Given the mimetic origin of conflicts, the rediscovered calm will not last very long. In order to protect themselves from the return of violence, men can resort to two rather evident strategies related to their recent experience of violence. The first is to reenact the original crisis and its resolution in an effort to reproduce its beneficial effect. From this faith in repetition proceed the institution of sacrifice and rituals in general. The second strategy is to forbid the actions that originally led to the crisis and fueled its development. This constitutes the origin of prohibitions and interdicts. However, because the actions that fueled the crisis and those that led to its "happy" outcome are to a large extent the same, there follows a tension between prohibitions and rituals, as the latter often prescribe acts that the first normally prohibit (Girard 1987, 28).

Girard does not claim that this mechanism always functioned, or even that it usually functioned. He does not claim that like natural selection it will take place in any population where certain conditions are satisfied, here a community of mimetic agents. In fact, according to him, many human groups may have destroyed themselves in an orgy of reciprocal violence. Rather, he claims that we descend from groups of individuals that were protected by this mechanism (Girard 1987, 27). According to him, all human culture proceeds from this mechanism, but, as we will see, it does not descend from it. (The fact is that there is no adequate parent-offspring relationship between different forms of human culture for them to really descend from each other.)

Why is this, in relation to violence, a self-regulating mechanism? Essentially, because what stops violence here is violence itself; violence does not cease because it has run its course to the end and destroyed every member of the group. Rather than the exhaustion of available resources, what curtails violence is violence itself, the very process that exacerbates conflicts and intensifies antagonism. No external intervention is needed; if certain conditions are satisfied, the intensification of violence will spontaneously bring about its own diminution. Violence does not as a consequence disappear entirely, but the way it functions as a form of interaction among members of the group changes. The agents themselves neither intended nor planned this result. They did not renounce violence, nor did they negotiate a social contract, a mutually advantageous agreement. They received their reconciliation like a gift from outside. Though it results from their own actions, there is a sense in which it is not their doing.

Culture and Descent

The first thing to note is that this abstract model of the sacrificial crisis and its resolution is less abstract than the earlier presentation of the core of Darwin's theory, in the sense that it imposes more constraints on the nature of the individuals involved. Any collection of individuals between whom there is a parent-offspring relation can constitute a Darwinian population, whether these individuals are molecules, viruses, cells, multicellular organisms, or groups of such organisms. This is not the case with Girard's model, which requires much more specific kinds of individuals. It requires mimetic agents who have relatively sophisticated cognitive abilities. The victimary mechanism could not take place in a population of molecules or of bacteria, though it seems clear that some forms of mimetism already exist at the cellular level. This of course is obvious, and this obvious fact indicates that mimetic theory is located at the level of specific mechanisms that are favored by natural selection, whose understanding requires specific empirical hypotheses concerning the nature of the elements involved, and often the history that brought them about.

Cultures only descend from each other in the sense that individuals in groups that experience a mimetic crisis and its resolution (mainly) descended from individuals that came from such groups. This form of descent, however, is quite different from what was postulated by the theory of the origin of culture labeled "diffusionism": the hypothesis that resemblance between cultures comes from the fact that they all proceed from a unique original source. In the Girardian scenario, there may have been many distantly related groups of early hominids who independently experienced a sacrificial crisis and its victimary resolution at different times, in complete separation from each other. Girard's thesis does not suppose a unique origin of human culture. Rather it argues that comparative data suggest that all known human cultures derive from the same type of events: the mimetic crisis and its resolution (Girard 1987, 27). To use a very imperfect analogy from evolutionary biology, one could say that between cultures there are more analogies (functional similarities) than homologies (similar structures by reason of common descent).

Now, it is possible to consider the mimetic crisis and its resolution, the basic mechanism of Girard's theory, as a form of reproduction of culture. When a crisis happens within a group, its present culture is destroyed—that is to say, it becomes unable to function as a culture should—and at the end of the crisis a new version of this same culture appears. This form of reproduction would to some extent resemble reproduction of a single-cell organism, which results from what appears as a catastrophic scrambling of the normal relations that exist between the elements of the cell. In this case, the main difference is that the parent, in general, only gives rise to one offspring, rather than splitting into two entities.[4] In this context, individual persons could be compared to individual cells within a multicellular organism, and social groups or roles to organs or cell lineages. Girard describes the intensification of conflicts during the crisis as transforming antagonists into doubles of each other, and as progressively destroying social differences. Here, if individuals compete, it is not because they are different, but because they are similar, and the more they compete, the more they become similar. In relationship to our previous analysis of Darwinian populations, this process of cultural loss of differences can be seen as a reduction of variability, and as making the fitness of individuals independent of their intrinsic characteristics.[5] This is evidently also true of the victim, if, as Girard argues, its designation is a random process. Conceived in this way, what the crisis does is to de-Darwinize the populations that make up human cultures. Furthermore, if the crisis itself can be viewed as the result of unbridled competition between agents, then de-Darwinization is also what culture itself does (Dumouchel 1982).[6] Here, as in the case of multicellular organisms, de-Darwinization of the lower-level populations is the condition for the emergence and maintenance of higher-level entities.

It may be objected that if this is the case, such higher-level entities can only exist if there is selection pressure at that level—that is to say, if human cultures or groups form a Darwinian population. It may be that such a pressure does exist, since as we all know, human groups have been in conflict throughout history. It may also be the case—and this has long been, and still is, a hotly debated issue—that this pressure, even if it exists, is/was not strong enough to obtain that result: the de-Darwinization of human populations. There may, however, be a different solution to that difficulty. As is sometimes the case in biology, natural selection can take place in the absence of any "struggle for existence" (Lewens 2007, 59–60). In other words, the way in which selection pressure for higher-level entities is expressed need not be direct competition between cultures. Organisms modify their environment; they create for themselves niches. As time goes by, their fitness depends more and more on having a certain type of niche outside of which they cannot survive (Odling-Smee, Laland, and Feldman 2003). One possibility is that the niche of the human species is essentially social and cultural. Humans have managed to survive and prosper, more or less, in just about every natural environment on earth, but they are nowhere to be found outside of culture and society, living alone or in herds. For us, outside the group there is no salvation: no survival and no reproduction. Cultures that favored the fitness of their members, that is to say their ability to live together in large and complex associations characterized by division of labor, would thrive even if there were no direct competition between cultures. In this case, pressure for the cultural de-Darwinization of human populations would be indistinguishable from the selection of fit individuals in the social niche of the human species.

Mimesis and Genes

At this most basic level, mimesis appears as a means through which the de-Darwinization of human population takes place. Like parameter *a*, competitive interaction with respect to reproduction, mimesis is a way in which members of a population are causally related, a way in which the actions of one individual affect those of another. The type of effects to which mimesis gives rise, as is the case for the parameters of natural selection, depends on the value it takes. When it is most intense, mimesis makes agents similar to each other. This similarity becomes a cause of increased competition and further similarity between them. The effects of mimesis also depend on the different actions to which it is applied (for lack of a better word). Through mimesis, the behaviors of members of a population become correlated. However, this process is accomplished at the sub-personal level. Agents are never directly aware of mimesis, only of its effect. This is a very important aspect of Girard's theory; mimesis is unconscious, but more importantly still, it is not an action. It is more like a constraint on the action of agents, but one of which they are totally unaware as a constraining force. Mimesis thus is best understood as a tendency towards various forms of similitude between agents' actions and mental states.

This invisibility of mimesis is the reason for the failure of participants in the mimetic crisis to understand the mechanism through which peace returns to the community. It also explains why they assign responsibility for the development and resolution of the violence that visited them to the action of an all-powerful being. Like Darwin's, Girard's theory is radically non-agential. It attributes not only the origin of religion and the belief in sacred beings to a blind, impersonal mechanism, but also the origin of society. It is this mechanism that explains agents' belief, rather than it is explained by them. And like Darwin, Girard does not need to make any particular hypothesis concerning the way in which mimesis is implemented as a characteristic of humans living in society. For it could very well be that like heredity, resemblance between parent and offspring, mimesis can be realized through many different processes.

Towards the beginning of *The Selfish Gene*, Richard Dawkins writes of replicators, of genes, which he views as the central agents of evolution.

> Replicators began not merely to exist, but to construct for themselves containers, vehicles for their continued existence. The replicators who survived were the ones which built *survival machines* for themselves to live in. . . . Four thousand million years on, what was to be the fate of the ancient replicators? They did not die out, for they are past masters of the survival arts. But do not look for them floating loose in the sea; they gave up that cavalier freedom long ago. Now they swarm in huge colonies, safe inside gigantic lumbering robots, sealed off from the outside world, communicating by tortuous indirect routes, *manipulating it by remote control*. They are in you and me; they created us, body and mind; and *their preservation is the ultimate rationale for our existence*. They have come a long way, those replicators. Now they go by the name of genes, and we are their survival machines. (Dawkins 1976, 21; my emphasis)

In this passage, genes appear as omnipotent, eternal entities that are responsible for our existence and that control our life from a distance. Godfrey-Smith argues that one of the difficulties of explanations of evolution in terms of substantial entities, like genes or memes, is that, unlike Darwin's original explanations, which referred to spontaneous mechanisms and conditions on populations, they tend to substitute one mythology for another. They relapse into thinking that there cannot be effects without agents who are responsible for them. This appears to me like another excellent reason to prefer Godfrey-Smith's interpretation to many more popular ones, and why it agrees so well with Girard's mimetic explanation of the origin of the sacred and of culture. Godfrey-Smith's interpretation gives us the means to understand how an articulation of Darwinism and culture is possible in a way that does not require the direct Darwinization or biologization of culture. From this point of view, we can see how Girard's theory can both be consistent with Darwinian explanations in terms of natural selection, and simultaneously explain why natural selection plays a limited role in the development and explanation of culture. Furthermore, this alternative explanation of culture remains faithful to Darwin's central discovery, the non-agential explanation of the development and evolution of complex forms and of sophisticated adaptations, much more than popular attempts to Darwinize culture.

Notes

1. Of course, everyone does not agree on the correct interpretation of mimetic theory. The situation, however, is different because disagreements bear mainly on whether or not the theory constitutes an important contribution, rather than on how exactly it should be understood.
2. Other types of interaction can also be represented—for example, mating between sexual organisms where the reproductive success of one adds to the reproductive success of another.
3. Recently there have been many discussions on the nature of imitation. Researchers distinguish three different types of behaviors related to what in everyday life we call imitation: mimicking, emulation, and imitation proper. The basis of these distinctions is cognitive. As we move from mimicking to imitation proper, the cognitive resources mobilized by the imitative behavior are assumed to grow. See Byrne 2005, 290–93; Gergely and Csibra 2006; Tomasello 1999. Girard's concept of mimesis cuts across these cognitive distinctions. He is more interested in the social results of imitative behavior than in the different cognitive mechanisms that may underlie it.
4. It may be argued that this is not reproduction, but there are many very strange forms of reproduction or of quasi-reproduction, and it may be that this comparison is not so far-fetched.
5. A point that was famously noticed by Hobbes in his description of the state of nature: "the difference between man and man is not so considerable, as that one man can thereupon claim to himselfe any benefit, to which another may not pretend, as well as he" (Hobbes 1976, 183).
6. I argue that the crisis, its resolution, and culture should be seen as forming a system where conflicts and loss of difference progressively lead to another crisis out of which culture comes out regenerated.

Works Cited

Allen, C., and M. Bekoff. 1997. *Species of Mind*. Cambridge, MA: MIT Press.

Barkow, J. H., L. Cosmides, and J. Tooby, eds. 1992. *The Adapted Mind*. Oxford: Oxford University Press.

Blackmore, S. 1999. *The Meme Machine*. Oxford: Oxford University Press.

Boyd, R., and P. J. Richerson. 1985. *Culture and the Evolutionary Process*. Chicago: Chicago University Press.

Byrne, R. 2005. "Do Parrots (and Children) Emulate Speech Sound?" In *Perspectives on Imitation*, vol. 1, *Mechanisms of Imitation and Imitation in Animals*, ed. S. Hurley and N. Charter. Cambridge, MA: MIT Press.

Callebaut, W., and R. Pinxten, eds. 1987. *Evolutionary Epistemology: A Multiparadigm Program*. Dordrecht: Riedel.

Dawkins, R. 1976. *The Selfish Gene*. Oxford: Oxford University Press.

Dennett, D. 1995. *Darwin's Dangerous Idea*. New York: Simon & Schuster.

Dumouchel, P. 1982. "Différences et paradoxes: Réflexions sur l'amour et la violence dans l'œuvre de Girard." In *René Girard et le problème du mal*, ed. M. Deguy and J.-P. Dupuy, 215–23. Paris: Grasset. Reprinted in P. Dumouchel, *The Ambivalence of Scarcity and Other Essays* (East Lansing: Michigan State University Press, 2014), 171–79.

Dupuy, J.-P. 1988. "Totalization and Misrecognition." In *Violence and Truth*, ed. P. Dumouchel. Stanford, CA: Stanford University Press.

Edelman, G. 1987. *Neural Darwinism*. New York: Basic Books.

Gergely, G., and G. Csibra. 2006. "Sylvia's Recipe: The Role of Imitation in Pedagogy and the Transmission of Cultural Knowledge." In *Roots of Human Sociality*, ed. N. J. Enfield and C. Levinson, 229–55. Oxford: Berg.

Girard, R. 1987. *Things Hidden since the Foundation of the World*. Translated by S. Bann and M. Metteer. Stanford, CA: Stanford University Press.

Godfrey-Smith, P. 2009. *Darwinian Populations and Natural Selection*. Oxford: Oxford University Press.

Hobbes, T. [1651] 1976 *Leviathan*. Edited by C. B. Macpherson. Harmondsworth, UK: Penguin Books.

Kauffman, S. 1993. *The Origin of Order*. Oxford: Oxford University Press.

Lewens, T. 2007. *Darwin*. London: Routledge.

Mayr, E. 1976. "Typological versus Population Thinking." In *Evolution and the Diversity of Life*. Cambridge, MA: Harvard University Press.

Nelson, R., and S. G. Winter, eds. 1982. *An Evolutionary Theory of Economic Change*. Cambridge, MA: Harvard University Press.

Odling-Smee, E. J., K. N. Laland, and M. W. Feldman. 2003. *Niche Construction: The Neglected Process in Evolution*. Princeton, NJ: Princeton University Press.

Rachels, J. 1991. *Created from Animals: The Moral Implications of Darwinism*. Oxford: Oxford University Press.

Tomasello, M. 1999. *The Cultural Origins of Human Cognition*. Cambridge, MA: Harvard University Press.

Maladaptation, Counterintuitiveness, and Symbolism

The Challenge of Mimetic Theory to Evolutionary Thinking

Pierpaolo Antonello

If we understand René Girard's generative hypothesis properly and take it with due seriousness, a number of conceptual issues and parameters currently discussed and used in theories of cultural evolution may come under challenge and may need to be rearticulated. Despite the apparently speculative nature of the scenario of origins it envisages, Girard's mimetic theory is capable of serving as a guiding framework that may help to make sense of vast tracts of archaeological, ethnological, and anthropological data, thus providing a coherent picture of cultural development as a function of an original culture matrix—a highly desirable outcome in scientific terms, which may probably remain elusive as long as we cling to a more straightforwardly cognitivist approach. The theoretical and terminological apparatus that is needed to make sense of specific anthropological and archaeological data (for instance, in relation to the emergence of agriculture, animal husbandry, or religious symbolism) would then be much simplified if we perform a conceptual, Copernicus-like shift: assuming, after Durkheim and Girard, religion and the sacred as the origins of the cultural order. A religion-centered perspective, as distinct from a genetic or cognitively centered one, would help to shed light on a number of the conceptual conundrums that still puzzle many practicing archaeologists, anthropologists, and cognitive scientists who frequently see religion as a later byproduct—either spandrel or parasitic—of specific cognitive and social skills developed independently for other reasons.

The scale and complexity of human societies, for example, present an important evolutionary puzzle for many. Standard evolutionary theory provides a perfectly good explanation for the social behavior of other primates, but not of humans (see for instance Smith 2003). The level of social organization, the time and effort involved in the construction of Neolithic temple sites such as Göbekli Tepe, for instance, is so vast that concepts like "counterintuitive" or "maladaptive" are themselves ill-adapted—are, indeed, misconceived and misleading—when it comes to explaining a social phenomenon of this order of magnitude, particularly when the feat of coherent social purpose we are observing is the work of hunter-gatherer proto-societies. It is clearly insufficient to invoke the projecting of forms of agency onto natural phenomena, or of accounting for cultural "fitness-reducing traits" in specific individuals; and it will not do to claim that human cooperation could have emerged simply as a side effect of other cognitive innovations (Boyd and Richerson 1983). We need, on the contrary, to understand the cultural, social, moral, and political persuasion or pull that was capable of moving and structuring a whole society, in performing such strenuous and—from a strictly utilitarian standpoint—"senseless" and highly "maladaptive," tasks.

Maladaptation

Maladaptation is one of the concepts that have common currency in evolutionary theorizing: it defines those genetic traits or cultural habits that tend to reduce the fitness of specific individuals, given certain environmental changes. In respect of cultural evolution in particular, Robert Boyd and Peter J. Richerson explain that "culture can respond independently to evolutionary forces, and therefore cultural inheritance can lead to the evolution of behaviors that are maladaptive in terms of genetic fitness" (Boyd and Richerson 1983, 211). However, this is a partial take on the issue. First of all, in terms of strictly biological evolution, the advantages conferred by any one adaptation are rarely decisive for survival when considered in isolation, but only decisive as taken together with other synergistic and antagonistic adaptations—i.e., factors that cannot change without affecting other factors. Also, in relation to the evolution of culture, we could argue that the term "maladaptation" is being misused, since theorists very often discount in this judgment the emerging nature of culture (and of religion in particular); they do so, moreover, most particularly in respect of its alleged biological underpinning: "Processes are described as emergent when they exhibit characteristics that are discontinuous with or even contrary to properties and tendencies observed at component levels" (Deacon and Cashman 2009, 493–94n1). What can be described as maladaptive at the component level could result, on the contrary, in being highly adaptive at the emergent level.

When speaking about maladaptation, we must also take into account different time scales and differences of magnitude between social groupings, as well as different levels of complexity within a given society, these variables being fundamental factors in accounting for the cultural evolution of our species. Referring, for instance, to the origins of food production, the domestication of animals and plants, and to sedentism—a major breakthrough in human cultural evolution—Woodburn (1980) made an attempt to distinguish between "delayed-return societies" and "immediate-return societies" (also termed "collectors" and "foragers," respectively [Binford 1980]). However, the fundamental question is how, and under what conditions, hunter-gatherers changed "from being immediate-return foragers to being intensified collectors with delayed return and ultimately having an increasingly complex social structure" (Byrd 2005, 236).

This is a question that, as we argue in this volume, is persuasively answered by Girard's mimetic theory. However, a preliminary remark is in order: we would need to highlight how the terminology used by many scholars in the field—"delayed-return," "allocation of resources," "controlled breeding condition for profit" (Bökönyi 1969, 219), "increased benefits and lower costs to individuals" (Harris 1979, 60)—betrays an ideological bias toward an individualistic and utilitarian understanding of the relationship between humans and nature that is anachronistically "modern." Frans de Waal sees this tendency as connected to the Western, especially American, ideology of individualism (de Waal 2001). It is not surprising that within this ideological frame of reference, the domestication of animals, or animal husbandry, is accounted for in purely functionalistic and utilitarian terms. Cultural materialists consider the proto-humans as rational agents, who could envisage the spectacular outcome of seizing, capturing, taming, and caging dangerous animals like bulls, wolves, bears, and wildcats for economic reasons. In fact, at first, domestication was quite uneconomical and maladaptive for both the animals captured and their human captors. The size of domesticated animals decreases in relation to wild species; they suffer all sorts of stress-related diseases due to captivity; captive animals fail to reproduce effectively; the number of germs and viruses that wild animals introduce into the human community is extremely high.

The same line of reasoning applies to the invention of agriculture. The Neolithic Revolution was the first agricultural revolution—the transition from hunting-and-gathering groups and communities to agriculture and settlement (the notion of settlement is itself currently being questioned). Archaeological data indicate that various forms of domestication of plants and animals arose in at least seven or eight separate locations worldwide, with the earliest known developments taking place in the Middle East around 10,000 BCE or earlier:

> From a scientific standpoint there is no generally accepted model accounting for the origin of agriculture, above all in the consideration that agriculture was anti-economic. Agriculture, far from being a natural and upward step, in fact led commonly to a lower quality of life. Hunter-gatherers typically do less work for the same amount of food, are healthier, and are less prone to famine than primitive farmers: why was this behaviour (agriculture) reinforced (and hence selected for) if it was not offering adaptational rewards surpassing those accruing to hunter-gathering or foraging economies? (Wadley and Martin 1993, 96; see also Lee and DeVore 1968; Cohen 1989)

Nutritional standards of Neolithic populations were generally inferior to those of hunter-gatherers, and life expectancy may, in fact, have been shorter, in part due to diseases. Average height, for example, went down—for men, from five foot ten to five foot six; for women, from five foot three to five foot one, respectively—and it took until the twentieth century CE for average human height to come back to the pre–Neolithic Revolution level. Irrigation, which was necessary for agricultural production in many areas, had negative consequences in various parts of the world, providing breeding places for the respective vectors of malaria and schistosomiasis (Cockburn 1971).

What was the vector of such clearly maladaptive cultural traits? And why have they been maintained for such a prolonged period of time? It is in fact widely acknowledged that the transition to agriculture was a long-term process rather than a short-term event, and one that did not occur uniformly in all places at all times, progressing differentially in fits and starts over the course of several millennia.[1]

This problem was addressed by Girard, with Antonello and de Castro Rocha, in *Evolution and Conversion* (2007), where it is pointed out that agriculture and animal husbandry are maladaptive in the short term and from an individual standpoint; whereas these things represent a form of enhancement in the long term and from a collective and social standpoint, for they go hand in hand with a progressive increase in the complexity of social organization, and with the development of religious and ritualistic practices. According to Girard, it is in fact rituals, together with their framing and generative culture matrix, said to be of a religious or archaic-sacral order, that enabled ancient populations to begin to recognize and, progressively, to fashion or refashion the whole of physical and spiritual reality. This was the most fundamental process at work, and it allowed humans to produce, thanks to the cognitively enhancing experiences proper to religious practices, the social and technical innovations that we now describe as civilizing.

The British archaeologist Ian Hodder, who directs the excavations at the Neolithic and Chalcolithic site of Çatalhöyük in Turkey, argues in similar terms that animal and plant domestication developed first of all for religious reasons: the earliest settled communities, and the Neolithic Revolution they represent, actually preceded the development of agriculture. Hodder believes that the Neolithic Revolution was the result of a revolutionary change in human psychology, a "revolution of symbols" that led to new beliefs about the world and shared community rituals (Hodder 1990; Cauvin 1994). The discovery of the site Göbekli Tepe is a clear testimony to that transition (as we examine further in section 4 of this volume), since it dates from a good three millennia before Çatalhöyük, and up to now no traces of domesticated plants or animals have been found on the site—from which we may safely infer that religion, rituals, and the sacred preceded settlement. More than that: according to Girard, they actually provoked and produced settlement:

> The hunter-gatherers started to settle permanently because of the increasing importance of ritual sites and the complexity of the rituals of which they were part, and which in turn produced, the domestication of animals and the discovery of agriculture. Climate changes or particular soil conditions were also important elements in this later development, but the discovery was very likely to have been made around the sacred burial sites in which any symbolic activity of the primitive community was carried out (such as burying seeds along with human beings, for instance). (Girard, Antonello, and de Castro Rocha 2007, 121)

Steven Mithen, on this score, argues in fact that invoking the changing climate and environment does not, in itself, provide an explanation for this dramatic change in lifestyles that laid the foundations for the early civilizations of Mesopotamia and Egypt (Mithen 2007, 711). Following James Frazer's anthropological study (1922), Girard noticed that the vocabulary and the ritualistic practices associated with proto-agriculture constantly relate to sacrificial rituals.[2] Roberto Calasso, for his part, remembers that "*Quechcotona*, in Nahuatl, means both 'to cut off someone's head' and 'to pick an ear of grain with one's hand'" (Calasso 1985, 135). Michel Serres points out that the Indo-European word for "to plant," i.e., *pak*—from which stem words like *paysage*, *pays*, pagan, peasant—refers to the tomb as the first *sign*, i.e., as the first human symbolic inscription deposited on the natural landscape (Serres 1985).[3] In *Hamlet's Mill*, Giorgio de Santillana and Hertha von Dechend make reference also to the role of the millstone as sacrificial instrument in Nordic mythology (de Santillana and von Dechend 1969, 90–94). In *Myth and Reality*, Mircea Eliade promotes the same understanding by reading the myth of the girl Hainuwele, recorded by A. E Jensen in Ceram, one of the islands of the New Guinea Archipelago:

> The next morning, seeing that Hainuwele did not come home, Ameta divined that she had been murdered. He found the body, disinterred it, and cut it into pieces, which he buried in various places, except the arms. The buried pieces gave birth to plants previously unknown, especially to tubers, which since then are the chief food of human beings. (Eliade 1963, 104)

Steven Mithen, following Humphrey (Humphrey 1984, 26–27), suggests that the "fortunate misapplication of social intelligence" may have played a key role in the origin of agriculture. However, according to Girard this misapplication was not a totally random and fortuitous process; it was governed rather by the logic of sacrifice and of the sacred. All cultural and natural elements in fact receive focalization and meaning only as processed through a religious matrix, thus displacing any "natural" causal link. Such links always derive their salience from a religious and ritualistic focalization, rather than from rational biological explanation (which many scientists anachronistically assume to have been part of the cultural and cognitive repertoire of primitive humans). As Girard puts it:

> Only if we understand the powerful causal link between ritual and nature, can we grasp the origins of practices like agriculture. Every natural element acquires meaning only if it is experienced within the space of ritual. We are not dealing with a "primitive" or "magical" mentality in cases like these: here is a form of ritual thinking in action, in which the effectiveness of ritual and religion is *actual*, it produces *real* effects. There you see how religion nurses human culture. (Girard, Antonello, and de Castro Rocha 2007, 120–21)

The domestication of animals also, Girard argues, is the "accidental by-product" of ritualized, sacrificial practices, a serendipitous outcome of religious rituals. Animals were introduced within the human community first of all in order to be sacrificed, substituting animal for human victims, or perhaps mixing these together, since the distinction between human and animal was not clear-cut in the prehistoric period (foragers generally regard animals as their equals; see Ingold 1984). The theriomorphism evidenced in myths and pictorial representation may be a testimony to this considerable phenomenon. In this process, animals were treated just like human beings, i.e., they were first of all symbolically and socially tamed, to make them part of the group.

As corroborating evidence, Girard refers to the Ainu tribes in northern Japan who tried to "enculturate" the polar bear, by treating it as a human within the human community for sacrificial purposes; there can be no thought that they wanted a convenient and self-preserving source of fresh food, nor could the bear be transformed, given its particular morphology and biology, into a fully domesticated animal (Girard 1987, 70). Girard also remembers that in historical times, there has not been any significant new domestication of wild animals; whereas there were areas in the world, like pre-Colombian Mexico, that did not have domesticated animals at all; where, on the other hand, there were massive ritual killings of human beings, because the process of substituting animals for human victims in ritual sacrifices had not occurred (Carrasco 1999). Similarly, William Durham in this volume refers to the fact that the Mundurukú, in their highly ritualized headhunting practices, used to refer to children from rival tribes as game. As a final remark on the subject, Girard also responded to Jonathan Smith's claim that "sacrifice is an exaggeration of domestication" (Smith 1987, 200):

> Smith gets closer to the link between religion and domestication, but he is too biased against the former to acknowledge the primacy of the religious. His functionalist reasoning prevents him from understanding that a primitive community cannot think in terms of "delayed payoff" because they have no clue of what is going to happen. Sacrifice is not an aberration of domestication, but the opposite. Domestication is not the art of "selective killing" but it is this ritualistic killing that produces selection. Domestication is the serendipitous "spin-off" of animal sacrifice. (Girard, Antonello, and de Castro Rocha 2007, 117–18)

Maladaptation and Coevolution

The perspective implicit in the theoretical approach proposed by Girard also addresses the problem of the coevolution of physical and cultural traits and their mutual interaction, an approach illustrated, for instance, by Durham in this volume. Jerome Barkow, discussing "the elastic between genes and culture," argues that any fitness-reducing or maladaptive cultural traits would be eventually eliminated by natural selection "if the information is stably transmitted for a sufficient number of generations while continuing to be maladaptive, then, assuming sufficient relevant genetic variance in the gene pool and assuming at least partial genetic isolation of the local population, natural selection will tend to eliminate the information" (Barkow 1989, 125). However, he also notices—though without providing any explanation for this phenomenon—that "long-term cultural stability may, however, have occurred during the Paleolithic, given the immense duration of the Oldowan and Chellean-Acheulean lithic traditions." Because of the religious importance of specific cultural elements and rituals, these allegedly maladaptive cultural traits, far from being eliminated from the cultural pool, would actually be maintained for prolonged periods of time, to the point of becoming an ecological conditioning that would progressively exercise forms of genetic selection—in the terms discussed, for instance, by Durham, with reference to lactose intolerance and milk-drinking at different latitudes (Durham 1991). Maladaptive cultural traits force biology to adapt to their imperatives, rather than the other way round. Culture *modifies* nature.

In *Coevolution*, Durham presents another interesting case of cultural maladaptation (or rather, to use his own terminology, of "opposition") within the gene-culture interplay: the case of Fore cannibalism. The Fore are a population living in the Highlands province of Papua, New Guinea, who practiced mortuary feasts involving the consumption of deceased kin (Durham 1991, 393–414), which led to the development of kuru, the deadly nerve degeneration disease first described by Ronald Berndt (known today as mad-cow disease), which was viewed by the locals as a product of sorcery. For opposition to exist, argues Durham, "the ideas and beliefs of highest cultural fitness must actually confer a lower average inclusive fitness upon their carriers than is conferred by some other available option. When this occurs, cultural selection will favor the evolution of phenotypical properties different from those that evolve through the influence of natural selection" (Durham 1991, 368); "most cases of opposition, especially enduring opposition, are socially imposed" (371). Durham defines these social impositions as ideas, values, and beliefs that are "controlled and manipulated in a number of devious, self-interested ways" by a small minority within a given population. Similarly, Barkow sees fitness-reducing cultural traits as emerging because of errors, environmental changes, or appropriation by elites ("powerful elites are likely to manipulate culture traits in the interests of maintaining their status and, therefore indirectly, their possible reproductive advantage" [Barkow 1989, 113, 118])—an argument that Durham also maintains in his chapter in this volume. This may have been true in historical time, when forms of social hierarchies and stratification became more complex and more crystallized. Once we go back to hunter-gatherer groups in the prehistoric period, a clear social stratification is harder to identify, and these "fitness reducing values or beliefs" were commonly shared by the entire social group. From recent research on the subject, it actually appears that the development of kuru-like illnesses related to cannibalistic practices did not stop hominids and humans from continuing with this practice, but it eventually produced a genetic selection at the prion protein gene locus in human populations (Mead et al. 2003), which seems to suggest that cannibalism was a very common practice that eventually produced a selection at the genetic level (White 2001). The strong selection documented at the prion protein gene locus is consistent with the growing view from archaeological evidence that cannibalism may have been widespread among prehistoric populations (see Fernandez-Jalvo et al. 1999; Marlar et al. 2000; White 2001). Moreover, the signal of this selection is apparently "the *strongest* yet documented for any gene in humans" (Stoneking 2006, 2003; my emphasis). The persistence of this cultural habit is surely testimony of its ritualistic and cultural significance and its vital relevance for the community involved; it cannot be explained simply via cultural materialistic interpretations.

It is also claimed that cannibalism emerged more systematically at the later stage of human cultural development, with the symbolic explosion and the agricultural revolution. Ethnological studies show that cannibalism appears almost exclusively in the practices of agrarian peoples—that is, at a later cultural stage—and is essentially bound up with religious or magical conceptions in which cultivated plants play a large role. Cannibalism and its link to kuru, albeit maladaptive from a short-term biological standpoint, produced a long-term benefit at the genetic level because of the selection this illness imposed; but, more than anything else, it was maintained because on the one hand, it was an enhancement in cultural terms, but on the other—and most importantly—it represented what structured the common beliefs of the whole society. When asked to comment on Carl Vogt and Edward Volhard's ethnological observation that "tribes devoted to cannibalism and to human sacrifices are in general more advanced in agriculture, industry, arts, legislation etc. than the neighboring tribes, who reject these horrors" (Vogt 1871, 298; Volhard 1939), Girard emphasizes the fact that "the ritualistic and symbolic complexity that needs to be developed in order to handle cannibalistic practice was such that, inevitably, it produced a cognitive, technical, artistic spin-off. Of course, it is not cannibalism in itself which favors knowledge: it is not the type of victim selected to be sacrificed, it is the sacrificial mechanism and its rituals which engenders knowledge" (Girard, Antonello, and de Castro Rocha 2007, 122). As we have said, the ritualization of human sacrifice became the template for the later (or coeval) ritualization of animal sacrifice, which in turn produced domestication.

This also points to the widespread lack of theorization on the role of violence in the emergence of culture and in the structuring of primitive society. Ritualistic practices, social layering, and normative control through the emergence of taboos and prohibitions were of course key to the control of intraspecific or intergroup violence. The kind of impositions that were administered through ritualistic practice and religious beliefs acted as a social organizational mechanism that increased cooperation, division of labor, internal solidarity, cognitive improvements, and normative control, providing an overall enhancement in terms of group fitness.

Counterintuitiveness

Another concept that has some currency in the field of cognitive science of religion is "counterintuitiveness," seen as "the lowest common denominator of all religions." "In counter-intuitiveness, the boundaries separating domains of intuitive ontology are violated, for example by transferring psychological properties to solid objects, or denying physical or biological properties to a person" (Pyysiäinen 2002, 110–12). "Counterintuitive" (or "counterontological") is a technical term introduced by Dan Sperber and Pascal Boyer (Boyer 1994; Sperber 1996; and see Atran 2002 and critical discussion in Bloch 2005, 105) to mean information contradicting some information provided by ontological categories, where the ontological categories are five in number: persons, tools, plants, natural objects, animals (Boyer 2001, 65).

However, the claim that there is an intuitive ontology, equating semantically to people's tacit expectation, seems, again, more the projection of a modern categorization than a clear definition of what religion or the sacred is or may be. It seems sufficiently clear that any natural and biological events or facts would always be framed by cultural constructs, and would need to be understood within the social and ideological parameters set by the discursive and ritualistic practices of a given society. Nature is, indeed, a physical constraint; but it has no meaning outside its relation to the symbolic.

Barkow offers the example of the difference between diseases caused by invisible agents, where soul eaters and germs are both considered as self-evident in different cultural contexts. They are counterintuitive in respect of each other, but they cannot be labeled such in absolute terms. "Much of culture is unverified and often unverifiable," Barkow concludes (Barkow 1989, 116). Also, it seems quite anachronistic to speak about physical properties or biological properties in the context of primitive religions (Pyysiäinen 2002). Nerissa Russell expresses a similar judgment while discussing Gregory Forth's book *Nage Birds: Classification and Symbolism among an Eastern Indonesian People*:

> Forth suggests that we see culture shaping knowledge most clearly where it is in conflict with science; that is, where beliefs are empirically incorrect. . . . Forth argues that even these mistaken beliefs are based to some degree on observation, but partial knowledge leads to erroneous interpretations. He does not consider that the symbolic role of birds plays much role in these false beliefs, but rather that the Nage simply do not systematically subject their inferences to experimental falsification in the manner of Western science. (Russell 2010, 10)

Interestingly, Girard himself borrows the term "counterintuitive" at various points of his argumentation (without making any reference to the way it is used by cognitivists), turning it topsy-turvy from a conceptual standpoint. It is not used to account for irrational beliefs in any superhuman agency, but rather for the kind of ideological inversion that modern rationality has performed in its understanding of the sacred. As mentioned previously, if one posits religion as the genetic principle of culture, what seems paradoxical, or counterintuitive, would start making sense, since it posits the strict a priori rationality of mythical thinking. What Girard stressed in his explanation is the intrinsically antinomic structure of the sacred, which defies any strictly Cartesian or modern causalist rationality; the fact that the sacred encapsulates both good and bad, purity and danger, positive and negative poles, may be seen by many as a philosophical sophism, rather than its intrinsic structure. Sacred is what is sacrificed, i.e., ostracized, expelled, victimized:

"it is criminal to kill [the victim]—but the victim is sacred only because he is to be killed" (Hubert and Mauss 1905). Sacred means both "holy" and "accursed"; it is what saves, but it is also what is impure and polluting. It is the *pharmakós*, at once poison and remedy; it is a principle of order and disorder. It is an example of the so-called *vox media*, which refers to terms that are ambiguous and with double entendre, as in the case of *agos*, which is both veneration and sacrilege; *anathema* is both offering and curse (the Latin *deus*, god, also originates from the Old Persian *daiva*, meaning "demon"). With different terminology, Mircea Eliade illustrates what he defines as "the mythical pattern": myths, rituals, and mystical experiences involve a *coincidentia oppositorum* (Eliade 1958, 419). Many myths, Eliade notes, "present us with a twofold revelation":

> They express on the one hand the diametrical opposition of two divine figures sprung from one and the same principle and destined, in many versions, to be reconciled at some *illud tempus* of eschatology, and on the other, the *coincidentia oppositorum* in the very nature of the divinity, which shows itself, by turns or even simultaneously, benevolent and terrible, creative and destructive, solar and serpentine, and so on (in other words, actual and potential). (Eliade 1976, 449)

According to Girard, the intrinsic ambivalence of the sacred is the product of the peculiar contradictory logic of its origin: the divinization of an emissary victim who is expelled and sacrificed by a riotous mob, by a social group on the verge of collapsing due to internal hatred and violence, and who find a convergence, a salvific outlet of all its endemic, mimetically generated violence, by discharging it against a random victim, deemed to be responsible for the disorder that disrupted the social order. Her collective banning, or killing, restores the natural order and peace inside the community. The simple fact that peace is immediately restored after her victimization, makes the culprit and scapegoat sacred. In this way the sacred victim becomes, according to mythical thinking, the principle of both evil and good.

For this reason, in the evolution of culture, there are many events and cultural inventions that strike us as counterintuitive from the standpoint of a rationalistic or functionalist explanatory approach, and they all have to do with the ambivalent nature of the sacred, and with the original sacrificial matrix. Another example is Girard's discussion of the emergence of taboos and anti-acquisitive behavior (again, in its etymology, the word "taboo" means not only "under prohibition," "not allowed," and "forbidden," but also "sacred," "holy"). He comments in particular on the system of exchange and gift-giving of the populations of the Trobriand Islands, off the northeast coast of New Guinea, as discussed by Bronisław Malinowski in *Argonauts of the West Pacific* (1922). In this book, the Polish anthropologist illustrates, among other things, the Kula ring ritual by which symbolic objects of value never remain for long in the hands of any recipient, but rather they must be passed on to other partners within a certain amount of time, thus constantly circling around the ring: "Everybody in turn must possess them," Girard adds, "because they are so *sacred* and so precious that they must shift from hand to hand, and this is part of a complex ritual, which keeps the Trobriand Islands in touch with each other, without conflict" (Girard, Antonello, and de Castro Rocha 2007, 127; Malinowski 1922, 81ff.). A similar behavior was also noted by John Pfeiffer in discussing Kalahari egalitarianism:

> If Kalahari men and women acquire valuable or beautiful objects . . . they are torn by conflicting emotions. They appreciate and treasure the object, and yet they feel exposed and threatened by having something which others do not have. The object becomes a psychological hot potato, something to be concealed for a while and gotten rid of as soon as possible. . . . People tend to feel more comfortable not having an outstanding possession, and thereby sinking back into a less conspicuous and less envied position within the group. Such behavior does not come naturally. It must be created, inculcated, by established custom. In the Kalahari, training to give things away starts from six weeks to six months after birth. (Pfeiffer 1982, 65)

Girard stresses the counterintuitive character of this behavior, providing an interpretation based on the premises of his theory on mimetic acquisition as a potential source of extreme forms of violence:

> One cannot explain taboos, prohibition and the complexity of symbolic exchange systems simply via biological explanations of the emergence of unselfish behavior. Exchange is at the center of this system. The gift is the opposite of grabbing everything for oneself, which is what the dominant

> animal does. The process of getting not only the dominating animal, but the *whole* culture to give up that grabbing attitude and give everything to the other in order to receive from the other—this is totally counterintuitive. There must be that upheaval which forced the change in behavior. This upheaval is absolutely indispensable. The only thing that can produce such a relational structure is *fear*, fear of death. If people are threatened, they withdraw from specific acts; otherwise chaotic appropriation will dominate and violence will always increase. Prohibition is the first condition for social ties and the first cultural sign as well. Fear is essentially fear of mimetic violence; prohibition is protection from mimetic escalation. (Girard, Antonello, and de Castro Rocha 2007, 109–10)

On this score, Girard also makes explicit reference to the biblical Decalogue, seen as a set of norms that try to limit acquisitive behavior (Girard 2001). Girard's general argument also implicitly answers to Mary Douglas's famous dichotomy between "purity and danger" (Douglas 1966): things that have been set apart as taboo because of their impurity and contagiousness are consubstantial to the sacred. In maintaining the socially legitimated order, individuals and social collectives create symbolic-cultural systems by setting apart impure objects, substances, places, or times, and emphasizing their cognitive status by taboo norms and rules of avoidance (see Douglas 1966; Sperber 1996; Parkin 1996). What is missing in Douglas's account is the reason for these forms of separations or confinement, which, according to Girard, is the violence intrinsic to the sacred. The sacred is generated by (collective) violence, and it is approached, ministered, handled, through sacrificial rituals that are the surrogate pharmacological forms of a primordial, apocalyptic, endogenous expression of social violence that it is feared will return to destroy the whole social order (as seen by the proto-culture as expression of a transcendental force equated to the divine or the sacred). If its linguistic root universally denotes "to cut," "to set apart," "to mark off" (see Paden 1991; Lutzky 1993; Anttonen 1996), it is because sacrifice is the principle of separation and categorization visible in the natural and social worlds, and which is performed, first of all, by an arbitrary closure of the social reality with the violent expulsion of one of its parts. According to Anttonen, the notion of the sacred calls into question "the dispositional properties of human beings in forming specific types of representations of some objects and things . . .

as aberrant, marginal, paradoxical, different, exceptional, or 'wholly other'" (Anttonen 2002, 30). According to Girard, in fact, the sacred is the source for this particular segmentation of natural and social reality, where specific objects, persons, animals, brought within the sphere of ritualized sacralization, acquire the paradoxical nature of the sacred.

Girard explains this dichotomization as a mechanism of sacralization: what the sacred does is to produce within the social order a reconfiguration of the inside/outside, self/other, good/evil dichotomies, which from the social domain are progressively extended to the understanding of the natural one, which acquire cultural meaning only from this original source of symbolization.

Cognitive Fluidity

A concept that is more naturally apt for the understanding of cultural evolution and the role of religion from the vantage point of mimetic theory is the concept of "cognitive fluidity." In *The Prehistory of the Human Mind*, Steven Mithen argues that the mind of modern humans has a particular cognitive fluidity: "ways of thinking and stores of knowledge about the social, natural and technical worlds flow unconstrained into each other, enabling us to live within a world of metaphors and analogies" (Mithen 1996). This needs also to be linked to the emergence of symbolism as the cultural product par excellence that sets nonhuman primates apart from humans:

> Neanderthals appear to have been very constrained in their range of behaviours and showed very limited, if any, signs of a creative intelligence: no visual art; no architecture; no body ornaments. . . . The Neanderthals became extinct doing much the same as they had been doing throughout the entirety of their existence hunting, gathering, making stone artefacts, sitting in caves, probably feeling rather cold and hungry even though they may have had third, fourth and possibly even fifth orders of intentionality. (Mithen 2007, 705)

Mithen traces the roots of cognitive fluidity back to the Middle Stone Age of Africa, "but the evidence becomes most striking after 50,000 years ago with the advent of the Upper Palaeolithic in Europe" (Mithen 2007, 706; see also Mithen 1996, 1998).[4] Mithen makes particular reference to the use of sexual metaphors in the processing of plant foods, but also to the symbolic complexity of the PPNA site of Wadi Faynan located in the southern Levant, making a remark very similar to Ian Hodder's about Çatalhöyük:

> As with other sites of this period, it has human burials below house floors, some of which appear to have had bones repeatedly added to and removed. . . . These burials are literally the imposition of the social, i.e. persons, into the natural, i.e. the ground, providing a dramatic material representation of what I suspect was a cognitively fluid understanding of the world. (Mithen 2007, 715)

There is an interesting corollary added by Mithen to this perspective, which is quite instructive in the understanding of any intuitive ontology: regarding the "imposition of a social way of thinking onto the natural world and physical objects, we must also note that an equally important characteristic of humans is to treat other persons as non-social objects. In this regard, people use ways of thinking appropriate to physical objects to manipulate other people without recourse to their feelings and relationships" (Mithen 2007, 706). The ethnologist Irenäus Eibl-Eibesfeldt affirms that, more than the invention of tools and weapons, what really triggers violence is the capacity we have for convincing ourselves that the adversary is not a human being, but an animal, often a monster. For instance, the Mundurukú divide the world in a significant way: themselves and *pariwat*, that is, the others. The others are simply considered animals to be preyed upon (Eibl-Eibesfeldt 1996; Girard, Antonello, and de Castro Rocha 2007, 115). These facts complicate the simple observation that religious (or magical) thinking would tend to attribute agency or animacy to nonliving things, or that there are ontological categories such as persons, tools, plants, natural objects, or animals. The sacred, rather, produced a constant dislocation of meaning, which bypasses and overcomes any strict ontological boundary with stable indexical attribution of meaning. On this score also, Nerissa Russell suggests that the domestication of animals, a later byproduct of sacrificial practices, as we have seen, favored a more hierarchical and unequal structuring of societies: "once domesticated animals existed in their permanent subordinate position within the human sphere, it became easier to conceive of humans subordinated like animals" (Russell 2007, 37). In a sense, sacrificial practices introduce a form of self-reflexivity in the social group that produces cultural "ripples" in all social domains, restructuring established categorization, and reconfiguring, as I said, the distinction between insiders and outsiders, self and other, animate and inanimate, subject and object, forming and shaping the cognitive fluidity that is proper to humans.

Homo Symbolicus

As we have seen, this cognitive fluidity was paralleled and actually made possible by the emergence of symbolic activities in humans, which is a crucial and central aspect in any general theory of the origins of culture. As empirical evidence gathered by primatologists suggests, primates already have culture; they have toolmaking, as well as forms of cooperation and proto-morality—but they do not have symbols. It is the symbolic order that produces a dissociation between referents and signs, allowing the free-floating of signifiers, enabling their recombination, hence the constitution of metaphorical and analogical thinking, and the possibility of language and myth-making.

Girard claims that evolutionists tend to minimize symbolicity by trying to derive it from purely anatomical or biological considerations (Girard, Antonello, and de Castro Rocha 2007). The emergence of language is explained in such theories purely in function of the evolution of the brain, and they tend to display a functionalist approach in accounting for its emergence (see for instance Atran 2002): the need for rapid and more effective communication in hunting is invoked, for instance, whereas the complexity of language and the emergence of symbolicity are, in reality, matters that go well beyond the reach of this explanation. Hominids such as Neanderthals no doubt hunted quite effectively without any complex symbolic system.

In discussing the origins of symbolization, Girard makes reference to one of the most important works on this topic: Terrence Deacon's *The Symbolic Species* (1997) (Girard, Antonello, and de Castro Rocha 2007, ch. 3). Deacon's perspective is in fact particularly cogent from the point of view of mimetic theory, providing evidence and a more insightful understanding of the emergence of the symbolic order. Deacon in particular is sensitive to some issues and problems that are fully addressed in explanatory terms by mimetic theory: key points are the role played by ritualization, sexual competition, and peacemaking (Deacon 1997, 400), as well as the need to think culture and the symbolic order in anti-reductionist terms, as an emergent modality, i.e., as the "spontaneous generation of a higher-order novel synergy arising from the interaction of component processes" (Deacon and Cashman 2009; see also Deacon 2006). Girard, in particular, underscores how Deacon emphasizes the opposition between indexation and symbolicity, arguing that symbolicity is counterintuitive from the viewpoint of indexation, because it dissolves the bond between the sign and the object (Girard, Antonello, and de Castro Rocha 2007, 109; Deacon 1997, 340–41). In Deacon's account,

> The earliest forms of symbolic communication were therefore likely not speechlike or manual sign languages. They almost certainly included vocalizations along with conventional/ritual gestures, activities, and objects, all of which together formed a heterogeneous melange of indices transformed to symbols, each systematically dependent on the other, and defining a closed set of possible types of relationships. (Deacon 1997, 407)

"Early hominids were forced to learn a set of associations between signs and objects, repeat them over and over, and eventually unlearn the concrete association in favor of a more abstract one" (402). What made this shift possible? Deacon's answer is "ritual," which is still "a central component of symbolic 'education' in modern human societies" (402). In similar fashion, Girard argues that religion, culture, and symbolicity developed through the slow process of the ritualization of sacrifice. For Girard, ritual is a central component in the self-pedagogy of humans—or rather in the religious pedagogy that allowed early exemplars of *Homo* to become *sapiens*, from both biological and cultural standpoints. Similarly, Deacon argues that

> The problem of symbol discovery is to shift attention from the concrete to the abstract; from separate indexical links between signs and objects to an organized set of relations between signs. In order to bring the logic of token-token relationship to the fore. . . . the ritual context allows highly redundant, therefore reliable, associations between the markers of these relationships to become established. Because of this, it is possible to

> abandon reliance on the indexical associations themselves and come to rely on the symbolic (but virtual) reference to hold. (Deacon 1997, 405)

However, there is something missing in Deacon's account. Ritualistic redundancy does not suffice in itself. What is needed in this primordial scenario, Girard argues, is a center of signification:

> In order to have a capacity for symbolisation you must have an origin and referent for the chain of meaning; and, to me, that is the scapegoat murder. In this way, one can explain how the increase in symbolic capacity is tied to ritual. This demands what philosophers used to call a "totality," so those things within the totality can refer to each other, and therefore acquire meaning through indexation and through analogical, metonymical and metaphorical connections between elements of the totality. (Girard, Antonello, and de Castro Rocha 2007, 104)

The sacrificial victim, in particular, is the focal point of the whole scapegoating event and of the construction of meaning subsequently built around it: "We can therefore understand why in so many myths the rules of culture spring directly from the body of the victim" (Girard 1987, 41). In an effort to prevent frequent and uncontrollable episodes of mimetic violence, acts of controlled, mediated, and ritualized violence were periodically enacted: a form of staged representation or replay that involved the killing of a surrogate victim. This victim is no longer presumed responsible for the crisis, but he/she is both a real new victim that has to be killed, and a symbol of the proto-event. And this is the first symbolic sign ever invented: it is the first moment in which something stands for something else—here is the ur-symbol. In this sense, Girard implicitly argues that the analysis of how symbolization emerged should also take into account the reference level of ritualization and myth-making, meaning the narrativization of the key emotional events that produced the emergence of religion, the sacred, and its ritualized structure, which morphologically point to the ritualization of human sacrifice.

On the other hand, mimetic theory assumes that at the origin of the cultural order there must be a form of radical upheaval that literally projected the human onto a different cognitive level, allowing for the symbolic to emerge. This is found by Girard in unanimous scapegoating and its ritualization. This produced, in turn, a social totality; a collectively emotional cognitive focalization, and an ecstatic moment of high intensity; a (pseudo) dichotomization of social reality; the compelling social need to reproduce this event ritualistically for thaumaturgic reasons; a progressive process of separation, through ritualization, between signified and signifier within the token-object association.

Totality

As we have also seen, an interesting and fundamental corollary from the perspective envisaged by Girard's explanation is the role played by the so-called totality. The kind of cognitive and social upheaval that may be the cause of the emergence of the symbolic requires that the *whole* social group be stirred and transformed by this experience; it is not a matter of individual preference for specific cultural elements in question, but a form of collective agency without any predetermined intentionality or rationality. As suggested by Girard, as in the case of mass panic or herd behavior—interestingly enough, the Greek etymology of the prefix *pan-* defines in fact a totality—this totality is at first opaque to itself, i.e., it is impressed, steered, transformed by the power of a collective, unanimous, mimetically driven form of intragroup violent frenzy, where the borders between insider and outsider are reconfigured, where an artificial externalization, due to forms of perceptual misrecognition, is produced by the group by singling out a victim who is deemed responsible for the social disorder and internal violence experienced by the group. As Jean-Pierre Dupuy argues, this totality, in a Durkheimian sense, embodies the quality of the divine as an emergent phenomenon (Dupuy 1985).[5]

It is also through these unanimous phenomena, which act as productive agents of cognitive and social change, that a transformation of strict natural and biological order based on dominance patterns and/or on kin may be radically reconfigured. In discussing competing theories of the origins of culture, Chris Knight underscores the key role played by the emergence of "counterdominance, egalitarianism, and collective intentionality." While unaware of Girard's hypothesis, he makes particular reference to the works of Michael Tomasello (1999, 2006) on the cultural origins of human cognition, and to Christopher Boehm (2001) on the evolution of egalitarian behavior. Tomasello links the evolution of symbolism with collaboration or cooperation in pursuit of a shared vision or goal held jointly in mind, which is a defining feature of humans (wild-living apes do not even point things out to one another). "Declarative pointing presupposes individuals so trusting and cooperative that they are willing to decide collaboratively on the perspective to be adopted toward the world. Humans during the course of evolution established such 'we'-intentionality" (Knight 2010, 202; Tomasello 1999). However, Tomasello has no idea as to why this development occurred (Tomasello 2003, 108–9). According to Knight, Christopher Boehm in *Hierarchy in the Forest: The Evolution of Egalitarian Behavior* (2001) offers a concrete proposal in response to the question raised by Tomasello. The vision that really mattered, Knight submits briefly, was a political one. However, the boundary between anachronistic modern categorial projections, such as a political consciousness and social organization, and hard evidence is blurred in Boehm's argument:

> The aim was to take hold of primate-style dominance and turn it upside down. According to Boehm, the strategy of resisting dominance leads eventually to fullscale revolution. But how exactly did this happen? Boehm asks us to envisage *a coalition expanding until eventually it includes everyone.* This is a demanding concept, since a coalition by definition presupposes a boundary between insiders and outsiders. (Knight 2010, 202, my emphasis; see also Boehm 2001, 167–69)

Boehm, possibly because of the typical Marxist suspicion for everything religious, barely mentions the role of ritual, religion, and language in his argument. However, what has been described as a clear example of social totalization, i.e., the so-called "identity fusion" of the group (also referred to as "mechanical solidarity" and "collective effervescence," in the words of Emile Durkheim [1893/1964; 1915/1995] or "spontaneous *communitas*" by Victor Turner [1969]), is present in ethnographic records particularly in the context, and as the effect, of rituals: "Identity fusion occurs when people experience a visceral feeling of oneness with a group. The union with the group is so strong among highly fused persons that the boundaries that ordinarily demarcate the personal and social self become highly permeable"

(Swann et al. 2012, 442). This is achieved particularly by highly dramatically and emotionally charged rituals:

> Consider participation in rituals such as the ordeals of initiation cults, millenarian sects, and vision quests. Such "imagistic" rituals (Atkinson and Whitehouse 2011; Whitehouse 1995, 2000, 2004) are typically emotionally intense events that are experienced rarely (only once in a lifetime in some cases). The intensity of such rituals is exaggerated by extreme forms of deprivation, bodily mutilation and flagellation, and psychological trauma based around participation in shocking acts. . . . To the extent that humans are "creatures of concreteness" (Nisbett, Borgida, Crandall, and Reed 1976), such experiences may be particularly compelling sources of fusion—sometimes resulting in allegiances that are stronger than those found between blood relatives. (Swann et al. 2012, 449–50)

The identity fusion of the group is also deemed to be critical for the promotion of cooperation among non-kin. The principle of inclusive fitness in fact "cannot explain the willingness of humans to fuse with large groups of genetically unrelated individuals (i.e., extended fusion)" (Swann et al. 2012, 448).

There are a couple of remarks we should make from the vantage point of mimetic theory. First of all, this form of identity fusion can be better understood and conceptualized if we assume a form of unreflexive imitation at its base, as amply conceptualized by Girard. Moreover, this fusion produces a form of totalization in which the boundaries between insiders and outsiders, and between individual identity and group identity blur—a key element, as we have said, for the kind of cognitive slippage required for the symbolic to emerge. The ritualistic reenactment of this artificial dichotomization prompted by the sacrificial proto-events would then be instrumental both for the cognitive reinforcement discussed by Deacon in reference to the emergence of the symbolic, and for the development of the ritualistic apparatus in which forms of sacrifice are vigorously displayed, as amply found in religious rituals all over the world and in the historical record. As a matter of fact, the most emotionally charged, attention grabbing collective rituals (Boyer 1996), subverting and dramatically overriding any biological constraints, are those where the group sacrifices one of its own kin; the ritualistic reenactment of this sacrificial gesture is the pure sign of what *religio* actually means: the binding of a community together through liturgies and rituals. Rites of passage as ritualistic regulations of moments of transition in society all reproduce mimetically, in the sense of representation, the ritualistic phases of the primordial (self-)sacrificial ritualistic practice. If all culture stems from this original moment, cultural artifacts would carry the fingerprint, the subtextual frame, of the original scene.[6]

Notes

1. The view of botanists seems to have swung away from the idea of a rapid process of domestication of cereals, towards a long period of "predomestication agriculture," that is, cultivation before the recognizable traits of the domesticated species were manifested. George Willcox and his colleagues have shown us domestication in progress over about 1,500 years from the late Epipaleolithic (Willcox, Fornite, and Herveux 2008).
2. In *The Golden Bough* (1922), Frazer writes, for instance, "The corn-spirit is represented sometimes in human, sometimes in animal form, and . . . in both cases he is killed in the person of his representative and eaten sacramentally. To find examples of actually killing the human representative of the corn-spirit we had naturally to go to savage races; but the harvest-suppers of our European peasants have furnished unmistakable examples of the sacramental eating of animals as representatives of the corn-spirit. . . . At the present day in Lithuania, when new potatoes or loaves made from the new corn are being eaten, all the people at table pull each other's hair. The meaning of this last custom is obscure, but a similar custom was certainly observed by the heathen Lithuanians at their solemn sacrifices" (L. Frazer, "Eating the God § 1. The Sacrament of First-Fruits").
3. The idea of burials as ownership landmarks has been suggested also by archaeologists (Smith 1995, 80).
4. As a key testing point, he again makes reference to the domestication of plants and the invention of agriculture, seen as a sort of "misapplication of social intelligence." As an example he claims that "the processing of plant foods at WF16, and possibly throughout the PPNA, was imbued with a sexual metaphor" (Mithen 2007, 715).
5. Dupuy, in "Totalisation et méconnaissance" (1985), underscores the relevant element of unanimity and totalization in this collective act of divinization: "It is nothing but this very collective movement that separates itself, by taking distance, and acquiring autonomy from individual movements, without ceasing to be the simple composition of individual actions and reactions. As Durkheim understood it very well, in those moments, especially in those moments, the social totality displays all the traits that humans attribute to the divinity: exteriority, transcendence, unpredictability, inaccessibility" (118).
6. Boehm provides a fitting example to illustrate this argument by making reference to Lee's ethnographic study of conflicts among a number of Kalahari forager band members, and the particular form of communal execution of a group member, in which Girard would easily detect a primitive formalization of the logic of emissary victimization as a form of pre-institutionalized justice (as discussed in the first chapter of *Violence and the Sacred*): "In the most dramatic case on record, a man named Twi had killed three other people, when the community, in a rare moment of unanimity, ambushed and fatally wounded him in full daylight. As he lay dying, all the men fired

at him with poisoned arrows until, in the words of one informant, 'he looked like a porcupine.' Then, after he was dead, all the women as well as the men approached his body and stabbed him with spears, symbolically sharing the responsibility for his death" (Lee 1979, 100). "This group execution," Boehm comments, "involved the entire moral community that made the decision, and active participation by each person obviated the possibility of precisely targeted revenge. It may seem puzzling that the females participated, but remember that they were full members of the moral community" (Boehm 2001, 180). This may be puzzling to Boehm or to other anthropologists. Not so to Girard, who discerns here the fingerprints of a primordial collective murder, later institutionalized as a normative form of ritualized practice.

Works Cited

Anttonen, V. 1996. "Rethinking the Sacred: The Notions of 'Human Body' and 'Territory' in Conceptualizing Religion." In *The Sacred and Its Scholars: Comparative Methodologies for the Study of Primary Religious Data*, ed. T. A. Idinopulos and E. A. Yonan, 36–64. Leiden: Brill.

———. 2002. "Identifying the Generative Mechanisms of Religion: The Issue of Origin Revisited." In *Current Approaches in the Cognitive Science of Religion*, ed. I. Pyysiäinen and V. Anttonen, 14–37. New York: Continuum.

Atkinson, Q. D., and H. Whitehouse. 2011. "The Cultural Morphospace of Ritual Form: Examining Modes of Religiosity Cross-culturally." *Evolution and Human Behavior* 32: 50–62. doi:10.1016/j.evolhumbehav.2010.09.002.

Atran, S. 2002. *In Gods We Trust*. New York: Oxford University Press.

Barkow, J. H. 1989. "The Elastic between Genes and Culture." *Ethology and Sociobiology* 10: 111–29.

Binford, L. 1980. "Willow Smoke and Dog's Tails: Hunter-gatherer Settlement and Archaeological Site Formation." *American Antiquity* 45: 4–20.

Bloch, M. 2005. *Essays on Cultural Transmission*. Oxford: Berg.

Boehm, C. 2001. *Hierarchy in the Forest: The Evolution of Egalitarian Behavior*. Cambridge, MA: Harvard University Press.

Bökönyi, S. 1969. "Archaeological Problems and Methods of Recognizing Animal Domestication." In *The Domestication and Exploitation of Plants and Animals*, ed. P. J. Ucko and G. W. Dimbleby, 219–30. Chicago: Aldine.

Boyd, R., and P. J. Richerson. 1983. "Why Is Culture Adaptive?" *Quarterly Review of Biology* 58, no. 2: 209–14.

———. 2005. *Not by Genes Alone: How Culture Transformed Human Evolution*. Chicago: University of Chicago Press.

Boyer, P. 1994. *The Naturalness of Religious Ideas: A Cognitive Theory of Religion*. Berkeley: University of California Press.

———. 1996. "What Makes Anthropomorphism Natural: Intuitive Ontology and Cultural Representations." *Journal of the Royal Anthropological Institute* 2, no. 1: 83–97.

———. 1998. "Cognitive Tracks of Cultural Inheritance: How Evolved Intuitive Ontology Governs Cultural Transmission." *American Anthropologist* 100, no. 4: 876–89.

———. 2001. *Religion Explained: The Evolutionary Origins of Religious Thought*. New York: Basic Books.

Byrd, B. F. 2005. "Reassessing the Emergence of Village Life in the Near East." *Journal of Archaeological Research* 13, no. 3: 231–90.

Calasso, R. 1985. *The Ruin of Kasch*. Cambridge, MA: Harvard University Press.

Carrasco, D. 1999. *City of Sacrifice: The Aztec Empire and the Role of Violence in Civilization*. Boston: Beacon Press.

Cauvin, J. 1994. *Naissance des divinités, naissance de l'agriculture: La révolution des symboles au Néolithique*. Paris: CNRS Editions.

Chase, P. G. 1994. "On Symbols and the Palaeolithic." *Current Anthropology* 35: 627–29.

———. 1999. "Symbolism as Reference and Symbolism as Culture." In *The Evolution of Culture: An Interdisciplinary View*, ed. R.I.M. Dunbar, C. Knight, and C. Power, 34–49. Edinburgh: Edinburgh University Press.

Cockburn, T. A. 1971. "Infectious Diseases in Ancient Populations." *Current Anthropology* 12: 45–62.

Cohen, M. N. 1989. *Health and the Rise of Civilization*. New Haven: Yale University Press.

de Santillana, G., and H. von Dechend. 1969. *Hamlet's Mill: An Essay Investigating the Origins of Human Knowledge and Its Transmission through Myth*. Boston: Gambit.

de Waal, F. 2001. *The Ape and the Sushi Master: Cultural Reflections of a Primatologist*. New York: Basic Books.

Deacon, T. W. 1997. *The Symbolic Species: The Co-evolution of Language and the Brain*. New York: W.W. Norton & Co.

———. 2006. "Emergence: The Hole at the Wheel's Hub." In *The Re-emergence of Emergence*, ed. P. Clayton and P. Davies, 111–50. Cambridge, MA: MIT Press.

Deacon, T. W., and T. Cashman. 2009. "The Role of Symbolic Capacity in the Origins of Religion." *Journal for the Study of Religion, Nature and Culture* 3.4: 490–517.

Douglas, M. 1966. *Purity and Danger: An Analysis of the Concepts of Pollution and Taboo*. London: Routledge and Kegan Paul.

Dunbar, R. 2004. *The Human Story*. London: Faber & Faber.

Dupuy, J. P. 1985. "Totalisation et méconnaissance." In *Violence et Vérité: Autour de René Girard*, ed. P. Dumouchel, 110–35. Paris: Grasset.

Durham, William H. 1991. *Coevolution: Genes, Culture, and Human Diversity*. Stanford, CA: Stanford University Press.

Durkheim, E. [1893] 1964. *The Division of Labor in Society*. New York: Free Press.

———. [1915] 1995. *The Elementary Forms of Religious Life*. New York: Free Press.

Eibl-Eibesfeldt, I. [1970] 1996. *Love and Hate: The Natural History of Behavior Patterns*. Translated by G. Strachan. New York: Aldine de Gruyter.

Eliade, M. 1958. *Patterns in Comparative Religion*. London: Sheed & Ward.

———. 1963. *Myth and Reality*. New York: Harper & Row.

———. 1976. *Myths, Rites, Symbols: A Mircea Eliade Reader*. Vol. 2. Edited by W. C. Beane and W. G. Doty. New York: Harper & Row.

Enquist, M., and S. Ghirlanda. 2007. "Evolution of Social Learning Does Not Explain the Origin of Human Cumulative Culture." *Journal of Theoretical Biology* 246: 129–35.

Fernandez-Jalvo, Y., et al. 1999. "Human Cannibalism in the Early Pleistocene of Europe (Gran Dolina, Sierra de Atapuerca, Burgos, Spain)." *Journal of Human Evolution* 37: 591–622.

Forth, G. 2004. *Nage Birds: Classification and Symbolism among an Eastern Indonesian People*. New York: Routledge.

Frazer, J. 1922. *The Golden Bough: A Study in Magic and Religion*. Abridged ed. Edited by T. H. Gaster. New York: Macmillan.

Girard, R. 1987. *Things Hidden since the Foundation of the World*. Stanford, CA: Stanford University Press.

———. 2001. *I See Satan Fall Like Lightning*. Maryknoll, NY: Orbis Books.

Girard, R., P. Antonello, and J. C. de Castro Rocha. 2007. *Evolution and Conversion: Dialogues on the Origins of Culture*. New York: Continuum.

Harris, M. 1979. *Cultural Materialism: The Struggle for a Science of Culture*. New York: Random House.

Hodder, I. 1990. *The Domestication of Europe: Structure and Contingency in Neolithic Societies*. Oxford: Blackwell.

Hubert, H., and M. Mauss. [1905] 1981. *Sacrifice: Its Nature and Functions*. Translated by W. D. Halls. Chicago: Chicago University Press.

Humphrey, N. 1984. *Consciousness Regained*. Oxford: Oxford University Press.

Ingold, T. 1984. "Time, Social Relationships and the Exploitation of Animals: Anthropological Reflections on Prehistory." In *Animals and Archaeology*, vol. 3, *Early Herders and Their Flocks* (British Archaeological Reports, International Series, No. 202), ed. J. Clutton-Brock and C. Grigson, 3–12. Oxford: British Archaeological Reports.

Knight, C. 2010. "The Origins of Symbolic Culture." In *Homo Novus: A Human without Illusions*, ed. U. J. Frey, C. Störmer, and K. P. Willführ, 193–211. Berlin: Springer-Verlag.

Lee, R. 1979. *The !Kung San: Men, Women, and Work in a Foraging Society*. Cambridge: Cambridge University Press.

Lee, R. B., and I. DeVore. 1968. "Problems in the Study of Hunters and Gatherers." In *Man the Hunter*, ed. R. B. Lee and I. DeVore, 3–12. Chicago: Aldine.

Lutzky, H. 1993. "On a Concept Underlying Indo-European Terms for the Sacred." *Journal of Indo-European Studies* 21: 283–301.

Malinowski, B. 1922. *Argonauts of the West Pacific: An Account of Native Enterprise and Adventure in the Archipelagoes of Melanesian New Guinea*. New York: Dutton & Co.

Marlar, R. A., et al. 2000. "Biochemical Evidence of Cannibalism at a Prehistoric Puebloan Site in Southwestern Colorado." *Nature* 407: 74–78.

Mead, S., et al. 2003. "Balancing Selection at the Prion Protein Gene Consistent with Prehistoric Kurulike Epidemics." *Science* 300: 640–43.

Mithen, S. 2007. "Did Farming Arise from a Misapplication of Social Intelligence?" *Philosophical Transactions: Biological Sciences* 362, no. 1480: 705–18.

Mithen, S. J. 1996. *The Prehistory of the Mind: A Search for the Origins of Art, Science and Religion.* London: Thames & Hudson.

———. 1998. "A Creative Explosion: Theory of Mind, Language and the Disembodied Mind of the Upper Palaeolithic." In *Creativity in Human Evolution and Prehistory*, ed. S. Mithen, 165–92. London: Routledge.

———. 2003. *After the Ice: A Global Human History, 20,000–5000 BC.* London: Weidenfeld & Nicholson.

Murphy, R. F. 1957. "Intergroup Hostility and Social Cohesion." *American Anthropologist* 59: 1028.

Nisbett, R. E., E. Borgida, R. Crandall, and H. Reed. 1976. "Popular Induction: Information Is Not Always Informative." In *Cognition and Social Behavior*, ed. J. Carroll and J. Payne, 227–36. Hillsdale, NJ: Erlbaum.

Paden, W. E. 1991. "Before 'The Sacred' Became Theological: Rereading the Durkheimian Legacy." *Method & Theory in the Study of Religion* 3: 10–23.

———. 1999. "Sacrality and Worldmaking: New Categorial Perspectives." In *Approaching Religion, Scripta Instituti Donneriani Aboensis* 17, part 1, ed. T. Ahlbäck, 165–80. Turku, Finland: Åbo Akademi University.

Parkin, R. 1996. *The Dark Side of Humanity: The Work of Robert Hertz and Its Legacy.* London: Routledge.

Pfeiffer, J. 1982. *The Creative Explosion.* New York: Harper & Row.

Pyysiäinen, I. 2002. "Religion and the Counter-Intuitive." In *Current Approaches in the Cognitive Science of Religion*, ed. I. Pyysiäinen and V. Anttonen, 110–32. New York: Continuum.

Russell, N. 2007. "The Domestication of Anthropology." In *Where the Wild Things Are Now: Domestication Reconsidered*, ed. R. Cassidy and M. H. Mullin. Oxford: Berg.

———. 2010. "Navigating the Human-Animal Boundary." *Reviews in Anthropology* 39, no. 1: 3–24.

Serres, M. 1985. *Les cinq sens.* Paris: Grasset.

Smith, B. D. 1995. *The Emergence of Agriculture.* New York: Scientific American Library.

Smith, E. A. 2003. "Human Cooperation: Perspective from Behavioural Ecology." In *Genetic and Cultural Evolution of Cooperation*, ed. P. Hammerstein, 401–27. Cambridge, MA: MIT Press.

Smith, J. Z. 1987. "The Domestication of Sacrifice." In *Violent Origins: Ritual Killing and Cultural Formation*, ed. Robert Hamerton-Kelly, 191–205. Stanford, CA: Stanford University Press.

Sperber, D. 1996. "Why Are Perfect Animals, Hybrids, and Monsters Food for Symbolic Thought?" *Method and Theory in the Study of Religion* 8: 143–69.

Stoneking, M. 2003. "Widespread Prehistoric Human Cannibalism: Easier to Swallow?" *Trends in Ecology and Evolution* 18, no. 10: 489–90.

———. 2006. "Investigating the Health of Our Ancestors: Insights from the Evolutionary Genetic Consequences of Prehistoric Diseases." In *Integrative Approaches to Human Health and Evolution. Proceedings of the International Symposium "Integrative Approaches to Human Health and Evolution" held in Madrid, Spain, between 18 and 20 April 2005.* International Congress Series, vol. 1296: 106–14.

Swann, W. B., Jr., J. Jetten, Á. Gómez, H. Whitehouse, and B. Bastian. 2012. "When Group Membership Gets Personal: A Theory of Identity Fusion." *Psychological Review* 119 no. 3: 441–56.

Tomasello, M. 1999. *The Cultural Origins of Human Cognition*. Cambridge, MA: Harvard University Press.

———. 2003. "Different Origins of Symbols and Grammar." In *Language Evolution*, ed. M. H. Christiansen and S. Kirby, 94–110. Oxford: Oxford University Press.

———. 2006. "Why Don't Apes Point?" In *Roots of Human Sociality: Culture, Cognition and Interaction*, ed. N. J. Enfield and S. C. Levinson, 506–24. New York: Berg.

Turner, V. 1969. *The Ritual Process: Structure and Anti-Structure*. London: Routledge & Kegan Paul.

Van Gennep, A. 1960. *The Rites of Passage*. Translated by M. B. Vizedom and G. L. Caffee. Chicago: University of Chicago Press.

Vogt, M. C. [1871] 1873. "Anthropophagie et sacrifices humains." In *Congrès International d'anthropologie et d'archéologie préhistoriques. Compte rendu de la cinquième session à Bologne*. Bologna: Imprimerie Fava et Garagnani.

Volhard, E. 1939. *Kannibalismus*. Studien zur Kulturkunde; 5 Bd. Stuttgart: Verlag Strecker und Schröder.

Wadley, G., and A. Martin. 1993. "The Origins of Agriculture: A Biological Perspective and a New Hypothesis." *Australian Biologist* 6: 96–105.

White, T. D. 2001. "Once We Were Cannibals." *Scientific American* 285: 58–65.

Whitehouse, H. 1995. *Inside the Cult: Religious Innovation and Transmission in Papua New Guinea*. Oxford: Oxford University Press.

———. 2000. *Arguments and Icons: Divergent Modes of Religiosity*. Oxford: Oxford University Press.

———. 2004. *Modes of Religiosity: A Cognitive Theory of Religious Transmission*. Walnut Creek, CA: AltaMira Press.

Willcox, G., S. Fornite, and L. Herveux. 2008. "Early Holocene Cultivation before Domestication in Northern Syria." *Vegetation History and Archaeobotany* 17, no. 3: 313–25.

Woodburn, J. 1980. "Hunters and Gatherers Today and Reconstruction of the Past." In *Soviet and Western Anthropology*, ed. A. Gellner, 95–117. London: Duckworth.

PART TWO

Imitation, Desire, Victimization: Examining Mimetic Theory on the Evidence

Convergence between Mimetic Theory and Imitation Research

Scott Garrels

Imitation, as Darwin already noted, is found throughout all orders and in all epochs of the natural world; but—so Girard contends—it is most powerfully present in humans, and most transformingly and decisively engaged in the process itself of hominization. The singular contribution of Girardian theory to evolutionary thinking can only be as good as this mimetic basis—which is why, at the threshold of these essays inspired by the Darwin-Girard linkage, it is worth exploring the current scientific standing of this key Girardian notion. Within the last decade, the empirical investigation of imitation in humans has registered a dramatic resurgence of interest, the results of which provide unprecedented support for, and clarification of, the foundational role of mimesis in intersubjective, mind-to-mind relationalities. Convergent evidence across the modern disciplines of developmental psychology and cognitive neuroscience has been forthcoming, which demonstrates that imitation based on mirrored neural activity and reciprocal interpersonal behavior is what guides and structures human development as such.

It has been shown not only that imitation functions powerfully in the mother-infant dyad to bring about experience-dependent neurocognitive development, but also that mimesis continues to provide in adulthood the most characteristic and structurally crucial scaffolding of human relations, since it significantly affects mental representation, empathy, language, and the entire range of intersubjective experience. Further, new discoveries from neuroscience continue to suggest the essential role of mimetic reciprocity in contributing to a wide-scale cerebral reorganization of brain function, allowing for the coevolution of more complex social and representational abilities from primates to humans. This is foundational for social intelligence and group dynamics: the very things most crucially involved in Girard's account of hominization.

If, despite these breakthrough findings at the frontier of research, imitation still remains largely misunderstood by many scientists (and others) as a secondary, rather than a fundamental, building block of human behavior, this is by reason of unobserved conceptual difficulties and cultural persuasions. Imitation is commonly misidentified as a kind of mimicry that simply copies the actions of others, as in children's games, or a temporary mechanism providing a restricted and passing role in child development. There is also a latent post-Romantic misvaluation we inherit unthinkingly, which believes in mere imitation, i.e., in a mechanical replication (e.g., in thought or art), carrying the implication of a deficiency in transforming creativity or originality. All these unhelpful "interferences on the wavelength" are, in the light of recent empirical evidence, destined to shrink and die away as objections.

There are also distinct restrictions of attention. Focusing primarily on dyadic relationships in infancy, empirical researchers have only just begun to look at the persistent role of imitation in adulthood and group dynamics. The questions that have occupied cognitive neuroscientists as well as developmental psychologists have mainly addressed the functional architecture of imitation as well as its role in the development of language, theory of mind, intentionality, and memory.

Most significantly of all, there still remains an eloquent and questionable silence within imitation theories on the role of reciprocal mimesis in generating acts of social rivalry, conflict, and ultimately violence. This is the Girardian challenge par excellence, not only for imitation researchers, but for the social sciences at large.

It is important here to understand that since the emergence of modern imitation research, relatively little dialogue has in fact taken place—between imitation researchers and mimetic scholars, assuredly, but even and also between imitation researchers themselves. This latter case has changed substantially in recent years. For example, while infant imitation has been an active and growing area of investigation since the late 1970s, it was not until 1999 that the first compilation of evidence from a variety of researchers was published in book form (Nadel and Butterworth 1999). That same year, one of the first conferences took place that created an interdisciplinary dialogue between developmental psychology and neuroscience researchers (Meltzoff and Prinz 2002). Two years later, the dialogue expanded from developmental psychology and cognitive neuroscience to the social sciences more broadly, including the philosophical and social importance of imitation, at a conference in Royaumont Abbey, France, in May 2002 entitled "Perspectives on Imitation" (Hurley and Chater 2005).

Yet there are two certainties. The first is that empirical research provided by disciplines such as developmental psychology and neuroscience is in a position to help establish Girard's theory of psychological mimesis and its broader implications in a similar way to that in which Darwin's theory achieved its substantive structuring and continued influence. Much of the criticism aimed at Girard's work has centered upon the absence of empirical data to support his broad conclusions about the role of imitation in human life and in his theory of human culture (Livingston 1992). This absence has allowed many critics to reject outright the broader implications of mimetic theory on this basis alone. Yet it is imperative—and increasingly possible—that the foundational claims of mimetic theory be readdressed in the light of new evidence from contemporary empirical research. Girardian scholars are in a position to substantiate the principal claims of mimetic theory in ways that also corroborate findings across the empirical disciplines relevant to it, as well as to make their conclusions "accessible to the enriching and modifying effects of discoveries in science at large."[1]

The second certainty is that mimetic theory, with its central focus on universal mimesis, and its freedom from these unobserved inhibitions we have mentioned, clearly has the greatest potential for relaunching and redirecting imitation research. Several decades before empirical research prompted a resurgence of interest in imitation and its significance to human development and psychosocial functioning, René Girard (1965, 1977) had already articulated a theory of imitation, which explained imitative phenomena and their broader anthropological implications with surprising power and economy.

What makes Girard's insights so remarkable is that he discovered and developed the primordial role of what we may call "psychological mimesis" (i.e., the mimesis of acquisitive and rivalrous desire, leading to social crisis and the resolution by emissary victimization); and this during a time when imitation was quite out of fashion. Equally remarkable was the fact that he did so through investigations in literature, cultural anthropology, and history, and ultimately returning to religious texts for further evidence of mimetic phenomena. The parallels between Girard's insights and the very recent conclusions established by empirical researchers concerning imitation (in both human development today, and the evolution of the species in proto-historical time) are extraordinary and deserve a more detailed and comparative review, which must extend beyond what is possible in the present discussion. What follows, therefore, is intended as a springboard, not as a summation or closure.

Universal Mimesis and the Generative Function of Imitation

Imitation researchers and mimetic scholars overlap most significantly in their view of imitation as a vital and positive force in both human development and evolution. Girard himself has stated that "Mimetic desire even when bad, is intrinsically good, in the sense that far from being merely imitative in a small sense, it's the opening out of oneself. . . . Extreme openness. It is everything. It can be murderous, it is rivalrous, but it is also the basis of heroism, and devotion to others, and everything" (Williams 1996, 64). In like fashion, empirical researchers speak of imitation as the primary source of one's access and attachment to the mind and being of the other, and that these mimetic connections foster the opening of intersubjective experience to deeper and more penetrating levels of relationality and social cognition.

It has already been established that imitation research validates and substantiates many claims made by Girard and Oughourlian concerning the foundational significance of universal mimesis as the cornerstone of cognitive and emotional life (Oughourlian 1982; Webb 1993). The research presented in *Mimesis and Science* increases such validation exponentially by providing necessary explanations of the fundamental neural, psychological, and anthropological mechanisms on which mimesis operates (Garrels 2011).

In addition to validating the universal pertinence and range of mimesis, imitation research completes Girard's mimetic theory in important ways. There are indeed gaps and limitations in mimetic theory considered as a tissue of explanation accounting for the origins and mechanisms that allow for positive mimetic effects to take place. The really interesting questions it raises no longer pertain to whether we imitate or at what age we begin imitating, but how? What are the mechanisms of mimesis? What are the differences between human and nonhuman primate mimesis and representation? And how do these differences play out in the evolution of the species? Could they indeed have generated the effects attributed to them in mimetic theory: supercharging the acquisitive rivalries of the hominid line to the point of provoking the threshold scenarios, at once catastrophic and creatively foundational, of mimetic crisis and scapegoat resolution? Empirical researchers from disciplines such as developmental psychology and neuroscience are among those pioneering a clearer understanding of our imitative origins that need to be accounted for by mimetic scholars.

Immediate Imitation in Infancy

The seminal work of Andrew Meltzoff and Keith Moore (1977, 1983, 1989) has played a key role in changing the depth and scope of imitation research. In the process of testing Piaget's developmental stages of infant preverbal learning, Meltzoff and Moore (1977) unwittingly discovered that newborn infants were able to learn via imitation immediately from birth.[2] What they found at first was that two- to three-week-old infants could immediately match body parts between themselves and adults, including the ability to imitate facial expressions and various hand gestures.[3] In order to confirm that such behaviors were not the result of prior associative experience or reinforcement training, they repeated their study with newborns averaging thirty-two hours old, the youngest being only forty-two minutes old (Meltzoff and Moore 1983, 1989). The results were the same, demonstrating that newborns possessed an innate ability to imitate in a way that could not be explained by conditioning or the triggering of other innate responses.

These findings came as a shock to developmental theorists. While emphasizing the valuable role of imitation for infant learning, the predominant Piagetian model of the time stressed that infants gradually progressed from non-imitation to imitation. Infants learned to imitate later in development through acts of representation, such as symbolically associating their own actions, seen in a mirror or through tactile exploration of their own movements, to the actions of others. Self-imitation led to hetero-imitation. According to Piaget and Inhelder (1969), imitation was an intrapersonal phenomenon first, and only later, with the infant's increasing memory and representational skills, did it become interpersonal. Thus, prior to the discoveries by Meltzoff and Moore (1977), "the existence of immediate imitation in development was hardly suspected and its role was ignored" (Nadel and Butterworth 1999, 1).

A variety of studies conducted by Meltzoff and numerous others have been replicated and validated cross-culturally, essentially debunking what was thought to be an obvious disconnect in infancy between action and perception, self and other.[4] Imitation was now seen as a powerful interpersonal mechanism facilitating infant learning from the very beginning of life. The question was no longer if infants could imitate immediately, but how? Attempts at elucidating the mechanisms and conditions underlying such reciprocal behaviors are, for the most part, the story of imitation research over the last several decades.

Meltzoff and Moore (1994, 1997) have developed an influential model in order to account for the unity of shared self-other experience that they observed. They argue that infant imitation is based on a process of active intermodal mapping or AIM. According to this model, infants are born with a very primitive and foundational body scheme that allows them to "unify the seen acts of others with their own felt acts in a common framework":

> The crux of this hypothesis is that imitation, even early imitation, is a matching-to-target process. The goal or behavioral target is specified visually. Infants' self-produced movements provide proprioceptive feedback that can be compared with the visually-specified target. Active intermodal mapping proposes that such comparison is possible because the perception and production of human movements are registered within a common "supramodal" representational system. Thus, although infants cannot see

> their own faces, their faces are not unperceived by them. They can monitor their lip and tongue movements through proprioception and compare this felt activity to what they see. Metaphorically, we can say that perception and production speak the same language; there is no need for "associating" the two through prolonged learning, because they are intimately bound at birth. (Meltzoff 1999, 8)

Based on earlier findings (Meltzoff and Moore 1977) of immediate imitation in human neonates, Meltzoff and Moore (1994) later developed the above model, which implied an innate matching process between action and perception, between one's own body scheme and that of another. While it became increasingly obvious that infants were imitating and thus unifying these cognitive modalities, it was not clear at the time how this actually worked—that is, what the underlying mechanisms were that made such unification possible—although it certainly suggested shared neural representations. It would only be a few years later that the AIM hypothesis would be substantially validated from the separate discipline and methodological domain of neuroscience.

As a matter of fact, Oughourlian (1982) referenced the original work of Meltzoff and Moore (1977) in his development of an interdividual psychology—a psychological system founded solely upon universal mimesis. In addition to supporting their conclusions on the innateness of imitation, Oughourlian (1982) provided the following critique of the model used to explain such phenomena:

> Is imitation the result of a matching process due to the intervention of a system of abstract representations, as Meltzoff and Moore seem to think? Certainly not, and I have already indicated my agreement with Piaget on this point. In fact the American psychologists, having disproved Piaget's observations experimentally, have wished to take up a theoretical position that simply reverses his. The only way to reconcile the indisputable observations of the Seattle psychologists and the sound conceptual intuitions of Piaget is to adopt the theory of universal mimesis. (9)

While not as abstract as Meltzoff and Moore may have initially implied, the solution to the problem of infant imitation indeed seems to be the result of an innate and universal matching process (Meltzoff and Moore 1997), albeit one that is supported by mechanisms at a level in the brain that no one thought possible at the time. Furthermore, simply stating that there exists a universal mimetic capacity at birth does not answer the question that Meltzoff and Moore were attempting to answer, which is, how do we account for or make sense of this early form of mimesis? To this point, Oughourlian asked the following questions, which at the time were unanswerable: "How does that mimetic force operate or get brought into operation? What sorts of neurological or neurophysiological systems are indispensable to its operation? These questions pertain to neurophysiology and perhaps also to biochemistry" (Oughourlian 1982, 9).

Mirror Neurons

The available research helps to clarify, and in many respects answer, these questions to a great degree of specificity. This is most evident in the work on mirror neurons. The significance of the recent discovery of mirror neurons is inestimable for cognitive neuroscience and psychology, and imitation research in particular. Not only do mirror neurons provide overwhelming support for models proposed by developmental psychologists concerning imitation, but they also take our understanding of mimetic reciprocity to a whole new level of research on underlying mechanisms, that of cerebral organization and neural integration. Mirror neurons seem to represent a primary and primitive form of reciprocal social experience, and are understood as the neural basis for learning by imitation (Billard and Arbib 2001). Further explorations of the properties and functionality of mirror neurons promise to alter outdated conceptions of the nature of primate representation and mimesis, as well as their role in the evolution of human representation. Theoretical speculations stemming from the discovery of mirror neurons address their significance in helping to explain not only the underlying mechanisms of such skills but their evolution across species. For example, contemporary theorists propose that differences between humans and nonhuman primates are due more to cortical rewiring than to brain size or the acquisition of unique brain structures (Roth 2002). Thus, the development of mirror neurons, which code and unify both perception and action, may have contributed significantly to a wide-ranging, large-scale cerebral reorganization, allowing for the coevolution of more complex social and representational skills (Rizzolati and Arbib 1998; Gruber 2002).[5]

The dual coding capabilities of individual neurons provide convergent validation for the AIM hypothesis of infant imitation forwarded by Meltzoff and Moore (1994, 1997). Mirror neurons support this hypothesis by demonstrating how the capacity to imitate by the matching of equivalent body parts, as well as action and perception, is innate and initiated at a very primitive level of human experience. From the very beginnings of life, infants are immediately immersed in a rich social matrix of self-other reciprocity. However, human imitation is vastly more important than the in vivo resonance of affective states and visual-motor information. For example, we know that monkeys do not imitate, even though they do have a basic mirror-neuron machinery that affords them the capacity to interpret complex actions (Meltzoff and Decety 2003). The human neuron machinery demonstrates a far greater development of imitative phenomena throughout the lifespan, both quantitatively and qualitatively. Such phenomena include our capacity for complex representation; for language, communication, and learning; for imaging other minds; and all subsequent relationalities.[6]

Girard (1987) has commented on the significance of mimesis in evolution and the emergence of the "distinctively human phenomena" of mimetic desire:

> For there to be desire according to our definition, the effects of mimesis must interfere, not directly with animal instincts and appetites, but in a terrain that has already been fundamentally modified by the process of hominization: in other words, the mimetic effects and a wholesale re-processing of symbols must develop in unison. All the elements of what we call normal psychology—and everything that constitutes us as human beings on the level that we call "psychic"—must result from the infinitely slow, but ultimately monumental work achieved by the disorganization and increasingly complex reorganization of mimetic functions. Our hypothesis makes it logical to imagine that the rigorous symmetry between the mimetic partners . . . must bring about two things among man's ancestors, little by little: the ability to look at the other person, the mimetic *double*, as an *alter ego* and the matching capacity to establish a

> *double* inside oneself, through processes like reflection and consciousness. (Girard 1987, 283–84)

The findings on mirror neurons detail the complex and intricate functioning of the socially interactive brain, allowing researchers to ask questions that promise to enrich our understanding of the process that Girard has described here in support of his own theory. For example, Stamenov and Gallese (2002) predict that

> The peculiar (first-to-third-person) "intersubjective character" of the performance of mirror neurons and their surprising complementarity to the functioning of the strategic (intentional, conscious) communicative face-to-face (first-to-second) interaction may help shed light from a different perspective on the functional architecture of the conscious vs. unconscious mental processes and the relationship between behavioral and communicative action in monkeys and humans. And they may help to re-arrange, at least to a certain degree, some aspects of the big puzzle of the emergence of language faculty, the relation of the latter to other specifically human capacities like social intelligence and tool use. (2)

This evidence also leads us to think about the nature of internal imitation as well. How does deferred imitation actually function in the internal world or mind of the adult? On what basis does the adult imitate old affect-laden schemas, which are represented in memory in the presence of new imitative models? Imitation plays a key role in learning and the representation of events and mental states that extend over time and in the absence of the initial model. In addition to immediate imitation, Meltzoff and Moore (1977, 1994) have also demonstrated that deferred imitation (the delayed re-presenting of past events) takes place much earlier than Piaget had suggested. Meltzoff and Moore (1977) found that infants could represent and imitate adult facial gestures after short or prolonged periods of time. Infants as young as six weeks old can store a model of a novel act or gesture through a single brief exposure and imitate it from memory after delays as long as twenty-four hours. At twelve months of age, infants can successfully imitate after delays up to four weeks, and by two years of age the delay can be as much as four months or longer (Meltzoff and Decety 2003).

Thus, while mimetic scholars have long stressed the primordial role of psychological mimesis, it is only recently that we have been able to account for and support such reciprocity of experience, even at a level as basic as individual neurons. Taken together, imitation research, while still in its infancy, is coming strongly alongside mimetic theory to provide a complementary set of theories that provide greater clarity and explanatory depth not to be found in Girard's work alone or in that of theorists who have advanced his ideas.

Acquisitive Mimesis and the Role of Imitation in Conflict

As I have just demonstrated, mimesis is universal in application (it affects all human subjects) and in its range of pertinence (it underlies all capacities we are most likely to call "human"). This does not, however, mean that all mimesis is pacifying and cooperative. For Girard, the positive mimetic phenomenon essential to human development and interpersonal relationships is simultaneously the basis for rivalry and ultimately violence. In 1979 Girard critiqued the corpus of extant work on imitation in the following manner:

> If you survey the literature on imitation, you will quickly discover that acquisition [the goal of obtaining an object] and appropriation [the goal of obtaining an object exclusively for oneself] are never included among the modes of behavior that are likely to be imitated. If acquisition and appropriation were included, imitation as a social phenomenon would turn out to be more problematic than it appears, and above all conflictual. (9)

Indeed, a contemporary survey, if taken now, would reveal the same results. If any connection is made between imitation and violence by empirical researchers, it is typically in relation to copycat behaviors either through social modeling or violence portrayed in films and the media (Eldridge 2002). Now this phenomenon is assuredly important and deserves to be addressed; yet Girard is quite acutely right. The connection it makes between imitation and violence overlooks the entire process by which our imitative nature facilitates the initiation, in the first place, of human acts of violence, before there is any prior violence to imitate. It fails, that is, to observe what is not obvious, but is observable and is of major significance; there is an inhibition of attention, blocking the progress of understanding.

If left to itself, the mimetic process between two persons goes through three identifiable stages: mimetic desire, mimetic rivalry, and mimetic violence. Mimetic desire is the response of one person's interest in another person's desire. Girard (1965) states that we come to desire what another desires; that is, we learn what to desire from a model, though we often do not recognize the function of the model in the experience (affect) of desire. Instead, what the imitator experiences is a linear process in which he or she is suddenly motivated or curious about an object. The essential misrecognition in this process is that it is the object of the imitator's desire that has somehow become valuable to the imitator. The reality is that the model's desire or interest in the object has effectively created value in the object by means of his simple attention to and interest in it. So mimetic desire consists of an awakened desire invested in an object (a thing, a trait in a person, etc.), which has come to fruition by means of a model who is already desiring the object.

The second stage in the mimetic process is the transition from awakened mimetic desire to mimetic rivalry. What occurs in the interpersonal matrix between imitator and the model being imitated (once the mimetic process is engaged) is a set of dynamic interactions that are driven by the intensity of reciprocal mimetic capacities found in the human brain. Once the desire is awakened in the imitator, he soon believes that the object of interest that is in the possession of the other person is now more valuable and thus more interesting. As a result, the imitator's interest increases. After this happens in the mind of the imitator, he reflects outwardly (in some degree or another that is communicated) some derivative of this interest, which then has a profound effect upon the imitated model. The interest of the model in the object he possesses, whether it remained high or was decreasing when the imitator came on the scene, now becomes influenced greatly by the effect of the imitator's desire. The model's desire now increases substantially due to the fact that the imitator's desire for the object now becomes a model for his own imitativeness. Thus, there is a fundamental dynamic of incremental reciprocity that emerges at lightning speed—it flares up, as we say—between the two participants, and that may erupt if left without social structures of inhibition, prohibition, or neutralization to restrain or disarm it.

As the desire of one influences the desire of the other, this process sets up an increasingly intense interest in the object and subsequent rivalry, since one becomes the model for the other while at the same time responding to the other's interest as a model. In the process of vying with, and outbidding, the model that each becomes for the other, both parties (whether they be individuals or social groups) become increasingly alike in their behavior, overriding all initial differences (not least the initial difference that one had an object of desire and the other did not).

Something new develops from this reciprocity: the models now become, mutually, model-obstacles to each other. Previously, one was the model, the other the imitator. Each in turn now responds by protecting or removing the object from the view of the Other, thus investing it with even more perceived value to the Other. Each gesture of appropriation is imitated, i.e., countered in kind, mirrorwise. Thus, mutual interest is excited more and more between the parties, and finally overrides the mere object that was once the stake—and is now the pretext—of their increasing rivalry. Their relationship lurches, therefore, via mutual striving into outright hostility and, eventually, rises towards an Other-directed rage that has murder in mind. Each becomes simultaneously a model for the other's desire and, inevitably and fatefully, an obstacle to the obtaining of it.

Girard (1977, 1987) calls this stage mimetic rivalry because what quickly becomes the focus is the rivalry itself and no longer the object. As the rivalry heightens and the accusations or attempts toward obtaining/defending the object increase (behaviors), the affect-awareness system of perception and the primitive fight-or-flight responses in the body increase dramatically. The focus is now on the other-as-obstacle, and as the mimesis or reciprocity increases, participants begin to undifferentiate in particular aspects of their movements, utterances, and sense of identities. They become what Girard, referring to the ultimate convergence of exact reciprocity, calls "monstrous doubles"—each becoming an exact replica of the other. This begins by movements and utterances (accusations), which are immediately taken up and reciprocated by the Other, and which turbocharge the process into more extreme forms of the mimetic entanglement. This vortex of fascination/abhorrence is already among the most powerful of human experiences. As the crisis of undifferentiation deepens, it propels the combatants (as we must now call them) into the third stage in the mimetic process.

The most imitative behavior in the human species is, precisely, violence. Mimetic violence is the last downward spiral in the deepening vortex of mimetic rivalry. At last, the doubles that have come to the emotional apex of rivalrous fascination and abhorrence now are so undifferentiated and lost in the abyss of emotions that one strikes out with a blow, which is preemptive of the feared reciprocal blow, and is therefore terminal—i.e., death ensues.

Save that this death, in a social environment, then becomes in turn the pretext for the reciprocity that was preempted. As the moral codes known to us specify: an eye for an eye, a tooth for a tooth, a life for a life (and, in citing these precepts, we forget that this really means: you may take revenge only at par, in strict rather than in runaway or inflated reciprocity). For, as Girard points out, what is to be feared above all things is that negative mimesis, propagating like wildfire among beings who are highly social in nature, creates a risk of extreme contagion and extreme peril. The entire social group can be drawn—via acts of revenge, feuds engaging families and clans, and long-term vendettas of collective resentment—into a vortex of social violence, such that the black hole created is powerful enough to swallow the entire social group and/or all warring social groups. Indeed, it is a force capable, in principle, of putting an end to the hominid line as such: then, at the threshold of hominization; but also, and all the more so now, in the world of nuclear weapons and climate change.

The temporary structural accommodation by which catastrophe was averted and which enabled us, precariously, to become human in evolutionary time is examined from many viewpoints in this present volume and in its companion volume, *Can We Survive Our Origins?* Theorists of human origins will perforce return to it as to an originary scene at once revealing and concealing the haunting knot of the enigma that has made us what we are. In its Girardian essence, this scene represents, in respect of mimetic potency in humans, a reversal of polarity or valency from negative to positive. It supposes a tipping point, which is mimetic in nature: a rage-modeling leader designates an emissary victim or scapegoat, and all follow through in the act of scapegoat murder. It supposes, via an awesome and marvelous pharmacology of group intelligence, involving the most subtle reaches of the human mimetic psyche, an outcome: namely, that a new dimension of reciprocity is created, mythically explaining and managing the transcendence so cataclysmically experienced by emergent hominids and early men. The violent potential of human mimesis is thereby contained, redirected. A sacred space is created, in which human culture—i.e., human divergence from animal antecedence—can develop.

Breaking Out of Disciplinary Confines

This short outline of Girard's theory of desire shows a consequent and very challenging reflection on the deeper and darker side of human mimesis. Girard has developed an anthropological theory that explains how all culture has emerged from this bi-personal and social experience. He claims that all social structures and institutions have developed from a process that is fueled by a mimetic desire that, in the transitional stages from primates to humans, had spontaneously (in a self-organizing sense) transformed itself into a contagious group phenomenon that found its only resolution in the murder of a communal victim. This scapegoat mechanism is a social resolution to the perilous excesses of mimetically supercharged human desire (in contrast to the instinctual dominance patterns seen in nonhuman primates) and can account for all the uniquely human social and religious structures that have evolved from the need to limit mimetic potentials in order to achieve some degree of social cohesion and order.

Thus, the challenge forwarded by mimetic scholars is: now that we know more clearly how it is we imitate, it is time to look at exactly what we are imitating and how this makes mimetic behavior even more enlivening, and potentially destructive. Of course what empirical researchers have yet to acknowledge is that the goal-directed gestures of acquisition and appropriation are imitated and subjected to the same generative effects as all other gestures involved in imitative reciprocity. So at this stage in the development of cognitive neuroscience, imitation researchers only speak of models, and never rivals. It is no surprise, however, that when two toddlers reciprocate the goal or intention to acquire and appropriate the same object, such as a toy, they converge upon one another in a manner that foreshadows the plethora of adult rivalry, conflict, and envy to come.

While the dimension of conflict as such has yet to be addressed by imitation researchers, over the last decade the scope of what can be imitated has already surpassed the limitations placed upon it by Plato: it now includes those pre-representational states of our intentions and goals, of which acquisition and appropriation are a type. It is suggestive that the study of intentions has recently become a hot topic in its own right and has developed parallel to, and in many respects separately from, imitation research, though the two have converged recently and most notably thanks to the efforts of Andrew Meltzoff (see Meltzoff and Brooks 2001; Meltzoff and Decety 2003).

This new trend in understanding intentions and intentionality is largely the result of Theory of Mind investigations that seek to understand how infants acquire knowledge about the mental states of other minds and to what extent nonhuman primates can do the same.

> The nature of intention and the means whereby we recognize one another's intentions has become a central issue not only in philosophy but also in psychological theory and research—and not just in psychology "in general," but in enriching our understanding of how the growing child comes to know his or her social world and, indeed, how *Homo sapiens* managed to take the crucial step of developing human culture. (Malle, Moses, and Baldwin 2001, xii)

I have already presented evidence demonstrating the link between imitation and intentions. Not only is imitation the means by which children acquire access to the mind of another, including their goals and intentions, but imitation itself is thought to be goal-directed or intention-oriented. Meltzoff's (1995, 1996) work demonstrates that infants can infer and imitate invisible goals and intentions based on human acts, and that the convergence of gaze between adults and infants "indicate[s] that infants understand the object-directedness of an adult act even when the adult has only a distal relationship with the object" (Meltzoff and Brooks 2001, 187). Furthermore, we have seen that individual neurons demonstrate a primary response orientation toward goal- or object-directed actions, and not simply types of behavior. The finding that most mirror neurons respond to object-directed grasping behaviors is all the more poignant in light of our discussion on acquisitive mimesis. What is grasping if not a gesture of acquisition? Thus, while not explicitly stated to be such, many of the ingredients of acquisitive mimesis have been recognized by empirical research.

Even if researchers do not yet recognize the escalation of rivalry inherent in the generative reciprocity of such acts, therefore, their findings nonetheless provide valuable information and support for Girard's ideas about the mechanisms of acquisitive mimesis. Further explorations on the nature and presence of acquisitive mimesis in human and nonhuman primates may be an appropriate topic for future work, commencing with a necessary dialogue between mimetic scholars and imitation researchers. Girard himself (1987) has stressed that the nature of acquisitive mimesis in causing conflict is an essential factor in understanding the ramification of mimesis, as elaborated by mimetic theory.

> That cause, we repeat, is rivalry provoked by an object, the acquisitive mimesis which must always be our point of departure. We will see now that not only the prohibition but also ritual and ultimately the whole structure of religion can be traced back to the mechanism of acquisitive mimesis. A complete theory of human culture will be elaborated, beginning with this single principle. (18)

Over the last several decades, the growing disciplines of developmental psychology and neuroscience have continually required psychologists, anthropologists, linguists, and philosophers alike to rethink, and often do away with, certain assumptions about human nature that were founded without such knowledge, as well as helping them to understand why they came to such false conclusions in the first place (Churchland 2000; Lakoff and Johnson 1999). Yet, while neuroscience and other modern modes of investigation have disclosed many valuable secrets inaccessible to other methodologies, they do not claim to insubstantiate the findings of other theories, nor do they insist on any sort of methodological hierarchy determining what can or cannot be said about reality.

Rather, convergent evidence concerning the structure and function of the brain, for example, is considered an integral reference point holding other disciplines accountable to a clearer understanding of their own claims and assumptions as well as helping them recognize certain blind spots, from which their own methodologies elude them. In a reciprocal manner, developing fields like neuroscience are influenced by disciplines such as anthropology, philosophy, literary analysis, and theology, all of which approach similar or unique questions from differing sources and points of view. Without these other disciplines, neuroscience would not be able to ask the questions that it does, or apply its findings to a meaningful and preexisting framework of knowledge.

It is interesting, finally, to note that the process of Girard's discoveries is comparable to the work of developmental psychologists and neuroscientists (i.e., Meltzoff and Moore, and Rizzolati) who, in a similar manner as Girard, unintentionally stumbled upon the profound depth and significance of imitation while actively pursuing other aims. Now, over the last several decades, various theorists with various methodologies and subject matters have converged upon the same phenomena and have concluded unanimously with the Aristotelian decree that the human ability to imitate is what makes us unique. However, unlike the concepts of classic philosophers and Enlightenment theorists, the concept of imitation that we now speak of is that which operates outside our conscious awareness, though it does not go unperceived; it is preverbal, meaning that it operates during a time in psychosocial development in which the verbal capacity to communicate with others is crude and nonsymbolic, though it does not go uncommunicated; and finally, it is an imitation that is ultimately guided not by the acquisition of gestures or modes of behavior but by the intentions and desires of the other. Together, the disciplines represented by mimetic scholars and those of the empirical sciences demonstrate the significance of mimetic phenomena as a fact to be reckoned with by the social sciences.

Conclusion

It is clear that a new environment exists in which mimetic theory needs to be cross-checked, explored, and developed. This new environment may allow for many of the gaps that exist in mimetic theory to be filled in, as well as making the theory available as a working tool to more recent domains of research.

The work of Girard provides an enormous contribution to a fuller understanding of imitative/mimetic phenomena and their social and anthropological implications. For the most part, empirical imitation research focuses on imitation at the individual or dyadic level of behavior, emphasizing short-lived imitative acts, with the goal of understanding how imitation is accomplished at the psychological and neuropsychological levels (Meltzoff and Prinz 2002). Most of this literature has focused on imitation in infancy or nonhuman primates, with little attention given to its continued and pervasive influence in human adult life. In addition, the most obvious neglect in imitation theory is the role of mimesis in generating conflict between a subject and its model, and the subsequent effects of contagion in group relations. While the discoveries of developmental psychology and neuroscience are profound in their own right and have been used to advance many interventions in medicine and psychology, they are still largely unaware of the broader anthropological implications of imitation that Girardian scholars address.

When imitation research is viewed through the lens of mimetic theory, one sees not only the building blocks of connectedness, mindfulness, and meaningfulness but also the mechanisms of distortion, disillusionment, and violence. That lens has proved its worth and its worthiness for further service.

Notes

1. Instructions to Researchers of the Templeton Foundation. The workshop funded by a Templeton Foundation grant that I organized and convened in 2006 and 2007 and the subsequent volume *Mimesis and Science* provide the first substantial platform for this potential mutually enriching dialogue.

2. The classical Piagetian view of child development did not credit infants with many of the cognitive abilities we now know them to possess—the most significant of which is the precocious ability to imitate. Meltzoff notes that "In the classic view, young infants were initially devoid of the ability to imitate, and they developed through stages. A landmark development occurred at about eight to twelve months of age when they first became able to imitate facial gestures, such as lip and tongue movements. Before this age it was said that they could watch the facial gestures of adults, but they had no way of connecting or associating the seen acts of another with the invisible acts of their own" (Meltzoff and Moore 1977, 254).

3. Remarkably, the infants did not confuse either body part or action. For example, when viewing a protrusion of the tongue by the experimenter, the infant's tongue, and not the lips, would first become activated, while other body parts such as the hands or limbs would become silent, demonstrating that they could accurately and immediately match the correct body part. The infant would then actively engage in moving that body part until it matched the specific action of the adult. In essence, the infant would isolate the what, and then proceed with the how (Meltzoff and Decety 2003).

4. For a comprehensive review of infant imitation research, see *Imitation in Infancy* (Nadel and Butterworth 1999).

5. For a more complete review of mirror neurons and their functional and evolutionary significance, see Stamenov and Gallese (2002).

6. Prior to the discovery of mirror neurons and the recent neurocognitive findings of imitation

research, there were (and continue to be) several diverse theories attempting to account for the Theory of Mind (i.e., the ability to attribute mental states—beliefs, intents, desires, pretending, knowledge, etc.—to oneself and others, and to understand that others have beliefs, desires, and intentions that are different from one's own), as well as the various processes involved in acquiring such a capacity (Carruthers and Smith 1996). While ToM research continues to be a vast area of investigation, cognitive neuroscience imitation researchers have pointed out that there exists an explanatory gap between the in vivo resonance afforded by mirror neurons and the later development of ToM (Meltzoff and Decety 2003). Meltzoff and Decety (2003) propose a "linking argument" demonstrating how complex representational skills and ToM develop from the building blocks of preverbal representations of visual-motor imitation laid down in the first two years of life. Their three-step argument is as follows: (1) Innate equipment. Newborns can recognize equivalences between perceived and executed acts. This is that starting state, as documented by newborn imitation (Meltzoff and Moore 1997). (2) Constructing first-person experience. Through everyday experience, infants map the relation between their own bodily acts and their mental experiences. For example, there is an intimate relation between "striving to achieve a goal" and the concomitant facial expression and effortful bodily acts. Infants experience their own unfulfilled desires and their own concomitant facial/postural/vocal reactions. They experience their own inner feelings and outward facial expressions and construct a detailed bidirectional map linking mental experiences and behavior. (3) Inferences about the experiences of others. When infants see others acting "like me," they project that others are having the same mental experience that is mapped to those behavioral states as in the self.

Works Cited

Billard, A., and M. Arbib. 2001. "Mirror Neurons and the Neural Basis for Learning by Imitation." In *Mirror Neurons and the Evolution of Brain and Language*, ed. M. Stamenov and V. Gallese, 343–52. Amsterdam: John Benjamins Publishing Co.

Carruthers, P., and P. Smith. 1996. *Theories of Theories of Mind*. Cambridge: Cambridge University Press.

Churchland, P. 2000. *The Engine of Reason, the Seat of the Soul*. Cambridge, MA: MIT Press.

Eldridge, J. 2002. "What Effects Do the Treatment of Violence on the Mass Media Have on People's Conduct? A Controversy Re-considered." *Perspectives on Imitation: From Cognitive Neuroscience to Social Science*. Royaumont Abbey, France, 24–26 May, 2002.

Garrels, S. 2011. *Mimesis and Science: Empirical Research on Imitation and the Mimetic Theory of Culture and Religion*. East Lansing: Michigan State University Press.

Girard, R. 1965. *Deceit, Desire, and the Novel: Self and Other in Literary Structure*. Baltimore: Johns Hopkins University Press.

———. 1977. *Violence and the Sacred*. Baltimore: Johns Hopkins University Press.

———. 1979. "Mimesis and Violence." *Berkshire Review* 14: 9–19.

———. 1987. *Things Hidden since the Foundation of the World*. Stanford, CA: Stanford University Press.

Gruber, O. 2002. "The Co-evolution of Language and Working Memory Capacity in the Human Brain." In *Mirror Neurons and the Evolution of Brain and Language*, ed. M. Stamenov and V. Gallese, 77–86. Amsterdam: John Benjamins Publishing Co.

Hurley, S., and N. Chater. 2005. *Perspectives on Imitation: From Cognitive Neuroscience to Social Science.* Cambridge, MA: MIT Press.

Lakoff, G., and M. Johnson. 1999. *Philosophy in the Flesh: The Embodied Mind and Its Challenge to Western Thought.* New York: Basic Books.

Livingston, P. 1992. *Models of Desire: René Girard and the Psychology of Mimesis.* Baltimore: Johns Hopkins University Press.

Malle, B., L. Moses, and D. Baldwin. 2001. *Intentions and Intentionality.* Cambridge, MA: MIT Press.

Meltzoff, A. 1995. "Understanding the Intentions of Others: Re-enactment of Intended Acts by 18-month-old Children." *Developmental Psychology* 31: 838–50.

———. 1996. "Understanding Intentions in Infancy." Paper delivered as part of an invited symposium entitled *Children's Theory of Mind* (A. Leslie, chair). 26th International Congress of Psychology, Montreal.

———. 1999. "Born to Learn: What Infants Learn from Watching Us." In *The Role of Early Experience in Infant Development,* ed. N. Fox and J. G. Worhol. Skillman, NJ: Pediatric Institute Publications.

Meltzoff, A., and J. Decety. 2003. "What Imitation Tells Us about Social Cognition: A Rapprochement between Developmental Psychology and Cognitive Neuroscience." *Philos. Trans. R. Soc. Lond. B Biol. Sci.* 358: 491–500.

Meltzoff, A., and K. Moore. 1977. "Imitation of Facial and Manual Gestures by Human Neonates." *Science* 198: 75–78.

———. 1983. "Newborn Infants Imitate Adult Facial Gestures." *Child Development* 54: 702–9.

———. 1989. "Imitation in Newborn Infants: Exploring the Range of Gestures Imitated and the Underlying Mechanisms." *Developmental Psychology* 25: 954–62.

———. 1992. "Early Imitation within a Functional Framework: The Importance of Person Identity, Movement, and Development," *Infant Behavior and Development* 15:479–505.

———. 1994. "Imitation, Memory, and the Representation of Persons." *Infant Behavior and Development* 17: 83–99.

———. 1997. "Explaining Facial Imitation: A Theoretical Model." *Early Development and Parenting* 6: 179–92.

Meltzoff, A., and R. Brooks. 2001. "'Like Me' as a Building Block for Understanding Other Minds: Bodily Acts, Attention, and Intention." In *Intentions and Intentionality: Foundations of Social Cognition,* ed. B. Malle, L. Moses, and D. Baldwin, 171–91. Cambridge, MA: MIT Press.

Meltzoff, A., and W. Prinz. 2002. *The Imitative Mind: Development, Evolution and Brain Bases.* Cambridge: Cambridge University Press.

Nadel, J., and G. Butterworth. 1999. *Imitation in Infancy.* Cambridge: Cambridge University Press.

Oughourlian, J. M. 1982. *The Puppet of Desire: The Psychology of Hysteria, Possession, and Hypnosis.* Stanford, CA: Stanford University Press.

Piaget, J., and B. Inhelder. 1969. *The Psychology of the Child.* New York: Basic Books.

Rizzolatti, G., and M. Arbib. 1998. "Language within Our Grasp." *Trends in Neuroscience* 21, no. 5: 188–94.

Roth, G. 2002. "Is the Human Brain Unique?" In *Mirror Neurons and the Evolution of Brain and Language*, ed. M. Stamenov and V. Gallese, 63–76. Amsterdam: John Benjamins Publishing Co.

Stamenov, M., and V. Gallese. 2002. *Mirror Neurons and the Evolution of Brain and Language.* Amsterdam: John Benjamins Publishing Co.

Webb, E. 1993. *The Self Between: From Freud to the New Social Psychology of France.* Seattle: University of Washington Press.

Williams, J., ed. 1996. *The Girard Reader.* New York: Crossroad.

The Deepest Principle of Life

Neurobiology and the Psychology of Desire

William B. Hurlbut

At the heart of human nature lies the dilemma of desire—and its disordered dynamics. The significance of this is everywhere evident in the testimony of traditional philosophical concepts and religious ideas. Yet, for the many millennia of human experience these traditions distill, new perspectives on the source and significance of desire are provoking a fundamental revision in our self-understanding. Grounded in evolutionary theory, informed by advances in the neurosciences and cognitive psychology, and rooted in a recognition of the importance of mimetic process, we can forge a new exploration of the biology and anthropology of desire and its central role in the foundations of human culture. Clearly, as the tools of advancing technology extend our powers and lift us beyond the natural limitations that frame and constrain our desires, such an inquiry becomes increasingly urgent.

If we pause to ponder the nature of desire, it is immediately evident that we are contending with a mysterious concept. At the foundations of matter are fundamental attractions—gravity, magnetism, and the weak and strong forces that bind subatomic particles into elements and elements into compounds—but we would not say that an electron "desires" a proton or a cation "desires" an anion. Yet it is clear that through these fundamental forces, the unfolding emergence of the natural order proceeds—matter and mathematics, playing out in a seemingly ceaseless transcendence of layer upon layer in the drama of creation. In Darwin's felicitous phrase, "endless forms most beautiful and wonderful have been, and are being evolved" (Darwin 1859).

"Beautiful," "wonderful"—clearly, any reflection on the nature of desire leads us beyond mere mechanism and directly to the phenomenon of life. Yet, that places us immediately within a more problematic conceptual realm, what Darwin described as the "war of nature" (Darwin 1859). Potent but perishable, animal life by its very character is precarious being. Desire, prefigured as need, forms the central axis of survival. Even bacteria express primordial preferences that seem to presage desire—swimming after and absorbing glucose until it is exhausted, and only then consuming other kinds of sugar.

With more complex animal forms, the fundamental vital activities of the organism come under the direct governance of desire. Desire distills as an inwardly felt sense of self, of integrated and purposeful identity urgently engaged in the essential tasks of life. As a self-subsistent being, an organism is the executive of its own existence: desire subordinates and coordinates the elemental parts into the cohesive unity of a larger, enlivened whole. It regulates and motivates, aligning, sustaining, and empowering effortful engagement that bridges the span across time and distance to the object of action. Desire is embodied intention at the foundations of life. In the words of Leon Kass, "As with action and awareness, the seeds of appetite are copresent with life. Indeed, the germ of appetite governs, guides, and integrates awareness and action: Appetite or desire, not DNA, is the deepest principle of life" (Kass 1994, 48).[1]

With progressive evolutionary elaboration, ever more intricate capacities for awareness and action, coordinated by desire, drive the organism outward into active commerce within the wider world. More capable and conscious animal kinds are interwoven in deeper articulation with the multifarious forms of an evolving ecological whole. The varied senses are extended and refined, allowing a fuller disclosure of the world, not just in breadth and precision, but in the causal connections across space and time. Desire is the seed of comprehension and control.

The emotions, which have their evolutionary origin in physiological regulation of basic body processes such as circulation, posture, and readiness of response, are drawn more deeply into the inward intensity of wider intentions, empowering persistence toward more distant goals. As the philosopher Hans Jonas explains, "Animal being is thus essentially passionate being" (Jonas 1966, 106). And passion motivates and sustains effortful action toward broader and more distant horizons of need. Lifted beyond the immediacy of fundamental physical and chemical conditions, life extends its reach and realm. Jonas continues, "Fulfillment not yet at hand is the essential condition of desire, and deferred fulfillment is what desire in turn makes possible" (Jonas 1966, 101).

In all of these ways, desire, as a primal principle of being, extends the scope of life, magnifying its freedom, intensity, and inward sense of meaning.

Darwin's research on orchids (surely a category of species to be included among the "endless forms most beautiful and wonderful") led him to conclude that the "final end of the whole flower . . . is the production of seed." John Ruskin, the foremost art critic of the Victorian era, objected: "the flower exists for its own sake . . . not for the fruit's sake" (Ruskin 1879). And though these controversies eventually undercut Ruskin's religious convictions, he was right—ask any organism.

Jonas explains, "Not duration as such, but 'duration of what?' is the question. This is to say that such 'means' of survival as perception and emotion are never to be judged as means merely, but also as qualities of the life to be preserved and therefore as aspects of the end. It is one of the paradoxes of life that it employs means which modify the end and themselves become part of it. The feeling animal strives to preserve itself as a feeling, not just a metabolizing entity, i.e., it strives to continue the very activity of feeling" (Jonas 1966, 106). Desire, not DNA, is the deepest principle of life.

The Neurobiology of Desire

Even as we reject the conclusion that the chicken is only about the egg, we cannot ignore the ruthless role of desire in the phenomenon of life, and its culmination as the crisis point in the origins of human culture—when desire spills over into uncontainable violence and threatens to destroy the entire community.

To understand this, we need to explore how desire operates in the individual life embedded within the matrix of social existence. Advances in neurobiology are clarifying the connections between desire and reward and their role in development and behavior. Considering the central significance of reward in consolidating learning, aligning intention, and motivating action—and the destructive power of its pathologies—it is surprising how little is actually known about the biology of desire. The famous "pleasure lever" experiments of postdoctoral students Peter Milner and James Olds provided a dramatic window into the primary power of reward (Olds 1956). Pressing the lever sent an electrical stimulus through electrodes placed deep into midbrain structures. Male rats would press the lever up to seven thousand times an hour, preferring this direct stimulation to food, water, and females in heat waiting willingly, and would even cross a footshock-delivering grid to get to the lever. At first the experimenters thought they had located a single pleasure center, but further studies delineated a more distributed reward circuitry with multiple connections and varied contributions in the mediation of pleasure and its purposeful connections.

The elucidation of these circuits has led to more recent work focused on the role of the neurotransmitter dopamine. Research studies have established the ancient phylogenetic origins of reward systems (including deep homology between humans and insects) and the pervasive role of reward in shaping the full range of animal behaviors (Berridge 2006). It is now clear that dopamine, far from being a pleasure chemical, is an essential element in circuits modulating and coordinating motivational, emotional, cognitive, motor, and endocrine functions; the biology of desire is the central axis uniting all aspects of animal life. These discoveries have, in turn, allowed scientists to identify distinct components of the reward system, and to begin to gain insight into the relationship between pleasure, performance, and pathologies of desire.

The current terms of inquiry parse the reward system into three specific psychological components: associative conditioning and learning, affect and subjective hedonia, and motivation. For our purposes, a few simple conclusions suffice to set the foundations for further discussion of the individual and cultural implications of the biology of desire.

First, it is clear that reward plays a crucial role in learning by setting up systems of anticipatory response and goal-directed actions. And, this connection between reward and learning can be below the threshold of consciousness. Moreover, the associative connections that trigger response are pervasive and subtle. Even subliminal cues using images of drug apparatus will trigger craving in former addicts. Likewise, in experimental settings, addicts' behavior (including performance of work tasks) can be altered by low dose levels of stimulants so small that they produce no subjective effects and no autonomic responses (Berridge 2006). Reward, encoded as conscious desire or preconscious conditioning, plays a powerful role in shaping behavior, including behavior we cannot justify or explain (Behrens and Hunt 2009).

Second, it appears that there are neurological differences in the operation of the appetitive behaviors and the consummatory behaviors. In the language of neuroscience, a distinction is now drawn between liking (the conscious awareness of subjective pleasure) and wanting (the motivational state of active anticipation that need not be accessible to conscious awareness).

Generally, when we use the term "desire," we are referring to both of these components of the reward system and their broader effects in shaping the attitudes and actions of animal life. However, this distinction turns out to have important implications for mimetic theory, where desire refers to a perceived deficiency or an acquisitive drive—a want. There is a rare neurologic condition known as athymhormic syndrome that is characterized by extreme passivity and apathy. From the outside it appears to be a loss of ability for voluntary motion, but from the inside it is experienced as a lack of self-motivation. These patients report a nearly complete absence of mental life—a mental blank. Yet, if commanded from the outside, they are entirely capable of thought and action. So, it appears that motivation constitutes more than meaning; it is the very infrastructure of mind. Desire is essential to having a mental life at all. In California we used to say "you are what you eat." It is, perhaps, more true to say "you are what you want." Desires, more than pleasures, define and sum up personal identity. "For where your treasure is, there will your heart be also" (Matthew 6:21).

Broadly speaking, liking appears to involve a common neural mechanism for primary natural pleasures such as food satiation and sex and the direct action of pleasure-producing drugs. Objective liking is manifest with observable motor response patterns and evident affective facial expressions that are homologous across a wide range of mammals from rats to humans. The outward and observable expression of liking provides an important component of the mimetic mechanism (Berridge 2006).

It is instructive to consider how deeply and thoroughly this basic component of experience is tied in with the mechanisms of mind that shape our personal and social identity. Neural structures involved in the cognitive dimensions of liking include the orbitofrontal cortex, which plays a role in mediating the planning behavior associated with sensitivity to reward, evaluative judgments and decision making, impulse control and empathy. Cognitive liking also involves the insula, a deep cortical structure crucial for internal body awareness and body representation, body regulation, and subjective emotional experience. The insula appears to mediate a mirror neuron–like link between external and internal experiences essential for self-identity, admiration of others, and the intersubjective awareness necessary for the social emotions and central to the mimetic process. Both of these areas, the orbitofrontal cortex and the insula, have been implicated in the fundamental abnormalities of sociopathy. Interestingly, the anterior insular cortex processes the sense of disgust toward offensive odors as well as toward images of contamination and mutilation (even if they are just imagined)—a possible link between mimetic desire and the bloody ritual sacrifices that seem to defuse its destructive power (Wicker et al. 2003).

Dopamine, once thought to be the pleasure chemical, turns out to be neither necessary nor sufficient for generating either the objective liking observed with taste rewards in animals or the subjective pleasure reported with drug rewards in humans. Rather, dopamine appears to play an important role in incentive salience, establishing the reward-learning connections that form the neurological basis of wanting, and the associated state of attention and arousal that constitute motivation (Berridge 2003). Of course, wanting and liking are functionally interconnected, but the dopamine-mediated learning that establishes incentive salience promotes a mere sensory input into a motivational magnet and evokes the instrumental response of anticipation and action. Berridge and Robinson report that this dopamine-mediated associative connection can be so compelling that pigeons will "make eating pecks at light cues that predict edible rewards but make drinking pecks at cues for liquid reward, and rats or monkeys often bite their [pleasure] predictive lever CSs [conditioned stimulus]" (Berridge 2003). Of course, the tragic consequences of inappropriate connections between stimuli and anticipated reward are everywhere evident in human life. The power of addiction appears to be not so much a desire for reward as a compelling sense of wanting driven by an overpowering feeling of lack, defect, or deficiency. Addicts often hate their addiction.

Several additional aspects of this associative link between motivation and reward are particularly relevant for our reflections. It appears that observing others experiencing states of arousal and reward can activate a resonant response, and even fanciful but vivid cognitive images (cognitive incentive representations) of reward can do the same (Behrens and Hunt 2009).

Of course the most extraordinary motivating power evident in human nature, that of the idealizing imagination, must be rooted in a tangible neural substrate tied in with desire. Without this cognitive connection between image, action, and motivation, there could be no effective goal-directed strategies beyond those produced by mere associative response.

Moreover, there is some evidence that even the arousal associated with motivational states, with their implicit expectations, may be accompanied by a general sense of well-being associated with reward—anticipation can be sweet. And even where strong desires create the tension and anxiety of frustration and conflict, there may be an intensification of feeling. ACTH (adrenocorticotropic hormone), which is released by the anterior pituitary gland in response to biological and psychological stress, has structural similarities to endogenous opiates, and may play a role in the sense of exhilaration that often accompanies circumstances of crisis or violent conflict. So, even the moment of crisis or confrontation can carry a compelling immediacy, lifting it above both present fear and prudential concern for the future.

Finally, the dual role played by dopamine in motivation and motor action provides a natural connection to aggression. Desire is not simply an abstraction, but an embodied mental and emotional state with a riveting reality; it is rooted in prerational and preconscious connections, and carries with it a compelling power driving in the direction of reward through action.

Imitation and Desire

These neural mechanisms play a central role in the most dramatic transition in the history of life: animal imitation, social learning, and the ascent to genuine culture—processes all mediated by the biochemistry of desire. The biological benefits of imitation are immediately obvious: an animal can draw on the experience of another to gain understanding without the risk or expenditure of resources necessary to establish experience-based learning. Moreover, the rapid spread of new behaviors through imitation allows a responsive adjustment to changing environmental challenges and opportunities. Imitation also allows the acquisition of information, emotional dispositions, and motor programs with a specificity far too complicated for the molecular mechanisms of genetic change.

Fifty years before the word "gene" even entered our vocabulary, Darwin noted that wild animals "learn caution by seeing their brethren trapped or poisoned," and proposed a mechanism whereby habitual dispositions and actions could be transmitted via gemmules—as acquired characteristics (Dugatkin 1999, 8). His contemporary, George Romanes, a strong advocate of Darwin's general theory, believed that imitation could provide such continuity, but he claimed that "there must first be intelligent perception of the desirability of the modification" (Romanes 1883). More recent studies of animal imitation, however, make it clear that such desire and the impulse to imitate need not require a high level of intelligence and intention. Indeed, it is now recognized that imitation is widespread in the animal kingdom, and of ancient origins.

Female guppies imitate the mate choices of other females and will even override genetically based natural preferences, such as for brightly colored males, at least up to a certain threshold of intensity—so, there is an interaction of genetic and cultural transmission (Dugatkin 1999, 24–25). Moreover, younger females imitate older females (62).

Many species of birds learn their songs, some of which are "war songs" associated with aggressive confrontations over mates and territories, by imitation. In some cases this learning occurs even through the eggshell—showing how early imitative learning can be retained until circumstances are appropriate for its expression. Moreover, in black grouse, females are more interested in a male with other females in his territory (Dugatkin 1999, 72). Since older females mate on average three days earlier than younger females, age-down imitation is again the pattern. This popularity effect means that a single male will get up to 80 percent of the mating opportunities (73).

But imitation is not just limited to mating behaviors; other dimensions of life grounded in desire also draw deeply on the benefit of experience transfer—most prominently, foraging. Cultural learning in foraging is recorded in many species. For example, young rats will overcome their own taste preferences and eat cayenne-laced foods if they see others doing so (Dugatkin 1999, 77).

And, of course, the most famous case of animal culture is that of Imo the Japanese macaque, who learned to wash the sand off of her sweet potatoes. This practice slowly spread, but never changed the behavior of the dominant males (Dugatkin 1999, 171).

Several additional points relevant to mimetic theory are evident from these animal studies. First, the rapidity and breadth of imitation in animals can, at times, be quite dramatic. In bird studies, such a snowball effect has been observed in which copiers copied other copiers up to six permutations, and the learned behaviors may be retained across several generations (Dugatkin 1999, 73–74).

Second, as Lee Alan Dugatkin notes, "One loud and clear message comes through from work on mate copying in guppies: a small brain is not a barrier to imitation. This counterintuitive finding turns everything we think about culture on its head. Culture is not just for 'higher' animals. Nor is it a sign of intelligence. The plain implication is that it is a much more fundamental force than we have ever thought before" (Dugatkin 1999, 70).

Third, and of great relevance to mimetic theory, this pervasive capacity for culture built on imitation may be ultimately maladaptive. Fish can learn to take an unstrategic foraging path by observing others (Dugatkin 1999, 189–90). Likewise, blackbirds have been trained to fear non-predators, an error that has then been copied in a chain of cultural transmission up to six blackbirds long—a phenomenon that can perhaps be best described as a form of emotionally mediated animal superstition (133).

Finally, although the neural mechanisms of imitation at such primary levels are not well understood, evidence suggests that more than mere motor mimicking is at work. Emotions, including the affective expressions of desire and fear, appear to play a crucial role. In youthful monkeys, the contagion of fear in early group encounters with snakes produces a learned imitation that is both effective and enduring.

Likewise, the affective impact of basic sensation, and the evident drive of primary appetitive behaviors can be employed as agents of display in communicating and evoking higher-level social desires. In certain bird species (and perhaps even insects) where nuptial food offerings induce mate receptivity, the affective expressions that accompany consumption may promote and facilitate female response—both the motor programs and emotions of eating (such as impassioned biting, licking, and sucking) are widely evident in animal sexual behavior. In any case, it seems likely that the mate choice preference associated with bright red feathers is an exploitation of a more fundamental affective response (incentive salience and arousal) associated with the ripeness of red fruit. In the service of survival, the competition over ripe fruit must evoke a primary response (perhaps genetically encoded) that includes excitement, disinhibition, and aggression—all emotionally grounded and easily exploited for purposes beyond nourishment. In human culture, this connection between redness and its emotional valence seems evident in the urgency and intensity evoked by red in everything from stoplights to valentines. Moreover, the redness of engorgement (detectable even in darkly pigmented skin) reveals states of arousal, anger, and imminent aggression—all employed in the service of primary sexual desire.

It is also possible that mate copying (and other communications of desire) may have more to do with emotions than simple popularity, since observing conspecifics in the charged arena of combat or copulation could convey far more than just motor programs or simple preferences. So, the arousal of desire may carry a spillover effect that generalizes and escalates a sense of urgency and confrontation. Moreover, males and females may respond to the same situation dramatically differently. Clearly, observing the prowess of the victorious dominant male evokes open receptivity in the female, but withdrawal and retreat in the vanquished male—though some might say that both exhibit a submissive response.

Desire and the Neurohormonal Foundations of Sociality

The primary powers of desire and imitation (including their dimorphic sexual valence) are further extended across the scope of evolution by the ancient molecule vasotocin and its more recent descendants oxytocin and vasopressin. These tiny neuropeptides play a powerful and pervasive role in a range of basic biological processes related to reproduction and sociality. In fish, during ovulation, vasotocin facilitates mating by reducing the female's natural fear of being approached by the male. In gregarious finches, a cognate peptide (mesotocin) influences affiliation and flock size. In voles, oxytocin and vasopressin play a crucial role in the intensity and permanence of pair-bonding, and in sheep oxytocin mediates the olfactory-based imprinting essential for the ewe's ongoing recognition of her newborn lamb (Zak 2008, 88–95). Moreover, in studies with rats, Michael Meany has shown that within this oxytocin-mediated relationship, maternal licking and grooming of neonatal offspring promotes the proliferation of oxytocin receptors, which later makes them more nurturing mothers with their own offspring (Meany 2001, 201).

More fundamentally, the oxytocin neuroendocrine system operates both centrally (brain and spinal cord) and peripherally in dynamic processes that coordinate basic biological regulation with the highest levels of sociality. Oxytocin plays important hormonal and neuromodulatory roles in the basic physiology of homeostasis, stress reduction, sleep, perceptual processing, motivation and reward, and other body processes essential for development, self-maintenance, and social engagement. These fundamental systems are first established within the early interaction between mother and infant. Studies in rodents have elucidated the crucial role of maternal touch, odor, movement, and body rhythms as "bio-behavioral regulators" essential for specific physiological systems in the pup, including autonomic functioning, thermoregulation, and attention (Hofer 1995).

Oxytocin researcher Ruth Feldman explains how, between mother and infant, this fundamental concordance of bio-behavioral synchrony establishes the unique bond that characterizes the rhythms, content, focus, and pace of the specific attachment relationship (Feldman et al. 2007, 2012). She goes on to argue that this bio-synchrony ultimately creates a "time-locked ongoing relationship" between the physiology and behavior that is the basis of broader social communication and coordination.

The basic mammalian reproductive and affiliative functions of oxytocin are further extended in human sociality—and suggest a biological influence on desires and preferences that appear from common human perspective to be matters of purely personal choice or rationally grounded moral imperative. Oxytocin is released (in both sexes) during sexual orgasm, maintains uterine contractions during childbirth, and plays a central physiological role in the production and release of breast milk.

These oxytocin-driven reproductive functions appear to set the relational foundations for broader dimensions of human sociality. Romantic affiliation activates oxytocin-rich brain areas (Ditzen et al. 2009). During pregnancy, oxytocin levels rise in both mother and father and show sustained synchrony at both the postpartum period and six months later (Feldman et al. 2007). Likewise, there is strong evidence for a neuroendocrinological foundation of human affiliation: plasma oxytocin levels across pregnancy and the postpartum period predict mother–infant bonding (Feldman et al. 2007). Moreover, mothers who deliver vaginally (rather than by caesarian section) are, according to one brain-imaging study, significantly more responsive to the cry of their babies and appear to be less at risk of postpartum depression. "Vaginal delivery, but not caesarian section, involves the pulsatile release of oxytocin from the posterior pituitary which appears to affect brain regions that regulate emotions, motivations and postpartum mood" (Swain et al. 2008). Likewise, the earliest and most intense interpersonal experiences of the infant are in the context of lactation's oxytocin-driven bonding.

Upward through life, oxytocin appears to establish and sustain prosocial exchange. It intensifies social salience; alters the speed and accuracy of affect registration for social information such as facial expressions, vocal tone, and body motions; and promotes the encoding and retrieval of social memory (Rimmele et al. 2009). Through these basic cognitive recruitments, oxytocin facilitates cooperation, promotes trust, and reduces anxiety over interacting with strangers. Moreover, this establishes a whole new level of biological inclination and reward. Neuroeconomist Paul Zak explains, "Oxytocin constitutes a positive side of personal interactions; it literally feels good when someone seems to trust you, and this recognition motivates you to reciprocate." He goes on to say that "oxytocin causes the release of dopamine in deep midbrain regions associated with rewarding behaviors such as sex and food acquisition" (Zak 2008).

This pleasure of social interaction appears to play a crucial role in binding children to parents, and later sustaining the social solidarity essential to cooperative community. In a progressive pattern of neurologic extension and integration, a child will undergo a process of development from facial and postural imitation and generalized emotional resonance, to an increasingly conscious capacity for cognitive empathy and direct and intentional imitative learning. And, at every stage it appears that primary desires and deeply satisfying fulfillments promote this ascent.

Shaped by common values, concepts, and beliefs, the child is drawn deeper into a social solidarity that carries enormous practical advantages and personal satisfactions. Social community itself becomes a new environment of essential adaptation, with its own challenges, demands, and fulfillments. Successful navigation and negotiation within community require highly refined perceptual skills, dispositional balance, and acuity of interpersonal attention. Like cultural "filters of fitness," the rapidly changing patterns of fashion, the subtlety of shifting status, and the varied requirements of cooperation have all, throughout human history, shaped and sculpted our species' basic biology and genetic heritage. Likewise, through community life, new needs, desires, and joys have solidified deep within our nature. Though we generally would not use the term "desire" for such a longing, there is, perhaps, no deeper sense of fulfillment in human life than to be socially affirmed, admired, and lifted up in honor. (Science may be interesting, but the culminating moment is walking onto the stage to receive the Nobel Prize.) Certainly there is no personal pain greater than that of stigma and social shame—the single most powerful force in reigniting the desperation of addiction.

This deep and abiding need, however, means that oxytocin is not simply the "cuddling hormone," as it is sometimes described, but a crucial element in establishing the medium of mimesis and its complex consequences in human life. Oxytocin potentiates social salience, intensifies social interactions, and compels the empathic intersubjectivity that establishes congruency of identity and common values (including objects of desire).[2] Primary patterns of biological need are increasingly subsumed and even displaced by more proximal and subjectively urgent social imperatives. Social approval and its correlative power become the dominant imperative of personal fulfillment, a kind of coinage for the realization and extension of self. The sense of social connection becomes more psychologically prominent than the content of that connection. Mimetic process colonizes and continuously reconstitutes the images and objects at the core of human desire, even to a degree at odds with basic biological needs. One might almost say that sociality is so prominent in human life that it transcends and displaces all other evolutionary imperatives—the medium (social connection) literally becomes the message.

The pernicious influence of this process is everywhere evident in human life. The power of social pressure to entrain and enthrall the identity and life energy of the hapless individual is widely recognized. What is not fully appreciated is the more primary dynamic of mimetic rivalry and its destabilizing and destructive role at every level of human social life. Here again, oxytocin appears to play a role, but now in potentiating and intensifying conflict. Studies by the Israeli psychologist Simone Shamay-Tsoory show that internasal administration of oxytocin increases envy and schadenfreude (gloating over others' misfortune) in a game of exchange—but only when the reciprocal player is perceived as arrogant and unconcerned with the welfare of others (Shamay-Tsoory 2009).

Building on studies that show a positive mutual reinforcement between empathy, perspective taking, and perceived concordance of identity, it appears that a prominent component of sociality is a strong tendency for individuals to compare themselves with others. This capacity can stir authentic personal aspiration and encourage the understanding essential for genuine compassion, but it can also create a corrosive sense of alienation and resentment. When social relations are perceived to contravene the promise of reciprocal respect and the benefit it implies, disturbing dimensions of human nature are revealed—most forcefully in circumstances where admiration of another and identity of self seem at first to meld our very being into the unity of the relationship. Admiration promotes imitation, which draws desire into the mirror of mimetic identity formation, and, ultimately, into competitive rivalry; disillusionment and disorder ensue.

This result correlates well with other human studies that suggest a role for the primary biological mechanisms of sociality in the root causes of aggression. Moreover, they seem consistent with observed differences in male and female sociality. In males, while oxytocin levels increase in response to female indications of trust, without it (with evidence of mistrust) levels of dihydrotestosterone spike, producing an aggressive response and promoting physical confrontation—a behavior not seen in human female subjects in equivalent circumstances of distrust (Zak 2008).

These bivalent responses seem consistent with an evolutionary explanation of sociality and its mimetic process—and with the natural connection between sociality, competition, combat, and mating. Mimetic desire may lead to a conflict over a mutually desired object of no particular biological value beyond its symbolic significance in personal pride and social status, but the reaction it provokes taps into an ancient evolutionary mechanism of violence in the service of self-promotion and self-defense. And, here again, the neurophysiology of reward may be a crucial component in the amplification of aggression. Animal studies have established that agonistic encounters are reinforced by dopamine-mediated mechanisms associated with reward properties—aggression feels good (Couppis and Kennedy 2010). Indeed, Shamay-Tsoory has observed that in rodents, oxytocin may, in certain circumstances, be associated with an increased intensity of aggression (Shamay-Tsoory 2009).

In nonhuman mammalian species, natural mechanisms of submission dampen the danger of escalating violence during confrontations over mates, territories, or scarce resources. In Syrian hamsters, agonistic behavior is directly modulated by vasopressin. An increase in vasopressin in the medial preoptic-anterior hypothalamus produces flank marking, a sign of territoriality and domination, but a decrease produces lordosis, the sign of submission (Albers et al. 2006). Humans, however, do not exhibit such clearly preestablished programs of submission. Rather, as Girard has observed, at the foundations of human sociality where mimesis is overlaid onto the more primary evolutionary patterns of needs (and their social control), it provokes the "over-activation, aggravation, and disorganization of the latter"—leading to the uncontainable cycle of aggression, retribution, and reciprocal revenge (Girard 1987).

When the chaos of unconstrained violence threatens to endanger the entire community, primary psychological and social mechanisms emerge that solidify coalition and coordinate collective action. Atavistic impulses at the bedrock of the human psyche resurface, unmasking the guiltlessness of the predatory conscience. The foundational impulse of sociality is revealed, not as a rationally constructed social contract, but as an instinctive cooperation centered on survival and rooted in the primary coordination (and unconstrained cruelty) of the hunt. The urgency of individual survival is riveted to social unity in a heightened arousal and intensity of collective mental and physical coordination that is at once fraught with terror and exhilaration.

The psychologist Victor Nell describes the Paleozoic roots of our primal proclivities for violence and their "savage joys," the fascination (even delight) associated with cruelty (Nell 2006). He argues that rooted in the "emotional loading" of the evolutionarily ancient hunting adaptation, the primary psychological and physical mechanisms essential for successful hunting—high arousal and strong affect—establish what he terms the "pain-blood-death complex." He points to the dangers and high-energy demands of chasing and killing, and their associated pains of injury, stress, and extreme muscle fatigue. He suggests that powerful dopamine- and endorphin-driven motivational and pleasure-producing mechanisms sustain and reward this behavior even in the earliest vertebrate predators. But while these physiological and psychological mechanisms of the predatory adaptation served immediate instrumental ends for our animal ancestors, in the human species they are extended in a more pervasive quest for private pleasure and social power, as is evident in their elaboration in violence-filled entertainment, coercive social control, and sacrificial rites.

Carsten De Dreu and colleagues have explored the role of oxytocin in sustaining human ethnocentrism and regulating intergroup conflict (De Dreu 2010). As with the social dynamics of the hunt, oxytocin appears to facilitate in-group trust, cooperation, and coordination, and out-group derogation. Moreover, in a context of conflict, this in-group bias is expressed as "infrahumanization," the tendency to ascribe less than full humanity to those outside the circle of social solidarity. These dichotomous dispositions may have an adaptive role in conditions of competition between groups, but they take a pernicious turn with the intragroup chaos provoked by mimetic rivalry.

For the individual, the imperative of identity-defining desires links the very sense of personal survival to the competitive rivalry provoked by the mimetic mechanism. This is at once a crisis that isolates the individual and threatens community survival as the rivalry escalates to the extremes. This crisis reaches toward its resolution only as the rivals are, by a seemingly magical transformation, bound together in a powerful unity against a surrogate victim. The pain of isolation is dissolved within a ferocious frenzy of blood and death. The original object of mimetic rivalry is displaced by an exhilarating social solidarity potentiated by the arousal and heightened effect of the most primary predatory mechanisms of the mind. Here the personal, social, and moral/spiritual are unified in the intensity of an act of righteous violence that carries the full symbolic power of blood and death—the predatory prerequisites of species survival. The frenzy of ferocity gives way first to horror and then to the catharsis and calm of a reestablished order that seems to confirm the transcendent power and cosmological significance of the sacrificial rite. Life is restored by death.

Conclusion

From an evolutionary perspective, there are notable precedents for an initially beneficial adaptation such as mimesis to become amplified to a degree that it becomes dysfunctional and even threatens the survival of a species. Such patterns of "runaway evolution" have been proposed to explain extreme forms of mate display such as peacock tails and giant antlers. Indeed, species specialization always carries the danger of overexploiting the immediate opportunity of a propitious adaptation at the expense of more general adaptability. It is ironic, however, that the very evolutionary strengths of the human species—our broad adaptability, functional freedom, and creative sociality grounded in mimesis—would culminate in a crisis of violence that threatens the entire order of creation.

The philosopher Hans Jonas spoke of the evolutionary drama as a "progressive scale of freedom and peril" (Jonas 1966, xxiii). As our advancing technology delivers new and increasingly effective means of working our will in the world, we would be wise to more earnestly explore the biological basis of mimetic desire and the violence it promotes.

Notes

1. It is important to note that Girard generally uses the term "desire" to refer to a specifically human capacity and disposition. He at once acknowledges the natural phylogeny of desire as "grafted onto needs and appetites" (Girard, Antonello, and de Castro Rocha 2007) evident in animal species, yet at the same time he affirms a decisive discontinuity in its human expression. This apparent contradiction in terms may be resolved if we look more carefully at evolutionary elaboration that established the neurobiological foundations of human desire.
2. It appears that oxytocin may potentiate the mirror neuron systems that mediate a congruence of awareness of self and other, and thereby intensify social behavior (Bos et al. 2011).

Works Cited

Albers, H. E., et al. 2006. "Role of V1a Vasopressin Receptors in the Control of Aggression in Syrian Hamsters." *Brain Research* 1073–74: 425–30.

Behrens, T., and L. Laurence Hunt. 2009. "The Computation of Social Behavior." *Science* 29: 1160–64.

Berridge K. C., and T. Robinson. 2003. "Parsing Reward." *Trends in Neurosciences* 26: 507–13.

Berridge, K.C. and T. E. Robinson. 2006. "Automatic processes in addiction: a commentary." In *Handbook of Implicit Cognition and Addiction*, ed. R. W. Wiers and A. W. Stacy, 477–81. New York: Sage Press.

Bos, P. A., et al. 2011. "Acute Effects of Steroid Hormones and Neuropeptides on Human Social-Emotional Behavior: A Review of Single Administration Studies." *Frontiers in Neuroendocrinology*. doi:10.1016/j.yfrne.2011.01.002.

Couppis, M., and C. Kennedy. 2010. "The Rewarding Effect of Aggression Is Reduced by Nucleus Accumbens Dopamine Receptor Antagonism in Mice." *Psychopharmacology* 197: 449–56.

Darwin, C. 1859. *On the Origin of Species*. London: John Murray.

De Dreu, C.K.W., et al. 2010. "Oxytocin Promotes Human Ethnocentrism." Http://www.pnas.org/cgi/doi/10.1073/pnas.1015316108.

Ditzen, B., M. Schaer, B. Gabriel, G. Bodenmann, U. Ehlert, and M. Heinrichs. 2009. "Intranasal Oxytocin Increases Positive Communication and Reduces Cortisol Levels during Couple Conflict." *Biological Psychiatry* 65: 728–31.

Dugatkin, L. A. 1999. *The Imitation Factor*. New York: Free Press.

Feldman, R. 2012. "Oxytocin and Social Affiliation in Humans." *Hormones and Behavior* 61.3: 380–91.

Feldman, R., A. Weller, O. Zagoory-Sharon, and A. Levine. 2007. "Evidence for a Neuroendocrinological Foundation of Human Affiliation: Plasma Oxytocin Levels across Pregnancy and the Postpartum Period Predict Mother-Infant Bonding." *Psychological Science* 18: 965–70.

Goldberg, S., R. Mui, and J. Kerr, eds. 1995. *Attachment Theory: Social, Developmental, and Clinical Perspectives*. Hillsdale, NJ: Analytic Press.

Girard, R. 1987. *Things Hidden since the Foundation of the World*. Translated by S. Bann and M. Metteer. Stanford, CA: Stanford University Press.

Girard, R., P. Antonello, and J. C. de Castro Rocha, 2007. *Evolution and Conversion: Dialogues on the Origins of Culture*. New York: Continuum.

Hofer, M. A. 1995. "Hidden Regulators: Implication for a New Understanding of Attachment, Separation, and Loss." In *Attachment Theory: Social, Developmental, and Clinical Perspectives*, ed. S. Goldberg, R. Mui, and J. Kerr, 203–30. Hillsdale, NJ: Analytic Press.

Jonas, H. 1966. *The Phenomenon of Life: Toward a Philosophical Biology*. Evanston, IL: Northwestern University Press First published 1963 by Harper and Row.

Kass, L. 1994. *The Hungry Soul: Eating and the Perfecting of Our Nature*. Chicago: University of Chicago Press.

Meaney, M. J. 2001. "Maternal Care, Gene Expression, and the Transmission of Individual Differences in Stress Reactivity across Generations." *Annual Review of Neuroscience* 24: 1161–92.

———. 2010. "Epigenetics and the Biological Definition of Gene X Environment Interactions." *Child Development* 81: 41–79.

Nell, V. 2006. "Cruelty's Rewards: The Gratification of Perpetrators and Spectators." *Behavioral and Brain Sciences* 29: 211–24.

Olds, J. 1956. "Pleasure Center in the Brain." *Scientific American* 195: 105–16.

Rimmele, Ulrike, et al. 2009. "Oxytocin Makes a Face in Memory Familiar." *Journal of Neuroscience* 29: 38–42.

Romanes, G. J. 1883. *Mental Evolution in Animals*. London: Kegan Paul, Trench & Co.

Ruskin, J. 1879. *Proserpina: Studies of Wayside Flowers, While the Air was Yet Pure among the Alps, and in the Scotland and England Which My Father Knew*. Orpington, England: Allen.

Shamay-Tsoory, S. 2009. "Intranasal Administration of Oxytocin Increases Envy and Schadenfreude (Gloating)." *Biological Psychiatry* 66: 864–70.

Swain, James, et al. 2008. "Maternal Brain Response to Own Baby Cry Is Affected by Cesarean Section Delivery." *Journal of Child Psychology and Psychiatry* 49: 1042–52.

Wicker, B., et al. 2003. "Both of Us Disgusted in My Insula: The Common Neural Basis of Seeing and Feeling Disgust." *Neuron* 40: 655–64.

Zak, Paul. 2008. "The Neurobiology of Trust." *Scientific American* 298: 88–95.

The Three Rs

Retaliation, Revenge, and (Especially) Redirected Aggression

David P. Barash

As you consider the following real-life situations, ask yourself what they have in common:

1. As a graduate student several decades ago, I was assisting a friend whose research involved banding golden eagle chicks. This required rappelling down to the animals' cliffside nests. On one such occasion, as I dangled closer to the nest and its chicks, the mother eagle screamed and repeatedly dove at me, always turning aside at the last minute, until finally she came uncomfortably close (probably for her no less than for me), whereupon she swerved yet again and chased a flock of canyon wrens for at least a kilometer. (It should be noted that golden eagles never prey upon canyon wrens; the latter are too small and too fast for such a large, comparatively clumsy predator. We can conclude that this particular animal was motivated by something other than simple hunger.)
2. One day when I was an hour or so late feeding our horses, my wife's mare kicked my normally good-natured gelding who promptly responded by biting the pony!
3. During the Middle Ages, victims of the Great Plague in Europe

commonly would react to their distress by attacking Jews, who came to fear their fellow villagers more than the Plague itself.[1]

4. Here and now in the twenty-first century, someone has a bad day at work, and on the way home he drives aggressively and dangerously, succumbing to road rage, and/or upon getting home he yells at his wife or kicks the cat.

The pattern should be clear. When individuals—animals no less than people—suffer pain, they often react by passing that pain along to someone else, frequently an innocent bystander. This phenomenon is, of course, representative of scapegoating, something that René Girard has examined closely and fruitfully. I believe, however, that the basic pattern is somewhat different from Girard's interpretation in that instead of surrogate objects and sacrificial victims, something more fundamental, rooted in human and infra-human biology, is being evoked. Moreover, whereas Girard locates the benefit of what he calls "mimetic violence" in the social payoff of reducing in-group conflict, I stand with mainstream evolutionary biology in attributing the behavior to adaptive benefit experienced by individuals, with group outcomes being largely (if not exclusively) the sum effect of such benefits.

In any event, the phenomena just described are all examples of what, in the mid-twentieth century, ethologists labeled "redirected aggression," occurring when individual A attacks B, who then takes it out on individual C. The term eventually fell into disuse, so that the phenomenon was only rarely investigated until recently. At last, however, we have the prospect of comprehensively understanding its biological underpinnings. My general point is that redirected aggression—with which I shall be especially concerned in this chapter—is a special case of a more widespread phenomenon whereby victims respond to pain in one of three ways, a troublesome version of the Three Rs: not "reading, writing, and 'rithmetic," but retaliation, revenge, and redirected aggression.

Retaliation involves an immediate and violent response to being attacked. It is quite widespread in the natural world and is readily understood. Revenge is similar to retaliation, except that the payback is delayed and typically exaggerated in severity. It is possible that revenge is unique to human beings, although something very similar has been reported for chimpanzees (de Waal 2007). The third "R," and the subject of this chapter, is redirected aggression. Despite its seeming illogicality, redirected aggression is a very important and typically unrecognized cause of violence, something that is so natural that most people take it for granted and typically don't give it the attention it deserves. Like the proverbial fish who would not describe its environment as wet, most of us experience, almost daily, an unspoken, unrecognized tide of redirected aggression. It is the ocean in which we swim.

Not surprisingly, when possible, a victim engages in either retaliation or revenge, which by definition is reflected back on the perpetrator, the original source of the pain. But if this cannot be achieved, perhaps because the actual victimizer is physically or socially inaccessible, then someone else is liable to be attacked in turn, regardless of his or her innocence. Modern science, at last, can explain why this happens.

Biologists recognize two fundamentally different ways of explaining things: "proximate" or "how" answers, and "ultimate" or "why" answers. Let's start with the proximate. If a rat is repeatedly subjected to an electric shock and then necropsied, it typically shows a characteristic syndrome including increased adreno-corticoid secretion, hypertension, reduced sex hormone levels, and often ulcers. This is known as "subordination stress." If the experiment is repeated but this time the rat is given a wooden stick, it will chew on the stick when shocked, and at necropsy, its subordination stress is reduced. Finally, when a rat is placed in the same cage as another rat, it then responds to the shocks by attacking the other rat, and upon necropsy, such an individual shows few if any indications of subordination stress (Barash and Lipton 2011).

Essentially, the animal has been reducing its own stress by literally passing it along to someone else. This phenomenon has been confirmed among free-living baboons, in which after having been attacked by a dominant male, victims who attack other baboons in turn show reduced stress levels compared to those who simply take it. Neurobiologist Robert Sapolsky notes the ubiquity of this phenomenon when he comments that it is reminiscent of the person about whom it is said "So-and-so doesn't *get* ulcers, he *gives* them" (Sapolsky 2004). In other words, at a proximate level, redirected aggression occurs as a means whereby a victim essentially self-medicates, reducing his or her own stress, at substantial cost to someone else, often an innocent third party.

This appears to explain one leg of the biologist's explanatory scheme. But what about the other, the ultimate or adaptive significance of redirected aggression? In short, why has natural selection produced a physiological/behavioral connection that appears so illogical? If redirected aggression occurs at the proximate level as a response to subordination stress, why has such a response been selected for? This is equivalent to asking whether a plausible case can be made that individuals who responded to their subordination stress by attacking someone else experienced a higher evolutionary fitness than those who did not do so.

Consider that in a social species, individuals are exquisitely aware of something equivalent to Lenin's famous question: Who, Whom? Who is doing what to whom? Who is up and who is down? Essentially, what is happening in the social sphere? There are numerous potential costs of being a victim, including the prospect of being physically injured as well as likely losing some important resource, such as food, a mate, a nest site, and so forth. Beyond this lies the very real prospect that individuals who are attacked and are perceived to not pass along their pain to at least someone else may well lose crucial status as well. I call this the "I am not a patsy hypothesis."

Seeking to test this idea, I reevaluated data compiled (for other reasons) over the course of many years studying animals known as hoary marmots, *Marmota caligata*, large terrestrial rodents found in the mountains of western North America. In my reanalysis, I compared the experiences of adult females who had been attacked by another adult as a function of whether or not these initial victims redirected aggression toward a third party during the ensuing fifteen minutes. The results were striking: individuals who redirected their aggression were significantly less likely to be attacked by other members of the social group during the next thirty minutes (Barash 1989). Other studies, involving other animal species, have supported this result.

Girard's pathbreaking work did not specifically mention redirected aggression, and was developed without reference to the underlying physiological and evolutionary bases that are only now becoming clear. Of course, Girard wrote extensively and creatively about the phenomenon of scapegoating (1979), which he interpreted as serving to unify a group that was otherwise at risk of disintegrating due to its interpersonally directed violence. What was new in Girard's day remains equally fresh today, however, and all the more compelling since it can now be connected to a growing body of theory and evidence concerning the evolutionary potency of pain-passing.

Let me be clear: just because redirected aggression is natural does not mean that it is good; in fact, I think it is very bad, something against which thoughtful people are called to struggle. But to combat it, we need to confront it, and to confront it, we need to understand not only its ubiquity but also its origins.

And confront it we must, because redirected aggression, and the general principle of passing along one's pain, has been seriously influential in generating violence not only in animals but also in human beings. For example, one day in 1858, a squadron of Mexican cavalry ambushed a group of Apaches, in peacetime, while the men were away. The following year, a large force of Apaches caught up with a detachment of Mexican soldiers—who may or may not have been those who committed the initial massacre—and a young man named Geronimo was given command. Why him? Because his mother, wife, and three young children had been among those slaughtered the previous year. Here are Geronimo's own words, from his autobiography:

> I was no chief and never had been, but because I had been more deeply wronged than others, this honor was conferred upon me. . . . In all the battle I thought of my murdered mother, wife and babies—of my father's grave. . . . Still covered with the blood of my enemies, still holding my conquering weapon, still hot with the joy of battle, and victory, I was surrounded by the Apache braves and made war chief of all the Apaches. Then I gave orders for scalping the slain. I could not call back my loved ones. I could not bring back the dead Apaches, but I could rejoice in what we had done. (Geronimo 2005, 33)

A similar process can operate at the level of entire communities as well. Thus, journalist Lawrence Weschler, writing in the *New Yorker*, recounted ethnic cleansing in the Bosnian town of Banja Luka. Although it used to consist of a majority of Muslims, when Weschler arrived, nearly all of them had just been murdered or driven out ("cleansed") by their Serb neighbors:

> As I was standing alongside the rubble-strewn parking lot on the site of what had until recently been one of the most splendid ancient mosques west of Istanbul, I asked a passing Serb student by what justification this and all the town's other mosques had been leveled. "Because of what the

> Ustasha did to us during the Second World War—they leveled our Orthodox churches," he replied without the slightest hesitation. Only the Ustasha were Croats. I somehow felt transported into a Three Stooges movie: Moe wallops Larry, who then feels entirely justified in turning around and smashing Curly. (Barash and Lipton 2011, 9)

There is also the U.S. invasion of Iraq. This little ditty (to the tune of "If You're Happy and You Know it, Clap Your Hands") made its way around the Internet shortly before that attack:

> If you cannot find Osama, bomb Iraq.
> If the market's hurt your momma, bomb Iraq.
> If the terrorists were Saudi and they've repossessed your Audi,
> and you're feeling kind of rowdy . . . bomb Iraq!

Thomas Friedman wrote the following in the *New York Times* article "Because We Could" on June 4, 2003:

> The "real reason" for this war, which was never stated, was that after 9/11 America needed to hit someone in the Arab-Muslim world. . . . Smashing Saudi Arabia or Syria would have been fine. But we attacked Saddam for one simple reason: because we could . . . and because he was right in the heart of that world.

According to former chief UN weapons inspector Hans Blix, in his book *Disarming Iraq*, "It's clear that the U.S. determination to take on Iraq was not triggered by anything Iraq did, but by the wounds inflicted by Al Qaeda" (Blix 2004). For all its bumbling incompetence and rigid ideology, the Bush administration was at least good at one thing: judging the desire of the U.S. public to pass along its post–9/11 pain. I am not suggesting, by the way, that in invading Iraq, the U.S. government itself was motivated by redirected aggression; the record seems clear that many influential members of the Bush administration came into office eager to invade Iraq, for numerous reasons. What they needed was an excuse motivating public opinion, something potent enough to move the American people. The events of 9/11 provided precisely this motivator, with redirected aggression—a strongly felt collective need for the country to pass along its pain—serving as the legitimizing force.

Numerous other examples of the Three Rs in general and redirected aggression in particular can also be adduced. Thus, the well-known and much deplored "cycles of domestic violence," whereby victimized children are liable to become victimizing adults, may be similarly underpinned. And of course there is scapegoating—a topic to which Girard devoted considerable attention—whereby entire communities appear to bind themselves together and cleanse themselves of their shared pain by symbolically and often literally passing that pain to an innocent third party. "In the frenzy of the mimetic violence of the mob," writes Girard,

> a focal point suddenly appears for whatever reason, in the shape of a culprit who is thought to be the cause of the disorder and the one who brought the crisis into the community. He/she is singled out and unanimously killed by the community. He/she isn't any guiltier than any other, but the whole community strongly believes he is, because of the mimetic reinforcement of unanimity. The killing of the scapegoat ends the [internal] crisis, since the transference against it is unanimous. Here is the importance of the scapegoat mechanism: it channels the collective violence against one arbitrarily chosen member of the community, and this victim becomes the common enemy of the entire community, *which is reconciled as a result.* (Girard, Antonello, and de Castro Rocha 2007)

Although I believe that Girard was prescient in this discussion, I also differ with him somewhat, in that I see no reason why reconciliation as such should result from successful scapegoating. What does result, according to all available biological evidence, is a diminution in each participant's subordination stress, which itself generates a degree of internal peace within those individuals who constitute the larger social assemblage. Under this interpretation, any pacifying impact on the group as a whole is simply a nonadapted, undirected byproduct of a benefit selected for at the level of individuals.

Interestingly, Girard was also aware of the work by classical ethologists such as Konrad Lorenz, who reported on the tendency of greylag geese to redirect aggression toward a third party in the service of their own pair-bonding. Girard called this "incipient scapegoating" (Girard, Antonello, and de Castro Rocha 2007), a phrase that may or may not be appropriate, although the phenomenon unquestionably is a case of redirected aggression, which presumably serves to diminish whatever subordination stress courting individuals might otherwise experience.

Paradoxically, Jews—who so often have been themselves scapegoated—may have invented it as an organized socio-religious phenomenon, when the high priest would place his hands on the head of a goat and recite various verses by which the sins of the community were transferred to the animal, who was then either ritually slaughtered or driven from the protection of the village, after which everyone presumably felt better.[2]

In more recent times, research by social psychologists Carl Hovland and Robert Sears (1940) examined southern lynchings between 1882 and 1930, and found that they could predict the frequency of these lethal events simply by knowing the wholesale price of cotton during the preceding year: When the price went down, economic conditions in the cotton-dependent South became worse and lynchings increased. When cotton prices went up, conditions improved and whites were less inclined to take out their pain on an innocent minority.

Scholars, including Girard in his monumental work *Violence and the Sacred* (1979), have examined the anthropology of religious sacrifices and substitute violence. One conclusion is that in their effort to make sense of a world filled with incomprehensible suffering, people have long assumed that when disaster comes upon them, it is because some higher power has been offended, and that a deity is passing its pain along to the rest of us. Hence, the bloody history of sacrifices, propitiatory offerings to mollify a divinity who must have been angered if not downright injured in order to be moved to treat his or her subjects so badly.

Girard's basic point—powerfully consistent with the Three Rs—is that human societies tend to seek surrogate objects, which they then subject to sacramental violence as a way of establishing social order.

There are many other circumstances in which the Three Rs in general and redirected aggression in particular likely reverberate in human experience. Think, for a moment, about justice, and consider the fine line that separates it from revenge. Thus, crime victims or victims' relatives traditionally deny that they are seeking revenge, and yet they consistently tell of their need to see the guilty punished in order to achieve personal peace or closure.

Of course, there are exceptions, reverently reported by observers, but I fear that what generates such attention is the fact that genuine forgiveness on the part of victims is so rare! It is entirely possible that in the aftermath of serious social and personal pain, powerful biological forces are evoked that demand someone be made to suffer in return. Indeed, it can be argued that to some extent civilization can be measured by the degree to which society steps in to make sure that this powerful impulse is handled decorously and by official practice not obviously connected to the initial victim. Notably, in the absence of such patterns of organized justice, individuals cross-culturally are prone to "take the law into their own hands."

Here, too, Girard prefigured the connection, noting in *Violence and the Sacred* that

> By definition, primitive societies have only private vengeance. Thus, public vengeance is the exclusive property of well-policed societies, and our society calls it the judicial system. Our penal system operates according to principles of justice that are in no real conflict with the concept of revenge. The same principle is at work in all systems of violent retribution. (Girard 1979, 16)

In a discussion that closely parallels many of the points I have sought to make in this chapter, Girard (1979) also speculated about the origin of science. His argument, in brief, is that when bad things have happened to innocent people, there has been a powerful tendency for these people to seek someone, or some group, to blame. Take, for example, the tale of Oedipus. When a terrible plague afflicted the people of Thebes, it was immediately assumed that such pain and suffering must have been caused by some human misbehavior, and that once the malefactor was discovered and suitably punished, the city would be healed. Eventually, of course, it was discovered that Oedipus himself, king of Thebes, was the secret sinner (unbeknownst even to himself), after which his mother hanged herself, Oedipus blinded himself, and normalcy was restored. This is a tale of primitive scapegoating, essentially one of witchcraft.

Girard's point is that we didn't so much stop burning witches because we had developed science, but rather, we developed science only when we were able to get beyond burning witches, past looking for victims to blame for our own distress, and started looking for natural causes of natural phenomena—e.g., microorganisms—and not reflexively blaming other people for our own painful experiences.

Armed with an understanding of the biology of pain-passing, we can subject other aspects of human behavior to a new explanatory lens. Take literature, especially those classics that have endured and that presumably reflect something genuine about underlying human nature. Rarely does such literature present evil for evil's sake, the mustache-twirling villain who gleefully ties the heroine to the railroad tracks simply because he is cruel, and that's that. Almost inevitably, for a bad actor to be believable, he or she must be shown to have suffered some injury. Then it all makes sense. Among the great villains of Shakespeare's creation, for example—Iago, Richard III, Edmund—all are depicted as having experienced their share of pain, as a result of which they elect to "dish it out" to others.

An especially revealing tale is portrayed in James Joyce's story "Counterparts," part of his collection *Dubliners*. It describes the travails of one Farrington, a lowly clerk who suffers indignities at work but is unable to get back at his overbearing boss. To make matters worse, after he stops at a pub on the way home (seeking to drown his sorrows), Farrington proceeds to lose two arm-wrestling matches to a young newcomer. Farrington, we learn, had been renowned for his physical strength. As a result, it was a sullen Mr. Farrington who headed home that evening,

> full of smouldering anger and revengefulness. He felt humiliated and discontented; he did not even feel drunk; and he had only twopence in his pocket. He cursed everything. . . . He had lost his reputation as a strong man, having been defeated twice by a mere boy. His heart swelled with a . . . fury that nearly choked him. (Joyce 1914, 64)

His young son comes running down the stairs to meet him, small and vulnerable, pitifully eager to do his father's bidding, altogether innocent of the latter's misfortunes, and unaware of the older man's pent-up rage, whereupon Farrington takes up a walking stick and mercilessly beats the boy.

Other examples are legion and could be multiplied almost indefinitely, but I trust the point has been made: We all know that violence causes pain.

What needs to be understood is that the connection works in reverse as well: Pain causes violence.

Unfortunately, the tendency for victims to respond to pain by reverting to one or more of the Three Rs is easier to diagnose than to treat. There is hope, however; indeed, the world's great ethical systems have long struggled to deal with this problem. For example, Buddhist tradition emphasizes that suffering is ubiquitous and unavoidable, yet can be minimized. The first of the Buddha's Four Noble Truths is that life inevitably entails pain, followed by specific suggestions for how to reduce suffering, called The Eightfold Path. In addition, among the fundamental teachings of Mahayana Buddhism is the *kshanti paramita*: "the capacity to receive, bear and transform the pain inflicted on you by your enemies and also by those who love you." The latter part of this is especially important since even those who have not been victimized by crime, war, or other serious stressors are liable to suffer the pain of illness and loss, inflicted even by those who love us—perhaps via unintentional slights, or, if nothing else, the fact that eventually they will die.

Hinduism—ancestral to Buddhism—focuses on the repeating cycle of death and rebirth, and of ways to break this pattern and achieve Nirvana. What about breaking the cycle of pain and the Three Rs? (It isn't quite so easy as simply adding a fourth and fifth: "restraint" or "reconciliation," even though these are altogether appropriate goals.) In this regard, one cannot avoid mentioning Gandhi, whose way of *satyagraha* and nonviolence was explicitly developed with an eye toward not demanding an eye for an eye, not passing along one's pain.

Christian tradition, too, venerates and validates the role of pain. Christ's agony is widely taken as crucially related to God's redemption of humanity. Hidden within dense layers of theology is this equation, one that is, however, rarely made explicit: The more pain (the more suffering on the part of Jesus), the more redemption for the rest of us. But why? Insight into the role of pain-passing suggests that perhaps the crucifixion of Christ, who is considered the epitome of innocence, provides an especially potent example of scapegoating as route to social cleansing. Also consistent with this thesis is the following possibility: Insofar as Christ suffered ("for our sins"), this enhances the social, personal, and even biochemical status of the rest of us, helping to overcome subordination stress among his followers.

According to Christian theology—and, so far as I can determine, Girard's interpretation of this event as well—Christ's suffering was intended to put an end to all such sacrifices involving collective ritualistic cleansing. I see no evidence, however, that this is true. Rather, Christ's agony is ritualistically repeated over and over, in numerous Christian Easter traditions and ceremonies worldwide, suggesting that its function may well be consistent with biological expectation in that it must be repeated periodically if the stress level of Christ's followers is to be decreased.

In any event, understanding the Three Rs helps us understand why it is so difficult to follow Christian tradition in its most emblematic form of turning the other cheek. As S. J. Perelman stated: "To err is human, to forgive, supine." Nonetheless, any potential solution to the numerous dilemmas posed by the deep inclination to respond to pain by the infliction of yet more pain must be based on a truth that is as deep and widely shared as that tendency for pain-passing itself: that human beings, perhaps unique among animals, are capable (at least on occasion, and once the issues are made clear) of acting against the promptings of their biology.

Accordingly, I conclude with a "Maxim of Minimizing Pain," offered as a kind of eleventh commandment: Given that there is already too much pain, whenever you contemplate alternative actions, ask yourself whether each will increase or decrease the world's burden, and always choose the latter.

Notes

1. This case is examined at length by R. Girard in *The Scapegoat* (1989).
2. This is not to claim that scapegoating itself was invented by the Jews, since there is clear evidence that it exists—via redirected aggression—even in nonhuman animals. Moreover, Girard may well be correct when he suggested that we have been scapegoating "since the foundation of the world," even though the term "scapegoat" evidently did not exist prior to the Old Testament. For further discussion on this point, see the introduction to this volume.

Works Cited

Barash, D. P. 1989. *Marmots: Social Behavior and Ecology*. Stanford, CA: Stanford University Press.

Barash, D. P., and J. E. Lipton. 2011. *Payback: Why We Retaliate, Redirect Aggression and Seek Revenge*. New York: Oxford University Press.

Blix, H. 2004. *Disarming Iraq*. New York: Pantheon.

Geronimo. 2005. *My Life*. New York: Dover Press.

Girard, R. 1979. *Violence and the Sacred*. Baltimore: Johns Hopkins University Press.

——— . 1989. *The Scapegoat*. Baltimore: Johns Hopkins University Press.

Girard, R., P. Antonello, and J. C. de Castro Rocha. 2007. *Evolution and Conversion: Dialogues on the Origins of Culture*. New York: Continuum.

Hovland, C., and R. R. Sears. 1940. "Minor Studies of Aggression. VI. Correlation of Lynchings with Economic Indices." *Journal of Psychology* 9: 301–10.

Joyce, J. 2010. *Dubliners*. Red Wing, MN: Cricket House. First ed. London: Grant Richards Ltd., 1914.

Sapolsky, R. 2004. *Why Zebras Don't Get Ulcers*. New York: Holt.

de Waal, F. 2007. *Chimpanzee Politics*. Baltimore: Johns Hopkins University Press.

PART THREE

Violent Origins Revisited

Violent Origins

Mimetic Rivalry in Darwinian Evolution

Melvin Konner

The essence of evolution as a process has been framed in the following way: "Animals engage in a struggle for existence; for resources, to avoid being eaten, and to breed. Environmental factors influence organisms to develop new characteristics to ensure survival, thus transforming into new species. Animals that survive to breed can pass on their characteristics to offspring."

These words could have been Charles Darwin's, but they were actually written by the natural philosopher Al-Jahiz, in Baghdad, in the ninth century. So it isn't a very complicated idea. Three things are needed for Darwinian evolution to take place: differential adaptation, which is partly heritable, and results in differential reproductive success. While Darwin emphasized a Malthusian struggle for existence, with animals and plants producing far more offspring than the world can support, so that they must fight one another for sustenance, this is actually not a necessary dimension of the process. What is necessary is that they have differential reproductive success due to partly heritable differential adaptation. They do fight for that.

In the closing passage of *The Origin of Species*, Darwin adroitly skirted the dark side of evolution: "There is grandeur in this view of life . . . from so simple a beginning endless forms most beautiful and most wonderful have been, and are being, evolved" (Darwin 1864, 425). That was in 1859. But a few years earlier he had written to botanist Joseph Hooker, "What a book a Devil's Chaplain might write on the clumsy, wasteful, blundering low and horribly cruel works of nature!" (Darwin 1901, 105). Yet, interestingly enough, the standard phrases we associate with the dark side of Darwin's theory were coined by others: "struggle for existence" by his great fellow biologist Thomas Huxley (also known as Darwin's Bulldog); "survival of the fittest" by sociologist Herbert Spencer, who applied and misapplied Darwin's theory to human life; and "Nature red in tooth and claw" by Alfred, Lord Tennyson. Nevertheless, all fairly express Darwin's own private thoughts (and fears) about the implications of his theory.

"Fittest," one must hasten to say, does not, in this theory, have anything necessarily to do with medical, muscular, or (least of all) moral fitness. I sometimes envision a runty, tubercular, charming, sociopathic man who persuades many young women to sleep with him. In a time before contraception and abortion, and even to some extent with their availability, he could have high reproductive success without living very long. This is the downside of Darwinian evolution. Certainly, "endless forms most beautiful and most wonderful have been, and are being, evolved" (Darwin 1864, 425). But at the same time, by the same process, some things that are neither beautiful nor wonderful have also been produced and preserved.

Darwin, who was in the first place a keenly observant and deeply insightful naturalist, understood early on that it was not just about survival. Also in *The Origin of Species*, he wrote "a few words about what I call sexual selection":

> This depends, not on a struggle for existence, but on a struggle between the males for possession of the females; the result is not death to the unsuccessful competitor, but few or no offspring. Sexual selection is, therefore, less rigorous than natural selection. Generally, the most vigorous males, those which are best fitted for their places in nature, will leave most progeny. But in many cases, victory will depend not on general vigour, but on having special weapons, confined to the male sex. A hornless stag or spurless cock would have a poor chance of leaving offspring. Sexual selection by always allowing the victor to breed might surely give indomitable courage, length to the spur, and strength to the wing to strike in the spurred leg, as well as

> the brutal cock-fighter, who knows well that he can improve his breed by careful selection of the best cocks. . . . The war is, perhaps, severest between the males of polygamous animals, and these seem oftenest provided with special weapons. (Darwin 1864, 83–84)

Despite the obvious sexism of the language, this is a clear statement of principle, and Darwin goes on to offer a brighter side of the process:

> Amongst birds, the contest is often of a more peaceful character. All those who have attended to the subject, believe that there is the severest rivalry between the males of many species to attract, by singing the females. The rock-thrush of Guiana, birds of paradise, and some others, congregate; and successive males display their gorgeous plumage and perform strange antics before the females, which standing by as spectators, at last choose the most attractive partner. . . . If man can in a short time give elegant carriage and beauty to his bantams, according to his standard of beauty, I can see no good reason to doubt that female birds, by selecting, during thousands of generations, the most melodious or beautiful males, according to their standard of beauty, might produce a marked effect. (Darwin 1864, 84–85)

So we have either the spectacle of males tearing at each other or that of males preening and strutting. Either way, it's a disturbing process by which much of the history of life has been played out. We now consider the role of violence in this process.

Violence in Nonhuman Species

Conflict, as observed in all motile animals, occurs over scarce resources such as food, space, or mates. In an older view, threats and other aggressive displays were thought to reduce violence by spacing individuals and stabilizing their hierarchies (Wynne-Edwards 1962). Humans, on this view, kill each other because weapons distance us from our victims, rendering submissive displays and other natural constraints on violence weak or useless (Lorenz 1970). This view persisted in part because of lack of opportunity to observe animal killings. If a baboon troop had the same violent death rate as Americans, it could take centuries to observe even a single killing (Wilson 1975, 246–47). As fieldwork expanded, many species were found to kill their own kind.

A crucial case is competitive infanticide, first studied in Hanuman langurs (Hrdy 1977, 1979). Matrilineal kin and their young make up the core of langur groups; adult males may stay for a year or longer but are ultimately transient. When new males appear, they try to drive off the resident males. If successful, they kill all infants below six months of age. Female resistance is brave but futile; they cycle back into fertility again and mate with the new males. Similar phenomena were described in chimpanzees, lions, wild dogs, and many other species (Hausfater and Hrdy 1984). In this and many other natural circumstances, violence evolved to help individuals and coalitions gain and keep resources, including mates. Dominant males mate with ovulating females in baboons (DeVore 1965; Hausfater 1975), rhesus monkeys (Wallen and Tannenbaum 1997), and other species; competition for fertile females is a main cause of conflict. Male violence against females is also common in monkeys and apes, and often leads to sexual coercion (Smuts 1992; Smuts and Smuts 1993).

Chimpanzee aggression can be extreme, including attacks on females by the larger males, competitive infanticide by females, and violence between groups at territorial boundaries (Goodall 1977, 1979, 1986; Manson and Wrangham 1991; Wrangham and Peterson 1996). One or two victims temporarily separated from their own group are stalked and attacked by a group of males that beat, stamp, drag, and bite them to death. Females may be killed but are more often absorbed into the other group. In the Gombe Stream Reserve in Tanzania, entire groups of males have been eliminated and females absorbed according to this pattern (Goodall 1986).

Similar chimpanzee ambush-killings occur in the Kibale National Park in Uganda, where they have been studied for over a decade. The best predictor of such an attack is a critical number of adult males. In a group of 150 chimpanzees of both sexes and all ages (Gibbons 2004), the critical mass was about eighteen congregating males. They would grow more excited before going out into the forest in single file, maintaining an unusual quiet, and bypassing hunting opportunities until they passed the outer bound of their own territory. If they found a lone male from the neighboring group, they jointly assaulted this victim, on five different occasions killing him.

It is important to note that bonobos, a species of ape as closely related to us as chimpanzees, do not show this kind or degree of violence (Kano 1992; Wrangham and Peterson 1996). The bonobo genome was recently sequenced, and comparative genetic analysis will ultimately tell us the extent to which we share the violent genes of the chimpanzee, the nonviolent genes of the bonobo, or some of both. Future field studies may suggest how much of bonobo nonviolence is related to the fact that they are on the verge of extinction. However, at present there is evidence for our greater similarity to chimpanzees in our own behavior and in the fossil record.

Violence during Human Evolution

For the first part of the proto-human fossil record, there is little evidence of violence, but there are in all only a few hundred specimens, mostly small parts of skeletons. The Neanderthals are the first hominins for whom there are large numbers of individuals represented. They are currently viewed as being mainly off the ancestral line to modern humans, although they probably interbred with our direct ancestors. They were very similar to us genetically, and were behaviorally similar as well. Neanderthal fossils, especially those found at the Shanidar site in Iraq, show a great many injuries, where the skeletons include many healed and unhealed fractures (Trinkhaus 1978; Trinkhaus and Howells 1979). One male has a partly healed scar on the top of his left ninth rib due to a sharp object that forcefully entered his chest (Trinkhaus 1995). He may have had a collapsed lung, and in any case survived just a few weeks after the injury. At Skhul, another Neanderthal site, one skeleton has spear damage in the leg and pelvis (LeBlanc and Register 2003). These remains show clearly that forty or fifty thousand years ago there was lethal violence among Neanderthals, and their high overall rate of injury is likely owing in some measure to violence.

There is also clear evidence of cannibalism (Culotta 1999; Defleur, White, et al. 1999). In the cave of Moula-Guercy in Ardèche, France, Neanderthal bones dated to one hundred thousand years ago were butchered with the same methods used on deer and goats in the same area. But from other evidence, cannibalism is probably much older than that, and it has persisted up to recent times, sometimes associated with mortuary rites, sometimes with violence (Sanday 1986; Villa et al. 1986; White 1992; DeGusta 1999; Wade 2000). The later fossil record of modern humans before the invention of agriculture also shows scattered evidence of violence.

After that, the evidence is abundant, and archaeology has demolished the myth of the peaceful savage (Keeley 1996; LeBlanc and Register 2003). In fact, we know now that belief in this myth required substantial blindness to evidence, in accounts that were in effect "interpretive pacifications" (Keeley 1996). The fossil record remains sparse for most of prehuman evolution, and even in violent human societies most people die nonviolently, so it is remarkable that we see as much as we do in the record. Homicidal violence has evidently been part of our own species' way of life for at least twenty-seven thousand years (Keeley 1996). At Grimaldi in Italy, a projectile point was found embedded in a child's spinal column. Czechoslovakian cemeteries from around the same time show substantial violent death, perhaps on a large scale. A Nile Valley man buried twenty thousand years ago had stone projectile points in his abdomen and another in his upper arm. Between fourteen thousand and twelve thousand years ago there are many more such cases in Egyptian Nubia, and pre-agricultural sites in Europe show that violence was common, including the "Iceman" of five thousand years ago, whose well-preserved body bears an arrow in the upper back. He was apparently alone in the mountains, had a last meal, was pursued by an enemy, shot from behind, and bled to death.

All this violence took place during the hunter-gatherer phase of human prehistory, many thousands of years before agriculture, which is widely thought to have worsened violence. Ethnographic and demographic research also reveals homicides in many recent hunter-gatherer societies, including the !Kung, Eskimo, Mbuti, Hadza, and others (Lee 1979; Knauft 1987). It is often said that hunter-gatherers did not have group-level violence, but this claim is no longer sustainable. One cross-cultural study showed that almost two-thirds of such societies had combat between communities at least every other year (Ember 1978). The sample in this particular analysis is questionable—for example, it includes numerous equestrian hunters of the Great Plains and elsewhere, not appropriate models for the general human past since our ancestors did not have horses.

Still, ethnographies of classical warm-climate hunter-gatherers show that their level of intergroup combat has been underestimated (Eibl-Eibesfeldt

1979). Southern African rock paintings, Australian aboriginal clubs and shields, and common spear wounds in two thousand-year-old skeletons in the American Southwest also point to group violence among recent hunter-gatherers (LeBlanc and Register 2003). Recent mathematical models of the evolution of cooperation, which is highly evolved in our species, suggest that it could easily have resulted from group selection in severe and widespread intergroup conflict among our hunter-gatherer ancestors (Bowles 2009; Bowles and Gintis 2011).

After the invention and spread of agriculture, archaeological evidence of warfare in widely separate parts of the ancient world becomes decisive. Many skeletons show embedded arrow and spear points, left-sided skull fractures (caused by blows with weapons in the enemy's right hand), and parry fractures of the lower arm sustained in warding off such blows. Numerous sites include graves with weapons and armor, and fortifications are ubiquitous (Keeley 1996; LeBlanc and Register 2003). *The Iliad* and the biblical books of Judges and Kings describe the continual clash of agricultural tribes and early civilizations. We can in fact summarize history since the hunter-gatherer period as a process of ongoing, expansionist tribal warfare (Schmookler 1983; Keegan 1993).

Extrapolating from ethnography, true warfare appears to have emerged with the transition from smaller to larger chiefdoms, followed by the emergence of the state (Earle 1991). Increasing population density made social stratification, division of labor, and taxation important. Alliances among religious, economic, and military elites led these societies, which continued to grow by conquest, but the process preceded the state; the Nuer, pastoralists of the Sudan, became an effective organization for predatory expansion at the expense of their Dinka neighbors, despite the relatively low level of social complexity in each group (Sahlins 1961; Kelly 1985).

Among people like the Aztecs and ancient Mayans, power was more centralized and the military more effective (Otterbein 1970). Such hierarchical societies emerged as states rather than tribes or chiefdoms, and their level of social organization corresponds to that of the legendary rivals of the Bronze and Iron Ages. Going from there to the wars of modern states is mainly a matter of advancing technology (Schmookler 1983; Cook 2003). Nationalism, as Arnold Toynbee put it, is new wine in the old bottles of tribalism (Toynbee 1972).

Violence in Small-Scale Recent Societies

The ethnographic record strongly suggests that violence is simply part of human behavior (Bohannan and American Museum of Natural History 1967; Otterbein 1970). Among the most violent traditional cultures were the Yanomamö of highland Venezuela, the Dani and Enga of highland New Guinea, the equestrian Great Plains Indians of the United States, the Aztecs, the Mongols, and the Zulus of nineteenth-century southern Africa. These cultures were very violent. Of all adult male deaths among the Enga, one in four were due to violence, and the Enga way of life was largely organized around it (Meggitt 1977). For the Yanomamö, known as "the fierce people" by themselves and others, conditions were similar (Chagnon 1968, 1992). Forty percent of Yanomamö men had committed homicide at least once, and those who had done so had more offspring than those who had not (Chagnon 1988). These and many other violent cultures have led some anthropologists to conclude that we are a very bloody species composed of "sick" societies (Edgerton 1992). Many older ethnographic accounts of warfare in traditional cultures, including some that have now been pacified, suggest that ethnographers, like archaeologists, have underestimated it (Eibl-Eibesfeldt 1979).

However, rates of homicide span three orders of magnitude among cultures, and these differences matter. Consider the least violent societies. The !Kung San of Botswana have been considered nonviolent (Thomas 1959; Marshall 1976), yet their homicide rate at least matched that of American cities (Lee 1979) and there were also many nonfatal individual assaults and fights (Shostak 1981, 2000). While they have not carried out intergroup conflict in recent times, their contempt for other ethnic groups and even for !Kung in neighboring areas suggests that they have the psychological disposition for group conflict, and historical data suggest that they conducted violent raids on neighboring village-camps in the past (Eibl-Eibesfeldt 1979).

Among the Semai, simple horticulturalists of Malaysia, violence was reported to be abhorrent and virtually absent. "Since a census of the Semai was first taken in 1956, not one instance of murder, attempted murder, or maiming has come to the attention of either government or hospital authorities" (Dentan 1968). Cultural ideology and child-care patterns seemed to explain this:

> A person should never hit a child because, people say, "How would you feel if it died?" . . . Similarly, one adult should never hit another because, they say, "Suppose he hit you back?" . . . The Semai are not great warriors. As long as they have been known to the outside world, they have consistently fled rather than fight, or even than run the risk of fighting. They had never participated in a war or raid until the Communist insurgency of the early 1950's, when the British raised troops among the Semai, mainly in the west. . . . Many did not realize that soldiers kill people. When I suggested to one Semai recruit that killing was a soldier's job, he laughed at my ignorance and explained, "No, we don't kill people, brother, we just tend weeds and cut grass." (Dentan 1968, 58)

However, in the 1950s, the Semai had become involved in British counterinsurgency against Communists, and in this their behavior was very different:

> Many people who knew the Semai insisted that such an unwarlike people could never make good soldiers . . . they were wrong. Communist terrorists had killed the kinsmen of some of the Semai counterinsurgency troops. Taken out of their nonviolent society and ordered to kill, they seem to have been swept up in a sort of insanity which they call "blood drunkenness." . . . "We killed, killed, killed. The Malays would stop and go through people's pockets and take their watches and money. We did not think of watches or money. We only thought of killing. Wah, truly we were drunk with blood." One man even told how he had drunk the blood of a man he had killed. (Dentan 1968, 58–59)

Yet after that war, Semai life returned to normal:

> Talking about these experiences, the Semai seem, not displeased that they were such good soldiers, but unable to account for their behavior. It is almost as if they had shut the experience in a separate compartment. . . . Back in Semai society they seem as gentle and afraid of violence as anyone else. To them their one burst of violence appears to be as remote as

> something that happened to someone else, in another country. The nonviolent image remains intact. (Dentan 1968, 59)

These events could merely suggest what happens when men are torn from their accustomed cultural context, and perhaps it was their very inexperience with violence that made their behavior as soldiers extreme. But in any case, the Semai experience shows that upbringing and cultural ideology are only part of what shapes the human tendency to violence.

Nevertheless, the differences among societies are important and should be understood. In a broad cross-cultural study designed to sample the ethnographic universe representatively, matrilocal societies had less warfare than patrilocal ones (Ember and Ember 1971; Divale 1974). Another study showed that where husband-wife intimacy is high—where husbands and wives sleep and eat together and share the child care—organized intergroup conflicts are less frequent (Ember and Ember 1971; Divale 1974). Societies organized around frequent or intermittent warfare tend to segregate men, with distinct men's houses for eating and sleeping, and often have men's societies that initiate boys under stress and actively train them for warfare. The social dynamic of male groups can foster violence (Tiger 1969), and this is apparently an important process in recent terrorist actions (Sageman 2008). This can be thought of as a slower, more complex, human version of the building excitement of groups of male chimpanzees that results in violence toward other groups.

It is clear from cross-cultural statistical research that after a society has been pacified by external powers, it becomes less interested in training boys to be aggressive (Ember and Ember 1994). Among the Enga, previously very violent, warfare has been reduced to very low levels (Wiessner and Pupu 2012). Similar reductions have been seen in other previously violent cultures such as the Gusii (Knauft 1987). And there is evidence that the levels of violence in industrial and postindustrial societies have declined substantially over the past few centuries (Pinker 2011). These trends indicate that the right social and cultural conditions can greatly reduce human violence. However, they do not necessarily show that the human capacity for violence, or our tendency to violence, has fundamentally changed. Also, the decline of violence under pacification of violent traditional societies should serve to make us more cautious about calling cultures nonviolent on the basis of ethnographic research done long after such pacification.

How Does Aggression Lead to War?

The evidence for biological mechanisms of aggression has been reviewed many times (Niehoff 1999; Konner 2002, 2006a, 2006b). A wide range of both animal and human studies leave no doubt that physical violence has a strong genetic component, that it develops in predictable ways only partly dependent on upbringing and enculturation, that it is carried out in increasingly understood brain circuits, and that it is influenced by hormones, especially androgens, having influence both during early development and after sexual maturation—a fact that accounts for the well-established, innate predominance of males in violent acts. These biological factors, together with psychosocial and cultural influences, will ultimately explain individual violence. But how does this become group violence?

Three processes, each drawing on a strong human tendency that is separate from the tendency to violence, can be identified: dichotomizing or splitting the social world, which psychoanalyst Erik Erikson called "pseudo-speciation"; emotional contagion and other processes of group psychology; and following leaders.[1]

Violent rivalries do not reflect just the proven human tendency to violence, but also the tendency to dichotomize the social world. It is partly a special case of dualistic thought in general, identified by Marcel Mauss, Claude Lévi-Strauss, and others as cross-culturally universal (Douglas 1966; Lévi-Strauss 1968; Maybury-Lewis and Almagor 1989). Divisions emphasized in the language, religion, and customs of varied cultures include night vs. day, human vs. animal, village vs. "bush," tame vs. wild, good vs. evil, polluted vs. pure, profane vs. sacred, male vs. female, right vs. left. The underlying reality is usually a weak dichotomy or a continuum, but it is exaggerated or distorted by mental processes into strongly contrasting divisions.

Splitting is related to the generally low human tolerance for ambiguity and cognitive dissonance (Festinger 1957). In language, this is crucial; there is a physical continuum between *p* and *b*, but we must decide which one we are hearing in order to preserve meaning (Jakobson and Halle 1971). This also applies to other cognitive processes. As we evolved, we often had to make rapid decisions, made easier by having two clear choices. We must classify every stimulus as familiar or strange and decide on approach or avoidance. In the social realm, dichotomies of kin and non-kin, us and them, real people versus barbarians, heathen, Gentiles, or strangers are found in almost all cultures.

Dichotomies also have an emotional dimension. Fear of the strange is characteristic of complex nervous systems, with a continuum from attention to arousal to fear. Weak stimulation of the amygdala can produce alertness, while stronger stimulation in the same area will produce fear (Ursin and Kaada 1960). Novelty, depending on the context, may produce either attention or fear in infants. Socially, the second half-year of life sees a rise of new distinctions, including attachment to a primary caregiver and wariness or fear of strangers (Bowlby 1969–77; Lewis and Rosenblum 1973). These reactions are ultimately the basis of adult xenophobia.

Social psychologists have traced the emergence and consequences of the us-them distinction. The Robbers Cave Experiment (Sherif, Harvey, et al. 1961) brought 22 average eleven-year-old boys to a summer camp. All were from middle-class white Protestant families, with similar educational backgrounds. At the camp they were randomly assigned to one of two matched groups that differed in no measurable way. Despite joint activities and attempts to discourage competition, the groups began to compete, naming themselves, speaking disparagingly of each other, and reacting to each other's incursions with territorial defense. Formal competitions with trophies and prizes followed, and "good sportsmanship" gave way "to name calling, hurling invectives, and derogation of the outgroup . . . [to the] point that the groups became more and more reluctant to have anything to do with one another" (101). Over several weeks, "derogatory stereotypes and negative attitudes toward the outgroup were crystallized" (210). This dichotomization proved reversible, but it is noteworthy how quickly bigotry was created in two groups with no initial differences between them. Similar findings have been made many times with adults and under more controlled conditions. They confirm that it is easy to establish prejudice against arbitrarily formed out-groups, and to exacerbate the prejudice by giving people frustrating experiences or challenging their self-esteem (Tajfel 1982; Robinson and Tajfel 1997).

Other aspects of group psychology are also well studied. Fear and anxiety in a complex and unpredictable world is partly relieved by reducing responsibility for our actions. We do this by following rules, taking collective action, or following a leader. Rules are often benign, but the mass or crowd psychology that sometimes arises in group action is far more problematic. Charles Mackay, in his nineteenth-century classic *Extraordinary Popular Delusions and the Madness of Crowds*, wrote:

> In reading the history of nations, we find that whole communities suddenly fix their minds upon one object, and go mad in its pursuit; that millions of people become simultaneously impressed with one delusion, and run after it, till their attention is caught by some new folly more captivating than the first. We see one nation suddenly seized, from its highest to its lowest members, with a fierce desire of military glory; another as suddenly becoming crazed upon a religious scruple; and neither of them recovering its senses until it has shed rivers of blood and sowed a harvest of groans and tears, to be reaped by its posterity.... Men, it has been well said, think in herds; it will be seen that they go mad in herds, while they only recover their senses slowly, and one by one. (Mackay 1932)

Mackay reviews a wide variety of collective actions: lynch mobs and witch hunts, reckless investment schemes such as the South Sea Bubble and the Tulip mania, fads, pilgrimages, revolutions, and wars. Collective violence may be seen as an instance of human susceptibility to emotional contagion, a phenomenon that has since been well studied by social psychologists (Hatfield, Cacioppo, et al. 1994). In terms of evolutionary background, humans are not herding animals but participants in small groups with more complex social patterns, yet the rudiments of these processes are present. Other classic psychological studies show that a person will deny the evidence of his or her senses, even with respect to something as simple as the relative length of printed lines, if a few others (stooges of the investigatory) are in agreement against his judgment (Asch 1951). However, the contagions Mackay describes may result partly from mass societies that violate the small-group dynamics we evolved with.

Irrespective of group size, a common expression of mass psychology is the identification and destruction of enemies, which may be called *contagious enmity*. It has two principal forms. The first identifies weak internal enemies, then isolates and destroys them, as in the examples of lynch mobs, witch hunts, inquisitions, and genocide. The victims are viewed as strange, confusing, evil, and dangerous to the spiritual and physical life of the larger group.

In an extension of Girardian principles of sacrificial violence (Girard 1977; Burkert, Smith, et al. 1987), killing them becomes a form of ritual purification.

The second form of contagious enmity identifies external enemies, who are similarly condemned but who are capable of group self-defense. If bloodshed is sacralized in primitive and ancient ritual, then the concept of holy war becomes more comprehensible; people send their children into battle, and when they are killed, their blood makes the cause sacred. Sacrifices purify the community by exporting sins to the victim, but raiding and ambush-killing of defenseless neighboring enemies may play an intermediate role. For example, Ilongot headhunting is directed against external enemies, yet "it involves the taking of a human life with a view toward cleansing the participants of the contaminating burdens of their own lives" (Rosaldo 1980, 140). Through mimetic emotional contagion, the collective fear of two groups engaged in reciprocal contagious enmity will each finally justify the other's responses. What may at first have been a largely irrational fear becomes quite rational as each side sees the real threat in the other.

Following leaders and obeying orders generally is, of course, necessary for most martial actions. The fearful infant flees to a protective caregiver, and if the infant's fear of strangers is transformed in adulthood into denigration or hatred, then the adult's flight to a protector may take the form of obedience, conformity, chauvinism, or loyalty. Freud, in *Group Psychology and the Analysis of the Ego*—"group psychology" being a debatable translation of the German word *Massenpsychologie*—argues that although the process operates with a leader (Freud 1949), something resembling mob psychology is apparent: "the lack of independence and initiative in their members, the similarity in the reactions of all of them . . . the weakness of intellectual ability, the lack of emotional restraint, the inclination to exceed every limit in the expression of emotion and to work it off completely in the form of action" (81–82). But Freud did not restrict his model to popular delusions:

> We are reminded of how many of these phenomena of dependence are part of the normal constitution of human society, of how little originality and courage are to be found in it, of how much every individual is ruled by those attitudes of the group mind which exhibit themselves in such forms as racial characteristics, class prejudices, public opinion, etc. (82)

Freud deemed group psychology as identical to hypnosis, especially in "the behavior of the individual to the leader" (78). In his view, both the leader and fellow group members have a hypnotic suggestive power. The flight to a protector—the "escape from freedom" (Fromm 1994)—is to the dichotomous certitude of leader and group alike. Freud's two main examples are armies and churches, both of which have an "us–them" distinction at their core; hypnosis thus becomes focused in relation to an enemy.

The submission of individual choice to authority is shown in Stanley Milgram's famous experiments: naive subjects were ordered to give what they thought were electric shocks to an unseen person (Milgram 1963, 1974). Most of the subjects delivered what they believed were very dangerous shocks when ordered to by a man in a white laboratory coat. Milgram later asked: "What is the limit of such obedience? . . . We attempted to establish a boundary. Cries from the victim . . . were not good enough. The victim claimed heart trouble; subjects still shocked him on command. The victim pleaded to be let free, and his answers no longer registered on the signal box; subjects continued to shock him" (Milgram 1974, 188). The encouragement of peers strengthened the subjects' obedience.

Milgram clearly states that this is "not aggression, for there is no anger, vindictiveness, or hatred in those who shocked the victim. . . . Something far more dangerous is revealed: the capacity for man to abandon his humanity, indeed, the inevitability that he does so, as he merges his unique personality into larger institutional structures" (188). Philip Zimbardo's extremely disturbing experiments in which Stanford students role-played as guards and prisoners underscored the power of these processes, which made the one group as brutal as the other was cowed. As Milgram said, "This is a fatal flaw nature has designed into us, and which in the long run gives our species only a modest chance for survival" (188).

Sacred Violence, Mimetic Rivalry, and War

In works such as *Things Hidden since the Foundation of the World* and *Violence and the Sacred*, René Girard confronted fully the possibility that bloodshed may be at, or close to, the heart of all human social life:

> To make these processes effective once again, people are tempted to multiply the innocent victims, to kill all the enemies of the nation or the class . . . and to sing the praises of murder and madness. (Girard 1987, 287)

This quote occurs in the context of a conversation about the theories and movements spawned by Marx, Nietzsche, Freud, and even Foucault, all of which might be characterized as enthusiasms for which Girard has limited sympathy. Although they all share his willingness to acknowledge the role of violence, they also share the conviction that with the right approach (communist revolution, the triumph of the *übermensch*, universal psychoanalysis, or the overthrow of illegitimate power), violence can be controlled and overcome.

This resembles what I have called the Tinker Theory (Konner 2002): Human life is terribly flawed, but if we tinker with the class structure, the unconscious, or the reins of power, we will transcend and even eliminate the flaws. Girard considers this kind of thinking naive and potentially dangerous. In reality, none of these approaches has succeeded in its goals, and in some cases the results have been horrifically destructive. Girard (rightly in my view) takes these failures as evidence that violence is, and will likely remain, central to human experience.

In fairness to Freud, some of his later writings—*Civilization and Its Discontents*, for example—seem close to Girard's in their acceptance of the ultimate tension between aggressive or "death" instincts and the cooperation needed for civilized life. But in his famous exchange of letters with Albert Einstein in 1932, it was Freud who played the optimist. The physicist began by bemoaning human susceptibility to propaganda leading to war: "How is it that these devices succeed so well in rousing men to such wild enthusiasm, even to sacrifice their lives? Only one answer is possible. Because man has within him a lust for hatred and destruction. In normal times this passion exists in a latent state, it emerges only in unusual circumstances, but it is a comparatively easy task to call it into play and raise it to the power of a collective psychosis" (Einstein [1932] 1963). This is a great oversimplification, since the posited "lust for hatred and destruction" exists only under certain circumstances. A more general and easily evoked human emotional state is the anger that arises in response to frustration, fear, and grief. Combined with an easy slide into dichotomous thought that may lead to pseudo-speciation, the outcome can be ethnic violence, including war or genocide. Freud wrote of his entire agreement regarding the lust for destruction, but they differed on a crucial point: For Freud, "whatever fosters the growth of culture works at the same time against war" (Freud 1932, 287). Einstein doubted the civilizing power of culture, and to the world's great sorrow, he proved the more prescient thinker. Girard appears to be closer to Einstein, but for subtler reasons.

Girard has made at least two major contributions to our discourse about violence. One is the concept of mimetic rivalry, according to which angry and competing individuals or groups in confrontation inevitably mimic one another, and in so doing escalate their rivalry into ever-greater risk of ever-greater violence. The other is the thesis of sacrificial violence, which holds that ritual sacrifice is a way of deflecting mimetic rivalry and exporting it from the community, defusing the process that otherwise results in what Hobbes called "the war of all against all." Whether impassioned and Dionysian, as in Euripides's *The Bacchae*, or controlled by the strictest ritual, as in the priestly sacrifices in the Israelite temple, the result is similar: the blood shed is that of a designated victim, and it is sacred because it prevents us from shedding one another's.

And woe to the social world if it does not. Then, to paraphrase Mark Antony in *Julius Caesar*, you "let slip the dogs of war," and the foul deed of a sacrifice not agreed upon "cries above the earth with carrion men groaning for burial." Thus, too, do the Montagues and Capulets, "both alike in dignity," destroy each other piecemeal through interminable vendetta. Not even the accidental sacrifice of poor, good, funny Mercutio, the would-be peacemaker, deflects the violence; it goes on until the (also unintended) sacrifice of what each house loves most brings both down to indignity in a common plague of ultimate loss; "*all* are punishèd."

Much earlier in the history of tragic drama, the mimetic rivalry of Eteocles and Polyneices, two sons of Oedipus, annihilates his house as they tear Thebes apart and kill each other. Then, when the one is buried with honor and the other left to rot, Antigone too must die, sealed up in the earth, for the sisterly crime of burying Polyneices. And with her she brings down the whole house of the man who condemns her.

Surely, we think, if a ritual sacrifice could avert such endless mirroring of death breeding death, it would be a gift of the gods. But the role of sacrifice is not always preventive; one-sided sacrifices can speed wars. Because in truth, "the face that launched a thousand ships and burnt the topless towers of Ilium"—and in the end toppled too the House of Atreus—was not that of Helen, but of Iphigenia, ritually slaughtered by her father Agamemnon, at Aulis, for the sake of wind.

Here we are closer to the dawn of civilization, but we are not there yet. Marx and Engels say in *The Communist Manifesto* that capitalism arose from the mud with blood oozing from every pore. This may or may not be metaphorically true of capitalism, but it is almost literally true of what we call civilization, which emerged from the mud of irrigated fertile land acquired and then protected by much slaughter.

Joining organized violence to religious zeal, early civilizations from the Yangtze to the Yucatan conquered and pacified large numbers of people who, through taxation and military service, provided resources for further expansion. Clashes with other, similar entities were frequent and inevitable. This dynamic has changed little in the thousands of years leading up to the modern age. We think we control the process, but human nature and human biology loom very large in the risk of ethnic violence and war.

In simpler ecological settings like that of the Nuer, a Nilotic people of southern Sudan, warlike tribal groups were able to form hierarchies of alliances and operate as organizations for predatory expansion. And in yet simpler and more static settings, people like the Dani and Enga of highland New Guinea and the Yanomamö of highland Venezuela sustain blood feuds and ritualized war over generations. Perhaps, as Girard suggests, the Kaingang of Brazil represent a degenerate form of this type of conflict, having slaughtered each other almost to extinction.

And yet it is possible to reach deeper, into the process of hominization, to find the origins of the violence at the heart of human life. Perhaps, in some ways, we transcended that background as we became human; perhaps ritual sacrifices enabled us to do this. But in other ways we are all too similar to our pre-hominid ancestors for whom violence may have bred violence in an unending, bloody mimetic cycle.

Conclusion

Girard's two concepts of mimetic rivalry and sacred blood spilled in sacrifice, so useful in literary and ethnographic analysis, also rest upon scientific evidence that gives bloodshed a central role in human experience. Nonhuman groups, especially those of chimpanzees, show that an elementary form of human ambush-raiding is present among them: periodically a group of males gangs up on and kills a helpless and hapless victim. Many cultures carry out violent raids with or without a ritual dimension; Ilongot headhunting and highland New Guinea raiding parties, in which multiple males ambush and crush a single victim, are two examples. In our own time, both terrorist attacks on civilians and drone strikes on suspected terrorists without due process (and their attendant civilian casualties) constitute the functional equivalent of ambush raids. Of course, as we went through the process of hominization, language, religion, and ritual made something different out of what may have been blind killing by our chimplike ancestors. But in humans too, males predominate, emotional contagion is important, and both group context and leaders facilitate bloodshed. This can at times be directed at in-group members, who cease to be protected when they are split off from all that is human. In other words, there may be a continuum from chimpanzee ambush-raiding, to human ambush-raiding, to headhunting, to ritual sacrifice, to witch hunts and lynch mobs, and finally to genocide.

However, if the enemy is not isolated and weak, but well organized and strong, and you attack him, you have the peculiarly human outcomes of pitched battle and even all-out war. Mimetic rivalry manifests itself fully, as mutual fear and contempt are increasingly justified by real changes on the ground. In a battle, two mobs mirror each other's emotional contagion, and if their leaders compel or inspire obedience, mass mutual slaughter may ensue, sometimes over generations. Religious, ethnic, and national loyalties and passions justify both sides, and with every death—every sacrifice—the cause becomes more sacred to one side or the other. Aggression is involved, but so are fear, contempt, dichotomization, emotional contagion, obedience, and the flight to the protector.

The reciprocal violence of equals may finally engender a sacrificial crisis. The twins Polyneices and Eteocles kill one another, accomplishing nothing, but soon their armies must carry out protracted mimetic slaughter. "Once violence has penetrated a community it engages in an orgy of self-propagation. There appears to be no way of bringing the reprisals to a halt before the community has been annihilated. If there are really such events as sacrificial crises, some sort of braking mechanism, an automatic control that goes into effect before everything is destroyed must be built into them. In the final stages of a sacrificial crisis the very viability of human society is put in question" (Girard 1977, 67).

And yet, Girard argues, such motives are subject to more severe and thorough repression in modern times than are the sexual motives that obsessed Sigmund Freud. There are thousands of competent behavioral and social scientists today, but only a few, mostly cited here, have grappled seriously with violence; yet the threat of violence dominates our lives as a species, and we cannot address it by escaping. In the final lines of *Violence and the Sacred*, Girard sees a coming sacrificial crisis:

> We have managed to extricate ourselves from the sacred somewhat more successfully than other societies have done, to the point of losing all memory of generative violence, but we are now about to rediscover it. The essential violence returns to us in a spectacular manner—not only in the form of a violent history but in the form of subversive knowledge. This crisis invites us, for the very first time . . . to expose to the light of reason, the role played by violence in human society. (Girard 1977, 318)

Or as Simone Weil put it in her great book *The Iliad, or the Poem of Force*: "I believe that the concept of force must be made central in any attempt to think clearly about human relations" (Weil 2006). This imperative has not been heeded by many social scientists, but the Darwinian worldview, deepened by the philosophic and literary insights of Girard, Weil, and others, urges us to stop turning away.

Note

1. A more extended discussion is available in Konner 2006b.

Works Cited

Asch, S. E. 1951. "Effects of Group Pressure upon the Modification and Distortion of Judgments." In *Groups, Leadership, and Men*, ed. H. Guetzkow, 177–90. Pittsburgh: Carnegie Press.

Bohannan, P., and American Museum of Natural History. 1967. *Law and Warfare: Studies in the Anthropology of Conflict*. Garden City, NY: Natural History Press.

Bowlby, J. 1969–77. *Attachment and Loss*. 3 vols. London: Hogarth Press.

Bowles, S. 2009. "Did Warfare among Ancestral Hunter-Gatherers Affect the Evolution of Human Social Behaviors?" *Science* 324, no. 5932: 1293–98.

Bowles, S., and H. Gintis. 2011. *The Cooperative Species: Human Reciprocity and Its Evolution*. Princeton, NJ: Princeton University Press.

Burkert, W., J. Z. Smith, et al. 1987. *Violent Origins*. Stanford, CA: Stanford University Press.

Chagnon, N. A. 1968. *Yanomamo: The Fierce People*. New York: Holt, Rinehart and Winston.

———. 1988. "Life Histories, Blood Revenge, and Warfare in a Tribal Population." *Science* 239: 985–92.

———. 1992. *Yanomamö: The Last Days of Eden*. San Diego: Harcourt Brace & Co.

Cook, M. 2003. *A Brief History of the Human Race*. London: Granta.

Culotta, E. 1999. "Neanderthals Were Cannibals, Bones Show." *Science* 286: 18–19.

Darwin, C. 1864. *On the Origins of Species by Means of Natural Selection: Or the Preservation of Favoured Races in the Struggle for Life*. New York: D. Appleton and Co.

Darwin, F., ed. 1901 *The Life and Letters of Charles Darwin*. Vol. 2. New York: Appleton.

Defleur, A., T. White, et al. 1999. "Neanderthal Cannibalism at Moula-Guercy, Ardache, France." *Science* 286: 128–31.

DeGusta, D. 1999. "Fijian Cannibalism: Evidence from Navatu." *American Journal of Physical Anthropology* 110 (October): 215–41.

Dentan, R. K. 1968. *The Semai: A Nonviolent People of Malaysia*. New York: Holt, Rinehart and Winston.

DeVore, I. 1965. "Male Dominance and Mating Behavior in Baboons." In *Sexual Behavior*, ed. F. Beach. New York: John Wiley.

Divale, W. T. 1974. "Migration, External Warfare, and Matrilocal Residence." *Behavioral Science Research* 9: 75–133.

Douglas, M. 1966. *Purity and Danger: An Analysis of Concepts of Pollution and Taboo*. New York: Praeger.

Earle, T., ed. 1991. *Chiefdoms: Power, Economy, and Ideology*. Cambridge: Cambridge University Press.

Edgerton, R. B. 1992. *Sick Societies: Challenging the Myth of Primitive Harmony*. New York: Free Press.

Eibl-Eibesfeldt, I. 1979. *The Biology of Peace and War: Men, Animals, and Aggression*. London: Thames and Hudson.

Einstein, A. [1932] 1963. "Why War? Letter to Sigmund Freud." In *Einstein on Peace*, ed. O. Nathan and H. Nordan. London: Methuen.

Ember, C. R. 1978. "Myths about Hunter-Gatherers." *Ethnology* 17, no. 4: 439–48.

Ember, M., and C. R. Ember. 1971. "The Conditions Favoring Matrilocal versus Patrilocal Residence." *American Anthropologist* 73: 571–94.

———. 1994. "Prescriptions for Peace: Policy Implications of Cross-cultural Research on War and Interpersonal Violence." *Cross-Cultural Research* 28, no. 4: 343–50.

Festinger, L. 1957. *A Theory of Cognitive Dissonance*. Evanston, IL: Row, Peterson.

Freud, S. 1932. "Why War? Letter to Albert Einstein." In *Standard Edition of the Complete Psychological Works of Sigmund Freud*, ed. J. Strachey. London: Hogarth.

———. [1922] 1949. *Group Psychology and the Analysis of the Ego*. London: Hogarth Press.

Fromm, E. 1994. *Escape from Freedom*. New York: H. Holt.

Gibbons, A. 2004. "Chimpanzee Gang Warfare." *Science* 304: 818–19.

Girard, R. 1977. *Violence and the Sacred*. Baltimore: Johns Hopkins University Press.

———. 1987. *Things Hidden since the Foundation of the World*. Stanford, CA: Stanford University Press.

Goodall, J. 1977. "Infant Killing and Cannibalism in Free-living Chimpanzees." *Folia Primatologica* 28: 259–82.

———. 1986. *The Chimpanzees of Gombe: Patterns of Behavior*. Cambridge, MA: Harvard University Press.

Goodall, J. v. L. 1979. "Life and Death at Gombe." *National Geographic Magazine* 155: 592–621.

Hatfield, E., J. T. Cacioppo, et al. 1994. *Emotional Contagion*. Cambridge: Cambridge University Press.

Hausfater, G. 1975. *Dominance and Reproduction in Baboons (Papio cynocephalus)*. Basel: Karger.

Hausfater, G., and S. B. Hrdy, eds. 1984. *Infanticide: Comparative and Evolutionary Perspectives*. New York: Aldine de Gruyter.

Hrdy, S. B. 1977. *The Langurs of Abu: Female and Male Strategies of Reproduction*. Cambridge, MA: Harvard University Press.

———. 1979. "Infanticide among Animals: A Review, Classification, and Examination of the Implications for the Reproductive Strategies of Females." *Ethology and Sociobiology* 1: 13–40.

Jakobson, R., and M. Halle. 1971. *Fundamentals of Language*. The Hague: Mouton & Co.

Kano, T. 1992. *The Last Ape: Pygmy Chimpanzee Behavior and Ecology*. Stanford, CA: Stanford University Press.

Keegan, J. 1993. *A History of Warfare*. New York: Vintage Books.

Keeley, L. H. 1996. *War before Civilization: The Myth of the Peaceful Savage*. New York: Oxford University Press.

Kelly, R. C. 1985. *The Nuer Conquest: The Structure and Development of an Expansionist System*. Ann Arbor: University of Michigan Press.

Knauft, B. 1987. "Reconsidering Violence in Simple Human Societies: Homicide among the Gebusi of New Guinea." *Current Anthropology* 28: 457–500.

Konner, M. 2006a. "Human Nature, Ethnic Violence, and War." In *The Psychology of Resolving Global Conflicts: From War to Peace*, vol. 1, ed. M. Fitzduff and C. E. Stout. Westport, CT: Praeger Security International.

———, ed. 2006b. *Human Nature, Ethnic Violence, and War*. Westport, CT: Praeger Security International.

Konner, M. J. 2002. *The Tangled Wing: Biological Constraints on the Human Spirit*. Rev. ed. New York: Holt/Times Books.

LeBlanc, S., and K. E. Register. 2003. *Constant Battles: The Myth of the Peaceful, Noble Savage*. New York: St. Martin's Press.

Lee, R. B. 1979. *The !Kung San: Men, Women and Work in a Foraging Society*. Cambridge: Cambridge University Press.

Lévi-Strauss, C. 1968. *The Savage Mind*. Chicago: University of Chicago Press.

Lewis, M., and L. Rosenblum. 1973. *The Origins of Fear*. New York: Wiley.

Lorenz, K. 1970. "What Aggression Is Good For." In *Animal Aggression: Selected Readings*, ed. C. H. Southwick. New York: Van Nostrand Reinhold.

Mackay, C. 1932. *Extraordinary Popular Delusions and the Madness of Crowds*. New York: Noonday Press.

Manson, J. H., and R. W. Wrangham. 1991. "Intergroup Aggression in Chimpanzees and Humans." *Current Anthropology* 32, no. 4 (August-October): 369–90.

Marshall, L. 1976. "Sharing, Talking, and Giving: Relief of Social Tensions among the !Kung." In *Kalahari Hunter-Gatherers: Studies of the !Kung San and Their Neighbors*, ed. R. B. Lee and I. DeVore, 349–71. Cambridge, MA: Harvard University Press.

Maybury-Lewis, D., and U. Almagor. 1989. *The Attraction of Opposites: Thought and Society in the Dualistic Mode*. Ann Arbor: University of Michigan Press.

Meggitt, M. J. 1977. *Blood Is Their Argument: Warfare among the Mae Enga Tribesmen of the New Guinea Highlands*. Palo Alto, CA: Mayfield Publishing Co.

Milgram, S. 1963. "Behavioral Study of Obedience." *Journal of Abnormal and Social Psychology* 67: 371–78.

———. 1974. *Obedience to Authority: An Experimental View*. London: Tavistock.

Niehoff, D. 1999. *The Biology of Violence: How Understanding the Brain, Behavior, and Environment Can Break the Vicious Cycle of Aggression*. New York: Free Press.

Otterbein, K. F. 1970. *The Evolution of War: A Cross-cultural Study*. New Haven, CT: Human Relations Area Files Press.

Pinker, S. 2011. *The Better Angels of Our Nature: Why Violence Has Declined*. New York: Viking.

Robinson, P., and H. Tajfel, eds. 1997. *Social Groups and Identities: Developing the Legacy of Henri Tajfel*. International Series in Social Psychology. London: Butterworth-Heinemann.

Rosaldo, R. 1980. *Ilongot Headhunting, 1883–1974: A Study in Society and History*. Stanford, CA: Stanford University Press.

Sageman, M. 2008. *Leaderless Jihad: Terror Networks in the Twenty-first Century*. Philadelphia: University of Pennsylvania Press.

Sahlins, M. D. 1961. "The Segmentary Lineage: An Organization of Predatory Expansion." *American Anthropologist* 63: 322–45.

Sanday, P. R. 1986. *Divine Hunger: Cannibalism as a Cultural System*. Cambridge: Cambridge University Press.

Schmookler, A. B. 1983. *The Parable of the Tribes: The Problem of Power in Social Evolution*. Berkeley: University of California Press.

Sherif, M., O. J. Harvey, et al. 1961. *Intergroup Conflict and Cooperation: The Robbers Cave Experiment*. Norman, OK: Institute of Group Relations.

Shostak, M. 1981. *Nisa: The Life and Words of a !Kung Woman*. Cambridge, MA: Harvard University Press.

———. 2000. *Return to Nisa*. Cambridge, MA: Harvard University Press.

Smuts, B. 1992. "Male Aggression against Women: An Evolutionary Perspective." *Human Nature* 3, no. 1: 1–44.

Smuts, B. B., and R. W. Smuts. 1993. "Male Aggression and Sexual Coercion of Females in Nonhuman Primates and Other Mammals: Evidence and Theoretical Implications." *Advances in the Study of Behavior* 22: 1–63.

Tajfel, H. 1982. *Social Identity and Intergroup Relations*. Cambridge: Cambridge University Press.

Thomas, E. M. 1959. *The Harmless People*. New York: Vintage Books.

Tiger, L. 1969. *Men in Groups*. New York: Random House.

Toynbee, A. 1972. *A Study of History*. New York: Oxford University Press.

Trinkhaus, E. 1978. "Hard Times among the Neanderthals." *Natural History* 87: 58–63.

———. 1995. *The Shanidar Neandertals*. New York: Academic Press.

Trinkhaus, E., and W. W. Howells. 1979. "The Neanderthals." *Scientific American* 241, no. 6: 118–33.

Ursin, H., and B. R. Kaada. 1960. "Functional Localization with the Amygdaloid Complex in the Cat." *Electroencephalography and Clinical Neurology* 12: 1–20.

Villa, P., et al. 1986. "Cannibalism in the Neolithic." *Science* 233: 431–37.

Wade, N. 2000. "If You Are What You Eat, Mind if I Move to Another Table? Reconsidering Cannibalism." *New York Times*, January 2, sec. 4, p. 3.

Wallen, K., and P. L. Tannenbaum. 1997. "Hormonal Modulation of Sexual Behavior and Affiliation in Rhesus Monkeys." *Annals of the New York Academy of Sciences* 807: 185–202.

Weil, S. 2006. *The Iliad, or, the Poem of Force: A Critical Edition*. New York: Peter Lang Publishing.

White, T. D. 1992. *Prehistoric Cannibalism at Mancos 5Mtumr-2346*. Princeton, NJ: Princeton University Press.

Whiting, J.W.M., and B. B. Whiting. 1975. "Aloofness and Intimacy between Husbands and Wives." *Ethos* 3: 183–207.

Wiessner, P., and N. Pupu. 2012. "Toward Peace: Foreign Arms and Indigenous Institutions in a Papua New Guinea Society." *Science* 337, no. 6102: 1651–54.

Wilson, E. O. 1975. *Sociobiology: The New Synthesis*. Cambridge, MA: Harvard University Press.

Wrangham, R. W., and D. Peterson. 1996. *Demonic Males: Apes and the Origins of Human Violence*. Boston: Houghton Mifflin.

Wynne-Edwards, V. C. 1962. *Animal Dispersion in Relation to Social Behaviour*. New York: Hafner Publishing Co.

Mechanisms of Internal Cohesion

Scapegoating and Parochial Altruism

Zoey Reeve

In the first few pages of *The Scapegoat* (1989), Girard presents a poem by Guillaume de Machaut, depicting the Jews as being responsible for the deaths of many during the plague of the mid-fourteenth century. For Girard, scapegoating captures and canalizes the socially destructive energies of acquisitive and rivalrous mimesis in humans, by discharging them against a single, arbitrarily chosen emissary victim or victim group. The Jews, in this case, were the innocent but conveniently marginal group persecuted by the masses for deaths that were in fact due to plague—i.e., to a natural disaster that no one could have possibly been responsible for. Scapegoating means taking it out on an innocent third party, under the cover of a self-mystifying and mythical accusation.

A different, but compatible, perspective on this poem (and similar events) is possible, utilizing the concept of "parochial altruism" familiar to all empirical scientists working in the field of evolutionary studies. This perspective views the drama unfolding as a form of intergroup conflict. The Jews are marked as the out-group, despite also being members of the wider community. The process of scapegoating provides this previously coherent community, currently in crisis due to the rampant spread of disease, with the occasion and the pretext for differentiating and excluding the Jews as devilish outsiders. The Jews, once members of this community, are now perceived to be intent on the destruction of that same community. The community has changed from including Jews, to excluding them. In so doing, the crisis is now relocated and redefined: it exists between groups (the community versus the Jews), rather than between all individuals who are victims of the crisis. While the process of scapegoating is the enabling mechanism, it is parochial altruism, within a context of intergroup conflict that forms the underlying plot; it directs the process of protecting the in-group, and expressing hostility towards the out-group.

Scapegoating and parochial altruism are compatible and complementary forms of explanation that can work in tandem. Both mechanisms serve to protect the in-group in contexts of perceived threat, and this is achieved primarily on the basis of categorization into "us" and "not us." The shift from a within-group to a between-groups scenario sets the scene, in an evolutionary perspective, for acts emphasizing the parochial character of group altruism; while, in mimetic theory, similarly, social unity is seen to fissure in times of crisis, producing a need to reprise the bonding pharmacology of "founding murder"—a process of which scapegoating is the consequence and the manifestation.

This reading is all the more cogent since in Girard's thought, human social bonding is, originally and always, guaranteed in the ultimate by exclusion. "We" are always one against the excluded Other: originally, the scapegoat victim of the paradigmatic "founding murder"—this act of unifying exclusion being regularly and ritually reprised in times of a return of social disorder, stress, and crisis (Girard 1989, 1978). The scapegoat mechanism, therefore, should figure on the map of evolutionary social scientists—at least as an interesting approach that offers to theorize and explain the internal cohesion of an in-group, most obviously one that is perhaps not afflicted by overt intergroup hostilities, or in which the in-group boundaries are not clear.

The Scapegoat Mechanism

Girard's theory, to recapitulate briefly, is extensive. It incorporates and explains the beginnings and evolution of religion, culture, society, and the institutions that exist to structure our society. The theory explains in particular the process of hominization—the move towards being human, and the divergence from in-group behavior in, say, chimpanzees—by homing in on the capacity of human imitation, or mimesis. The difference in humans is that they imitate one another's represented desire; and, more potently and single-mindedly than animals, they desire what the other desires because the other desires it. Humans are unique in the animal kingdom for their capacity for imitation, and it is this singular multiplier that drives human social groups into a supercharged and incremental violence. This is particularly true in moments of material or social crisis where prereflective or instinctual responses like imitation are more likely to influence behavior. Such situations include crises of internal structure, produced by pressures of increasing group size, or by natural disaster, as well as crises due to common-or-garden internal conflict, disorder, and anarchy.

Desire is not, therefore, an expression of the individual self merely; rather, and more fatefully, it is imitative and reflective of the social world the individual inhabits, and it is thus directed by culture (Garrels 2011). It is not that the object has an irresistible intrinsic value that draws individuals and groups into striving rivalrously to appropriate it. Rather, it is the very fact that the object is desired by an Other who invests it, thus conferring a superadded and overriding fascination value. Mimetic desire, therefore, points us towards the tissue of social reciprocities and social relationalities (Gallese 2011).

It also forms a special case of the functioning/malfunctioning of enhanced group intelligence in humans. For Girard, mimetic desire leads to an intolerable undifferentiation, which results as each individual separately (and all individuals corporately within a given social community) pits himself/themselves against each other/one another: first, as rivals for the object of desire (whatever that may be); but then also, as the incremental dynamic of mimetic rivalry comes into effect, as victims of the desperate attempt at asserting difference and existing more intensely and distinctly. (Girard identifies here a hidden metaphysical stake, not present in animal rivalries.) In which process, the (original) object soon becomes symbolic and is forgotten entirely. The focus becomes the business itself of the rivalry and antagonism between individuals vying for the unlimited good of more-potent-being or identity. As rivalry spirals into violence, the adversaries indeed revert to undifferentiation. They come to imitate one another in the very logic of violence that unites and drives them—an outcome that is, ironically, the reverse of their initial aspiration. Unless it is restrained or contained, the contagious dynamic of mimetic violence will spread and infect all others until society crumbles. (This runaway dynamic of contagion explains why, according to Girard, plague and flood often function in mythologies as working metaphors obliquely describing human violence.)

What Girardian scapegoat theory suggests, then, is that by channeling mimetic violence towards a seemingly random individual (or group) pointed out (or "fingered") by sometimes minute signs of marginal difference (including prior victimization), violence can be unleashed in a manner that serves to discharge the pent-up energies of violence, thus reuniting the community against this one victim (or set of victims) (Girard 1995). The scapegoat qualifies for this role by being, in some sense, from the community but not of it. Through scapegoating, the victim becomes recategorized as a dangerous outsider. As he is blamed for all its sins, the scapegoat unites the community. What is crucial here is that the persecutors do not realize that he is arbitrarily chosen and innocent; nor, indeed, that they are persecutors of innocence. The scapegoat sacrificed (i.e., made the victim of some non-ritual or [later] ritual form of bloody immolation) purges the community and enables it to recover its pre-mimetically nonviolent stage, albeit in a fragile and provisional way. The scapegoat is thus first declared responsible for the harm inflicted on the community, but then, once this mythic catharsis through scapegoat violence has pacified and transformed the collective psyche mimetically, he is declared a "divine savior," the bearer and origin of the new peace experienced (Girard 2009). The scapegoat resolution process has, therefore, the dual function of halting mimetic rivalry and violence, and of uniting the community together under a sacred sign. It is this process that accounts for the foundation of human culture (in particular, for the religious matrix within which institutions, rituals, laws, and myths develop, and which they offprint).

Parochial Altruism

Parochial altruism is a combination of altruistic, or at least cooperative, behaviors that are costly to oneself but beneficial to others—a determination having, as its obverse face, hostility towards others from outside the in-group

(Choi and Bowles 2007). The concept has also been considered in a slightly more flexible way: altruistic and cooperative tendencies are sometimes said to be parochial in the sense that they are directed only towards in-groups and in-group members and not extended to out-groups and out-group members (Bernhard, Fischbacher, and Fehr 2006; Ginges and Atran 2011; De Dreu et al. 2010; García and van den Bergh 2011). Thus this concept can range from merely withholding some benefit from out-group members, biasing and favoring in-group members, to overt aggression and hostility towards out-groups. The latter assertion is seemingly the most relevant to intergroup conflict. However, this matter is not straightforward, since the withholding of benefits from out-groups by in-group members may, of itself, give occasion and cause for conflict (De Dreu et al. 2011).

Group living is said to have evolved due to the benefits of increased group size, such as coalitional hunting, access to wider territories, capacity to gather more food, food sharing, communal caregiving for offspring, information sharing, and protection from predators, including other human groups (Buss 2005; Van Vugt and Schaller 2008).[1] If all human groups are motivated to increase group size for these benefits, then groups become potentially more threatening to one another, since larger groups require more resources and territory, and weaker (smaller) groups will lose these to bigger, stronger groups (Alexander 1974). In addition to this, out-groups may bring disease and parasites to which the in-group has no immunity, thus potentially presenting a real threat to entire groups (Schaller and Duncan 2007).

Within this logic, it would seem that humans were destined to be prone to intergroup conflict, as well as to intragroup rivalries and violence. If we follow a Girardian model, both risks, indeed, go hand in hand. The human social group, as it increases its size, confronts phases of internal instability, due to looser internal social ties—at which point it is more vulnerable to external competition and assault. It seems structurally possible, indeed probable, that the scapegoat mechanism came into play, or at least gained traction, as a way of uniting the group under pressure of external threat (and, as we have seen, the assaults of nature can appear to those suffering them to be modeled on human assaults). The scapegoating of Jews in medieval times under the threat of plague could thus have clear evolutionary antecedents, if we admit the confusion and/or self-mystification at work in the matter of causality and of subject agency within it. In the politics of later times, and indeed in our own, we very readily recognize the pattern whereby societies under stress, in crisis, or subject to external threat seek to enhance internal cohesion and combat readiness by discovering an internal enemy or scapegoat. We recall some classic cases: the French establishment "fingering" Dreyfus, in the revanchist climate prevailing in France after defeat in the Franco-Prussian War; or Hitler, denouncing the "Jewish conspiracy" during Germany's descent into anarchy after the First World War.

There is, it is recognized, a critical point at which social ties can be maintained and cohesion and cooperation remain, and this is typically limited to cliques of approximately one hundred to two hundred individuals (Dunbar 1993). Beyond this point, internal stability is threatened. It is through these smaller cliques that larger group sizes can be maintained (Dunbar 1992). There are thus two paradoxical pressures with regard to group size that are relevant. One is that increased group size would have been beneficial to fitness on the basis of protection from the threat from increasingly large out-groups. The second is that we have the cognitive capacity to deal with limited numbers of others before the group starts to fracture. The pressure then is at once to increase group size, so as to fend off encroaching and threatening out-groups, and to reduce group size to maintain internal cooperation and stability.

Choi and Bowles address the question of why out-group hostility and intergroup conflict were so common in our ancestral history, with their model of the coevolution of war and parochial altruism (2007). They suggest that parochialism and altruism could coevolve in the correct conditions: if most altruists were parochial and vice versa; if most parochial altruists were members of a group with other parochial altruists; and if competition over resources favored groups high in parochial altruists (individuals willing to risk life and limb in conflict with out-groups, for the benefit of in-group members) (Bowles and Gintis 2013). The benefits of parochial altruism would thus have compensated the costs of such behavior at an individual level (within-group selection). Such benefits would amount to the obtaining or maintenance of resources, territory, and mates, which are all vital to the fitness of all individuals, and all groups of individuals.

If one group of individuals has more of these resources than another, then that group is more fit (in terms of survival and reproductivity); thus all groups will be motivated to increase or maintain access to those resources.

Out-groups are therefore potential threats to in-groups because they are likely to be in competition for resources (food, water, shelter, territory, mates) (e.g., McDonald, Navarrete, and Van Vugt 2012). Intergroup conflict in terms of parochial altruism occurs because an in-group is favoring and defending its members from a potentially threatening out-group. While neighboring tribes need not be threatening in some contexts (e.g., times of plenty), they may well be when resources run scarce, or disease has reduced the population (or the group's capacity to hunt and gather food). In any case, the in-group is always favored because it is vital to the fitness of the individuals within it. In cases where resources become scarce, whether due to increasing population size or natural disasters, in-group members—in the form of coalitional groups—may encroach on the territory of neighboring others in order to sustain their in-group members, even if this is to the detriment of other groups. Those other groups, whose territory may be encroached upon, are similarly motivated by sustaining or enhancing their own group fitness, to defend that territory and those resources or risk the demise of their in-group. It is in this way that groups are parochially altruistic or cooperative—they seek to maintain and enhance their own group's survival and fitness, even if that means reducing that of another group. The combination of parochially altruistic members, and the threat of death by intergroup competition suggests that the parochial altruism mechanism would have enabled group cooperation and cohesion in times of conflict with out-groups (Choi and Bowles 2007).

The claim by Girard that the wars of early human history are not reducible to this sole logic of parochial altruism as triggered by material context (with its attendant motivations of resource control and defense/gain) is, however, worthy of attention at this point. Some wars are purely ritualistic/antagonistic in origin.[2] The Yąnomamö, for instance, practice a type of low-level warfare that is a graded form of conflict, and is thus ritualized, enabling males to practice and display their skills and courage in battle, but in conditions less likely to lead to death (although death rates are still remarkably high for this tribe) (Chagnon 1968).

The Biological Basis of Parochial Altruism and Its Adequacy as Explicator

Empirical research on parochial altruism is sparse and has mostly favored economic games, punishment experiments, economic models, and the hormone/neurotransmitter oxytocin (Bernhard, Fischbacher, Fehr 2006; Choi and Bowles 2007; De Dreu 2012; Baumgartner et al. 2012; Abbink et al. 2012). A majority of the research has been conducted using oxytocin. Oxytocin is a hormone and neurotransmitter that has been associated with empathy and parochial altruism (De Dreu et al. 2011, see also Churchland and Winkielman 2012; Hurlbut 1997). It has been shown to induce categorization of in-group and not in-group, regulate intergroup conflict; increase trust and cooperation for the in-group; influence noncooperation with out-groups, particularly in situations of perceived out-group threat; modulate social recognition and avoidance of socially relevant potential pathogenic threats; trigger risk-averse behavioral responses in the event of a dearth of social information; decrease fairness and adherence to norms in contexts in which interaction is with members of a perceived out-group; influence ally choices; and facilitate accurate perceptions of intergroup conflict—in males, but not in females.[3] The latter study is important because it indicates sex differences in perceptions of intergroup conflict, which has been proposed in other research.[4] This indicates that oxytocin may be a crucial element in mimesis (Hurlbut 1997, 2011). However, due to the nature of mimesis, conflict may result because inter-individual comparisons are important in sociality, and admiration of positively perceived others may lead to mimetic rivalry (Hurlbut 2011).

This brief section on oxytocin is included because it indicates that there may be a biological basis of parochial altruism. Trust and cooperation may be bounded by parochialism—or group membership, particularly in intergroup scenarios, which also means that oxytocin is vital to the categorization process (De Dreu 2012). This effect is enhanced by the presence of perceived threat from an out-group. Two other features of oxytocin and parochial altruism are relevant here. One is that these studies have not typically shown oxytocin to influence levels of out-group hostility, which remain stable whether participants are given a placebo or oxytocin (De Dreu et al. 2011).

This could suggest that there is a sort of base level of out-group hostility, and/or that its manifestation is influenced by individual differences, including perceptions of the out-group (Hein et al. 2010; Konner 2011). Even the seemingly most nonviolent tribes could be roused to violence when the situation inspires it, indicating the importance of context, and suggesting that culture and upbringing cannot solely explain our penchant for violence, although they may certainly be influential in directing it (Konner 2011). In order to act on out-group hostility, one must be able to perceive differences between the in-group and out-groups. The capacity to recognize and adhere to group boundaries is at the heart of the concept of parochialism. The capacity to differentiate between friend and foe, in-group and out-group, kin and strangers, would have been vital for human survival, and since strangers (including out-group members) would have presented individuals and groups with particular threats, being wary of them rather than merely indifferent or ambiguous would also have been an important survival strategy. Thus, as Konner suggests, our "tendency to dichotomize the social world" as a result of mimetic rivalry and the propensity to violence is related to a low tolerance for ambiguity and cognitive dissonance that would have been vital for our ancestors to ensure fast and accurate behavioral responses to novel and/or threatening contexts (Konner 2011, 165).[5]

The second important feature is that there are sex differences in intergroup conflict, in that males are typically considered the more belligerent, the warriors, and this is also why most research using oxytocin uses male subjects (Van Vugt 2009; De Dreu et al. 2010). Research that has compared males and females in oxytocin conditions has shown that it increases the capacity of males to perceive intergroup conflict, but not of females, whose capacity to discern kinship is instead enhanced (Fischer-Shofty, Levkovitz, and Shamay-Tsoory 2012). This sex difference is important here because Girard's mimetic desire and rivalry does not seem to distinguish between males and females, yet they appear to have differential responses to oxytocin and perceptions of intergroup conflict.

The strongest evidence for sex differences is found in aggression, with males being more aggressive than females, and some have suggested that aggression is the antithesis of nurturance—the latter, of course, being typically a more feminine trait (Konner 1982, 119). Importantly, aggression has been shown to be mediated by testosterone, and testosterone levels can be influenced by situation (Konner 1982). In competition, particularly intergroup competition, males will typically have raised levels of testosterone before the competition, and after, providing they (or their group) win; testosterone levels tend to be lower in the losers of competition (Oliveira, Gouveia, and Oliveira 2009; Booth et al. 1989). This can extend even to vicarious competition, in which individuals identifying with a competing winning or losing group will also show similar patterns of testosterone levels by merely watching the events unfold[6] (Bernhardt et al. 1998). Other studies have shown that aggression, overconfidence, and a willingness to attack without provocation are a distinctly male set of traits that is linked to testosterone levels (Johnson et al. 2006). Interestingly, however, some studies have shown that this influence of testosterone in intergroup competition is also found in females (Oliveira, Gouveia, and Oliveira 2009). This indicates that although testosterone plays an important role in competition, it is perhaps not the sole explanation for sex differences in aggression, and may be tied to differences in male and female brain structures (Konner 1982). However, another important consideration to bear in mind is that in competition, males express not only higher levels of testosterone but also increased levels of cooperation (Huoviala and Rantala 2013; Van Vugt, De Cremer, and Janssen 2007). This suggests an important and intricate interaction between biology and context that is mediated by culture, the latter because males are typically encouraged to be warriors and females are not (Gelfand et al. 2012; Konner 1982, 2011; McDonald, Navarrete, and Van Vugt 2012).

Scapegoating and Parochial Altruism

Parochial altruism enables cooperation and cohesion in situations of intergroup competition and conflict. What must also be present, however, is the capacity to maintain cooperative and cohesive groups, especially in larger numbers. While pressure from external groups (i.e., large out-groups) brings an in-group together to fight for its survival and fitness, internal pressures from weak social ties and instability (perhaps in the absence of external pressure and threat) also threaten the survival and fitness of the group by way of inhibited cooperation and cohesion, and a propensity towards mimetic rivalry and violence. The scapegoating mechanism therefore enables groups to direct internal instability that would otherwise lead to debilitating violence within the group, towards particular sections of the group, thus enabling the maintenance of cooperation and cohesion in increasingly large groups, and outcompeting other groups lacking such internally stabilizing mechanisms.

Both parochial altruism and scapegoating mechanisms work to emphasize the group over individuals, and protect the in-group from some sort of threat. Cooperation, cohesion, and unity within the group are improved by the presence of an enemy that is perceived to threaten the safety of the in-group. The enemy (scapegoat or out-group) is considered to be the cause, or potential cause, of problems faced by the group, and that cause is always located outside of the group. For Girard, this is the manner in which mythical thinking is constructed—a new act of differentiation quelling the violence and the threat created by *un*differentiation within a community (Girard 1995). In situations that are very threatening, such as natural disasters and disease, the blamed enemy's destruction is considered just and necessary in order to rid the group of the (potential) problems it faces. The cohesion of individuals within the group is vital to the functioning of the group, and is enhanced when a threat is perceived as outside of the group (rather than internal to it). What constitutes and defines myth, for Girard, is largely the fact that causal agency is externalized and disguised in the telling of the story.

Durham (1991) provides some telling examples of the link between externally directed violence and internal cohesion. In directing conflict outwards, to non-Mundurucú tribes, coherence and cooperation between Mundurucú villages was maintained, and mimetic rivalry within the tribe was avoided. This is clearly at odds with the Yąnomamö who were frequently warring between villages of other Yąnomamö (Chagnon 1983). In terms of parochial altruism, the Mundurucú were clearly protecting the in-group from resource encroachment by other groups, and they were scapegoating their enemies in the interests of their own group coherence and well-being. There was a shift to males marrying outside of natal groups, which meant that intragroup competition between Mundurucú villages would have led to competition and aggression between kin groups. Although neighboring Mundurucú villages were as much competition for scarce game as neighboring non-Mundurucú villages, directing competition and aggression against non-Mundurucú, and imposing sacred beliefs onto the trophy heads, enabled cooperation and coherence within the group, and enhanced the fitness of that group by reducing the capacity of other groups to impinge on the scarce resources needed to sustain the Mundurucú communities.

Whereas the scapegoating mechanism protects the group from its own violence, parochial altruism intervenes to protect the in-group from the out-group; unless we choose to follow the logic of the example given above and conclude simply that these two perspectives of theory are so intertwined and largely exchangeable that the difference is finally one of semantic footprint, perspective, and focus—and preferred terminology. Either way, it is perhaps the threat to the community that triggers the assertion of group interest, so that individuals within it shift their mimetic violence away from each other and onto a victim who is mythically perceived to be the cause of this threat. This shift, therefore, promotes group interest and directs a community's own violence away from itself via the scapegoating process. At which point, the rejected insider becomes a prefigure or avatar of the Other group encountered in externally directed warfare. In both cases, there is a mobilized in-group self-assertion and a scapegoating of the Other; and there are shifting boundaries in the perception of Self-and-Other.

From a parochial altruism perspective, individuals are typically viewed as group members, as the fitness of the group overall is vital to the fitness of individuals within the group, which is why it must compete with other groups for fitness-enhancing resources (De Dreu et al. 2010). However, this can also be regarded as self-interest since individuals within a group benefit from parochial altruism because if their group is strong and fit (with access to resources and territory), the members will be as well (Gelfand et al. 2012). Thus, there is an element of both self- and group interest with parochial altruism that influences the way in which individuals within a group behave towards one another (i.e., they cooperate with each other but do not lend that cooperation towards out-groups), and the same can be said in the operation of the scapegoat mechanism. In addition, research with oxytocin has shown that it (oxytocin) works at a group level in that individuals administered with it will seek to protect vulnerable in-group members from threatening out-group members, even where his/her individual self-interest is not threatened (De Dreu, Shalvi, et al. 2012). This suggests that cooperation within the group rather than rivalry, and group interest rather than pure self-interest, is already present to an extent within the group, even in intergroup competition situations, and that it has a biological underpinning. The process of scapegoating, then, may well be viewed as one in which cooperation and group interest can be spawned out of the chaotic partisan violence of the mimetic crisis—which is certainly compatible with the scenario of good mimesis replacing bad, as often envisaged in Girardian thinking.

Individuals, in both theories, are not always bound to mimetic desire and rivalry, even in situations such as intergroup threat. When oxytocin was given to males in an intergroup competition scenario, they were more likely to choose more threatening allies than those given a placebo, who typically chose low-threat allies (De Dreu, Greer, et al. 2012). If oxytocin triggers group interest, homing in on intergroup threats to the in-group, the focus of individuals will be in terms of allies that can protect the group according to that threat. When intergroup threat was less relevant to the individual, self-interest in ally choice occurred such that *less* threatening allies were preferred. Yet where intergroup threat was perceived, ally choices were *more* threatening to the individual but also more useful in intergroup conflict. This suggests that there may be something different about intergroup conflict that is not sufficiently explained by Girard's theory—even if mimetic rivalry between groups is a potent explicator and a superactive form of parochial altruism, mirroring the intragroup situation in external projection. It will be well in clarifying this thought to look at the ambiguous social location and identity profile of the scapegoat—like the community (and therefore able to represent it in ritual sacrifice), but rejected from it (and therefore like its Others and potential enemies).

Context of Threat

With regard to parochial altruism, the out-group (which is a position also held by the in-group) is always a potential threat (Choi and Bowles 2007). It is a threat by way of disease and parasites, encroaching on vital, scarce resources and territory, and overt threats to the appropriation of territory and resources (Schaller, Park, and Faulkner 2003; Neuberg, Kenrick, and Schaller 2011; Faulkner et al. 2004; Van Vugt and Park 2009; Girard 1989). Related to this is the perception of objects. For Girard, the objects of desire themselves are not as important as the desire of obtaining that object held by others. It is the value placed on the object by the individual who desires it, rather than the intrinsic value of the object itself that triggers mimetic desire in others. Individuals model themselves on the other who desires (or has obtained) that object. Desire for the object becomes increasingly symbolic, but the object is soon forgotten as rivalry takes over. Clearly, this does not exclude the view that the objects of mimetic desire (resources) would have been directly related to fitness for our ancestors. Desires for food, territory, and other resources, including mates, are all directly related to reproductive success and fitness. Even the desire for something as seemingly abstract as status brings with it tangible benefits for fitness (e.g., Von Rueden, Gurven, and Kaplan 2011). The desire for objects therefore occurs between groups, in intergroup contexts, as the later Girard also acknowledges (but see Bowles 2006, 2012), and the objects themselves often have some kind of fitness value. Of course, desire for these fitness-enhancing objects can and does occur within the group also, and this is why there are dominance hierarchies and leveling norms designed to attempt to inhibit the potential for overly destructive within-group competition. The distinctive Girardian emphasis here would seem to be that where mechanisms inherited from animal nature fall short and fail to meet the mimetic desire surge in man, or the perils that come with it, the scapegoat mechanism does bring a cultural containment—and indeed founds all culture as a matrix of containment and group identity.

The Kwakwaka'wakw are interesting in this context, because they use a form of gift-giving ("potlatch") to address socioeconomic conditions and redistribute wealth and resources, particularly in winter, a procedure that has supposedly replaced warfare as a form of competition (Paper 2007). Gift-giving is related to prestige, with enhanced status and validation of social rank being proportionate to the gifts being offered. Those with higher status give more, and are held in higher esteem because of that. In a sense, competition between these tribes tends to entail attempts to be the best giver, thereby enhancing the status and prestige of the giver. But this also includes the destruction of gifts. In order to outcompete another clan, a clan would be required to destroy more of their own gifts, or those of higher worth. And so the cycle continues. The destruction of gifts symbolizes the wealth and surplus of the destroying group, which further bestows on them prestige and status relative to less wealthy others.

Perhaps these gifts are symbolically utilized in the same way that Girard argues that agriculture and domesticated animals were—as sacrificial substitutes (Girard 1995). Or perhaps during these gifting competitions, the intrinsic value of the goods become mimetically distorted as clans seek to outcompete other clans by indicating that their wealth is so prosperous that they can afford to destroy gifts. In this case, the ritual becomes as much about status as resource redistribution, and this is indicative of the way in which mimetic desire and rivalry can take hold.

Fortunately for the Kwakwaka'wakw, their mimetic rivalry is bound up with group altruism and redistribution of material resources. But competition between groups often takes on a more negative form, particularly for males. The sex differences found in perceptions and participation in intergroup conflict do not seem, at first sight, to fit well in Girard's framework given that if it evolved as a mechanism, then presumably all individuals irrespective of their sex would present mimetic desire and mimetic rivalry in the same way. As it happens, males and females react very differently to intergroup conflict, but presumably not to scapegoating.[7]

However, there may be a clue to this apparently awkward exception, if we consider that mimetic rivalry generates at its apex a transcending (sacred, divine) persuasion, i.e., a cogency that compels—and so unites—all. If so, the exception points to the exceptional significance of the mechanism of emissary victimization or scapegoating. Something as unique as this, operating at this strategic crossroads of intra- and intergroup dynamics, having this degree of potency for the archaic mind, could indeed explain by which processes, in which sacred space, the novelty of human culture actually came into being.

Sex differences in intergroup conflict can be related to the influence of hormones, neurotransmitters, and brain structures, as well as societal and cultural pressures. It has been suggested that these sex differences are due to sexual selection because pressures and mating preferences were different for ancestral males and females (Wrangham 1999). Females required resources and protection for themselves and their offspring, and were thus likely to prefer males that could provide these. Males were therefore motivated to seek status in terms of resources and be willing to defend that status (i.e., resources including females) from other males in order to gain/maintain reproductive access (Von Rueden, Gurven, and Kaplan 2011). This can occur both within and between groups (Wrangham 1999; Wrangham and Peterson 1997).

Females respond to in-groups in the same way as males: with preference and bias. However, female perceptions and behavioral responses to out-groups differ in terms of inclinations towards fear and avoidance rather than to hostility and aggression, as is the general inclination of males (Van Vugt, De Cremer, and Janssen 2007; McDonald, Navarrete, and Van Vugt 2012; Van Vugt and Park 2009). This in-group bias is an important similarity and is perhaps why the scapegoating process can occur with reasonable consistency across both sexes. This would indicate, however, that the particular function of scapegoating is in-group bias and not out-group hostility, supporting the notion that scapegoating may have evolved to protect and unite the in-group, but suggesting that the latter requires another level of explanation to deal with the violence attributed to males (Van Vugt 2009; McDonald, Navarrete, and Van Vugt 2012).

Given that the core of both scapegoating and parochial altruism entails the capacity to effectively categorize and dichotomize between the in-group and the out-group/scapegoat, this aspect of the process is perhaps not differentiated according to sex. Yet, the underlying causes or the roots of the attitudes may be different. Males are threatening to other males (within and between groups according to context) because their capacity to retain access to territory and females dictates their reproductive fitness (Von Rueden, Gurven, and Kaplan 2011; Wrangham 1999). Females, however, are at risk of sexual coercion and infanticide by other males (typically in between-group situations, though possibly within-group also, although this is context dependent) (Navarrete et al. 2009; Wrangham and Peterson 1997). These different roots lead to differences in behavioral response (male aggression versus female avoidance), but still the capacity to recognize and adhere to group boundaries is the same.

Thus, the two theories of scapegoating and parochial altruism may appear convergent in this respect, despite agreed differences over sex difference. More fundamentally, we have touched on the possibility that no incompatibility exists between a perspective of theory that explains in one logic, at one level, and another perspective of theory that attempts to show why that first level and its logic are, in specified circumstances, transcended. It would seem we need both of these perspectives if we are looking at one and the same time for continuity and for the emergence of novelty—if we are hoping to catch up (in a cognitive sense) with evolutionary process.

Process of Categorization

The unity of the group is achieved in both scapegoating and parochial altruism, in the face of apparent threat by some outsider. The contexts in which unity and group interest are achieved are somewhat different, but the processes lead to the same outcome. For scapegoating to occur, a tipping point at which mimetic crisis boils over inhibits the capacity of social structures to maintain order. At this point, individuals appear self-interested as they engage in a struggle to survive the relentless tide of mimetic violence. Thus, violence within a group occurs because of undifferentiation between individuals and parties or factions, and this is particularly likely in the event of natural disasters and disease. When factions compete and conflict with one another, they are increasingly undifferentiated as they become embroiled in a cycle of reciprocal violence and vengeance (Girard 2009). Desire to obtain important (reproduction-enhancing) objects leads to initial between-group rivalry, and the inevitable mimetic violence that drives conflict makes rival groups seem identical in terms of attitudes and behavior, their strategies of mastery, and their bloodlust.

Where scapegoating and parochial altruism appear to converge is at the point at which the in-group unites against a perceived threatening outsider. The apparent difference is that, in intergroup conflict, at the point where group altruism declares itself parochial by active hostility, the distinction between the in-group and out-group is already extant and evident. Where internal infighting develops within the mimetic crisis, the point at which the victim is designated as threatening outsider is due to the mimetic process of scapegoat designation: a rage-modeling leader points the finger and all throw themselves upon the victim. Yet, as we have seen, the first situation is prefigured in the second: the scapegoat, if he were not killed, becomes like the enemy, and had he not been killed, might have joined the enemy. The in-group will similarly have such rage-modeling leaders who finger the external enemy and mobilize mass feeling in preparation for intergroup warfare. So that what we see in these two "different" images is that, when superimposed one on the other, they show at work—actually moving through its various possible figures—the fundamental dynamic plotted in different terms by both theories. Categorization and dichotomization are the same in different figures, at different moments.

The distinction between intragroup and intergroup violence becomes decidedly blurred if one considers tribes like the Tupinamba. The Tupinamba ritually sacrifice captured out-group members after a period in which they are symbolically incorporated into the community. The victim is thus an outsider who becomes a member of the community, albeit peripherally and provisionally so, since he is always destined ultimately to be a scapegoat. His immolation dispels the tensions and violence within the community, leading it back to cohesion (Girard 1995). Here is the case that, we said, might repay attention. For what we are seeing here is that a very strange and special category is being created: a category of "citizen" sufficiently incorporated to be representative of the community, yet sufficiently different and peripheral to be sacrificed in both archaic and modern senses. Unless both conditions are fulfilled, the scapegoat will have no potency, and no purgation of the ills of the social group will occur. His civil status and his destiny are dictated solely by the ritual function for which he is being prepared. It could not be clearer that human society functions ritually and symbolically, and not simply in terms of the instinctual-environmental pressures that entirely explain the functioning of animal groups.

This intergroup distinction is a vital notion for parochial altruism because parochialism above all implies a recognition of, and adherence to, group boundaries (Bernhard, Fischbacher, and Fehr 2006; Ginges and Atran 2011; De Dreu et al. 2010; García and van den Bergh 2011). The Tupinamba case bends the theoretical perspective, because an enemy is deliberately brought into the community and symbolically incorporated as a group member. However, the purpose he serves is still to protect the group from the peril of internally or externally generated violence. At which point, this case points us towards something else: the representative victim has also to elicit a credible verdict of "not *really* one of us," and especially the verdict "not a victim, rather an enemy." Otherwise the sacrifice, instead of curtailing violence and pacifying disorder, will do the opposite; it will relaunch violence motivated by revenge from within the community. Here Girardian theory, because it bends the rules, helps us to think outside the box. It does not abolish the rules, since the general process observed still rests on differentiating an individual as a scapegoat from the rest of the group. But it does defer their application, at least for the time it takes to achieve a more comprehensive and balanced understanding.

And here is a something more that it helps us understand. The scapegoat figure or emissary victim, now designated a threatening outsider, is considered less than human by his persecutors in much the same way as threatening out-groups are considered less than human by in-groups. The victim is differentiated and dehumanized by the rest of society—he is not one of them, despite his in-group status (albeit hybrid and marginal). In intergroup scenarios, in-groups and out-groups are already categorized as separate, and in-groups tend to be ethnocentric and may perceive out-groups as less than human, particularly if they are perceived to be threats to the in-group (Waytz and Epley 2012). This dehumanization may act to enhance justification for killing the enemy. It could also be suggested that this is part of the function of categorization and in-group bias (e.g., Reicher, Haslam, and Rath 2008). We do know that archaic tribes often used terms designating themselves as "the people" or "the human beings of the tribe," implicitly or explicitly reserving for other groups the label or category of "non-people," "nonhumans."

In other words, instances of in-group bias can appear as if they were instances of out-group hostility, and it is very difficult to tease them apart (De Dreu et al. 2011; see also McDonald, Navarrete, and Van Vugt 2012). The Yąnomamö, for example, consider themselves to be the only real humans, from which the rest of the (inferior) human race was spawned (Chagnon 1983). This is despite the rest of the human race not necessarily posing the same level of immediate threat as neighboring Yąnomamö. Two issues seem important here: one is that context is crucial. The Yąnomamö derogate and dehumanize their neighbors in times of conflict with them, yet when the comparison is between the Yąnomamö and the rest of the human race, the Yąnomamö as a collective are considered superior. Secondly, the notion that the rest of the human race is inferior is not necessarily an example of out-group hostility, though it is certainly dehumanization. Rather, it is a statement of in-group bias and differentiation. The Mundurucú have similar distinctions. Differentiation allows these groups to know who they are, based on who they are not, in particular contexts. In both cases, the Yąnomamö and the Mundurucú are superior and distinct from all other human groups. This in itself provides internal cohesion. The other is considered less than human, particularly when he presents (or is perceived to present) a threat to the group. In-groups may always be biased against out-groups and potential scapegoats, and therefore dehumanize them, but it seems that it is only under contexts of threat and perceived threat that dehumanization becomes related to justification for killing (e.g., Reicher, Haslam, and Rath 2008; Waytz and Epley 2012).

The targeting and killing of the scapegoat has the power to halt the progression of mimetic rivalry so that violence does not destroy the community, directing it unanimously onto one individual (or a group), thereby uniting the previously disparate community, albeit temporarily. If successful in intergroup conflict, to the extent of destroying the opposing group, an in-group will not only halt the violence between the groups, assuring its own safety; it may obtain more resources, thereby enhancing its fitness (and that of its members). Scapegoating is probably, in its initial impetus at least, a self-organizing (rather than a calculated and deliberately engineered) movement; while the decision to engage in intergroup conflict for the purpose of defending an in-group (by way of destroying the threatening out-groups' capacity to encroach on resources, etc.) is a perhaps rather more rational and pragmatic process. Yet, as Girard points out (1978, 1989), scapegoating itself undergoes a ritual elaboration in time, which does imply an increasing quotient of awareness and calculation.

However, if the intergroup conflict is along the lines of the raiding parties typical to ancestral intergroup conflict scenarios (e.g., Wrangham 1999), then the groups will be engaged in a self-perpetuating spiral of revenge attacks such as those seen by Chagnon in the Yąnomamö (Chagnon 1983; Wrangham 1999; Wrangham, Wilson, and Muller 2006). While this is likely to strengthen ties within the group (due to the constant threat of out-group attack), the violence between the groups is escalated rather than reduced (Girard 1978). Yet, as we have seen, the scapegoating mechanism avoids this to an extent because the sacrificial victim is often peripheral to the community, rather than integral. In such cases, the cycle of violence is halted because the choice of victim is unlikely to trigger vengeance in response (Girard 1995).

Indeed, Chagnon noted an event in which conflict between two groups of Yąnomamö had spiraled into reciprocal vengeance, over a woman. Ultimately, the woman was killed, as she was considered to be the cause of the violence and her death served to inhibit it (Chagnon 1983). So it would appear that even in intergroup conflict situations, the cycle of revenge may be halted by the expedient of sacrificing a victim.

Conclusion

The scapegoat mechanism, we said at the outset, should figure on the map of evolutionary social scientists—at least as an interesting approach. We can now clarify: it should figure, at least, in explaining the internal cohesion of an in-group that is perhaps not afflicted by overt intergroup hostilities, or in which the in-group boundaries are not clear. Perhaps then also: the scapegoat theory may provide insight into the way in which groups might redefine their boundaries in the grip of internal crises. And beyond that, one glimpses a sense in which the very transmission of parochial altruism itself, as a viable and survival-enhancing *mode d'être* from the higher primates to specifically human groups, might have happened in continuity, via transforming variations, through the uniquely sensitive and strategically placed mechanism of emissary victimization, or scapegoating as described by Girard.

I do not in the least claim here to have assessed the validity or otherwise of Girard's theory of hominization; but I do see clearly that scapegoating had a great deal to do with "how we became human." What theory, as such, certainly does for the empirical practice of evolutionary science is to envisage a larger picture vividly, allowing the practitioner to hypothesize advisedly and fruitfully in creating testable proposals of sense.

Does not Darwin's own theory of the evolution of species by natural selection itself claim just that—very major—virtue?

Notes

1. This is despite the many costs of group living, such as increased competition within and between groups for resources (including mates), and increased risk of contagious disease and parasites (Alexander 1974).
2. See also William Durham in this volume. A recent study on the subject is Douglas P. Fry and Patrik Söderberg, "Lethal Aggression in Mobile Forager Bands and Implications for the Origins of War," *Science* 341, no. 6143 (19 July 2013): 270–73.
3. See De Dreu, Greeg, et al. 2012; De Dreu, Shalvi, et al.; De Dreu et al. 2010; De Dreu 2012; Van IJzendoorn and Bakermans-Kranenburg 2012; De Dreu et al. 2011; Kosfeld et al. 2005; Israel et al. 2012; Kavaliers and Choleris 2011; Declerck, Boone, and Kiyonari 2010; Radke and De Bruijn 2012; Fischer-Shofty, Levkovitz, and Shamay-Tsoory 2012.
4. See Van Vugt, De Cremer, and Janssen 2007; Van Vugt 2009; McDonald, Navarrete, and Van Vugt 2012; Yuki and Yokota 2009.
5. Oxytocin alone, however, may be an insufficient explicator in the game of evolutionary causalities.

For Girard, culture and biology are continuously operative in the same field, woven and rewoven into a kaleidoscope of patterns. But if by "culture," we mean the structuring practices and institutions, the bonding rituals and values, that structurally order the life of the social group, then the larger role of culture in human origins is to provide the fail-safe mechanisms that limit the potential harm done by the oxytocin rush. Culture balances out or compensates for nature—and the more crucially so as the effects of biological nature are supercharged by the novel power and the novel peril of human mimesis. The scapegoat mechanism looks here to be a lightning conductor and a fine-tuning mechanism, developing at the point of intersection of intra- and intergroup conflicts, in a way that is crucially enabling to the novelty-in-nature that is humankind.

6. However, this pattern of results has not always been found to be consistent (see Gonzalez-Bono et al. 1999; Van der Meij et al. 2012).

7. In mythology, however, women participated in ritual sacrifice, as in the case of the Erinyes, literally the avengers, from Greek *erineinÿ*, "pursue, persecute."

Works Cited

Abbink, K., et al. 2012. "Parochial Altruism in Inter-group Conflicts." *Economics Letters* 117, no. 1: 45–48.

Alexander, R. D. 1974. "The Evolution of Social Behaviour." *Annual Review of Ecological Systems* 171: 325–83.

Baumgartner, T., et al. 2012. "The Mentalizing Network Orchestrates the Impact of Parochial Altruism on Social Norm Enforcement." *Human Brain Mapping* 33, no. 6: 1452–69.

Bernhard, H., U. Fischbacher, and E. Fehr. 2006. "Parochial Altruism in Humans." *Nature* 442, no. 7105: 912–15.

Bernhardt, P. C., J. M. Dabbs, J.A. Fielden, and C. D. Lutter. 1998. "Testosterone Changes during Vicarious Experiences of Winning and Losing among Fans at Sporting Events." *Physiology & Behavior* 65, no. 1: 59–62.

Booth, A., et al. 1989. "Testosterone and Winning and Losing in Human Competition." *Hormones and Behavior* 23, no. 4: 556–71.

Bowles, S. 2006. "Group Competition, Reproductive Leveling, and the Evolution of Human Altruism." *Science* 314, no. 5805: 1569–72.

———. 2012. "Warriors, Levelers, and the Role of Conflict in Human Social Evolution." *Science* 336, no. 6083: 876–79.

Bowles, S., and H. Gintis 2013. *A Cooperative Species: Human Reciprocity and its Evolution*. Princeton, NJ: Princeton University Press.

Buss, D. M. 2005. *Handbook of Evolutionary Psychology*. Hoboken, NJ: Wiley.

Chagnon, N. A. 1968. "Yanomamö Social Organization and Warfare." In *War: The Anthropology of Armed Conflict and Aggression*, ed. M. Fried, M. Harris, and R. Murphy, 109–59. New York: Natural History Press.

———. 1983. *Yąnomamö: The Fierce People*. London: Holt, Rinehart and Winston.

Choi, J.-K., and S. Bowles. 2007. "The Coevolution of Parochial Altruism and War." *Science* 318, no. 5850: 636–40.

Churchland, P. S., and P. Winkielman. 2012. "Modulating Social Behavior with Oxytocin: How Does It Work? What Does It Mean?" *Hormones and Behavior* 61, no. 3: 392–99.

Declerck, C. H., C. Boone, and T. Kiyonari. 2010. "Oxytocin and Cooperation under Conditions of Uncertainty: The Modulating Role of Incentives and Social Information." *Hormones and Behavior* 57, no. 3: 368–74.

De Dreu, C.K.W. 2012. "Oxytocin Modulates Cooperation within and Competition between Groups: An Integrative Review and Research Agenda." *Hormones and Behavior* 61, no. 3: 419–28.

De Dreu, C.K.W., L. L. Greer, et al. 2012. "Oxytocin Modulates Selection of Allies in Intergroup Conflict." *Proceedings of the Royal Society B: Biological Sciences* 279, no. 1731: 1150–54.

De Dreu, C.K.W., S. Shalvi, et al. 2012. "Oxytocin Motivates Non-cooperation in Intergroup Conflict to Protect Vulnerable In-group Members." *PloS One* 7, no. 11: 1–7.

De Dreu, C.K.W., et al. 2010. "The Neuropeptide Oxytocin Regulates Parochial Altruism in Intergroup Conflict among Humans." *Science* 328, no. 5984: 1408–11.

De Dreu, C.K.W., et al. 2011. "Oxytocin Promotes Human Ethnocentrism." *Proceedings of the National Academy of Sciences of the United States of America* 108, no. 4: 1262–66.

Dunbar, R.I.M. 1992. Neocortex Size as a Constraint on Group Size in Primates. *Journal of Human Evolution* 20: 469–93.

———. 1993. "Coevolution of Neocortical Size, Group Size and Language in Humans." *Behavioural and Brain Sciences* 16: 681–735.

Durham, W. 1991. *Coevolution: Genes, Culture and Human Diversity*. Stanford, CA: Stanford University Press.

Faulkner, J., et al. 2004. "Evolved Disease-Avoidance Mechanisms and Contemporary Xenophobic Attitudes." *Group Processes & Intergroup Relations* 7, no. 4: 333–53.

Fischer-Shofty, M., Y. Levkovitz, and S. G. Shamay-Tsoory. 2013. "Oxytocin Facilitates Accurate Perception of Competition in Men and Kinship in Women." *Social Cognitive and Affective Neuroscience* 8: 313–17. doi:10.1093/scan/nsr100.

Gallese, V. 2011. "The Two Sides of Mimesis: Mimetic Theory, Embodied Simulation, and Social Identification." In *Mimesis and Science*, ed. S. R. Garrels, 87–108. East Lansing: Michigan State University Press.

García, J., and J.C.J.M van den Bergh. 2011. "Evolution of Parochial Altruism by Multilevel Selection." *Evolution and Human Behavior* 32, no. 4: 277–87.

Garrels, S. R. 2011. "Human Imitation: Historical, Philosophical, and Scientific Perspectives." In *Mimesis and Science: Empirical Research on Imitation and the Mimetic Theory of Culture and Religion*, ed. S. R. Garrels, 1–38. East Lansing: Michigan State University Press.

Gelfand, M., et al. 2012. "The Cultural Contagion of Conflict." *Philosophical Transactions of the Royal Society of London B: Biological Sciences* 367, no. 1589: 692–703.

Ginges, J., and S. Atran. 2011. "War as a Moral Imperative (Not Just Practical Politics by Other Means)." *Proceedings of the Royal Society B: Biological Sciences* 278, no. 1720: 2930–38.

Girard, R. 1978. *Things Hidden Since the Foundation of the World*. London: Stanford University Press.

———. 1989. *The Scapegoat*. Baltimore: Johns Hopkins University Press.

———. 1995. *Violence and the Sacred*. Baltimore: Johns Hopkins University Press.

———. 2009. *Battling to the End*. East Lansing: Michigan State University Press.

Gonzalez-Bono, E., et al. 1999. "Testosterone, Cortisol, and Mood in a Sports Team Competition." *Hormones and Behavior* 35, no. 1: 55–62.

Hein, G., et al. 2010. "Neural Responses to Ingroup and Outgroup Members' Suffering Predict Individual Differences in Costly Helping." *Neuron* 68, no. 1: 149–60.

Huoviala, P., and M. J. Rantala. 2013. "A Putative Human Pheromone, Androstadienone, Increases Cooperation between Men." *PloS One* 8, no. 5: 1–8.

Hurlbut, W. B. 1997. "Mimesis and Empathy in Human Biology." *Contagion: Journal of Violence, Mimesis, and Culture* 4, no. 1: 14–25.

———. 2011. "Desire, Mimesis, and the Phylogeny of Freedom." In *Mimesis and Science: Empirical Research on Imitation and the Mimetic Theory of Culture and Religion*, ed. S. R. Garrels, 175–92. East Lansing: Michigan State University Press.

Israel, S., et al. 2012. "Oxytocin, but not Vasopressin, Increases both Parochial and Universal Altruism." *Psychoneuroendocrinology* 37, no. 8: 1341–44.

Johnson, D.D.P., et al. 2006. "Overconfidence in Wargames: Experimental Evidence on Expectations, Aggression, Gender and Testosterone." *Proceedings of the Royal Society B: Biological Sciences* 273, no. 1600: 2513–20.

Kavaliers, M., and E. Choleris. 2011. "Sociality, Pathogen Avoidance, and the Neuropeptides Oxytocin and Arginine Vasopressin." *Psychological Science* 22, no. 11: 1367–74.

Konner, M. 1982. *The Tangled Wing: Biological Constraints on the Human Spirit*. Middlesex, England: Penguin Books.

———. 2011. "Violence, Rivalry, and War." In *Mimesis and Science: Empirical Research on Imitation and the Mimetic Theory of Culture and Religion*, ed. S. R. Garrels, 155–74. East Lansing: Michigan State University Press.

Kosfeld, M., et al. 2005. "Oxytocin Increases Trust in Humans." *Nature* 435, no. 7042: 673–66.

McDonald, M. M., C. D. Navarrete, and M. Van Vugt. 2012. "Evolution and the Psychology of Intergroup Conflict: The Male Warrior Hypothesis." *Philosophical Transactions of the Royal Society of London B: Biological Sciences* 367, no. 1589: 670–79.

Navarrete, C. D., et al. 2009. "Race Bias Tracks Conception Risk across the Menstrual Cycle." *Psychological Science* 20, no. 6: 661–65.

Neuberg, S. L., D. T. Kenrick, and M. Schaller. 2011. "Human Threat Management Systems: Self-protection and Disease Avoidance. *Neuroscience and Biobehavioral Reviews* 35, no. 4: 1042–51.

Oliveira, T., M. J. Gouveia, and R. F. Oliveira. 2009. "Testosterone Responsiveness to Winning and Losing Experiences in Female Soccer Players." *Psychoneuroendocrinology* 34, no. 7: 1056–64.

Paper, J. D. 2007. *Native North American Religious Traditions*. Westport, CT: Greenwood Publishing Group.

Radke, S., and E. R. De Bruijn. 2012. "The Other Side of the Coin: Oxytocin Decreases the Adherence to Fairness Norms." *Frontiers in Human Neuroscience* 6 (June): 193.

Reicher, S., S. A. Haslam, and R. Rath. 2008. "Making a Virtue of Evil: A Five-Step Social Identity Model of the Development of Collective Hate." *Social and Personality Psychology Compass* 2, no. 3: 1313–44.

Schaller, M., and L. A. Duncan. 2007. "The Behavioural Immune System: Its Evolution and Social Psychological Implications." In *Evolution and the Social Mind: Evolutionary Psychology and Social Cognition*, ed. J. P. Forgas, M. G. Haselton, and W. von Hippel, 293–307. New York: Psychology Press.

Schaller, M., J. Park, and J. Faulkner. 2003. "Prehistoric Dangers and Contemporary Prejudices." *European Review of Social Psychology* 14: 105–37.

Van der Meij, L., et al. 2012. "Testosterone and Cortisol Release among Spanish Soccer Fans Watching the 2010 World Cup Final." *PloS One* 7, no. 4.

Van IJzendoorn, M. H., and M. J. Bakermans-Kranenburg. 2012. "A Sniff of Trust: Meta-analysis of the Effects of Intranasal Oxytocin Administration on Face Recognition, Trust to In-group, and Trust to Out-group." *Psychoneuroendocrinology* 37, no. 3: 438–43.

Van Vugt, M. 2009. "Sex Differences in Intergroup Competition, Aggression, and Warfare: The Male Warrior Hypothesis." *Annals of the New York Academy of Sciences* 1167: 124–34.

Van Vugt, M., D. De Cremer, and D. P. Janssen. 2007. "Gender Differences in Cooperation and Competition." *Psychological Science* 18, no. 1: 19–23.

Van Vugt, M., and J. H. Park. 2009. "Guns, Germs, and Sex: How Evolution Shaped Our Intergroup Psychology." *Social and Personality Psychology Compass* 3, no. 6: 927–38.

Van Vugt, M., and M. Schaller. 2008. "Evolutionary Approaches to Group Dynamics: An Introduction." *Group Dynamics: Theory, Research, and Practice* 12, no. 1: 1–6.

Von Rueden, C., M. Gurven, and H. Kaplan. 2011. "Why Do Men Seek Status? Fitness Payoffs to Dominance and Prestige." *Proceedings of the Royal Society B: Biological Sciences* 278, no. 1715: 2223–32.

Waytz, A., and N. Epley. 2012. "Social Connection Enables Dehumanization." *Journal of Experimental Social Psychology* 48, no. 1: 70–76.

Wrangham, R. W. 1999. "Evolution of Coalitionary Killing." *American Journal of Physical Anthropology*, suppl. 29: 1–30.

Wrangham, R. W., and D. E. Peterson. 1997. *Demonic Males: Apes and the Origins of Human Violence.* London: Bloomsbury.

Wrangham, R. W., M. L. Wilson, and M. N. Muller. 2006. "Comparative Rates of Violence in Chimpanzees and Humans." *Primates: Journal of Primatology* 47, no. 1: 14–26.

Yuki, M., and K. Yokota. 2009. "The Primal Warrior: Outgroup Threat Priming Enhances Intergroup Discrimination in Men but Not Women." *Journal of Experimental Social Psychology* 45, no. 1: 271–74.

A Mediatory Theory of Hominization

Giuseppe Fornari
Translated by Daniel A. Finch-Race

My aim in this essay is threefold: (1) to confront the question of human origins by resorting to a phenomenologico-genetic method, beginning from observational, documentary, and structural data that, if identified correctly, manifest a cognitive value in relation to an origin independent of predetermined interpretations into which we would like to insert them; (2) to apply a new critical methodology, "mediatory theory,"[1] based on the key role of mediation in human societies and cultures (by mediation, I mean a symbolic point of convergence capable of giving meaning and form to objects in the [cultural] world, in a dimension that I define as "objectual"[2]); (3) to show that defining the origin of humanity is not only a challenge for science, but also a philosophical problem, as it involves the origin of the very possibility of undertaking such research, indeed any research: it therefore implies a radical question about ourselves as cultural beings. That *Homo sapiens* is an animal capable of things beyond any other is an indisputable fact, whether this is for us the sign of a zoological particularity or of divine descent, and "culture" is a useful label to underline the peculiarity of our species and of the other species of the genus *Homo*, namely, the capacity to attain a symbolic world beginning from experiences of mediation.

Paleoanthropological research demonstrates that we derive from a long and multifarious process that has seen develop, with respect to a recognizable evolutionary lineage, many different mutations and adaptive solutions that, in growing measure, have found their principal means in the increase not only in the size of the brain but also in its plastic and cognitive capacities, up to the point at which a moment of biological homeostasis has been achieved, with the emergence of *H. sapiens* corresponding to an unprecedented cultural explosion. From one perspective, we cannot think in terms of a single process of hominization; rather, there have been different ones, not succeeding each other in time, but existing in parallel and contending for overlapping positions over millions of years. It is known that *H. sapiens* cohabited with at least another two species of the genus *Homo*: *H. neanderthalensis* until about thirty thousand years ago and a pygmy species derived from *H. erectus*, *H. floresiensis* until a little more than ten thousand years ago (Stringer and Andrews 2005, 164–65, 175). On the other hand, however, this extremely variegated and plural process has worked in favor of the species with a higher degree of ductility and plasticity: the most adaptable to the environment, and the most capable of adapting the environment to itself. The "modern" human species, in particular, has done what no other biological species has been able to do: freeze its own macroevolutionary development (Manzi 2007, 130–31), so as to trigger a very rapid cultural evolution, to which we all belong.

An integral part of such observations is a more historical and philosophical aspect, namely, the affirmation that the enigma of man has already been in part explored by a series of thinkers whom we cannot ignore if we want to advance on such a question (see Fornari 2012). I limit myself to quoting those who are the most important for my purposes: Friedrich Nietzsche, with his theory about the death of God, understood as the killing of the god from whom all of humanity is derived (Nietzsche 1882); Sigmund Freud, who was the first to enunciate an originary scene from an act of collective killing (Freud 1913); Georges Bataille, who pinpointed the genesis of humanity in its symbolic capacity to endanger that on which it depends, certifying through this its own value, which is irreducible to nature (Bataille 1951, 1973); René Girard, according to whom culture is born from the mimetic processes of the rivalries that, having exploded in the group, are offloaded onto a sole reconciling and deified victim (Girard 1978; Girard, Antonello, and de Castro Rocha 2007). I will limit myself to mentioning certain relevant or debatable passages from the theories developed by these authors, but in each case their undoubted weight and significance in the debate must be recognized. The development of this tradition of philosophical-scientific enquiry could start a more participatory and dialogic reflection about human origins.

In the background should doubtless be placed the work of Charles Darwin, who was the first to apply an evolutionary paradigm to humans (Darwin 1871), furnishing the aforementioned thinkers with the premise from which they began, directly (in the case of Freud and Girard) or indirectly (as with Nietzsche and Bataille). Darwin confronts human origins as a naturalist, and thus does not pose to himself the problem of culture, although he does take it on board obliquely when he highlights a particular aspect of humans, namely, sexual dimorphism and its influence on the somatic and behavioral evolution of humanity—as we shall see, this has significant repercussions in respect of how we conceive the cultural origins of *Homo sapiens*.

All these authors contributed to showing that the problem of nature, if systematically studied, raises per se the enigma of culture, and that both avenues of investigation return to the enigma of that which we were and are.

A Phenomenologico-genetic Method

My phenomenologico-genetic and mediatory formulation begins from a simple operation: identifying those phenomena that are so structurally and universally applicable to human essence that a provenance from a very ancient originary scenario can be hypothesized from them—namely, the originary circumstances from which culture arose, which I aim at reconstructing, but which nonetheless have concrete value as a real historical event. If humans derive from an originary scene, the forces that triggered it have not only continued to manifest themselves throughout the course of time and molded us, leaving traces and vestiges of their action, but are, in fact, present and operative in our current constitution as cultural animals. It is a matter not only of distant archaeological remains, but also of fully active and vital factors, the force of which consists of the unlimited capacity for development that they possess, and in the transformational plasticity that makes them apparently unrecognizable, in their variety, as beginning from a common matrix. My aim is to give evidence of each convergence between, on one hand, phenomenological results and, on the other, paleoanthropological, historical, and ethnographic data.

I would like to start with phenomena that are fundamental: here, our analysis must follow several gradual stages at once, since it is not a matter of distinct phenomena, but rather of a generative process, the sense of which it is possible to penetrate if we grasp their essential structure as a whole. The first, most general observation is concerned with meaning (meaningfulness)[3] as an essential dimension of humanity. Everything for humans has meaning, understood as an emotional and cognitive relationship ordained towards an end that goes beyond immediate and instinctually controlled aims. This equates to saying that meaning is found in the relationship of human beings to objects understood as *objecta*: as objective and external things that they encounter and have to reckon with. The notion of meaning linked to an object that is not instinctual—corresponding to that level of experience which I call "objectual"—opens up the dimension of the symbolic, or rather that of a semantic indicator potentially capable of transmitting meaning to anything whatsoever (this latter capacity is linked to the development of linguistic abilities; see Deacon 1997). On this first level, culture presents itself as the domain of meaningfulness and symbolicity. However, it is not adequate to presuppose a dimension of meaning as simply in existence, since that which is simply in existence returns to nature and does not acquire autonomy in and from nature. Animals cannot spontaneously per se have cognizance of an object endowed with meaning.

The phenomenological characteristics of such objectuality are not limited to the constitution of meaning, since its meaningfulness responds to two conditions: it coincides with an object, such that the symbolic is one with the process of a meaning corresponding to an object, and of the object assuming a meaning; it presents itself as a meaningful source—in other words, it establishes itself as a superior and original reality that bestows meaning. No spontaneous biological process could lead to a similar perception, which introduces into the animal dimension an element of transcendence, in the literal sense of something that goes beyond instinctual reality. This presupposes a factor, a force, that could have exercised such an influence on prehuman animals that would have compelled them to fracture their perceptive and instinctually controlled behavioral horizon, and such a factor cannot but be radically traumatic and extraordinarily creative.

Can we trace phenomenological signs that structurally correspond to the aforementioned traumatic and creative force? Human experience is not simply organized around various *objecta* that confer symbolic meaning on it, but derives its organizing and finalizing force from superior and immeasurable standards of meaning, with respect to which all other standards arrange themselves hierarchically, thence deriving their legitimacy and motivation. I call this phenomenon the "hierarchical organization of meaning," and its structure is above all collective, even at a predominantly individual level. Each of us has a life organized around fundamental objectives and objects (*objecta*), with respect to which all other objects and objectives pass into second place, not because they do not matter, but because only thence do they derive their significance.

The clearest example comes from our own most important affective relationships, which are per se in continuity with the considerable expressions of affectivity existing in higher mammals, and which nonetheless are characterized by their aptitude for meaningfulness, as attested by a rich series of meaningful and symbolic expressions having the function of constantly confirming affective investment and the unlimited value of this.[4] A loving and affectionate relationship demonstrates its heuristic and cognitive power by stimulating initiatives and representations of every type, confirming and broadening a vision of reality and its overall meaning (its meaningfulness), or rather the objectual and meaningful nature of the world. Personal identity, the relationship with one's own body, relationships with others, the optimal utilization of one's own abilities are all triggered and strengthened by the intensity of this affective and cognitive sense of fulfillment. This means that the relationship itself is a form of mediation between subjects and reality, which in this process is recognized and interpreted in the most intense and broadest way—we can even say, being thus molded and defined as reality (this is particularly evident in the relationships of children to their parents). These processes are of such importance that a very rich series of symbolic expressions reproduces their intensity and significance, as is evident in the huge range of artistic expressions that are familiar to us. Artistic and ecstatic phenomena exhibit a discontinuous and hierarchical structure analogous to our most intense emotional experiences, and their meaning derives from an expressive point around which their communicational act is organized. This is particularly evident in music. Our very cognitive and mental structure demonstrates a responsiveness to this signifying hierarchy, given that it fully operates only when it selects centers of meaning from which everything else derives, creating representative and conceptual wholes that are organic and coordinated.

These examples mainly refer to individuals and relationships between individuals. However, there are also wider experiences endowed with the same hierarchical and meaningful structure. One need only think of collective demonstrations linked to politics, sport, performance, or art. Our hierarchical and signifying structure does not change; we always have an absolute center of meaning (the political leader, the champion capable of phenomenal performances, the musical or cinema icon, the artistic genius, the climax of a ceremony, etc.) that justifies each moment of enthusiasm and effort, and the social dimension of these phenomena only serves to reinforce them, sometimes reaching peaks of collective hysteria. The potency of such collective phenomena leads one to think that they may be decidedly more ancient than their individual and inter-individual equivalents, such that their constructive or destructive effectiveness, according to the focus that they acquire, cannot be overestimated. The mediation that such events introduce between the community and its object becomes enormous, and historical pieces of data indicate that such a powerful mediation had to be religious at its roots and origin. Contemporary religions are the result of more ancient religious forms, and the history of religion shows us that their collective character is gradually accentuated as we travel backwards in time; all the social behaviors to which I previously referred appear to have their distant origins in religious experiences, just as affective phenomena reproduce in themselves a symbolic structure based on a religious matrix. It is reasonable to surmise that our supreme center of meaning was thus, at its shaping and informing origin, of a religious, divine, and sacred nature.

These are not sociological analyses, since they aim to isolate a mediatory foundation on which society depends, through how it appears to the actors involved. From a phenomenological standpoint, it is society that derives from hierarchical mediations around which it organizes itself, more than the other way around; the organizing efficacy and self-authenticating effect of such a hierarchical mediation comes to coincide with the perception of it that everyone has while obeying it. Freud's idea of collective identification (Freud 1921) has some points of resemblance with what I am trying to describe. In positing this intuitional starting point, my reflections do not follow any metaphysical assumptions: a phenomenologico-genetic method has the advantage of not being connected to any precise religious or ideological presupposition. It is crucial to understand the historical and anthropological function of religion, regardless of the most personal conclusions we may wish to derive from it.

If we accept the idea that we have an origin and *are* the result of that origin, we should also accept that there are primordial phenomena that transmit to us essential pieces of information about our genesis and condition as cultural animals. My hypothesis, based on a phenomenological analysis of our inner constitution as cultural beings, is that this genesis organized itself around a force that imposed itself on an animal community, starting from an event as traumatic as it was creative, which we can only define as proto-religious. Such a proto-religious event made conceivable to the prehuman animal an object no longer instinctually determined; therefore it could be seen as the first event of significant mediation for humanity, in the double sense that I understand by mediation: that of mediating with respect to an object, but also, that of making possible such mediation because there is a supreme mediatory source. The creatively traumatic nature of the event and its transcendental nature, as previously outlined, configure it as an ecstatic experience, in the literal sense of the Greek term *ek-stasis*: going beyond oneself, beyond a purely biological condition, not through an irrationally mystic experience, in the style of Rudolf Otto's notion of the sacred (Otto 1917), but rather through attaining a stable experience, a state (suggested by the term *stasis*) of new orientation in reality, or new object acquisition. This ecstatic experience provides a new link to the foregoing biological objects, imbuing them with an unprecedented detachment from the instinctual sphere of interest, and this powerful link, both mystic and proto-rational, corresponds to the phenomena of magic and of the sacred (De Martino 1948). In confronting the direction relative to the object, we can derive useful indications by discussing the theoretical tradition to which I referred at the beginning.

An Originary Scene

The best scene to explain all of these features, derived from phenomenologico-genetic analysis, is similar to that proposed by Freud and Girard of a situation of serious internal tension, both mimetic and instinctual, resolved through its discharge on a similarly internal victim. This crisis likely had to do with the closest biological object suitable for arousing competition, i.e., sexual mating (Freud), and this competition was essentially mimetic (Girard). I believe that the sexual cause was not deterministic as Freud implies, and was not completely detached from biological objects as Girard assumes; for this reason, I speak of an objectual crisis, consisting of the traumatic shift from biological to (proto-)symbolic objects. The object-oriented instinct of prehuman animals became a problem and, thanks to the process of the one victim identified by Freud and more consistently developed by Girard, found a new orientation thanks to a collective experience of mediation (a reason for which I also call the crisis mediatory, considering its final point of resolution). Henceforth, any critical situation for proto-human groups, both mimetic and linked to survival, could trigger such collective solutions of "at-one-ment." No gradual and peaceful natural phenomenon, nor any violent and external natural phenomenon (such as a catastrophe or a dire state of necessity), is capable of explaining radical mutations such as those presupposed by the human animal. The only remaining answer is thus an internal and intraspecific catastrophe, and this leads in the direction of the originary scene advanced by Freud and Girard, who trace humanity to the sacrifice of a founding victim—the primordial Father for Freud, a randomly selected victim for Girard.[5] Neither of these authors has posed the problem, however, of showing the phenomenological data essential to an originary scene, let alone succeeded in providing an explanation: Freud takes for granted an object, which for him is natural, and does not illuminate the theme of culture; Girard begins from a devaluation of the role played by objects, due to the mimetic escalation of rivalry, and does not dwell sufficiently on the cultural revisitation of those objects, thus remaining within a mechanical vision of the origin of culture. Nietzsche and Bataille, with differing levels of clarity and articulation, perceive the ecstatic power of an originary event, but do not provide a complete explanatory theory, to which the aforementioned two thinkers come closer.

In order to articulate my originary scene, it is important to turn to the central question of objectuality. A human object cannot be in perfect continuity with biology, as Freud positivistically assumes with his libido, since objectuality presupposes a break with respect to a natural datum, which is subject to severe proscriptions. This is particularly true in the case of sexual couplings (as Bataille emphasizes, there are no proscriptions in nature). Nor, however, can a human object be in perfect discontinuity with nature, as Girard postulates, considering an intragroup rivalry that makes natural objects of secondary importance, and eventually destined to disappear.[6] In Freud, we have an instinctive object, whereas his psychoanalysis shows, in fact, that objectuality is, rather, the result of a long and tormented process of development. In Girard, we have the nonobjectual and destructive break from instinctual patterns, overcome thanks to a sacralization of the victim seen as an external divinity that must be exorcised and kept at a distance; so that within a culture the object continues to lack a role, remaining—on the level of need—a precultural biological object, or vice versa disappears into the hysterical polarization of mimetic rivalries.[7]

What is also overlooked is the finality, proper to human cultures, of discovering the object as a source of meaning and stable orientation of collective existence. The centrality of the experience of *ek-stasis* is also not considered, along with its orientation towards objectuality, its tendency towards an internal homeostasis—towards a *stasis* based on external reality.

The emphasis on the phenomenology of objectuality provides us, on the contrary, with a scene of greater coherence. The victim has all the characteristics of a primordial object—not according to Freud's and Girard's naturalistic terms, but as an event that destabilizes the precultural objects, thus allowing for their re-elaboration in symbolic terms. Freud correctly attributes such a crisis to a precise instinctual object, namely, mating with females, which is by far the most frequent cause of intraspecific conflicts in the animal kingdom; but such an object is then transformed, bypassing the control of instinctual regulation, in a scenario similar to the mimetic crisis of Girard. It constitutes, rather, an objectual crisis in which conflict does not entirely defuse instinctual points of reference, but rather undermines them and makes them in need of a new anchorage that can no longer be biological. This is exactly what the foregoing ecstatic experience furnishes: an experience capable of revisiting the preceding instinctual object, conferring on it a new value of symbolic meaning, which will be, first of all (but not exclusively), that of sexual regulation.[8] This ecstatic and mediatory force becomes the key factor capable of containing and giving meaning to human mimesis: unlike Girard, I deem mediation, not mimesis, to be the prime energy source of human beings.

We must suppose two phases: one intra-cultural, not yet completely stabilized, and a cultural one, stabilized in the ritualization of an originary event. The distinction, introduced by Girard (Girard 1987, 100), is very useful because it suggests a criterion of reconstruction that is both elastic and plausible, linked to different possible scenarios, although it is necessary to articulate its origin with a more satisfying definition of the two different phases. In the intra-cultural phase, moments of crisis and their violent resolution happen spontaneously, and this could be attributed to the most important genus preceding that of *Homo* (although overlapping in its period of initial development): the genus of *Australopithecus*. The advantage of a two-phase explanation comes in postulating situations that are explicable on the basis of biological mechanisms, but also have the potential for development not limited to biology. In this respect, there exists an important clue. During the pre-cultural phase, there must have been a series of evolutionary modifications linked to growing dimorphism, evidenced at least in *Australopithecus afarensis*, and such dimorphism was favored by increasing sexual competition (Manzi 2007, 41). The intensification of factors of sexual attraction, which could also be linked to a prolongation of estrus, must have also intensified relationships of coupling, and favored a series of relational and communicational abilities at the basis of eventual cognitive and linguistic acquisitions. At the same time, prehuman sexual dimorphism must have avoided excessive differentiation, above all in body size, in order to render effective and mutual the collaboration of the couple (see Deacon 1997, 392–94). We are dealing with an intermediate phase, since the biological and sexual object begins to assume a valence that is no longer fully biological, but pre-symbolic, although in an as-yet uncodified manner. This emerges from highly unstable situations of collective pre-mediation.

According to my hypothesis, some form of stabilization must have operated during more violent crises, favored by the growth of mimetic capabilities and the intensification of the sexual impulse, which rendered mating rivalries potentially more catastrophic, overcoming and deconstructing relationships of dominance. Confronting crises graver than any preceding ones, the prehuman community, through the killing of an internal victim, underwent its first out-and-out ecstatic experience and related it to instinctual objects, conferring upon them a proto-symbolic significance. This event guided the group and indelibly engraved itself on the memory of the members; from this moment, the proto-human community repeated the event regularly, not out of simple automatism, but rather out of obedience to a superior and mysterious power from which the community felt itself to be derived, and towards which it had to establish a relationship that was no longer instinctual in itself. This is how the most archaic form of religion was born, and such a beginning coincides with the birth of the genus of *Homo*, along with the evolutionary and cultural acquisitions that the new stabilization allowed. After pre-humanization followed proto-humanization, attributable to what we know at present about *H. habilis* (Leakey 1994). All of the characteristics of the prehuman animal persist and resurface in a strengthened manner, signified by an immaterial center of collective objectual mediation, which orientated life and the behavior of the group, developing its collective and communal perceptive, cognitive, and explorative abilities.

In Search of a First Sacrifice

The conjecture, recently sustained by various scientists, that hominization may be linked to a carnivorous diet, with its greater intake of protein (Manzi 2007, 54–55), acquires a different value if read from a sacrificial perspective. A simple dietary modification would be disproportionate with respect to the massive changes that determined the rise of the new genus of *Homo*, and by itself remains inadequate to explain them, whereas a sacrificial hypothesis is perfectly adequate because it provides an intraspecific factor through which hominids developed not only different alimentary habits, with the nutritional advantages brought by this change, but above all the cognitive and explorative resources that put them in a position to compete with other predators, even if only by way of the opportunistic methods that we must imagine in a yet-inchoate state of cultural development. The prehuman animal began to become human by having recourse to a diet to which neither its dentition nor its digestive apparatus were predisposed, and this leads back to a leap that was somewhat unnatural—no longer entirely reducible to biological and instinctual processes or to simple adaptive variants. This introduces us to a scenario that is conjectural, though anything but arbitrary.

The reasoning behind the introduction of a carnivorous diet, which has an independent scientific value, reveals to us the glimmer of a possible originary scene. There is, in fact, a ritual that, on account of its extremely archaic characteristics, attracted the attention of William Robertson Smith (1907, 338ff.) and, in his wake, Freud (Freud 1913): homophagic sacrifice, consisting of the butchering and devouring of a still-living victim, often beginning with the genitals. Based on this rite, Smith elaborated his theory of a totemic meal, according to which the most ancient form of sacrifice is that wherein all the members of a group create among themselves a simultaneously physical and symbolic union by consuming the flesh and drinking the blood of a victim killed by all of them in an act of extreme agitation and violence. The theory of a totemic meal is so suggestive that its reading by Freud signaled the decisive turning point in the compilation of the fourth essay in *Totem and Taboo*, with its scene of the primordial Father being devoured by his children in unison—even if Smith committed the error of considering the animal version of this sacrifice to be more originary, since correct reasoning should normally begin from a "human" target more at hand, within a group. However, in analyzing this sacrificial form, we find ourselves in a gray area where the distinction between man and animal is still fuzzy. There are several reasons why I believe homophagic ritual to be the most archaic form of sacrifice among all of those known to us.

The homophagic rite does not necessitate per se any technology, and was frequently carried out with bare hands, thence deriving one of its denominations. This is a remote phase in which not only was fire still undiscovered, but also in which flint had not even been developed into a weapon (Fornari 2006, 119–21, 291–92). If my reasoning is correct, we are in the presence of a relic that leads us back to the passage between *Australopithecus* and the birth of the genus of *Homo*, more than two-and-a-half million years ago. The observation of behavior among chimpanzees hunting other isolated monkeys, which are surrounded and torn to pieces in order for the predators to feed on meat in periods of scarcity (Deacon 1997, 393, 395–96), shows us that similar episodic behaviors are perfectly possible in some species of primates. In the case of the prehuman primate, similar behavior would have been within a group and species, on account of the outbreak of a crisis of particular severity.

Such a rite does not necessitate per se the intervention of a divinity. Its efficacy consists, first of all, in the proto-magical communion allowed by the manducation of flesh and the sprinkling of blood. The act is effective in itself, and this is the sacral experience that leads the group that underwent it towards a new symbolic and social dimension. This can signify that we are in a phase so totally remote that it makes the intervention of a divinity in any form, even a rudimentary one, inconceivable.[9] The totemization of the Father postulated by Freud and the divinization of the victim hypothesized by Girard are implausible at this stage of human development because at the dawn of humanity there could not have been the representational capacity to conceive of similar inferential abstractions. The act of homophagic sacrifice, so traumatic and portentous, engraved itself indelibly on the memory of all, so as to be occasionally repeated as part of a primary rudimentary ritualization and elementary experiential association. The substance devoured by the group then became with time a being endowed with great power, totally deprived of a personality, capable of undergoing transformation in respect of its signifying elements.

The homophagic ritual demonstrates a perfect intermingling of a natural act (devouring) and a cultural one (attribution of meaning); of a spontaneous action and a planned one. Physical and symbolic aspects become inseparable, and are also strictly tied to the effectiveness of the rite, with the consequence that their structural and elementary pattern is demonstrably more ancient than an intervention by an external divinity. We are envisaging the situation of an animal, which acts on a biological level, surpassing a certain threshold of intensity, and doing something no longer entirely reducible to a biological level.

The detail that the dismemberment often began from the genitals of the victim emphasizes that the victim was intraspecific and that the sexual object bore a key role in the crisis that led to the collective action.[10] The attention given to the genitals leads back to an anatomical conformation, both protuberant and prehensile; thus it presupposes a masculine victim, against whom the other males were seemingly carried away by rivalry for females. We can even suppose that the trigger may have been, in some cases, or even in many cases, a coupling no longer protected by the relationships of dominance, and in such a case the oldest or strongest males could have been the most suitable candidates, according to Freud's idea. There is not, however, any Oedipal exclusivity, since the mechanism could have been unleashed against any other male, with a younger individual challenging an older one. The unanimity required by the homophagic proto-ritual implies, however, that females also took part in it, carried away by the frenetic general agitation. The indication of masculine precedence also makes one think that the attraction towards the genitals of a sexual rival may have been in its turn ritualized in the form of homosexual connections.

A rite that can be connected to this originary scene is that of hierogamy (attested in both prehistoric and historical time), of which the conclusion would be the killing of one of the two members of the couple, or both (Taylor 1997, 112–14; Fornari 2006, 61–62, 83–86). In ancient Mesopotamian cultures, hierogamy played a central role, and in mythological strata we find the motif of a female divinity's lover dying prematurely in tragic circumstances. Behind such a fairly widespread motif, we may recognize the more distorted and revised (and thus more ancient) motif of the death of the feminine deity. However, in a probably even more ancient stratum, we find the presence of a virile partner, with the features of the king of the underworld or the bull of the sky, which would point to a more originary masculine victim. Another striking example from the historical era is the Indian rite of the horse, in which the animal was killed and dismembered, and a woman copulated with its severed penis: the horse, of which the ritual butchering gave rise to a startling series of substitutionary killings, can certainly correspond to an originary masculine victim, and the consequent symbolic intercourse with its severed penis could combine an originary dismemberment with the coupling linked to it.

Another indication, less demonstrative but more universally present, is given by the worldwide diffusion of creationary myths in which the universe originates from the dismemberment of a primordial being, whose limbs become the various parts of physical and social reality. Such universal diffusion could correspond to a particularly ancient motif, dating back to the most distant era of prehistory—even if already purified of the cannibalistic component, substituted by a cosmological re-elaboration. Another universally widespread motif is that the parts of the dismembered victim release a particular beneficial power: for example, fertilizing fields and propitiating a harvest—an interpretation, in this case, dating back to the Neolithic era.

Another element for reflection, endowed with its own independent documentary attestation, is the frequency of cannibalistic practices in a very large number of archaic cultures and not a few ancient historical cultures, confirmed by several prehistoric finds bearing the traces of butchery on human bones (Facchini 1992 125, 135, 141). Any utilitarian motivation, linked to food scarcity, is not sufficient to explain the diffusion of such practices, which were, moreover, performed ritually, and thus not under the occasional pressure of alimentary emergencies. A further proof of the ancientness of these alimentary customs comes from the discovery, in samples originating from populations on every continent, of genetic mutations due to prion-based illness (bovine spongiform encephalopathy, or Mad Cow Disease), a pathology that is particularly widespread among populations addicted to cannibalism (Lusetti 2008, 82–83). Even if they do not obviously demonstrate that the most archaic form of sacrifice was homophagy, these circumstances make such an eventuality more plausible. Homophagic sacrifice would then have evolved, over a rather brief period, into a variety of cannibalistic rites at the expense of members of other conspecific and congeneric groups.

There is, ultimately, a final piece of the inductive puzzle, relating to the traces of red ochre that have been found in archaeological strata of relevance to humans, dating back to one-and-a-half million years ago (Facchini 1992, 34–35; Fornari 2006, 28–29). Red ochre is also documented in other prehistoric finds, and is universally widespread among innumerable archaic cultures, within which it habitually symbolizes blood, and, in significant measure, human blood. My interpretative hypothesis is that the most remote red ochre may have the same significance, and, besides proceeding by means of analogy from these documented usages, is founded on the consideration that such a precocious use of chromatic symbolism may date back to an event strongly imprinted on the memory of these archaic communities, responding to the same reasons for which a sacrificial victim had to be intra-community in origin. In a manner analogous to homophagic proto-sacrifice, but with a further symbolic development, we have a process of symbolization even more closely mimicking the performative reality that it represents, with a further indication of memorization, since red ochre reproduces not fresh blood, which would be a vibrant red, but solidified and dried blood. The ritual usage of such a color thus implies that these archaic communities may have observed human blood that had previously been spilled, and may have done so because such blood had been spilled as part of a memorable experience in which the community had participated. In this case, too, the originary scene described above best answers the task of interpreting such finds.

◆ ◆ ◆

I am aware that this is a case of highly speculative readings, especially given the exorbitant requirement of going back to events that occurred two-and-a-half million or more years ago, but, besides the partial support of the thinkers to whom I have referred, there is also convergence with the phenomenological analysis from which I initially departed. Anyone who may be skeptical about the possibility of using more recent proofs for such remote reconstructive ends must realize that the myths and human beliefs envisaged here are, to an extraordinary degree, enshrined in a conservatism founded on the fact that our ancestors had to overcome a brutal and continuous conflict against their external environment *and* internal difficulties. No institution or custom that had proved its efficacy on this score could end up neglected, and the catastrophes that from time to time struck these communities reinforced their use. Moreover, to maintain the validity of my reasoning, it is not strictly necessary that a homophagic solution is the only possible one, but that it is the most shocking and incisive one—the one most capable of engraving itself indelibly on the memory and experience of these small communities. Starting from the first mediatory experiences of sacrifice, proto-human communities became capable of using them as an explorative and cognitive tool for discovering new sacrificial objecta (both objects and objectives) in the surrounding environment. Within a relatively brief period, therefore, it became necessary for the sacrificial victim to be external, too.

It is hardly conceivable, moreover, that a victim was periodically selected within groups comprising a few dozen individuals, nor is it any more plausible that this always happened at the expense of the strongest and most experienced males—an observation that brings to mind a variety of internal victims, associated in one way or another with the original one. By force of circumstance, the choice must soon have fallen on external victims taken from other groups. The danger of internal mating may have quickly made it indispensable to procure females from elsewhere (abductions and raids being amply attested in mythological and ethnographic materials), and this probably led to the extremely rapid development of the institution of warfare. War, however, was also the perfect way to procure external victims to be substituted for internal ones.

I believe that collective organized hunting arose later, since animal victims capable of substituting for human ones had to possess characteristics and dimensions such as to make them sufficiently potent in the substitutionary rite, which required the acquisition of adequate technology and sophisticated hunting procedures. I have no doubt that the ritual impulse was, however, of chief importance in the development of such techniques, far from alimentary needs, which could have been profitably satisfied through recourse to very much less risky processes. The most interesting fact is that the ritual hunting of the latest period of the Paleolithic era, reserved for large animals because they were most loaded with sacred potency, was born from the most ancient hunting practice of all: the "hunting" of other human beings, understood either as substitutive victims or as females with whom to mate.

Fire and Burial

In order to complete my theory on human origins, there remain two fundamental passages to consider, corresponding to different speciations and stages of culturalization. The first concerns the domestication of fire, an event that it is impossible to overestimate, due to its multiple effects, beginning from the improvement in alimentation with regard to the hygienic condition of food, the greater possibilities of conserving comestibles, the extent to which these were masticable and digestible, and their overall nutritional value, along with the growth in fertility that this favored (see Wrangham 2009). To this should be added the further technological improvements that fire made possible regarding the working of flint, and the immense gain in security from wild animals, particularly at night—a change that must have contributed to the upright posture of our ancestors (whereas the species of *H. habilis* maintained the tree-dwelling behavior that was necessary for it to pass nights in relative security). These changes were so radical as to make one legitimately think that the discovery of fire should be placed in a more archaic epoch, at the foundation of a new speciation of *H. habilis*, attributable to *H. erectus* or *H. ergaster* according to the taxonomic classification of the evidence at our disposal.[11] The use of fire to colonize cold environments and to make hunting more efficient should be placed, instead, in a chronologically later phase, during which human populations achieved particularly evolved capabilities of coordination and control, which presuppose the ability to generate combustion artificially (Delson et al. 2000, 244–46).

The most relevant aspect in the domestication of fire is, in fact, its subdivision into two phases: passive domestication (when humans learned to gather and preserve fire, but did not know how to ignite it) and active domestication (when different methods of artificially producing a flame were elaborated).[12] The first phase is very much more rudimentary, hence evidence is more inconclusive and scanty, whereas the second phase took place much later—with indisputable proofs dating back to one hundred fifty thousand years ago, though less certain pieces of evidence put us in the region of some hundreds of thousands of years earlier—and offers the earliest unequivocal signs of combustion technology, which are nevertheless necessarily related to a long preliminary phase of passive utilization. It is very much the unreflecting use of the concept of "technology," in fact, that has so far impeded scholars from arriving at a clearer vision of the argument, favoring the quite fallacious representation of instrumental knowledge, directed at practical purposes conceived as natural.

According to these conceptualizations, archaic man would have discovered fire through simple trial and error, imagining that it was of use to him. Such a scenario, however, is quite improbable, despite its scientific façade. All animals, from the weakest to the strongest, react with terror in the face of fire, and there is no reason whatsoever not to attribute to *H. erectus* or *H. ergaster* the same instinctive response. If man overturned such a biologically spontaneous reaction in the face of the primordial danger of fire, transforming said reflex into the capability to approach the flame and establish a relationship with it, this must have been due to a more powerful force, or rather by means of an impulse that was no longer biological, but rather cultural, which must have been founded on a sacred and religious mediation that taught this no longer simply animal species to look in a new way at a natural phenomenon that was otherwise terrifying. There is, perhaps, nothing like the domestication of fire for restoring a vivid idea of what a cultural animal meant in deepest prehistory, and here the phenomenological quality of the more general data at our disposal supports us, above all.

Fire was approached, rather than avoided, because a certain form of sacredness was attributed to it, favored by the overwhelming power of certain natural phenomena that produced it (such as thunderstorms, volcanic eruptions, spontaneous combustions): a power interpreted as significant on the basis of mediatory and objectival experiences within human groups, which taught them to perceive natural phenomena as significant and imposing realities. The domestication of fire presupposes an otherwise unknown primordial religion of Fire, of which we find certain traces in available historical and ethnographic evidence. Sacredness implies in one way or another a link with sacrifice, of which fire became one of the most effective instruments (that of total destruction); however, my hypothesis does not need to postulate any more precise details, which would only have the effect of increasing skepticism without adding further evidence. There were probably various ritual occasions that introduced combustion into these very ancient communities, and that all had in common the adoration of this divine force and its employment in various functions (certainly interpreted as its gifts), which needed to be propitiated by means of appropriate ritual and, consequently, technological procedures.

The myths and rites linked to fire transmit to us precious pieces of information in this regard, deriving from the particularly long phase of passive domestication (such as in the Roman rite of Hestia's eternal flame, guarded by the Vestal Virgins, and which led to the sacrifice of one of them if it went out). It is also extremely instructive to note that such rituals, dating back to the remote times of *H. erectus* and *H. ergaster* (about one-and-a-half million years ago), may have reached right up to the historical era, after hundreds of thousands of years dominated by the new technologies (that is to say, by the new rituals) of active domestication. This reveals to us not only a quite remarkable conservatism, but also the extent of the power contained in the sacred value assigned to the hearth on which the life of everyone depended—such a considerable value that for hundreds of thousands of years, its cult was preserved next to the new reality of fully mastered fire, transmitting into the bargain analogous traditions from one human species to the other. The ancient Greeks certainly did not err in making the birth of humanity relate back to the gift of fire from Prometheus, where we find both the divine origin of fire and the subsequent punishment by Zeus's hand, which recalls the cultural connection between pyrotechnic technology and sacrifice.

The second important stage on the road to hominization is the invention of the tomb.[13] The most ancient known burial sites date back to about one hundred thousand years ago, and were discovered on Mount Carmel in Israel, in different localities of this massif; at Es Skhul and Qafzeh, diverse inhumations practiced by populations of *H. sapiens* have been identified, while a burial site due to *H. neanderthalensis* has been found at Tabun (Vandermeersch 1991). The sites are in caves that were not used for the purposes of habitation; the bodies have a bent or tucked-in arrangement, similar to the fetal position. The most striking burial site is that of a young woman, found at Qafzeh, at whose feet was placed a child of about six years old, perhaps her offspring. In two cases, at Es Skhul and Qafzeh, animal remains (a pig and a deer) were placed on the corpses. Other ancient burial sites have been discovered in Europe (dating back to the Neanderthals) and in the Middle East, dating to between seventy thousand and forty thousand years ago: they are almost always in uninhabited caves or shelters, comprising skeletons in a contorted position; in more than one case, the intentional removal of the cranium, for evidently cultic ends, has been discovered. The find at the grotto of Regourdou in the Dordogne Valley is unique: the body was not buried in a tomb, but inhumed under a pile of rocks, next to the abundant remains of a bear, subject to another inhumation.

As a first observation, we could say that inhumation in caves complies with the purpose of sheltering bodies from carrion feeders, but this is an insufficient explanation; they had to have, first of all, a sacred and ritual connotation, as is suggested by the practice of several burials at the same site, the manipulation of some bodies, and the presence in several cases of animal remains associated with the funeral ceremony, or themselves the object of inhumation. The contorted position of the bodies makes one think of a fetal analogy, and consequently of a symbol of rebirth. The animal offerings, moreover, introduce another very important element, namely, a sacrificial one, since it is quite likely that the remains of large animals found in these sites are of organisms that were immolated. It is, however, unquestionable that such archaic burial sites express a precise vision of death and a system of mythico-religious beliefs. We are in the presence of an already sophisticated interpretation of reality, in which a plane of invisible existence (in which the deceased participate) overlaps with the plane of the living world. Before reflecting, however, on this capacity for mental partition that constitutively accompanied burials, and hypothesizing an explanation of it, it is necessary to extricate the field from a misunderstanding and underline a strange particularity noticeable in the earliest tombs.

The misunderstanding from which it is necessary to liberate oneself is that prehistoric man had a natural perception of death and feared it as we do. It is an interpretational error as frequent as it is insidious, since it distorts data on the basis of an experience that appears unquestionable and elementary to us, but which, in truth, is culturally articulated and complex. In ancient and archaic cultures, death was never perceived as pure expiration, as a total interruption of the biological and mental activity of a corporeal organism, accompanied by a feeling of total absence—of personal disappearance. Death, on the contrary, was something like a change in state, certainly critical and destabilizing, but inserted into a broader vision that did not recognize stark interruptions or irreversible discontinuities, but rather transformations that were qualifying and admitted to different states, without clear distinctions between them, that were ill-defined as well as defining, but were, to all intents and purposes, not personal. There was discontinuity and subtraction, with corresponding emotional states of affliction or joy according to whether it was the case of a relative or enemy, but such experience expressed per se the transition from one state of existence, in which the living participated, to another, belonging to the dead and gods (or those who would have become gods). This phenomenological reconstruction, in the circularity and reversibility that characterizes it, allows us to understand the fragility and precariousness of such a transition, and overturns our overhasty readings: the insurmountable caesura, the vital interruption that ignites our grief and seems to us so natural, was for more ancient societies, indeed, an outcome that had to be achieved with effort. The primary preoccupation, in very ancient periods, was to fix a stable distinction between the world of the living and that of the dead, which allowed a representable and controllable transition from one plane to the other, and permitted the surviving members of the group to continue to exist.[14] This explains the compelling and dramatic need to neutralize death, to impede it from returning among the living, that is visible in a whole series of ritual procedures amply evidenced in archaic cultures and also noticeable in prehistoric finds, such as taking away the most dangerous parts of the dead person (the head or limbs), up to the more radical solution of incineration.

My analyses, like our experience of death, presuppose a vision of reality articulated and split, which is that of us *H. sapiens*, and that is closely linked to burial, which must lead us to reflect, on one hand, that we move within the mental and symbolic configuration of our species, and, on the other, that such a configuration is not at all a particular organization that stands beside other particular mental organizations, but in a certain way makes them real and relaunches them, stabilizing a split between immediate and mediated experience that belongs to the events and processes whence the genus of *Homo* originated. The symbolic transition of burial is certainly decisive, even if we must still determine why. The exclusion of a natural feeling of death allows us, for one thing, to exclude any psychological or romantic reading of the most ancient burials as a gesture of piety towards the dead.

I thus come to what is perhaps the most peculiar strangeness of such finds: the fact that they concerned only a small minority of the population. As Bernard Vandermeersch writes, "burials were accorded only to a restricted number of people, perhaps on the basis of precise criteria that, however, totally escape us" (1991, 49). It should be possible to remove the "perhaps" without causing upset, since rites of such importance could not have been undertaken without precise criteria, which induced the population that carried them out to choose localities responding to determined characteristics, and doubtless with a ceremonial accompaniment of which no trace has remained, apart from odd animal or vegetal remains and a peculiar treatment reserved for the body. In the historical era, the civilization that developed the most imposing funerary and cemetery-based apparatus—namely, the Egyptians (during the Old Kingdom)—saw burial as something reserved for pharaohs and the highest dignitaries, and only with time was it extended, with the privileges of salvation that burial promised, to the lower social classes. We are thus right to add that such a distinction remained in force throughout the Middle and Lower Paleolithic, up to the entirety of the Neolithic, and beyond.

In summary, nobody has yet been able to respond to the following questions: Why were such burial sites also placed in locations that were difficult to access and uninhabited? If they were based on a certain feeling of *pietas* towards the dead, they should have been found in more convenient localities, and the necessity of defending the dead from wild animals could, moreover, have been more easily satisfied in the presence of the community. Why are they associated with large animals, to the point (at the grotto of Regourdou) of interchangeability between man and animal? Why do they concern only a small portion of the population—a circumstance that does not appear, in my view, to be traceable to a caste-based social structure, such as is the case with the pyramids in Egypt? Such motivations, which were nonetheless based on a matrix that was sacred and not simply founded on class, imply much more differentiated societies, and in the first tomb finds of the Paleolithic there is not even the slightest symbolic trace: this is a preceding phase, which was to develop in a caste-based direction, but in which the imposing monarchical institutions that were to arise from the Neolithic Revolution did not yet exist.

The only rational explanation of all these particularities is that such burial sites concerned sacrificial victims. Such a reading appears perfectly congruous with the association to animal sacrificial victims, as well as with the practice of the removal of the cranium, which in some cases was certainly linked to cannibalistic rites, such as suction of the brain. A sacrificial interpretation provides, moreover, a valid explanation of the double burial at Qafzeh, in which the child was inserted at the feet of the woman "with a certain brutality," as Vandermeersch writes (1991, 41), because the ditch had been dug with insufficient dimensions. Any attitude of *pietas* is scarcely compatible with the treatment reserved for the body of the child; hence the simplest hypothesis is that we are dealing with a double sacrifice of mother and child, which would have interesting mythical and historical equivalents.[15] If every pietistic or naturalistic interpretation is excluded, in any case, this does not at all leave us in a void of possible rationalizations, since it delivers us to the only plausible explanation: the very lack of alternatives makes the sacrificial interpretation, although quite circumstantial, absolutely coherent with the strong sacrificial connotation possessed by the most ancient burial sites of Egypt, Mesopotamia, China (until the fifteenth century), and many other civilizations, in which the burial of the king was accompanied by the ritual killing of members of his family and court, besides that of the slaves and animals dear to him. This hypothetical trace also directs us towards an internal, phenomenologico-genetic understanding of the formidable innovations that the tomb introduced.

If the earliest tombs—as I maintain—involved the sacrificial and sacred victims on whom the community depended, they permitted an enormous advance of symbolic and ritual technology, linked to new possibilities of surviving for a good while as the intended mediatory victim of the community, as well as to the revolutionary mental distinction that such a greater temporal duration made available. The idea of burial must have been formed empirically on the basis of certain modalities in the killing of human or animal victims, involving the covering of them with the instruments of the killing (as in the case of lapidation), or in making them disappear in a place that swallowed them (such as a precipice or a stretch of water), which consequently remained associated with the figure and powers of the victim buried there. The analogical linking of pyramids with piles of stones resulting from lapidation has been noted—for instance, by Walter Burkert (1983, 55)—but a structural analogy has never been extended to the very principle of burial, which is to make the victim disappear beneath something that becomes both a symbolic and physical substitute, offering a simultaneity of the two aspects that is typical of the inchoative phases of cultural processes. We therefore have a disappearance that is simultaneously a conservation, hence a paradoxical co-presence of two states that exclude and recall each other, in turn.

This is perhaps the moment to confront the problem of the different impact that burial must have had on the two competing species of *H. neanderthalensis* and *H. sapiens*. The tendency for cultural and symbolic development is the same, but evidently interacted to the fullest extent with the characteristics of modern man, who translated them entirely into a new cognitive endowment, transforming (so to say) the duplicative and meta-representative resources of the tomb into mental ones. In Neanderthals, an analogous process somehow appears half-finished. My impression is that the duplicative symbolism of the tomb did not suffice for our archaic cousin, such that supplementary practices were necessary in order to neutralize and propitiate the dead (e.g., the removal of the cranium and suction of the brain, which reinforced and confirmed the role of the tomb). Analogous rituals in *H. sapiens* end up having a developmental autonomy that concludes by undoing them from their corporeal matrix, transmitting their force by both magical and intermedial representational supports, as would have happened in the earliest artistic depictions. These indicative reflections justify the conclusion that only *H. sapiens* fully developed the potential of the tomb, nonetheless fulfilling a tendency, a movement, that was also present in other human species. In this sense, we are also permitted to make conjectures about the symbolic and cognitive developments of the other species congeneric to us, and it is tomb-based symbolization that allows us to do so.

Once a ritual habit implying both the disappearance and conservation of the victim had been artificially reproduced, so-practiced intentional burial resolved itself in *H. sapiens* into a formidable symbolization that appropriated this paradox, transforming it into an instrument of mental multiplication:

the tomb, in fact, conceals the victim and substitutes for it at a symbolic level, making the dead figure at once secure and constantly present. It is indicative that the first burials were excavated outside the residential areas of the various communities, at a safe distance and with methods of access that must have depended on particular celebrations. With the passage of time, modern human communities would have learned to master this symbolic instrument, taking it as far as the striking example of Çatalhöyük, one of the first cities of the Neolithic era, where burials were performed inside the same residences in which the population lived. The first cities seem to have been born and developed not as agglomerations of the living, but as inseparable agglomerations of the living and the dead, strengthening each other, in turn, in terms of religious beliefs and their cult.[16]

It is the very mind of *H. sapiens* that was modeled by the paradoxical combination of absence and presence that is the tomb. Humans thus learned to master the mnemonic representation of something by means of the visual and physical representation of a totally different object, which was nevertheless indissociably linked to that which was remembered but not seen. The first form of abstraction was born, nothing more than a burial transformed into a mental process. It is no surprise that a few tens of thousands of years later, the first artistic depictions came into being, reproducing in a stable manner such capacities for representational doubling. At this point, *H. sapiens* abandoned de facto, as it were, its macroevolutionary course, in order to embrace the path of cultural evolution entirely. The brain and the mind of the species attained its maximum ductility for learning, interpretation, and the transformation of reality, making it possible today to investigate these beginnings buried in a distant past, as well as actively buried in our present, in ourselves.

Notes

This essay develops, in a new theoretical approach, research undertaken in the 1990s, following dialogue and critical debate with René Girard. A first sample of my research on hominization is in Fornari 2000.

1. I derive the adjective "mediatory" from the history of political thought, where it indicates the function of authority as a go-between; "mediatory" in my sense also refers to the function of symbolic and cultural models in human societies. On my idea of mediation, see Fornari 2012 and 2013.
2. The adjective is used both in psychology and philosophy to signify the relational or symbolic

meaning of an object and to express the general meaning of objects for human beings. I also employ the associated noun "objectuality."

3. "Meaningfulness" is a philosophical term indicating the specific domain of cultural meaning: the specific power of culture to have and generate meaning. The same applies to a similar word related to symbols: "symbolicity."

4. See Hurlbut's chapter in this volume.

5. We may add that theirs is the only hypothesis consequent on the announcement of the death of God by Nietzsche, who had in mind a Dionysian sacrifice of a victim butchered and devoured by its sacrificers; even the origin elaborated by Bataille, despite being less coherent, is understandable only from this perspective.

6. Girard (1972, 320): *Pour renoncer complètement à l'ancrage objectal du désir, pour admettre l'infini de la* mimesis *violente, il faut comprendre, simultanément, que le sans mesure de cette violence peut et doit être maîtrisé dans le mécanisme de la victime émissaire* [In order to completely renounce the objectival anchorage of desire, to admit the infiniteness of violent *mimesis*, it is necessary to understand simultaneously that the immoderacy of this violence can and must be mastered in the mechanism of the sacrificial victim]. See Girard (1987, 95), about the disorganization of the instinctual pattern of the prehuman animal, a process to be understood as radical, to the extent that it involves mimesis.

7. Girard's answer in *Evolution and Conversion* (Girard, Antonello, and de Castro Rocha 2007) fully confirms my remarks as he distinguishes between pre-mimetic and natural needs (i.e., natural objects) and mimetic contamination giving rise to rivalry (i.e., destruction of objects): in such a way, no cultural creative role nor objectuality is attributed to human objects.

8. The importance attributed by Darwin to dimorphism and sexual competition in humans thus receives fair recognition, but within a vision that ceases to be naturalistic. Particularly interesting are the pieces of data attesting the tendency, noticeable in some mammals, to transform competition between males into a rite of alliance against a single rival (Darwin 1871, 562). Girard supposes his mechanism of a sole victim to be the intensification of a tendency that must be overcome, in a similar way to the rivalry between two contenders already observed by Konrad Lorenz (Girard 1987, 89–93).

9. On the implausibility of a representation of the divine in the earliest phases of humanity, Darwin makes correct arguments, even if applying inadequate explanatory categories (Darwin 1871, 116–17).

10. See Girard and Durham in this volume.

11. The dating of the first traces of combustion controlled by man is uncertain, and ranges from one-and-a-half million years ago to more recent times; for the reasons that I articulate, the most ancient dating should be privileged (see Tattersall 1998, 139–40). In terms of the species to whom this discovery should be attributed, there is today the tendency to recognize *H. ergaster* as the most ancient African species, thus responsible for this innovation, and *H. erectus* as an Asian species derived from *H. ergaster* (Stringer and Andrews 2005, 139).

12. On this fundamental distinction are based the excellent mythico-ritual interpretations contained in Frazer (1930).

13. Interesting observations on burial can be found in Morin (1973, 107–11), and in Girard (1987, 80–83), who, in fact, confuses the cultural origin of modern *Sapiens* with burial and the very first origins of culture.

14. This corresponds to the concept of a "crisis of presence" developed by De Martino (1948 and 1958)—an idea that corresponds not as much to the mimetic crisis of Girard as to the active cultural elaboration of an originary crisis, bearing an interesting proximity to my idea of objectual crisis.

15. In the myths related to the Cretan labyrinth and Dionysus, we find motifs of the killing of the mother (Pasiphae, Arianna, Phaedra, Semele, etc.) and of her son (the Minotaur, the infant Dionysus, etc.); these motifs are probably related to the Mesopotamian mythology of hierogamy, which must have originally entailed a sacrificial coupling, involving the sacrifice of one or both partners and sometimes their symbolic child (Fornari 2006, 83–86, 141–43).

16. See Girard in this volume.

Works Cited

Bataille, G. 1957. *L'érotisme*. Paris: Editions de Minuit.

———. 1973. *Théorie de la religion*, ed. P. Klossowski. Paris: Gallimard.

Burkert, W. 1983. *Homo Necans: The Anthropology of Ancient Greek Sacrificial Ritual and Myth*. Translated by P. Bing. Berkeley: University of California Press.

Darwin, C. [1871] 2004. *The Descent of Man, and Selection in Relation to Sex*. London: Penguin Books.

Deacon, T. W. 1997. *The Symbolic Species: The Co-evolution of Language and the Brain*. New York: W.W. Norton & Co.

de Martino, E. 1948. *Il mondo magico: Studi sul magismo*. Turin: Einaudi.

———. 1958. *Morte e pianto rituale nel mondo antico*. Turin: Einaudi.

Delson, E., I. Tattersall, J. A. Van Couvering, and A. S. Brooks, eds. 2000. *Encyclopedia of Human Evolution and Prehistory*. New York: Garland Publishing.

Facchini, F. 1992. *Premesse per una paleantropologia culturale*. Milan: Jaca Book.

Fornari, G. 2000. "Alla ricerca dell'origine perduta: Nuova formulazione della teoria mimetico-sacrificale di Girard." In *Maestri e scolari di non violenza: Riflessioni, testimonianze e proposte interattive*, ed. C. Tugnoli, 151–201. Milan: Franco Angeli.

———. 2006. *Da Dioniso a Cristo: Conoscenza e sacrificio nel mondo greco e nella civiltà occidentale*. Genoa: Marietti.

———. 2012. *Mediazione, magia desiderio in Leonardo e nel Rinascimento*. Poggio a Caiano: CB Edizioni.

———. 2013. *La conoscenza tragica in Euripide e in Sofocle*. Ancona-Massa: Transeuropa.

Frazer, J. G. 1930. *Myths of the Origin of Fire*. London: Macmillan & Co.

Freud, S. [1913] 1955. "Totem and Taboo." In *The Standard Edition of the Complete Psychological Works of Sigmund Freud*. Vol. 13 (1913–1914): *Totem and Taboo and Other Works*. Translated by J. Strachey, xii–162. London: Hogarth Press.

———. [1921] 1955. "Group Psychology and the Analysis of the Ego." In *The Complete Psychological Works of Sigmund Freud*. Vol. 18 (1920–1922). Translated by J. Strachey. London: Hogarth Press.

Girard, R. 1972. *La violence et le sacré*. Paris: Grasset.

———. 1978. *Des choses cachées depuis la fondation du monde*. Paris: Grasset.

———. 1987. *Things Hidden since the Foundation of the World. Research undertaken in collaboration with Jean-Michel Oughourlian and Guy Lefort*. Translated by S. Bann and M. Metteer. Stanford, CA: Stanford University Press.

Girard, R., P. Antonello, and J. C. de Castro Rocha. 2007. *Evolution and Conversion: Dialogues on the Origins of Culture*. New York: Continuum.

Leakey, R. 1994. *The Origin of Humankind*. New York: Basic Books.

Lusetti, V. 2008. *Il cannibalismo e la nascita della coscienza*. Rome: Armando.

Manzi, G. 2007. *L'evoluzione umana: Ominidi e uomini prima di Homo sapiens*. Bologna: Il Mulino.

Morin, E. 1973. *Le paradigme perdu: La nature humaine*. Paris: Editions du Seuil.

Nietzsche, F. [1882] 1974. *The Gay Science: With a Prelude in Rhymes and an Appendix of Songs*. Translated by W. Kaufmann. New York: Vintage Books.

Otto, R. [1917] 1923. *The Idea of the Holy: An Inquiry into the Non-rational Factor in the Idea of the Divine, and Its Relation to the Rational*. Translated by J. W. Harvey. New York: Oxford University Press.

Smith, W. R. 1907. *Lectures on the Religion of the Semites*. London: A. and C. Black.

Stringer, C., and P. Andrews. 2005. *The Complete World of Human Evolution*. London: Thames & Hudson.

Taylor, T. 1997. *The Prehistory of Sex: Four Million Years of Human Sexual Culture*. New York: Bantam Books.

Tattersall, I. 1998. *Becoming Human: Evolution and Human Uniqueness*. Oxford: Oxford University Press.

Vandermeersch, B. 1991. "Le sepolture musteriane." In *La religiosità nella preistoria*, ed. F. Facchini, M. Gimbutas, J. K. Kozlowski, and B. Vandermeersch. Milan: Jaca Book.

Wrangham, R. 2009. *Catching Fire: How Cooking Made Us Human*. London: Profile Books.

PART FOUR

Interpreting Archaeological Data: Mimetic Readings of Çatalhöyük and Göbekli Tepe

Animal Scapegoating at Çatalhöyük

René Girard

My aim is to discuss the relevance of mimetic theory for the analysis of certain cultural artifacts of the prehistoric period, more specifically, the Neolithic. That was the time when humans adopted farming and began to use permanent housing, by creating something we could call a "town" (even if we are not sure this would be quite the right word). The very idea of putting people together in permanent housing, together with what makes towns possible in the first place—streets, squares, administrative centers, etc—was, as far as we know, still missing at that time (Hodder 2006, 95). More than a modern town, this agglomeration of dwellings should be compared to a beehive. It is not that the walls were genuinely like cells, i.e., common to adjacent houses; rather, they formed narrow passages in between the houses. Quite fortunately for the archaeologists, these passages were used for garbage disposal—garbage being one of the most important ways we have of knowing about prehistoric settlement.

We know that civilization followed a westbound movement, from the Persian region to Anatolia and then to Europe; but for a long period of time, archaeologists did not realize that there were a lot of Neolithic settlements in Turkey. Then in 1959 James Mellaart, at that time director of the British Institute of Archaeology in Ankara, discovered one of the biggest and most fascinating of these Neolithic settlements in Çatalhöyük, situated in south-central Anatolia. It is particularly striking for its art, which focuses on wild animals. It was discovered very easily because Neolithic settlements were always implanted at the same spot, and houses were always rebuilt on the ruins of preceding houses. Çatalhöyük existed from approximately 7,500 BCE to 5,700 BCE: not a hugely distant period in prehistorical terms, but very early in terms of civilization, as far as we are able to tell. These houses were built of mud—some kind of clay, which is pretty strong, but nevertheless they were rebuilt every fifty to ninety years (Hodder 2006, 220); many of the decorations that were inside were kept and repainted. There are eighteen levels of occupation, and archaeologists calculate that, at the height of its expansion, there were up to eight thousand people living there. Çatalhöyük is not the oldest settlement of this area, but it is the largest and best-preserved Neolithic site found to date. James Mellaart was a very flamboyant man, who was aware of the need for publicity, so he cut very quickly through the various layers of the settlement in order to find spectacular things, and he did even better than he expected, because the paintings he found in Çatalhöyük are more sophisticated than anywhere else at that time.

They are not sophisticated in the sense of the Paleolithic art we find in the caves of Southern France and Northern Spain, at Lascaux, Chauvet, or Altamira. The art there is different. In Çatalhöyük it is more natural, more spontaneous. What I think people often fail to realize about Paleolithic art—with its magnificent profiles of the animals of the time, which are so perfect that they seem inspired by absolute realism—is that if you shift your attention from Lascaux to the painting at Chauvet, across a gap of some eighteen thousand years,[1] they are exactly the same. I think experts have not insisted enough on this aspect, which is very important,[2] and which shows that we are dealing with religious art. These paintings were not forms of primitive artistic expression; they had a very codified, ritualistic function. The pictures from Çatalhöyük I am interested in are not "good" compared to Paleolithic art, but they are "good" compared to the normal run of the most primitive art. In terms of modern, true-to-life realism, the animals in particular are more realistic; and they are distinct also in that they encapsulate a ritualistic and religious function.

Çatalhöyük is situated one hour southeast of the present-day city of Konya, a fairly large city with more than a million inhabitants, known for its

FIGURE 1. Reconstruction of the aurochs hunting scene in the Neolithic mural from Çatalhöyük. Photograph: Omar Hoftun. © Alan Mellaart.

fundamentalist religious and nationalist politics. The only housing present in proximity to the settlements is that built by the archaeologists themselves to operate close to the excavation sites.[3] Mellaart was actually, in the end, expelled by the Turkish government, under accusation of stealing material from the site, and from 1965 to 1993 the excavation was interrupted. The archaeologist who took over the site was Ian Hodder, chair of the Cultural Anthropology Department at Stanford. His team started excavating according to more up-to-date scientific methods. However, these eighteen levels of occupation proved to be both an incredible blessing for archaeologists and the worst curse possible, since they get mixed up all the time, and keeping them separate is a very challenging job. The site is still very much underexplored, and only 5 percent of it can be said to be thoroughly well known. I have not been able to visit the site: my analysis is entirely based on Hodder's book *The Leopard's Tale: Revealing the Mysteries of Çatalhöyük* (2006).[4]

Some of the scenes pictured in the book are not the originals, for the original pictures are too faint to be easily visible. It was Mrs. Mellaart who drew these pictures for the sole purpose of making them intelligible, eliminating the dirt and the irregularities in the surface, and trying to keep only the intention of the author of these pictures.[5] Most of the pictures I will discuss come from Level 5. One of these represents the auroch (figure 1), which was the ancestor of the European bull; it was widely hunted at that time, but is now extinct.[6]

As a matter of fact, there is a big difference between cave paintings like Lascaux, which were reserved for initiates, and these paintings, which are usually found in what we could call "private houses."

We may ask: Were these houses really private? Are they really religious? There are no temples or churches in Çatalhöyük, so any house was a shrine, or a kind of temple, and in some of them there were paintings that had a religious and ritualistic function.[7] The geography of the house was very important: the north wall was the sacred wall, on which the majority of these paintings can be found. It was also a custom to bury people in their houses, particularly underneath platforms against the north and east walls (Hodder 2006, 137).[8]

What is magnificent about Paleolithic painting is the depiction of animals—it is assumed that it was done through outlines on the wall, with the actual animal being present; however, human figures in Paleolithic art are practically nonexistent. This was the time when animals were domesticated for the first time, which is confirmed by the quantity of meat these prehistoric men were eating, as attested by the bones of the leftovers that were found in the refuse. Their meals consisted of domesticated sheep and domesticated goats, probably kept around the town or very close to it; while cattle and other wild animals were not a major part of the diet (Hodder 2006, 48). There was quite a bit of hunting, although the term "hunting" may sound controversial in reference to the scenes depicted in Çatalhöyük. Ian Hodder in fact defines these images as the "teasing and baiting" of an animal (Hodder 2006, 31).[9]

In order to discuss Hodder's claim, I wish to refer here to one of Mrs. Mellaart's reproductions (figure 2). It is a scene similar to the one representing the aurochs. What is striking from my point of view is the human mob surrounding the animal: it is quite a disorganized mob, although one can detect a circular or semicircular pattern. Some of the people are wearing what looks like a leopard skin as a garment: leopards, we know, have a strong symbolic value in the culture of Çatalhöyük, as the title of Hodder's book also testifies.[10] Ian Hodder defines this picture as the "teasing and baiting of a

FIGURE 2. **A stag is surrounded by bearded men. Reconstruction of a Neolithic mural from Çatalhöyük. © Alan Mellaart.**

stag." There is indeed an element of sexual teasing of the animal. The animals are always male and have their penis erect. It seems that the stag has lost its balance, and that the crowd is purposely aiming at its sexual organs. These mobs are essentially masculine, and it is important to underscore the fact that they are essentially hunting masculine animals.

The fact that the animal is always male, displaying an evident erection, of course has also some weight in respect to the ongoing discussion of Çatalhöyük as a community characterized by the devotion of female figures, from a statuette that was found on the site. The statuette that Çatalhöyük is famous for is a woman sitting between two leopards. This is a tiny figurine and it was found in a grainstore; that is, its purpose was most probably to protect the grain. It seems clear enough that there was some participation by women in the local culture of food procurement and preparation. Archaeologists tend to associate these statuettes to fertility rituals, following the standard understanding. In the case of Çatalhöyük, this has encouraged a peculiar type of female tourism to the site: groups on "goddess tours" visit the site from the United States, Germany, and elsewhere (Hodder 2006, 39). For this reason, the—by now—well-known tiny figurine is reproduced in

FIGURE 3. Copy of a Çatalhöyük mural showing a boar and a deer surrounded by sacrificers. Photograph: Omar Hoftun. © Alan Mellaart.

gigantic proportions in all presentational literature, principally for the sake of publicity by local authorities, even though hard evidence of her actual significance is scanty.[11]

There is in the modern mind a romanticizing attitude in respect to the prehistoric world: archaic man is deemed to be a Rousseauistic creature who is fundamentally good. Talking about brutality and violence in the Neolithic is perceived as incorrect or out of fashion, which is why there is such an emphasis on the artistic aspects of their culture and the constant search for matriarchal elements (Hodder 2006, 39). However, as you can see from this picture, what we have here is a violent act against an animal. There are people pulling the front of the animal, or holding its front legs, while there are others who seem to have handy objects with which to maim the animal.

There is another interesting picture (figure 3) that seems to confirm this violent scenario. It looks very similar to the previous one, although the animal seems a bit different. The stag here is sexually aroused, while the people are fighting him, moving towards him, baiting, teasing him. I should refer to the animal by saying "it," but from the point of view of the mimetic theory, it is important to consider the animal as a surrogate of a human being. A second animal is also present: a boar; and the teasing and baiting seem to target the boar as well. The hackles are very visible, which is the sign of irritation in the animal. This also flags up the concern for realism of the authors of these paintings—something that is really fascinating. The people surrounding the boar form a smaller group, but they are mocking the animal in the same way. Speaking in mimetic terms, I should use the word "scapegoating," as for mimetic theory, archaic scapegoating plays a crucial role because it is considered the origin of religion. In this case, animals are scapegoats, and they are killed in ritualistic fashion by a converging human mob.

None of the archaeologists who are studying these pictures are thinking in these terms, but I believe that these paintings, and the whole Çatalhöyük settlement, are an enormous discovery from the point of view of the mimetic theory. If you look at these pictures with no knowledge of mimetic theory, they would make little sense; but if you think in terms of a ritualistic reenactment of a sacrificial event, all the various elements of the picture fall into place. For instance, few members of the crowd are visibly damaged. There is one on the left in figure 2 who has a missing leg, representing the menacing power of the animal. Another important element is the presence of a woman in the bottom right corner of figure 2, who seems to be simply observing the scene, while in figure 3, the woman seems to participate in the event by sexually teasing the boar. The three men on the bottom right of the picture seem contaminated with the mood of the event, and they are also involved in reciprocal teasing and baiting as they are doing with the animals. Some kind of sexual orgy is taking over.[12]

The question is: what does this mean? The two animals in figure 2 and figure 3 are evidently different, as one could tell by their different horns. In figure 2, there is a man reaching for the front legs, although is unclear what he is doing. Most of these people are not really armed. The man on the back of the animal, pulling its tail, has some kind of sheath that could be for holding a dagger. The only efficient weapons that these people had were obsidian knives, which were short and very sharp. This made it impossible to kill an animal of this size from any distance; and that is the most probable reason why they performed this type of close-range hunting. If you compare figure 2 and figure 3, you understand the intention and the aim of the man heading to the front legs of the animal: that is, the cutting of the animal's ankles with his knife. I am not saying that these pictures are in sequence; what I am saying is that the technique of killing the animal was highly ritualized.

If figure 2 and figure 3 can be read in sequence, this is indeed because the gestures were very ritualized. Figure 2 represents an earlier moment in the hunting of the animal, while in figure 3 the hunting is over, the animal has already fallen on his front legs, and he becomes totally vulnerable to the mob. The animal suddenly deprived of its feet is about to collapse, and will never rise again. When this happens, the mob will probably rush forward, and quickly finish off the stag. The animal will be lynched with total impunity. The "teasing and baiting" is certainly present in our painting and its presence must be acknowledged, but it is not the sum total of the painting's significance. It is not acceptable as a definition of it. We cannot accept the "teasing and baiting" formula as an adequate summarisation of the action. It is not an end in itself for the community, but it might well be a means to an end. It distracts the stag's attention from a most vulnerable part of its own body, its front legs; it increases the animal's vulnerability to the real danger that threatens it: the loss of its own feet. The mob is never represented killing the animal. But obviously when the animal is down, the mob is going to rush upon the animal. So what we are witnessing here is the mob tormenting-to-death of an animal. The mob destruction of a single human individual is very important in the history of religion, but what I did not suspect is that the mobbing of an animal may be seen as the first form of sacrifice, precisely of ritual sacrifice. Here we have a ritual sacrifice coupled with hunting techniques, probably because these animals were eaten in big festivals. Only during festivals of this sort was wild venison consumed; normally, as I mentioned previously, these populations were eating sheep and goats (Hodder 2006, 198–99).

Such forms of ritual, the killing of wild animals, were not strictly necessary for alimentary purposes; this is all about looking towards the past—i.e., an act of collective memory recalling origin and provenance. It is past passion remembered; and it is passion for the past as a trace of origin and provenance—something religion always and necessarily does, both in myths and in rituals. The ritualistic aspects of these paintings point to a form of remembrance, to an account of ritual practices that present mythical characters.

It is as if they were looking back at the Paleolithic, so to speak, when the wild animal was all-important, because of the lack of domestication. If

FIGURE 4. Plastered bull heads or bucrania from Çatalhöyük. Image provided by Çatalhöyük Research Project.

you want to understand fully that this teasing and baiting of an animal had a strong ritualistic component and was not really a form of hunting, the first thing to consider is—counterintuitively, but in accord with actual fact—the economic aspect. These drawings show a sense that wild animals still retain a higher importance—which is why these representations focus on them. The problem that the domestication of the animals solved is not registered at all in the collective imagination of this people. Domesticated animals have no place in the iconography of that period, despite the fact that these populations consumed mainly meat meals. The second aspect to consider is the technological one, that is, the lack of weapons. From these pictures, one can notice that these people had bows, but there are no arrows. It might be that these bows were not powerful enough to kill these animals with thick skin and heavy fur. So they had to have the physical contact of close encounter with the animals to bring them down.

Another proof that these images represent the ritual killing of an animal is the way the horns of the stag are represented: in figure 2, they are on the head of the animal; in figure 3 it looks as if the horns are in the process of being removed and transported somewhere else. The archaeologists, in fact, have found clear evidence of their ritual use.

Figure 4 shows one of the benches where the ancestors were buried. This is the north wall, which is the sacred wall, and these are the horns of the animals that were hunted in the pictures we saw before. It is clear from this image that there was a sacred purpose in their hunting. However, one may ask, how do you shift from the image of an animal as an enemy that you persecute, that you treat badly because you are really mad at him, because he does not let himself be caught as he should, and he resists as much as he can, to a picture where his horns are protective, since they are inside the house and they stay inside the house for generations (they were repainted and reused when the new house was built on top of the preceding one)? Once the animal was dead, its significance changed completely and became protective; that is why it was put inside the house. It became divine. The logic of this is to be found in mimetic theory: the scapegoating united the mob against the animal. There is something mythical about these pictures: if you look at the members of the mob, they are wounded, and the idea that the image wants to convey is that they are wounded by the animal, who is responsible for this damage to humans. Arms, and even heads, are neatly cut off. However, an animal like this stag could hardly inflict that type of wound on these people. I think there is a purpose to this representation, and that purpose is to show that the animal was vanquished with great difficulty—whereupon peace is finally restored. The exaggeration of the animal's size is also part of the scapegoating process, since it represents the projecting of a menacing aspect onto an animal that is not particularly violent per se—a stag.

The explanation brought by mimetic theory to these pictures would suggest that there was probably internal disorder and violence inside this society; and the hunt, or at least the ritualized collective killing of these animals, was a measure invented to give back unity to the group. This procedure allowed the group to shift the violence internal to the community onto an external agent, which was ritually and collectively killed. The powerful phase shift from community violence to restored peace was perceived as divine. Religion is never senseless or purposeless as the modern world believes.

We could compare these ritualistic images to the Spanish bullfight, which could be defined as a "teasing and baiting" of the bull, because the first part of the bullfight, which is the longest, with the planting of the *banderillas* into the shoulders of the bull, the play with the *muleta*, and so forth, are not deadly for the bull; but they do get him tired, exhausted, and into a state where it is possible for the matador to kill the animal in the appropriate ritual fashion: facing the horns of the animal and planting the sword deep into the heart of the animal in a single, elegant gesture, which is the climax of the bullfight. The "teasing and baiting" definition is just as wrong as it would be in the case of a bullfight. If we defined a bullfight as the "teasing and baiting of a bull," we would say something true and yet we would miss the killing of the bull which is the real end of the bullfight. and this killing is complex and ritualized. Goya has captured these moments in magnificent fashion, for instance in *Scene at a Bullfight: Diversión de España* (1825); his bullfights have huge crowds being part of the ritualistic spectacle, and in some ways, they look very similar to this Neolithic art. The *Rg Veda* also traces the origin of religious ritual back to bull sacrifice. Bull sacrifice, bull baiting, and bull leaping are in fact shown on the oldest Vedic seals. Later scriptures rejected the practice, but the veneration of the cow is a clear example of how the animal was felt to be a savior, a deity, an animal capable of producing peace in various ways. The prohibition on killing the cow is due to a sacrificial past that is repented of, and rejected. This seems to confirm that wild animals were at first domesticated for the purpose of sacrifice rather than for meat. Wild animals were first sacrificed and then domesticated. The theology of the cow in India certainly seems to suggest this: the classification of this animal fell into a gray zone in between sacredness and domestication. It has become domesticated because it was needed in sacrificial rituals, but then as the sacrificial rituality was progressively abandoned, the animal never reached a secularized status, becoming edible, but remained invested with a sacred aura.

We are dealing with a form of religion that is very difficult to situate, because one of the images that have fascinated archaeologists, and Ian Hodder in particular, is the image of the leopards (figure 5). Leopards were present in the region at that time, and Hodder spent a lot of time looking for bones and remains of leopards, which are represented in other pictures. They are mostly represented motionless and face-to-face, in complete balance. While all the other images are of motion and turmoil, the image of the leopards is one of equilibrium, of total balance, despite the fact that it seems to suggest violence: they touch, but they do not fight. My sense is that they

FIGURE 5. Leopard relief from Çatalhöyük. Images provided by Çatalhöyük Research Project.

represent an older religion that is still in existence to a certain extent, and it is in conflict with the new one, which involves the animal ritual described above. This is just a vague hint. Not a single leopard bone was found in this site; the only element that was discovered was one claw of a leopard, which was turned into an ornamental object, a necklace (Hodder 2006, 260). That is why I tend to think that the Leopard religion was an earlier one, which is in conflict with this one, although the details cannot be worked out at this stage of the archaeological findings.[13] We are dealing with worlds that are dynamic from a cultural standpoint.

One may say that these images attest what Walter Burkert claimed in *Homo Necans* about the origins of sacrifice emerging from ritual hunting, a book where he also makes reference to the consecrated horns of the home sanctuaries of Çatalhöyük (Burkert 1983, 12–15). I think that this finding would strengthen his hypothesis, and I am willing to bend the explanatory logic of mimetic theory to this evidential finding. I think, though, that the human is always there at the beginning, because the animal is attributed with human feelings.[14] I think that the best way to interpret these pictures is to look for a combination of the explanatory principles of mimetic theory and Burkert's hypothesis. If animal hunting was the primary source of the sacrificial logic, evidence is abundant of human beings also being sacrificed, and in one way or another, one could certainly claim that for these populations, such a distinction was not as definite and sharp as we have it now. In the logic of sacrifice, the sacrificial victim ought to be at the same time different and similar to the members of the community. We cannot take for granted that the difference between man and animal always meant what it means to us today.[15] This question touches the problem of the incomplete separation of the outside/inside structure, which is rather a continuum.[16]

Notes

This text represents, authorized by René Girard, a reconstitution by the editors from video recordings of a lecture given at the COV&R Conference in Riverside, California, in June 2008. All references and footnotes are added by the editors of the present volume, who have also incorporated into the presentation certain replies to questions.

1. Chauvet in France, the paintings of which may be thirty-five thousand years old according to radiocarbon dating, and date back to 33,000 BCE (Upper Paleolithic); at Lascaux in France (ca. 15,000 BCE) and Altamira in Spain, where the painting died out about 10,000 BCE.
2. Ian Hodder mentions this fact in his book (Hodder 2006, 163–64).
3. "Nine laboratories have been built on the site, covering topics such as: faunal analysis; archeobotanical analysis; conservation; computing and data management; human remains; pottery; groundstone and obsidian analysis; micromorphology and so on" (Hodder 2006, 43).
4. Girard was involved in an interdisciplinary working group organized by Ian Hodder at Stanford in 2007 (Hodder 2010, 13).
5. The 2008 Riverside text adds: "They are remarkably accurate and I refer to them simply because they facilitate the comparative analysis of these paintings."
6. During the Neolithic Revolution, which occurred during the early Holocene, there were at least two auroch domestication events: one related to the Indian subspecies, leading to Zebu cattle; the other one related to the Eurasian subspecies, leading to taurine cattle.
7. Hodder observes that "all buildings give abundant evidence of both ritual and mundane activity. Indeed, it has become impossible to separate these two spheres" (Hodder 2010, 16). "Çatalhöyük is as much a cemetery as a settlement. It is as much a ritual centre of production. These various functions are integrated in the house" (Hodder 2006, 99). From the point of view of mimetic theory, these buildings were erected first of all as ritualistic spaces that gradually were converted into mundane housing. This becomes clear considering an earlier settlement like Göbekli Tepe, where the ritualistic function of the buildings predates any forms of settlement, and of domestication of animals and plants.
8. As Hodder explains, "Many (if not all) daily acts seem to have been embedded in ritual. . . . Daily practice within the building at Çatalhöyük was also formalized by division of space and activity" (Hodder 2006, 119).

9. It is clear that for Hodder this "teasing and baiting" did have a ritualistic function, and that animals were killed to gain trophies, which were displayed in the houses. Hodder also refers to the action represented in terms of "hunting/teasing/killing" (Hodder 2006, 203). Yet it is clearer still that Girard objects against Hodder that the ritualistic aspects of these practices are not emphasized enough. The objection is more explicitly asserted as such in the written version of the Riverside 2008 presentation. Girard writes of figure 2: "The teasing and baiting is certainly present in our painting and its presence must be acknowledged, but it is not the sum total of the painting's significance. It is not the be-all and end-all as it is for Hodder. The deed [of killing] is never shown, but is no invention of mine. If the definition in terms of teasing and baiting are inadequate, the reason is not that teasing and baiting are [not] really present: they certainly are, but they are not what Ian Hodder thinks they are, the main significance of the pictures. They are a means to the real end of the mob which is the hunting and killing of the animal." When he comes to discuss the religious meaning of removing the antlers and their installation at the sacred north wall of the houses, where the dead are buried, he writes, in implicit correction of Hodder: "The reasons for this display had certainly nothing to do with the reasons [why] hunting trophies are exhibited in private rooms today, for the celebration of individual courage and personal vanity. In Catalhoyuk the horns and antlers were exhibited as an object of reverence and worship. They certainly had a positive value for all those who lived and were buried in these houses."

10. The 2008 Riverside text points out that leopards are not represented in these pictures among the adversarial animals, surrounded by human tormentors and open to ritual killing. The reason may lie in the immediate identification of hunters with the top animal predator, whose qualities are appropriated ritually by the very wearing of the leopard-skin loincloth, and/or in the classification of sacrificial animals as offering simultaneously both a potency to be appropriated and a source of meat. Compare the similarities with animal representations at Göbleki Tepe.

11. For a discussion of gender roles in the Neolithic period, see Bolger 2010.

12. As Girard explains in *Violence and the Sacred*, sacrificial rituals often display orgiastic elements, as in the case of Dionysian Mysteries (Girard 1977, 134ff.).

13. However, it is possible to speculate a bit further from the point of view of mimetic theory and see in this representation an image of the "fearful symmetry" of the so-called monstrous doubles discussed by Girard in *Violence and the Sacred*: "Under the heading Monstrous Double we shall group all the hallucinatory phenomena provoked at the height of the crisis by unrecognised reciprocity. The monstrous double is . . . to be found whenever we encounter an 'I' or an 'Other' caught up in a constant interchange of differences" (Girard 1977, 165). Rather than two actual animals, this would be the representation of the collective mimetic rage, which escalates due to the mimetic mirroring of rivalrous conflicts, giving way to the scapegoating process, and therefore to the emergence of the sacred. The image is therefore symbolic rather than representational in strictly mimetic terms. More than the leopards themselves, the emphasis lies on the rosettes of the bodies, which are carefully designed and crafted, and take a variety of forms. In one of the images reproduced in Hodder's book (Hodder 2006, 1), the rosettes look like a cluster of eyes, while in figure 3, they seem to take the shape of a stylized body image of humans, which resemble some splayed figure reliefs inserted in the walls of some buildings of Çatalhöyük, where also the belly buttons are visible (Hodder 2006, 201). This would also explain the absence of any remains of leopards in the settlement. The leopard is the mythical form of the collective mimetic rage: "The double and the monster are one and the same being. . . . There is no monster who does not tend to duplicate himself or to 'marry' another monster, no double who does not yield a monstrous aspect upon close scrutiny" (Girard 1977, 170).

14. Hodder's interpretation seems to be closer to Burkert's, arguing about the precedence of animal ritualistic representation (and therefore sacrificial practices) to the human ones: "It is possible

to see an increase in the representation of humans, expecially active humans, gradually emerging after the Ice Age. Mary Helms argues that a shift from animal gods, to ancestors, to human gods may accompany the development of farming and settled village life" (Hodder 2006, 205). Hodder refers to M. W. Helms, "Tangible Materiality and Cosmological Others in the Development of Sedentism," in *Rethinking Materiality: The Engagement of Mind with the Material World*, ed. E. DeMarrais, C. Gosden, and A. C. Renfrew (Cambridge: McDonald Institute for Archaeological Research, 2004).

15. "A number of archeologists . . . now argue that personhood in the Neolithic was less whole, more divided and more continuous with the surrounding object world than in modern Western thought" (Hodder 2006, 219–20).

16. In discussing the findings at Göbekli Tepe, Ian Hodder writes that "the specific symbolism on the large stone pillars indicates a centrality of the human form, dominating and dwarfing the world of wild animals. This central human agency was perhaps a necessary precursor to the relationship with animals that we term 'domestication'" (Hodder 2010, 20).

Works Cited

Bolger, D. 2010. "The Dynamics of Gender in Early Agricultural Societies of the Near East." *Signs* 35, no. 2: 503–31.

Burkert, W. 1983. *Homo Necans: The Anthropology of Ancient Greek Sacrificial Ritual and Myth*. Translated by Peter Bing. Berkeley: University of California Press.

Girard, R. 1977. *Violence and the Sacred*. Translated by P. Gregory. Baltimore: Johns Hopkins University Press.

Hodder, I. 2006. *The Leopard's Tale: Revealing the Mysteries of Çatalhöyük*. London: Thames & Hudson.

———, ed. 2010. *Religion in the Emergence of Civilization: Çatalhöyük as a Case Study*. Cambridge: Cambridge University Press.

Self-transcendence and Tangled Hierarchies in Çatalhöyük

Jean-Pierre Dupuy

In this essay I am pursuing a very limited goal: to facilitate the conversation between empirical social sciences as well established as archaeology and anthropology, on the one hand, and a specific interpretative theory whose epistemological status remains in large part to be defined—the mimetic theory that René Girard has elaborated over several decades and that has been taken up, developed, discussed, and tested by a growing number of scholars across the world. One possible way of connecting those two corpuses is to do it at the formal level rather than at the level of content—as it is done, for instance, in this volume by Girard himself, by Fornari, and by Antonello and Gifford. The models and networks of concepts that structure the two approaches to human and social reality have indeed many resonances that seem more cogent than simple analogies. It seems worthwhile to analyze and assess them on their own merit. I will engage primarily with Ian Hodder's reflections on possible interpretative approaches to the findings at the nine thousand-year-old Neolithic site of Çatalhöyük in central Turkey, the excavation of which he has directed since 1993, and which has attracted the interest of many archaeologists, anthropologists, and scholars interested in mimetic theory. My own formalized thinking turns around the following concepts: path dependency, tangled hierarchy, self-transcendence, endogenous fixed points, and collective self-opacity (*méconnaissance*). These concepts, in their legitimate extensions, partially overlap, like the red tiles on a Mediterranean roof. After a theoretical premise, I will apply these concepts to the interpretation of some of the key symbolic religious representations found in Çatalhöyük in the light of mimetic theory.

Entanglement, Path Dependency, and Emergence

In his book *Entangled: An Archaeology of the Relationships between Humans and Things* (2012), Ian Hodder manifests clearly the ambition to give new foundations to the (empirical) social sciences by putting center stage the concept of entanglement. Any science rests on a certain form of determinism, and the kind of determinism proper to the sciences of man is entanglement. Hodder writes:

> The determinative factors in human action are neither material nor ideal. What is determinative is the entanglement itself, the totality of the links which hold and produce individual events, things, humans. The notion that humans dig themselves into the holes of human-thing dependences does indeed appear very determinative. Once a hole has been dug, there are very few options left moving forward. (Hodder 2012, xx)

In chapter 5 of his book, Hodder defines entanglement more precisely as follows:

> The previous three chapters have examined how humans depend on things (HT), how things depend on other things (TT), how things depend on humans (TH). If we add the obvious point that humans depend on humans (HH), then entanglement, at one level, is simply the addition of these four sets of dependences and dependencies.
>
> Entanglement = (HT) + (TT) + (TH) + (HH)
>
> The defining aspect of entanglement with things is that humans get caught in a double bind, depending on things that depend on humans. Put another way, things as we want them have limited ability to reproduce

> themselves, so in our dependence on them we become entrapped in their dependence on us. . . .
>
> There is thus a dialectic relationship between dependence, often productive and enabling, and dependency, often constraining and limiting. Humans and things, humans and humans, things and things depend on each other, they rely on each other, produce each other. But that dependence is in continual tension with boundaries and constraints as things and humans reach various limits (of resources, of material and social possibility) that are overcome by, that demand, yet further dependence and investment. Entanglement can thus be defined as the dialectic of dependence and dependency. (Hodder 2012, 89)

The interest of this notion, which is very cogent for mimetic theory as well, is that it provides a supplement or a replacement for the two basic models that have been proposed by way of conceptualizing a widely recognized fundamental characteristic of evolutionary processes: namely, that they are self-organizing. A fundamental distinction must be drawn between two principles or models of evolution: the first one is dubbed "order from noise," and the second "complexity from noise."[1] To illustrate their difference at a formal level, I would refer to two very simple mathematical thought experiments. The first—Buffon's needle—is just an illustration of the so-called law of large numbers, one of the pillars of the probability calculus: the frequency of a random event tends over time towards its a priori probability.[2] The second thought experiment illustrates the remarkable morphogenetic power of imitation. Dubbed the "Polya's urn scheme," after the name of Hungarian-born mathematician George Polya, it has become the matrix of a wide variety of scientific models.

An urn contains one white ball and one black ball; one ball is drawn randomly from the urn and its color observed; it is then placed back in the urn together with another ball of the same color. Hence the number of balls in the urn increases by one every time. The question is, how does the proportion of white balls, say, evolve over time? It is very easy to simulate this evolution with a simple calculator coupled with a generator of random numbers. We realize the experiment and observe with surprise that the system seems to have the same kind of dynamics as the Buffon's needle case: a series of oscillations dampen out and converge towards a certain value. A second surprise is that this value is not 0.5 (in which case half the balls in the urn would be white). Why is this a surprise? Because the setting is perfectly symmetrical, so that the observed breach of symmetry seems to come from nowhere. No rational explanation seems capable of accounting for it.

Note what makes this model the simplest formalization of a mimetic dynamic. Every random event (here, the drawing out of a ball of a certain color) changes the conditions for the next draw by reinforcing the odds of the color in question. This self-reinforcing process is very much akin to the mimetic pattern that Girard called "double mediation": imitating a desire that itself imitates one's own desire. There is no original desire, and the object on which rival desires converge is the emerging production of the mechanism itself.[3]

There is a fundamental difference with the case of Buffon's needle. Every time the experiment is carried out again, the same phenomenology obtains, but the value towards the convergence of dynamics is different. It is entirely contingent on the experiment in question. The dynamics seem to be converging towards a preexisting value, but the value is generated by the dynamics themselves. From within, it is impossible to realize that a preexisting end does not guide the course of evolution. From without—that is, if we are able to pull ourselves up by our own bootstraps and contemplate from there the set of all possible trajectories—our specific world appears in all its contingent singularity to be one among a manifold of possibilities. It is a case of "complexity from noise." Chance here brings about a form of necessity or tautness that appears as such only retrospectively.

The relationship between the dynamics and its asymptotic behavior (called, in the jargon of the mathematical theory of dynamical systems, an "attractor") takes on the form of a loop that is the signature feature of a self-organizing system—that is, a loop between an emerging level (the attractor) and its conditions of production (the dynamics) (see figure 1). In *Introduction aux sciences sociales: Logique des phénomènes collectifs*, I have shown that all the mimetic and sacrificial figures that mimetic theory has put forward or brought out (double mediation, pseudo-narcissism, pseudo-masochism, the pattern of the "Stranger," the scapegoating mechanism) are particular instances of this bootstrapping scheme (Dupuy 1992).

Any theory of evolution, in biology or elsewhere, that is structured by the "order from noise" model suffers from a fatal flaw: it is unable to account

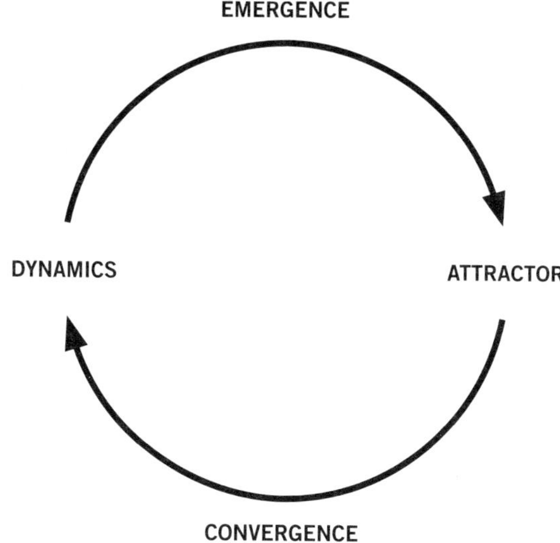

FIGURE 1. Complexity from noise: the dynamic converges toward an attractor that is generated by itself. The evolution is said to be path-dependent (author).

for the diversity of the world. The dynamics are bound to converge towards preexisting states. Neo-Darwinism, in biology or, worse, in the social sciences, when it refers to a principle of selection, such as the "survival of the fittest," falls under that fundamental critique. Darwin himself saw the danger. He did not think that selection, the sacred cow of vulgar Darwinism, was the only factor in evolution. Today, one could even say that it is not even the most important one. In the sixth edition of *On the Origin of Species*, Darwin wrote: "I am convinced that selection has been the main, *but not the exclusive*, means of modification." He added: "Ever since the first edition, I have repeated this claim again and again. This has been of no avail. Great is the power of misrepresentation" (Darwin 1872, 395).

In order to escape that fate, mechanisms capable of generating "complexity from noise" are required. Mimesis is the ground (or at least a major ground) from which they stem.

Tangled Hierarchies in Anthropology and the Deconstruction of the Sciences of Man

"There is a *tension* between the historical build up of ever more intricate and constraining dependences and the open and contingent nature of entanglements," Hodder writes (2012, xx). If the model of entanglement is path dependence/y, "tension" is not the right word. The contrast between the tautness of an apparent quasi-necessity and the openness and contingency proper to entanglement stems from the existence of two different viewpoints on the same process—the former being the viewpoint from within, the latter from without.

The phrase "tangled hierarchy" was actually coined by cognitive philosopher Douglas Hofstadter in his book *Gödel, Escher, Bach* (1979). One would think that the concept is perfectly appropriate to defining entanglement in Hodder's sense. Hodder is keen on distinguishing his approach from such intellectual tools as Actor Network Theory, which are essentially symmetrical approaches. The very word "dependence," let alone "dependency," implies a hierarchical relation between two terms: if A depends on B, then B has precedence over A.

However, in the case of entanglement, the hierarchy is inverted within itself, as it were. M. C. Escher's famous *Print Gallery* illustrates this notion beautifully (see figure 2). The print that the young man is admiring in an art gallery represents a harbor that turns out to be the town in which the print gallery and the young man find themselves.[4] This is very much consistent with Hodder's characterization of entanglement in terms of path dependency. There is indeed a tangled hierarchy between the path-dependent dynamics and its attractor(s). The attractor guides the dynamics from above, as it were, as a lodestar, but it is the dynamics itself that self-transcends and generates the attractor. It turns out that this structure has played an essential role in the intellectual environment (essentially French) in which Girard has developed mimetic thoery.

Anthropologist and Indianist Louis Dumont characterized the relation between a whole and an element of that whole as being a hierarchical relation. But he used the word "hierarchy" in a special sense, which must not be confused with its meaning in the army, for example. It is not a linear relation

FIGURE 2. M.C. Escher, *Print Gallery* (1956). The M.C. Escher Company—The Netherlands. All rights reserved. www.mcescher.com.

of mere superiority, but instead a relation of hierarchical opposition between the encompassing (the whole) and the encompassed (the element). Dumont dubbed this relation the "encompassing of the contrary" and showed that in holistic societies, like India, there is always a reversal of the hierarchy within the hierarchy. Take the Brahmin and the king, for instance: the Brahmin represents the sacred, the encompassing level, and is hierarchically superior to the king. But in certain domains to which the social hierarchy assigns an inferior rank, the hierarchy is reversed and the king stands above the Brahmin. As Dumont puts it, the Brahmin is above the king because it is only at inferior levels that the king is above the Brahmin.

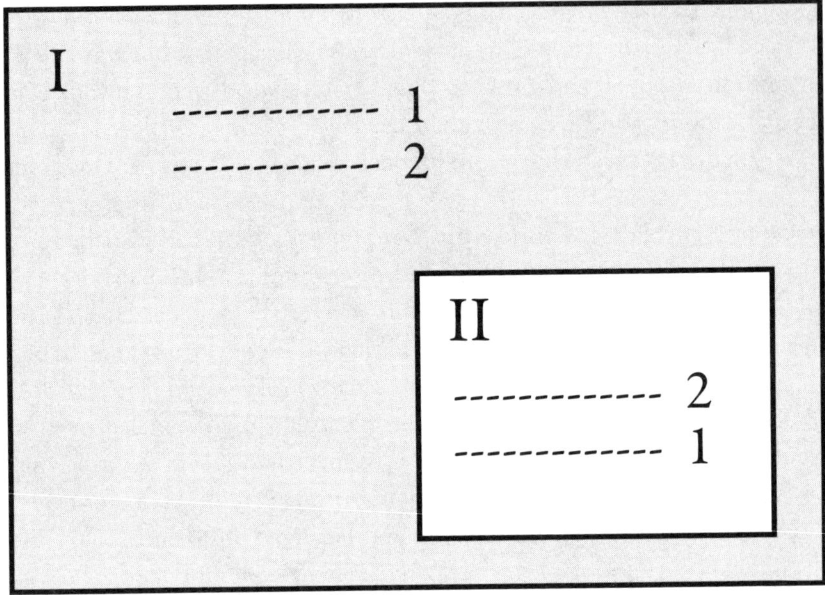

FIGURE 3. Louis Dumont's "reversal of a hierarchical opposition." Figure by the author.

What Dumont called "hierarchy"—he gave this term a meaning to conform to its etymology as "sacred order," i.e., the logical form of holist societies, molded by religion—is none other than what Hofstadter calls "tangled hierarchy." Its structure can be represented in figure 3. In the Indian case, for instance, I, the superior domain, represents the sacred, and II, the profane, while 1 represents the Brahmin and 2, the king. For Dumont, this form characterizes the preeminence of a social totality "always already" there, very much in keeping with the structuralist motto of the time.

At approximately the same period, Jacques Derrida used the same pattern and the same phrase, "reversal of a hierarchical opposition," to establish the impossibility of conceiving or achieving any autonomous totality at all (Derrida 1967). The very same form of tangled hierarchy was for the "deconstructionists" the signature of the self-destruction of any pretension to self-sufficiency or autonomy. They dubbed this form the "logic of the supplement."

The conflict of interpretations between the followers of Dumont (among them some of the most important political philosophers of the time, such as Claude Lefort and Marcel Gauchet) and the deconstructionists had important political implications—particularly so in the case of the traditional hierarchical relation between man and woman. For Dumont, the reversal of this hierarchy was part and parcel of the hierarchical relation; it was the sign of the totality, the unified whole constituted by the couple. As he put it, "The mother of the family (an Indian family, for example), inferior though she may be made by her sex, in some respects nonetheless dominates the relationships within the family" (Dumont 1981, 241). For the Derridians, on the other hand, reversal of the hierarchy was a major deconstructionist task. From Dumont's viewpoint, it was equality that was the major threat to hierarchy; for the Derridians, as Jonathan Culler put it, "it does not suffice to deny a hierarchical relation in the name of equality, it does little good simply to claim equality . . . for woman against man. . . . Affirmations of equality will not disrupt the hierarchy. Only if it includes an inversion or reversal does a deconstruction have a chance of dislocating the hierarchical structure" (Culler 1982, 166).

It is possible to transcend the opposition between those two interpretations of the same logical pattern; and that is what Girard did. He resorted to a third interpretation, one that was made available, unbeknownst to him, in a completely distinct area of human thought: the logic of complex, self-organizing systems that had been developed since the 1950s in the sciences of nature and life (Dupuy 2000).

The concept of a self-organizing (autopoietic, autonomous) system was in particular constructed by biologists belonging to the cybernetic tradition, in their attempt to characterize what it is for a system to be endowed with autonomy (Varela 1979). Dissatisfied by the dominant metaphor in molecular biology, the metaphor of the genetic program, they asserted that it made it impossible to conceive the autonomy of the living organism. Now, it is well known—and molecular biologists were the first to recognize this—that if one takes the metaphor of the genetic program seriously, one runs immediately into a strange paradox: one has to admit that this program is a self-programming program, or rather, a program requiring the outputs of its execution in order to be executed—the operators that perform the transcription and the translation of DNA into proteins are themselves proteins. They are coded within the DNA in such a way that in order for the translation to be possible, it has always already to have taken place. This paradox may be

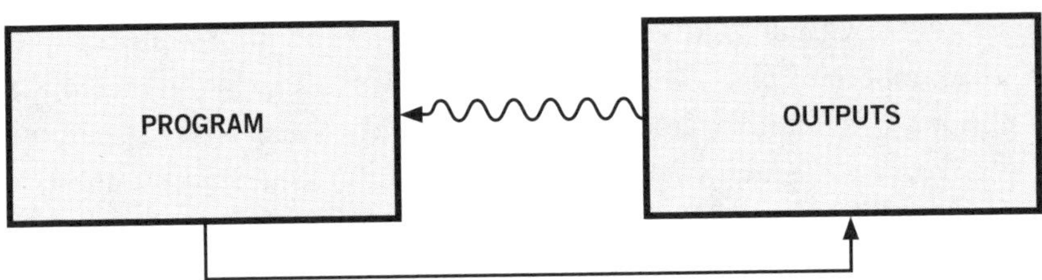

FIGURE 4. The paradox of a program requiring the outputs of its execution in order to be executed. Figure by the author.

depicted in figure 4. One recognizes here the very form that Derrida calls the "logic of the supplement" and Ian Hodder "entanglement." Now, the amazing fact is the following: it is this very same paradox that has been taken by the theoreticians of autonomous systems as the distinctive characteristic of what they call autonomy. On the other hand, the same paradox is the Derridians' main weapon for the deconstruction of any pretension to autonomy or self-sufficiency.

The attentive reader will have noticed that this "strange loop," as Hofstadter calls it, is not the same pattern as (tangled) hierarchy in Dumont's sense. If the latter is well represented by Escher's *Print Gallery*, it is another, more famous, print by the same Escher that represents the former: *Drawing Hands* (see figure 5). This figure is paradoxical because it is static. With the inclusion of time in the picture, the paradox resolves itself through a wild oscillation between the two terms. Between the operator and the operand, the program and the data, the cause and the effect, the metalanguage and the language, there is a continuous reversal of levels, in which each in turn sits on the higher level, then on the lower, and so on—not unlike two rivals, each alternately gaining the upper hand for a short time without ever completely defeating the other. Figure 6 is one of violence and vengeance, fully exemplified by one of the most extraordinary images found in Çatalhöyük: the two leopards facing each other in a perfectly symmetrical position.

There is, however, a relation between this representation of tangled hierarchy and the Dumontian one. Suppose we were to film the oscillation engendered by these hands, using a camera prone to afterimage. In each image, one hand would dominate the other, but the viewer would perceive superimposed the faded trace of the previous moment when the dominated

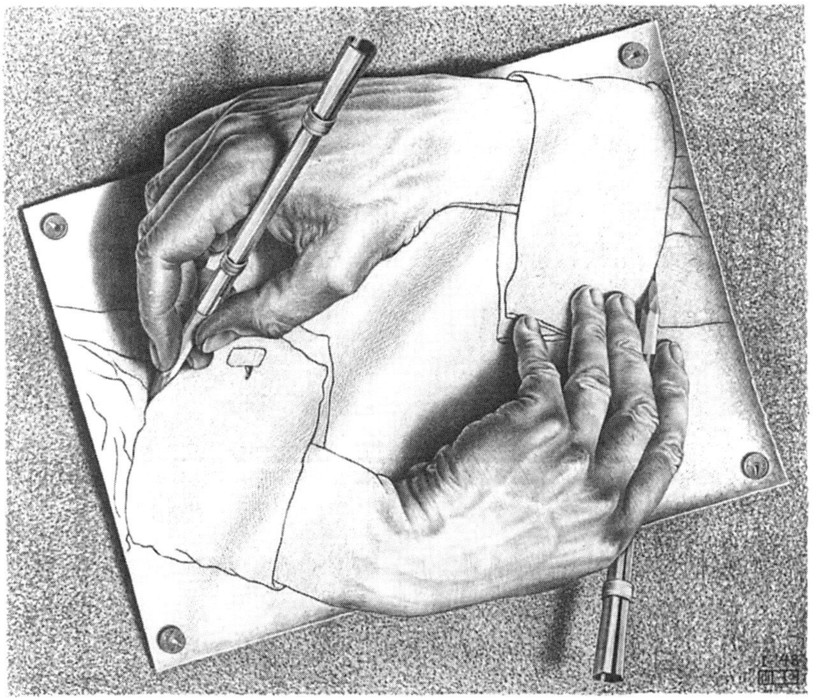

FIGURE 5. M.C. Escher, *Drawing Hands* (1948). The M.C. Escher Company—The Netherlands. All rights reserved. www.mcescher.com.

hand was dominant and vice versa. Each image is a figure of tangled hierarchy à la Dumont. The entanglement of the hierarchy is like the recollection that the vanquished was once the victor and could be the victor again. It betrays a feeling of fascination mixed with fear vis-à-vis the vanquished. The possibility of that reversal is contained within the encompassing hierarchy.

Mimetic theory could be summarized as a momentous conceptual edifice that rests on the ambivalence of the verb "to contain" in our Latin languages. To contain is to have within oneself, but it is also to stem, to keep in check.

In mimetic theory, the mechanisms responsible for the self-constitution of the social order are also responsible for its always possible reversal and self-decomposition.[5] We now perceive the symmetrical blind spots in the visions of Dumont and Derrida: Dumont sees only order; Derrida sees only

FIGURE 6. Leopard relief from Çatalhöyük. Images provided by Çatalhöyük Research Project.

the crisis that lurks beneath—with both of them missing the key point that order contains the crisis that undermines it.

Self-transcendence or the Machine for Manufacturing Gods

"Self-transcendence" (or "self-exteriorization") is the English translation of the German word *Entäußerung*, which belongs to the Hegelian terminology and was used by two Vienna-born scholars: psychotherapist Viktor Frankel, the author of the celebrated *Man's Quest for Meaning*, and social philosopher and Nobel Laureate in Economics Friedrich Hayek.

A similar expression, "transcendence within immanence," has been the motto of the phenomenological school from Edmund Husserl onward. The phrase "pulling oneself up by one's bootstraps" expresses the same idea of a system capable of creating its own exteriority in order to act upon itself. It finds its origin in a book by Rudolf Erich Raspe published in 1785 under the title *The Surprising Adventures of Baron Münchausen*.

In his contribution to the volume edited by Ian Hodder (2010), cognitive anthropologist Maurice Bloch wrote, very much in tune with his colleagues Dan Sperber, Scott Atran, and Pascal Boyer:

> I am confident that there was no religion in Çatalhöyük, any more than there was among the Zafimaniry before Christianity arrived there. Looking for religion is therefore a misleading wild goose chase. The English word "religion" inevitably refers to what English speakers have known, and no amount of redefinition or manipulation of the term can escape the associations that a particular history has created.... The kind of phenomena that the English word "religion," and the associated word "belief," can be made to evoke have, at most, a history of five thousand years. This is thousands of years after the establishment of Çatalhöyük. (Bloch 2010, 161)

If Bloch sees no religion in Çatalhöyük, it may simply be that he isn't looking in the right direction. Anthropologists in the Lévi-Straussian (turned cognitive) tradition very often reject words like "sacrifice," "religion," "belief," because they take them to reflect the hidden influence of Christianity on their discipline. The irony is that there are other, well-established anthropological traditions stemming from the works of Max Weber, Emile Durkheim, or Marcel Mauss that explain the process of secularization—what Weber called the "disenchantment of the world"—as a paradoxical consequence of the spread of Christian faith that in its turn prepared the way for the flourishing of economic rationality.[6] A number of these thinkers have described Christianity as "the religion of the end of religion." To some extent, mimetic theory synthesizes those traditions. Christianity, most assuredly, has no place whatsoever in Çatalhöyük. But, where Christianity is not, it is entirely likely that religion—or better, the sacred—lurks somewhere.

If mimetic theory is correct, the best way to find the place where religion resides is to look for violence. When Girard chose the phrase "Violence and the Sacred" as the title of his 1972 book, the "and" had more the value of a copula than of a conjunction. The sacred is the externalization of violence, or better, violence transcending itself. And there was much violence in

Çatalhöyük. However, that violence existed in the representations, in the imagery, but not, or very little, in real life. As Hodder writes:

> There is much evidence coming out of the human remains laboratory that the people at Çatalhöyük lived nonviolent lives. There were few indications of the cuts, wounds, parry fractures and crushed skulls that are so common on many other sites. So how had the potential for violence been so well managed at Çatalhöyük? (Hodder 2010, 343)

In the light of mimetic theory, it is tempting to surmise that it was the religion of Çatalhöyük, whatever its form, that kept that momentous "potential for violence" in check and managed it cleverly. Hodder is not far from making this assumption when he writes:

> Social violence was dealt with by living within a *symbolic, transcendent world of violence* in which conflicts were resolved and social structures made permanent. . . . Through violent *imagery* and *practice* the person was drawn into a social world in which long-term transcendent social institutions were increasingly prevalent. (Hodder 2010, 343, 349)

The question is: what kind of violence can be labeled "symbolic" and "transcendent"? Is it a violence that makes no victims, no harm, because it exists only in representations? The fact that the imagery is violent is in itself remarkable, notes Hodder. It contrasts with classical representations of female fertility and images of birth and rebirth and seems to be contemporary with the first large agglomerations and the development of agriculture.

Let us step back for a while. Any secular account of religious life has necessarily the form of a tangled hierarchy. It must posit that men make the gods that make them. But it is not any kind of tangled hierarchy since it must reflect the fact that one term retains some precedence over the other, such as in a Dumontian (tangled) hierarchy in which the sacred remains above the profane. I will speak of an oriented tangled hierarchy to contrast it with Escher's *Drawing Hands*, which are purely undifferentiated.

The mechanism that brings about this orientation is what I call self-transcendence. Mimetic theory posits the existence of a universal mechanism of this kind by which violence, due to its imitative (contagious) properties, is capable of transcending itself and creating stable institutions, which we call "the sacred." I will flesh out in a highly schematic and formal way the major steps of Girard's demonstration.

In building his theory, René Girard has renewed the great Franco-British tradition of religious anthropology that was brought to a premature halt by decades of structuralism and post-structuralism, and now, by the cognitivist paradigm. Before vanishing from the intellectual stage, religious anthropology had reached the following basic conclusions:

1. All non-modern social and cultural institutions are rooted in the sacred. Durkheim, in his great work *The Elementary Forms of Religious Life*, congratulated himself on having established that "the fundamental categories of thought, and therefore of science, have religious origins." As a result, he concluded, "it can be said that nearly all great social institutions are derived from religion" (Durkheim 1979, 598).
2. The sacred has three components: myths, rituals, and prohibitions (that is, beliefs, practice, and morals).
3. The most fundamental component is ritual.
4. The most primitive ritual form is sacrifice.

At the heart of the Girardian hypothesis is the proposition that the sacred is nothing other than the violence of men, expelled, exteriorized, hypostatized. The god-making machine runs on imitation, namely, the contagious character of violence. At the paroxysm of the "sacrificial crisis," when a murderous frenzy has shattered the system of differences that makes up the social order and sparked a war of all against all, violent contagion produces a catastrophic convergence of every enmity upon an arbitrary member of the collectivity. Putting that member to death is what abruptly restores peace. The result is religion in its three component parts. First comes mythology. The interpretation of the founding event makes the victim out to be a supernatural being, capable at once of introducing disorder and of creating order. Next comes ritual. Always sacrificial at the outset, it begins by miming the violent decomposition of the group so that it may go on to stage the reestablishment of order through the killing of a surrogate victim. Last comes the system of prohibitions and obligations, the effect of which is to prevent a new eruption of the conflicts that previously engulfed the community.

The sacred is fundamentally ambivalent: it uses violence to hold back violence. It contains violence, in both senses of the word. This is clear in the case of the sacrificial gesture that restores order. It is never other than one more murder, even if it is meant to be the last one. That is equally true of the system of prohibitions and obligations. The social structures that unify the community in normal times are the very same ones that tear it apart in times of crisis. When a prohibition is transgressed, the obligations of solidarity, leaping over the barriers of time and space (as in the mechanism of the vendetta), draw into an ever wider conflict people who were in no way concerned with the original confrontation.

These "things hidden since the foundation of the world" are not unknown to us. They have become an open secret, so to speak. All one needs to do is glance through a newspaper. The term "scapegoat" is served up at every opportunity. Just think about the word. This expression declares the innocence of the victim. It reveals the mechanism of the exteriorization of violence.

For Girard, that knowledge working through us has a Christian origin. The account of the death of Jesus on the Cross is, as nineteenth-century anthropology has accurately observed, similar to the stories one finds at the heart of so many religions. If one sticks to the facts, there is no important difference between Christianity and a primitive religion. But it is the interpretation that changes everything. Here, Girard is an inverse image of Nietzsche. The gospel account is the first not to be narrated by the persecutors. It sides with the victim, whose perfect innocence it proclaims—which is why Nietzsche accused Christianity of being a slave morality.

According to Girard, this knowledge has clogged up the works of the machine for making the sacred, damaging it irreparably. As it sacralizes less and less well, it produces more and more violence, but a violence that has lost the power to impose order on itself. Such is the modern world, described as a "low-gear mimetic crisis," "without catastrophic escalation or resolution of any kind" (Dumouchel 1979, 177). The catastrophe is constantly deferred until the final Apocalypse.

To sum up, according to mimetic theory there are two forms of violence: V1, the war of all against all, which is a generalization by contagion of the duel; and V2, the collective killing of a single victim. From V1 to V2, given certain conditions,[7] the passage is automatic, due to the contagiousness of violence. V2 itself has two varieties: the spontaneous event and its ritualistic

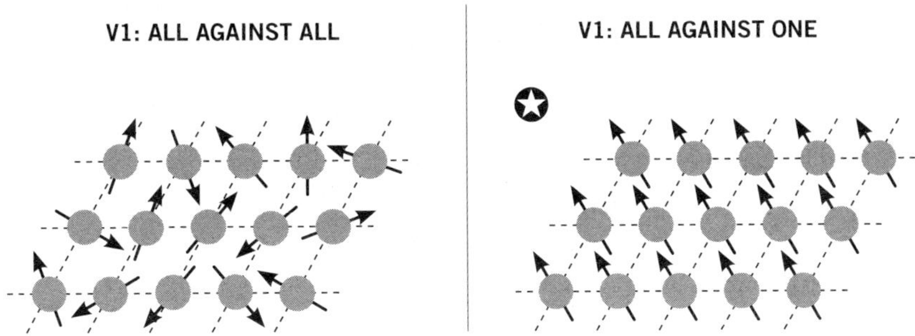

FIGURE 7. The war of all against all vs. the collective killing of a single victim. Figure by the author.

reproduction. This is, according to mimetic theory, how the sacred emerges from violence. The two forms can be represented in figure 7.

What, then, about Çatalhöyük? It is easy to understand what is perhaps in the nature of the comments made by Girard in response to Ian Hodder's book:

> The animal suddenly deprived of its feet is about to collapse, and will never rise again. When this happens, the mob will probably rush forward, and quickly finish off the stag. The animal will be lynched with total impunity. The "teasing and baiting" is certainly present in our painting and its presence must be acknowledged, but it is not the sum total of the painting's significance. It is not acceptable as a definition of it. We cannot accept the "teasing and baiting" formula as an adequate summarisation of the action. It is not an end in itself for the community, but it might well be a means to an end. It distracts the stag's attention from a most vulnerable part of its own body, its front legs; it increases the animal's vulnerability to the real danger that threatens it: the loss of its own feet.[8]

Looking carefully at one of the famous pictures representing a mob "teasing and baiting" a big animal (figure 8), Girard warned that this shouldn't be interpreted as an image of a "symbolic, transcendent world of violence," in the sense that this world would be devoid of actual violence. The big animal is not only teased and baited—that is merely the "foreplay"—it is actually put to death. Girard concludes:

FIGURE 8. Copy of a Çatalhöyük mural showing a boar and a deer surrounded by hunters. Photograph: Omar Hoftun. © Alan Mellaart.

> The "teasing and baiting" definition [of the scene that is represented in those pictures] is just as wrong as it would be in the case of a bullfight. If we defined a bullfight as the "teasing and baiting of a bull," we would say something true and yet we would miss the killing of the bull which is the real end of the bullfight.[9]

For mimetic theory, the sacred is not the sublimation of violence, its sheer symbolization. It is actual violence under a new regime brought about by the capacity of V1-type violence to transcend itself. In the same way, the distinction made by Oxford anthropologist Harvey Whitehouse, and taken up by Ian Hodder, between two types of rituals—the doctrinal mode, i.e., high-frequency, low arousal routine actions, and the imagistic mode, i.e., low-frequency but high-arousal traumatic rituals (Whitehouse 2004; Whitehouse and Hodder 2010)—cannot satisfy the student of mimetic theory.

In a good Durkheimian tradition, all social practices derive from sacred rituals, to be sure, but that does not imply that they themselves are ritualistic, in the specific sense given this term by mimetic theory. Man descends/

derives from the ape, but that does not entail that Man is an ape. Exchanges in a monetary economy derive from the sacred,[10] but that does not entail that modern money is sacred—if one sets aside loose metaphors in the King Dollar manner.

It is important to realize that this key idea of mimetic theory, namely, that violence has the capacity to transcend itself, goes against the grain of the central figure of the modern conception of rationality: Leibniz's metaphysics. Louis Dumont discussed it from the vantage point of anthropology, because he saw in it a "modern version of a pre-modern conception of the world" (Dumont 1977). Leibniz took up the question of theodicy, or divine justice, and the vexed problem of reconciling the presumptive benevolence and omnipotence of the Creator with the inescapable fact of the existence of evil on earth. His solution is well known: the world in which we live is the best of all possible worlds. What appears to us as evil seems to be so because we have only a finite, individual view of the world. But if we could have a view of the totality—if we could look at the world from the divine point of view—we would see that what appears to us as evil is a necessary sacrifice for the greater good of the totality. Had evil not been permitted to intervene, our world would not have been the best of all possible worlds. Dumont was therefore led to characterize the essence of theodicy by this memorable phrase: "Good must contain evil while still being its contrary." Here the verb "contain" has the sense of encompassing, and the relation it describes is (tangled) hierarchy, which is to say the "encompassing of the contrary."

It has always seemed surprising to me that Dumont and his school of anthropology should have seen hierarchy as nothing more than the sign of a stable order, guaranteed by religion. One has only to recognize that the verb "contain" has another meaning—of blocking, inhibiting, repressing—in order to construe hierarchy, understood as the encompassing of the contrary, in an entirely different and much more disturbing sense, namely, as a system that is constantly in danger of being overturned. Just so, the most stable social order is the one that contains the threat of its own collapse, in the two senses of the verb "to contain."

If one considers hierarchy only in its relation to order, as Dumont does, it is one of the most familiar ideas in the philosophy of history and society. It has been developed in different ways and under various names—"ruse of reason," "ruse of history," dialectical materialism, the "invisible hand" of the market, etc. In each case one finds the same idea, which is the foundation of modern rationalism: evil is, at bottom, only a lesser evil, a necessary evil, for it is placed in the service of the good; evil is only apparent, for it is an integral part of the good.

But once a hierarchical order enters into crisis and, under the pressure of the ensuing panic, totters on the edge of collapse, a quite different picture emerges. Its levels, distinct and well ordered until now, come to be confused with one another in a way that reveals their kinship. Whereas before good was thought to govern evil, its contrary, now evil seems to have governed itself—by distancing itself from itself, by putting itself outside of itself—with the result that the higher level, having been self-externalized, self-transcended, so to speak, takes on the aspect of the good.

This idea can be stated less abstractly if we consider the singular relationship that unites murder and sacrifice in a society where sacrifice constitutes the founding ritual. In that case, sacrifice contains the outbreak and spread of murder; though it is in one sense just another murder, it promises to put an end to violence. Capital punishment performs the same function in certain criminal justice systems. But when the religious order ("hierarchy") is overthrown by disorder and violence, ritual killing can no longer be distinguished from murder. Before the onset of crisis, however, sacrifice was both murder and something other than murder. This "something other" is the sacred.

The Sacred as Endogenous Fixed Point

In his *Formes élémentaires de la vie religieuse*, Durkheim describes the paradoxical situation of the orator:

> His language has a sort of grandiloquence that would be ridiculous in ordinary circumstances; *there is something dominating* about his gestures; his very thinking is impatient of proportion and easily allows itself to go to every sort of extreme. That is because he feels as if he were overflowing with an abnormal plethora of forces that tend to spread out from him; sometimes he even has the impression that *he is dominated by a moral power that transcends him* and of which he is but the interpreter. . . . Now, this exceptional surplus of forces is quite real: it comes from the very group that

> he is addressing. The feelings that his words arouse come back to him, but swollen, amplified, and they reinforce his own feeling to the same degree. (Durkheim 1979, 300–301)

The two phrases in italics do not contradict each other; together they define a tangled hierarchy, and an oriented one at that: the crowd depends on the leader to get a sense of direction, but the leader depends on the crowd to get the resources necessary for him to achieve this task. The leader is the keystone of the crowd, to use an architectural image, or its fixed point, to use a mathematical metaphor. But this fixed point is not exogenous: the leader does not gain his central position because of any intrinsic features, such as his supposed narcissism or charisma, as Max Weber supposed. The qualities that allow the leader to play his role come from the crowd itself. This fixed point is produced by the crowd, although the crowd sees itself as having been produced by it. Such a tangling of different levels is a distinguishing feature of a self-organizing system. The leader is, by definition, an endogenous fixed point.

It is possible to write a history of the human and social sciences (and, before them or in parallel, social and political philosophy) centered around this concept. Among the many incarnations of the endogenous fixed point, one would find: God in Leibniz's *Monadology*, power (the Leviathan) in Hobbes's political philosophy, the system of prices in neoclassical economics, money in Marx's and Keynes's economies, public opinion and the centralized State in Tocqueville's theory of democracy, and so on and so forth. If mimetic theory is right, though, all these incarnations derive from a single source: the divinized victim of a collective lynching and its various ritualistic reproductions.

The question for us is: what is the incarnation of the endogenous fixed point in Çatalhöyük? Two animals seem to vie for this glorious position: the leopard and the bull. The possible interpretations from the perspective of mimetic theory seem then twofold. Are there good arguments that would allow us to adjudicate between these two claims?

Why would the leopard occupy this role and be the *sacred* animal, which is to say at once hidden and divinized, internal and external? Benoit Chantre, in a workshop on mimetic theory and the finding of Çatalhöyük organized with Ian Hodder at Stanford University (March 11–12, 2013), answers in this way:

> The leopard, inasmuch as it is an "internal monster," is, for its part, closer to what Girard calls an "emissary victim" (or "internal victim"), the hallucinated prey of the "scapegoat mechanism" (or of lynching) thanks to which human groups save their unity in extremis. It is thus because the leopard hunt is closer to the founding murder that: 1) there are no leopard bones in the "town"; 2) the hunters wear leopard skins to hunt aurochs.

"At once internal and external" is indeed a phrase often used by Girard and the Girardians to describe the situation of the scapegoat, but it does not render full justice to the logic of the endogenous fixed point. According to Chantre, if the leopard is internal, this is because it lives among the citizens, but also because it resembles them, and its spotted skin seems even to provide the pattern for the layout of the city; but also external, since virtually no leopard bones have been found on the site, as though the leopard had to be held at bay.

However, the logic of the endogenous fixed point is not the mere juxtaposition of two opposite predicates, interior and exterior. It has the form of an oriented tangled hierarchy since it consists in the endogenous production of an exteriority. Nothing in what we know about the leopard in Çatalhöyük suggests a mechanism capable of bringing that about.

On the other hand, Mark Anspach, in his own contribution to the aforementioned workshop, follows rigorously the transformation of a V1 type of violence symbolized by the leopard into a V2 type of violence symbolized by the bull, the deer, or the auroch. Bringing together the basic concepts we have analyzed so far and their iconic representations, we can summarize his demonstration by the tableau in figure 9.

In order to become able to generate an endogenous fixed point—i.e., the sacred according to mimetic theory—V1 must first be transformed into V2, the bull, stag, auroch, or boar taking the place of the leopard. Given this, Anspach can argue:

> We might try to make a logical deduction based on the opposition between the leopards and the other dangerous animals. Girard asserts that relics of the latter are introduced into the houses because they embody a *positive, protective, unifying* form of violence. If he is right, it would be logical to suppose that leopards are banned from the houses because they are identified with a *negative, threatening, divisive* form of violence. The existence of

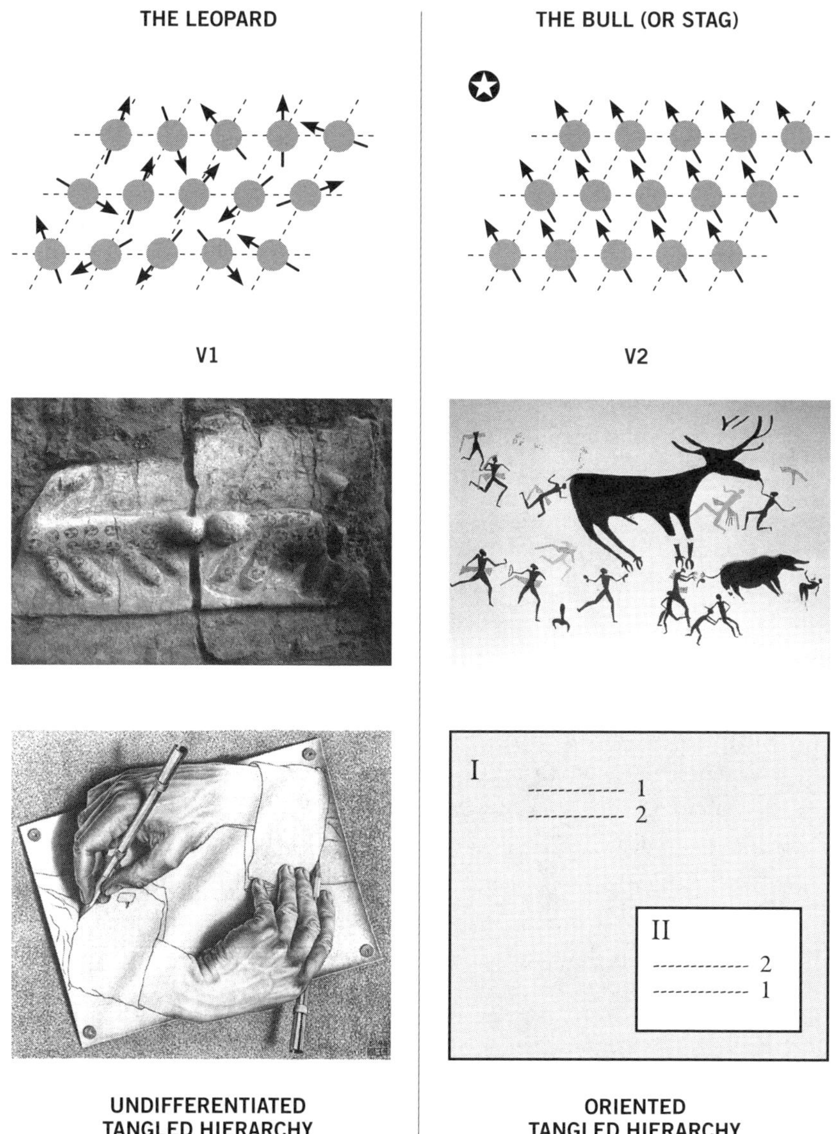

FIGURE 9. Undifferentiated tangled hierarchies vs. Oriented tangled hierarchies. Figure by the author.

> such an opposition between two forms of violence is a fundamental tenet of Girardian theory. The negative form that threatens the peace of the community is the reciprocal or symmetrical violence of warring mimetic doubles. Thus, if we were to extrapolate from Girard's analysis, we would be led to the hypothesis that leopards represent the latter form of violence.

The "reciprocal or symmetrical violence of warring mimetic doubles" is, of course, V1. Anspach concludes his paper with:

> The leopards represent the source of violence; the others are its object. A bull, stag, or boar is dangerous when aroused, and the baiting it undergoes brings out its aggressivity. But its sacrificial death leaves it changed, changed utterly—its violence metamorphosed into a force for peace and unity.

The bull is transformed by sacrifice; the leopard is not. At Çatalhöyük it may truly be said that a leopard never changes its spots. In passing, Anspach runs into a difficulty. He writes:

> Whether or not leopards were killed, the wall paintings never depict them as victims in the animal baiting scenes. However, leopard symbolism does show up in the spotted skins worn by many of the human figures. I take this to mean that the human participants assume the identity of leopards *precisely because* leopards embody the divisive violence that must be neutralized through sacrifice. If the ritual is meant to replicate an original crisis and its resolution, the participants must begin by miming the fearful symmetry of the doubles.

Indeed, a "good" ritual in Girard's sense has two stages, as it must represent/reproduce not only the successful (sacrificial) resolution of the crisis, but also, in a first moment, the crisis itself: V1 before V2, the leopard before the bull.

However, Anspach's account raises a general issue, which turns out to be a bone of contention within the Girardian community. If a sacred ritual entails some form of "playing with fire" by the entire community, to what extent can it reveal the intimate kinship between V2 (the "good" violence) and V1 (the "bad" violence) without jeopardizing the very foundations of the City? In other words, what can be shown and what must remain concealed in the games of the sacred?

That leads us towards a discussion of the last important concept of mimetic theory, which I cannot consider here: the issue of *méconnaissance* (literally: misrecognition), which I propose to translate in the present context as collective self-opacity. Girard's answer to this latter question, if we compare it to other anthropologists and sociologists such as Marcel Mauss and Pierre Bourdieu (for instance, in relation to the much-discussed practice of gift-giving), must appear stunning: what the strategy of *différance* in gift-giving serves to dissimulate is not what reciprocity is conventionally and traditionally supposed to reflect (for example, economic interest). It is reciprocity itself, inasmuch as reciprocity is the very form of violence. The first time human beings experienced the form of reciprocity, it was not through the exchange of goods; it was through the exchange of ills, of evils, of blows.[11]

The fact that reciprocity is taken to be the signature of violence is illustrated by the way vengeance in traditional societies is institutionalized, ritualized, codified, in the form of vindicatory systems. Everything occurs as if these systems' main concern was to conceal the very reciprocity inherent in vengeance. Vengeance can be an institution that consolidates the foundations of the City only on condition that what constitutes its very form—reciprocity—remain concealed.

This conclusion seems to me to vindicate the formal approach that I have pursued here. Focusing on the abstract, quasi-geometrical form of the phenomena brought out by anthropology is not only a game for philosophers or epistemologists. It is the very nature of the phenomena that ascribes content to form.

Notes

1. Those phrases have been coined by the neo-cybernetician tradition, from Heinz von Foerster to Francisco Varela to Henri Atlan. A history of those concepts can be found in Dupuy 2000.
2. This experiment has been carried out at the Palais de la Découverte (Paris) science museum, ever since its foundation in 1937. All visitors are invited to participate. They are requested to cast a needle onto a grid of equidistant lines. The length of the needle is half the distance between two neighboring lines. Either the needle intersects one of the lines or it does not. The setting is electrified, which permits a counter to compute the frequency of the cases in which there is an intersection. Over time, tens of millions of visitors have cast their needle, and the proportion of intersection cases has oscillated around and converged towards a value that is now determined

with thousands of decimals of which the beginning is 0.318309886183791. It turns out that this value is the inverse of pi (pi being the ratio of any circle's circumference to its diameter). It is thus that the value of pi can be experimentally determined with a precision that is, if we wait a sufficiently long time, as high as one wishes.

3. We may think of two absent-minded professors going together to attend the same event. Neither of them knows the venue; each one believes the other knows. A trajectory emerges, endowed with some stability, from the fact that each partner follows in the other's footsteps.
4. Note that the curvature of the structure is necessarily incomplete—a loose variation on Gödel's theorems of incompleteness, if you will. At the center, there is a hole, a vacuum, a nothingness in which the God of this universe, that is, Escher himself, has put his signature.
5. Mimetic theory is not the first theory to make this assertion. It can be found in Adam Smith, Tocqueville, Durkheim, Mauss, and many others. See Dupuy 1992.
6. Girard himself discusses this issue in a series of dialogues with the Italian philosopher Gianni Vattimo, in Vattimo and Girard 2010.
7. French economist André Orléan has studied the formal conditions that render V1 structurally unstable and lead inevitably to the stable pattern V2. They concern the connectivity of the graph V1—i.e., the distributions of probabilities that link the behavior of each node to the behavior of its neighbors. See Orléan 1988.
8. See Girard's chapter in this volume.
9. Ibid.
10. The economic vocabulary in our modern languages betrays this origin. See Benveniste 1969 and Dupuy 2014.
11. A development on the double meanings in the Indo-European vocabulary relative to exchange would be appropriate. For example, the English word "gift" comes from the German "das Gift," which means "the poison" (Benveniste 1969).

Works Cited

Benveniste, E. 1969. *Vocabulaire des Institutions Indo-Européennes*. Paris: Éditions de Minuit.

Bloch, M. 2010. "Is There Religion at Çatalhöyük . . . or Are There Just Houses?" In *Religion in the Emergence of Civilization*, ed. I. Hodder. Cambridge: Cambridge University Press.

Culler, J. 1982. *On Deconstruction*. Ithaca, NY: Cornell University Press.

Darwin, C. 1872. *On the Origins of Species by Means of Natural Selection*. London: John Murray.

Derrida, J. 1967. *De la grammatologie*. Paris: Éditions de Minuit.

Dumont, L. 1977. *Homo aequalis: Genese et epanouissement de l'ideologie economique*. Paris: Gallimard.

———. [1970] 1981. *Homo hierarchicus*. Translated by M. Sainsbury. Chicago: University of Chicago Press.

Dumouchel, P. 1979. "L'ambivalence de la rareté." In *L'enfer des choses: René Girard et la logique de l'économie*, ed. P. Dumouchel and J-P. Dupuy, 137–253. Paris: Seuil.

Dupuy, J.-P. 1992. *Introduction aux sciences sociales: Logique des phénomènes collectifs*. Paris: Ellipses.

———. 2000. *The Mechanization of the Mind*. Princeton, NJ: Princeton University Press.

———. 2014. *Economy and the Future: A Crisis of Faith*. East Lansing: Michigan State University Press.

Durkheim, É. [1912] 1979. *Les formes élémentaires de la vie religieuse*. 6th ed. Paris: Presses Universitaires de France.

Hodder, I., ed. 2010. *Religion in the Emergence of Civilization*. Cambridge: Cambridge University Press.

———. 2012. *Entangled: An Archaeology of the Relationships between Humans and Things*. New York: John Wiley & Son.

Orléan, A. 1988. "Money and Mimetic Speculation." In *Violence and Truth*, ed. P. Dumouchel. Stanford, CA: Stanford University Press.

Varela, F. 1979. *Principles of Biological Autonomy*. New York: Appleton & Lange.

Vattimo, G., and R. Girard. 2010. *Christianity, Truth, and Weakening Faith: A Dialogue*. Edited by P. Antonello. New York: Columbia University Press.

Whitehouse, H. 2004. *Modes of Religiosity: A Cognitive Theory of Religious Transmission*. Walnut Creek, CA: AltaMira Press.

Whitehouse, H., and I. Hodder. 2010. "Modes of Religiosity at Çatalhöyük." In *Religion in the Emergence of Civilization*, ed. I. Hodder, 122–45. Cambridge: Cambridge University Press.

Rethinking the Neolithic Revolution

Symbolism and Sacrifice at Göbekli Tepe

Paul Gifford and Pierpaolo Antonello

Çatalhöyük, dating from 6,400 to 6,200 BCE, presents evidence of one of the earliest human settlements: its construction, its social organization, its symbolic, artistic, and ritual life. A lesser known, but much earlier and potentially even more significant link in the evidential chain of the story of "how we became human" is provided by another archaeological site, situated some 450 miles east-southeast of Çatalhöyük. This site, generally recognized to be a temple complex, has been discovered at Göbekli Tepe (literal translation: "Potbelly Hill") in southeastern Turkey, near the present-day frontier with Syria. It lies about fifteen kilometers northeast of the present-day city of Şanlıurfa, at the highest point of an extended mountain range that can be seen from many kilometers away. To this day, it is a landmark visible from afar. Looking toward the Middle East's fertile crescent, it may be said to be sited at a nodal point of the great migration "out of Africa."

Crucially, it has been authoritatively dated to the astonishingly early period of 9,600–8,200 BCE, corresponding to the Epipaleolithic, or Pre-Pottery Neolithic A (PPNA). It dates, that is, from some three millennia before Çatalhöyük. According to the late director of excavations, Klaus Schmidt of the German Archaeological Institute (DAI), the still unexplored deeper layers of this nine-hectare site will show that "the place has a history stretching back over several thousand years to the Old Stone Age [that is, to before the Ice Age, which lasted from c. 10,800 to 9,600 BCE]" (Schmidt 2010, 245).

Here, in the words of Patrick Symmes, the reporter who broke the story to the wider world in *Newsweek*, has been discovered

> a vast and beautiful temple complex, a structure so ancient that it may be the very first thing human beings ever built. The site isn't just old, it redefines old: the temple was built . . . a staggering 7,000 years before the Great Pyramid, and more than 6,000 years before Stonehenge first took shape. The ruins are so early that they predate villages, pottery, domesticated animals, and even agriculture—the first embers of civilization. In fact, Schmidt thinks the temple itself, built after the end of the last Ice Age by hunter-gatherers, became that ember—the spark that launched mankind toward farming, urban life, and all that followed. (Symmes 2010)

Here, if anywhere, we might hope to be able to discover evidential traces tending to confirm or disconfirm empirically Girard's theory of hominization, in particular its claim that religion predates, and is actually the origin of, any form of sophisticated (i.e., evidently human) technical, economic, and social organization (Girard 1987; Girard, Antonello, and de Castro Rocha 2007).

But what is it, first of all, that has been discovered? And why is this discovery already, in advance of the test of Girardian theory we are proposing to conduct in this chapter, considered to be of five-star significance?

A Remote Hilltop in Southern Turkey and the Dawn of Civilization

The American author and scientific journalist Charles C. Mann, who has visited the site for *National Geographic*, describes Potbelly Hill as "vaguely reminiscent of Stonehenge, except that Göbekli Tepe was built much earlier and is made not from roughly hewn blocks but from cleanly carved limestone pillars splashed with bas-reliefs of animals" (Mann 2011, 39). A team from the University of Chicago visited the site in the 1960s for the purposes of a survey; it saw evidence of human activity in the broken pieces of limestone

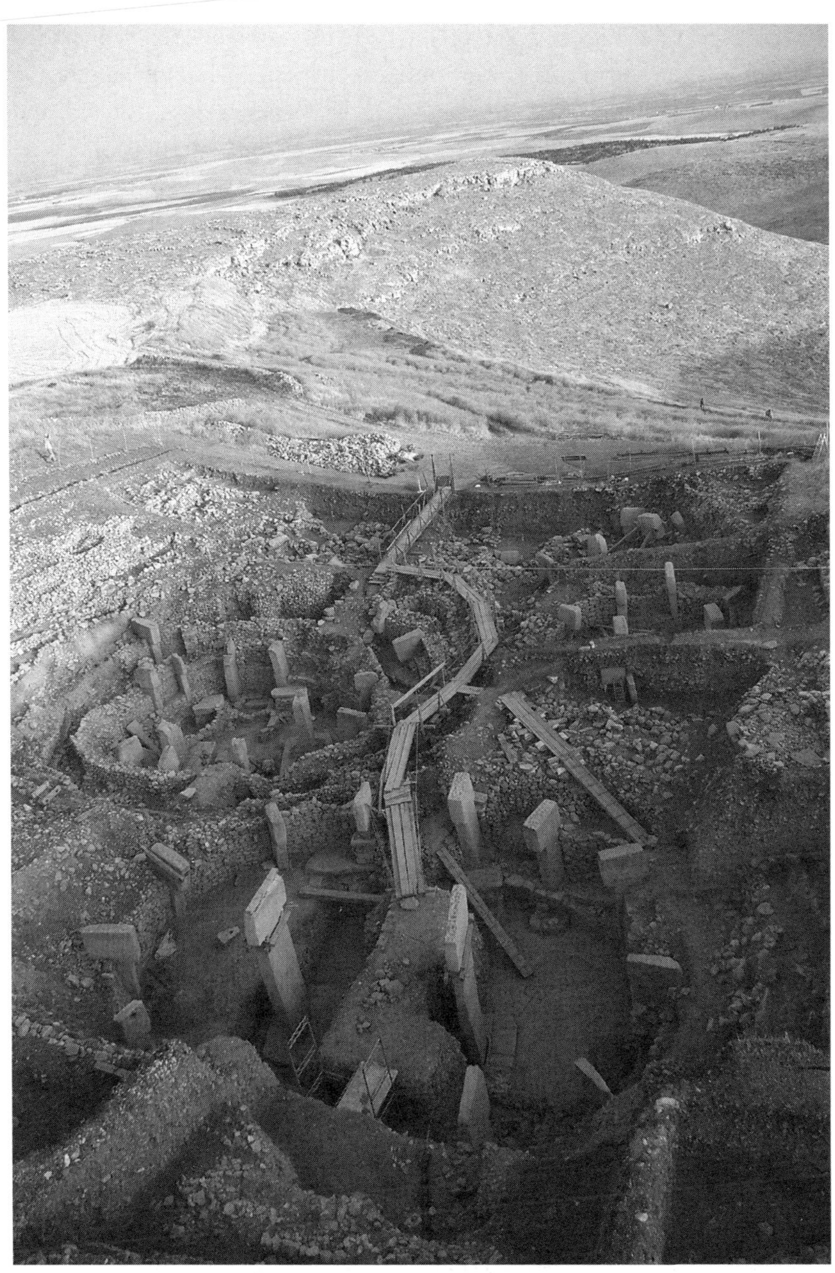

FIGURE 1. Göbekli Tepe: overhead view of the main excavation area. Photograph: N. Becker. © DAI, Orient Department.

that festooned the hilltop, but it took these to be gravestones and concluded that this was the site of a Byzantine military outpost, without great interest. The real discovery occurred in 1994, when Klaus Schmidt revisited it and knew within minutes that this was a major find. Initially alerting signs were the huge numbers of flint chips, indicating that scores or even hundreds of people had worked there in millennia past. Then, inches below the surface, he found a large, elaborately fashioned monumental stone, soon followed by similar others—a ring of standing-stone pillars. From 1995, when excavation began, Schmidt's German-Turkish team found a second and a third and then ever more numerous standing-stone rings, until at length, in 2003, a series of geomagnetic surveys revealed at least twenty rings, piled together higgledy-piggledy, under the earth.

Gradually, it was understood that this was a pointer to the most curious feature of the site: the fact that the standing-stone rings, whatever their function, had seemed to lose their virtue or their potency, so that fresh, near-identical structures (albeit progressively less elaborate) had, over a period of nearly 1,400 years, been built nearby or else simply on top of previous constructions, first filled in for the purpose—seemingly in the hope of making good some mysterious yet central deficiency. "Every few decades, people buried the pillars and put up new stones—a second, smaller ring inside the first. Sometimes, later, they installed a third. Then the whole assemblage would be filled in with debris, and an entirely new circle created nearby. The site may have been built, filled in, and built again for centuries" (Mann 2011, 48).

In short, the labor devoted to this temple complex was "never-ending," since it had to be constantly improved and even replaced (on average every seventy years). A similar technique of cyclical filling and reconstruction is recognizable as having applied to the houses of the Çatalhöyük settlement, with similar periodic frequencies—this correspondence perhaps pointing to a cultural and ritualistic continuity between these prehistoric sites, in spite of their structural difference and separation in time.[1] And yet,

> bewilderingly, the people at Göbekli Tepe got steadily worse at temple building. The earliest rings are the biggest and most sophisticated, technically and artistically. As time went by, the pillars became smaller, simpler, and were mounted with less and less care. Finally, the effort seems to have

> petered out altogether; by 8,200 BC, Göbekli Tepe was all fall and no rise. (Mann 2011, 48)

What ritual enterprise could have motivated such rare and remarkable persistence? What manner of ritual, what social functionality, could have generated such hope and/or such despair?

The pillars discovered were big—the tallest 18 feet in height and weighing sixteen tons. "By the end of the 2002 excavation season, 37 pillars [had] been found *in situ* in Layer III, 22 of which have animal decoration in relief" (Peters and Schmidt 2004, 182). The circles follow a common design. All are made from limestone pillars shaped like giant spikes or capital T's. Bladelike, the ring-forming pillars are easily five times as wide as they are deep. They stand an arm span or more apart, interconnected by low stone walls.

In the middle of each set of concentric rings are two taller pillars, symmetrically facing each other, with a perceptible interval or space between them. Their thin ends are mounted into shallow grooves cut into the floor ("they had not mastered engineering," says one German engineer at the site, who surmises that wooden props or posts would have been needed to keep the taller pillars upright). To Schmidt himself, the T-shaped pillars at the center of the rings are stylized human beings, an idea bolstered by the carved arms that angle from the shoulders of some pillars, reaching towards their loincloth-draped bellies. All the standing stones, a category embracing both the support ring stones and the central pair of T-shaped *figurae*, face the center of a circle—as at a meeting-place or dance, says Schmidt—a representation, perhaps, of a religious ritual.

As to the prancing, leaping animals carved on the pillars and, to a lesser extent, on the T-shaped central stones—Schmidt notes that they are mostly ferocious or dangerous creatures: snakes, scorpions, boars, lions. There are naturalistic representations showing, for instance, a male wild boar "signalling its readiness to attack, its mouth opened in order to display its impressive tusks. . . . below the wild boar is the head of a fox flashing its teeth" (Peters and Schmidt 2004, 184). The human figures represented by the central, dolmenlike T-shapes may be guarded by them, or appeasing them, or incorporating them as totems (Peters and Schmidt 2004, 209).

Related in some way to this puzzle is another. Other parts of the hill were littered with the greatest store of ancient flint tools Schmidt had ever

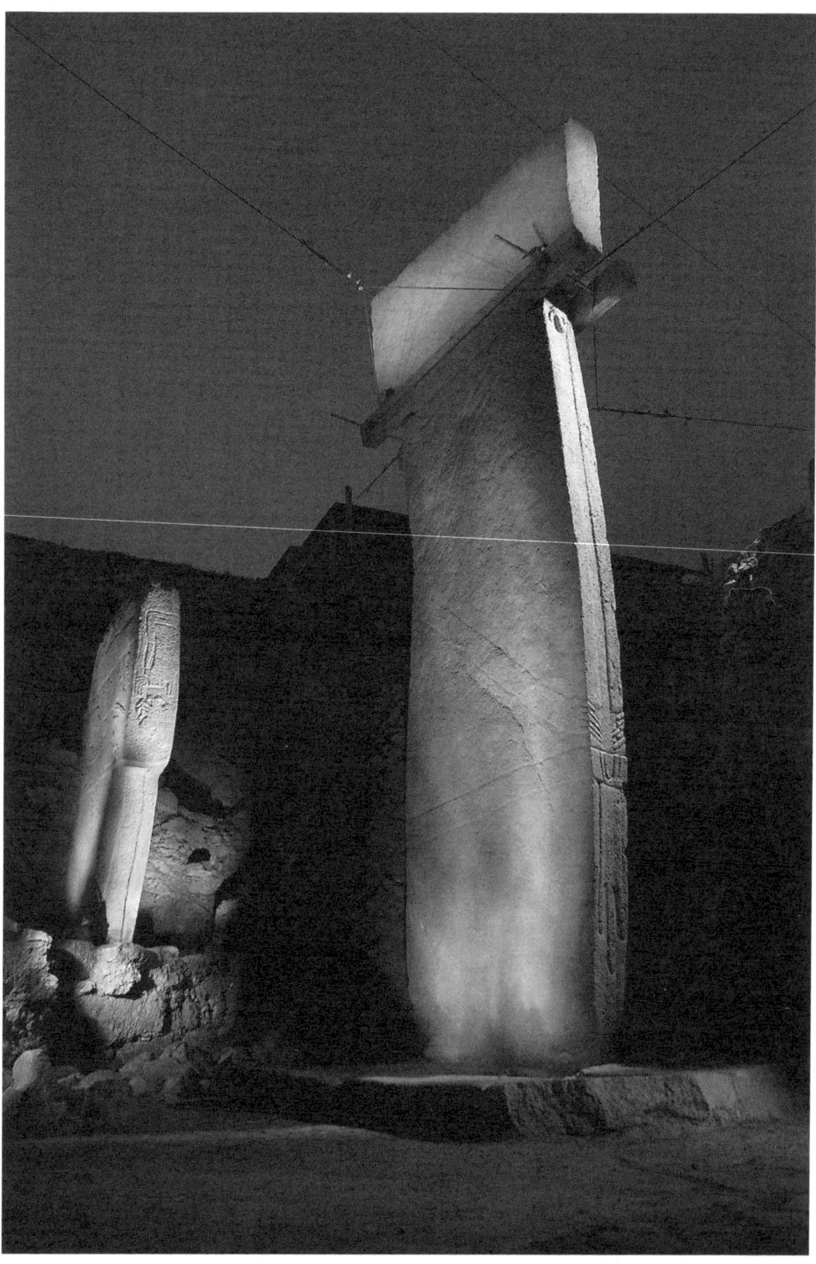

FIGURE 2. Arms, hands, and elements of clothing reveal the anthropomorphic character of the pillars (pillar 31 in the center of Enclosure D); photograph: N. Becker. © DAI, Orient Department.

come across—a veritable Neolithic warehouse of knives, choppers, and projectile points. ("There were more flints in one little area here, a square meter or two, than many archaeologists find in entire sites," he confided to Mann [2011, 41]). Again, this is a highly suggestive datum—to the point of suggesting to American anthropologist Karl W. Luckert the hypothesis that the function of Göbekli Tepe must have been that of a weapons factory, and that the violence recalled and addressed at this site generated, in some way or other, its own need for ritual purification (Luckert 2013).[2] We may perhaps put this theory on hold, while noting clearly that the pointer it is following towards human violence is, at all events, inescapable—and, of course, entirely Girardian. Göbekli Tepe is the oldest known example of monumental architecture—the first structure human beings put together that was bigger and more complicated than a hut. It is also, in its technological realization, a stupendous feat. It involved quarrying the tall T-stones in the rock and prizing them loose from it, then transporting them, often many kilometers, by large teams of men using a roller-log method, not far short in ingenuity of the later roller-sled technology thought to have been used at Stonehenge, or the stone-walking technology used on Easter Island. It involved temple design, artistic polishing and carving, erection of the stones, the building of intermediary walls of the ring linking the support stones, and further operations of artistic chiseling and decoration—finally, an art of ritual and mythic symbolism, the form and meaning of which are still largely hidden from us. All of which supposes a degree of social integration and an organization far greater than anybody had ever thought of attributing to the small, wandering bands of hunter-gatherers who made up the quasi-totality of humanity in the tenth century BCE. (While the site formally belongs to the PPNA, up to now, in fact, no traces of domesticated plants or animals have been found.) Mann underlines this monumental novelty:

> At the time of Gobleki Tepe's construction, much of the human race lived in small nomadic bands that survived by foraging for plants and hunting wild animals. Construction of the site would have required more people coming together in one place than had likely occurred before. Amazingly, the temple's builders were able to cut, shape, and transport 16 ton stones hundreds of feet despite having no wheels or beasts of burden. (Mann 2011, 39)

The Neolithic Revolution under a New Sign

Yet the truly monumental significance of the site lies not solely in the technological exploit it constitutes, nor even solely in the precocious realization of human group intelligence and cooperation that it supposes. For the implications of these things have still to be seen within the wider context of a momentous culture shift proceeding in the late Neolithic. They are to be deciphered afresh, that is, in relation to the way in which this change is traditionally thought to have proceeded:

> Archaeologists are still excavating Göbekli Tepe and debating its meaning. What they do know is that the site is the most significant in a volley of unexpected findings that have overturned earlier ideas about our species' deep past. Just twenty years ago most researchers believed they knew the time, place, and rough sequence of the Neolithic Revolution—the critical transition that resulted in the birth of agriculture, taking *homo sapiens* from scattered groups of hunter gathers to farming villages and from there to technologically sophisticated societies with great temples and towers and kings and priests who directed the labour of their subjects and recorded their feats in written form. (Mann 2011, 39)

The Neolithic Revolution was once viewed as a single, unilinear-plot story: almost as a single event, representing, Romantically enough (since the scenario just quoted is an invention of Victorian ethnology and anthropology), a sudden flash of genius occurring in a single location (Mesopotamia, between the Tigris and the Euphrates: spreading out then to India, Europe, and beyond). It was believed by most archaeologists that this sudden blossoming of civilization was driven largely by environmental changes: a gradual warming, as the Ice Age receded, allowing some people to cultivate plants and begin herding domesticated food animals. New research of our own times suggests, on the contrary, that the Neolithic Revolution was actually carried out across a huge area and over thousands of years. The view of botanists seems to have swung away from the idea of a rapid process of domestication of cereals, towards a long period of "predomestication agriculture," that is, cultivation before the recognizable traits of the domesticated species were manifested. George Willcox and his colleagues have shown us the process towards domestication in progress over about 1,500 years from the late Epipaleolithic (Willcox, Fornite, and Herveux 2008). Another recent study proposes that cultivation may have begun as early as the middle Epipaleolithic (Allaby, Fuller, and Brown 2008; Watkins 2010, 624).

One of the things not found at Göbekli Tepe is any trace of human habitation. This is a considerable paradox:

> Hundreds of people must have been required to carve and erect the pillars, but the site had no water source—the nearest stream was about three miles away. These workers would have needed homes, but excavations have uncovered no sign of walls, hearths or houses—no other buildings that Schmidt could interpret as domestic. They would have had to be fed, but there is no trace of agriculture. For that matter, Schmidt has found no mess kitchens or cooking fires. It was a purely ceremonial center. If anyone ever lived at this site, they were less its residents than its staff. To judge by the thousands of gazelle and auroch bones found at the site the workers seem to have been fed by constant shipments of game, brought from faraway hunts. (Mann 2011, 49)[3]

"These people were foragers," Schmidt himself concludes: people who gathered plants and hunted wild animals. "Our picture of foragers was always just small mobile groups, a few dozen people. They cannot make big permanent structures, we thought, because they must move around to follow the resources. They can't maintain a separate class of priests and craft workers, because they can't carry all the extra supplies to feed them. Then here is Göbekli Tepe, and they obviously did all that" (Mann 2011, 48). Clearly enough, then, the scattered groups who came together to this hilltop to construct this temple did not live here. They came in order to engage in ritual activities.

Who were they? They may originally have included some Natufian settlers (i.e., hunter-gatherers who also built, for occasional or temporary use, stacked stone huts, roofed with animal hides, typically comprising eighteen or so people). Just conceivably, some among the later of them may have been among the first settlers of the early PPNA: ex-hunter-gatherers, who were beginning to live in villages of mudbrick huts, comprising up to ninety people, and which included places of food storage (evidence of plant domestication is debated, but some wild grains were cultivated). Göbekli Tepe is so very significant precisely because it spans the great transition and attests to it.

Lest we miss the cumulative point made by these combined factors (monumentality, antecedence, transitionality, and religious function), and lest we underestimate the significance of their coming together in this site, *National Geographic* interprets in the form of a schematized graphic the "two paths to civilization" recognizably set in opposition by the discovery of the Göbekli Tepe site. The graphic interprets recapitulatively, on the one hand, the scenario envisaged by a traditionalist anthropology (going back to V. Gordon Childe), and, on the other, the new understanding of cultural development represented by contemporary researchers in archaeology and anthropology, among them Klaus Schmidt, Ian Hodder, and William Durham of Stanford University.

The traditional view, pursued by the Victorians and their twentieth-century epigones, holds that when the last blast of the Ice Age ended (ca. 9,600 BCE), more abundant vegetation and wild game led to domestication of plants and animals, to agriculture, and so to permanent settlement. After people began settling in villages, as farmers, religion arose to promote social cooperation.

For the newer school, wonderment at changes in the natural world led to organized ritual cults or religion—which in turn produced the effects of domestication of plants and animals, agriculture, and permanent settlement. On this view, people came together for rituals, creating the need to grow food for large groups gathering near sacred sites—a perspective often held alongside a functionalist and socially useful view of religion, while yet insisting on the lead role of religion as driving, shaping, and enabling reality.

Girard, following a Durkheimian lead, is clearly among the tenents of the second perspective of interpretation. He insists, for instance, that animal domestication and agriculture arose out of ritual practice, rather than the other way round; and that "humanity is the daughter of the religious dimension of things" (Girard 1987, 70–71; Girard, Antonello, and de Castro Rocha 2007).[4] Yet his assent to *National Geographic*'s formulation of the matter, as given above, would still be conditional, since it does not—or does not yet—acknowledge the preponderant role of violence, the management and the attempted exorcism of which must, in his view, condition the very notion of archaic religion and our entire understanding of its ritual practice.

For the moment, however, we may retain the simpler and more general point about temporal antecedence and lead-role functionality. Göbekli Tepe dates from a good three millennia before Çatalhöyük, and the conclusion to be drawn from this simple fact alone is clear and inescapable: *religion preceded settlement.* Which is to say that the "Ascent of Man" narrative, forged by Childe in the 1920s, owed more to the ideological conviction of this passionate Marxist than to any empirical data.[5] Childe thought that agriculture came first, and that this innovation—"the greatest in human history after the mastery of fire"—had allowed humans to seize the opportunity of a rich new environment, to extend their dominion over the natural world, only then developing a series of late-flowering cultural achievements, such as religion and writing. The discovery of Natufian sites of the Levant has since come along, suggesting strongly that settlement had occurred first and that farming arose later, as a product of crisis.[6] Equally, the idea of the Neolithic Revolution driven solely by climate change is now seen to have owed a great deal of its resonance to the fact that in the 1990s people became increasingly aware of environmental and planetary factors, often driven by concern about the effects of modern global warming.

Meanwhile, a suggestion from French archaeologist Jacques Cauvin was generally taken on board. Chauvin's suggestion was that the fundamental factor enabling the formation of mass settlement and of agriculture was the facility for using symbolic culture that enabled communities to formulate their shared identities and their cosmos. The Neolithic sea-change was at bottom a flowering of symbolic behaviors (recognizable in elementary forms from some 100,000 years BCE) (Mann 2011, 57).

The discovery of Göbekli Tepe is, in fact, the latest in a series of disconfirmations and rethinkings that have come as so many rocks thrown through the ideological windows of the basically nineteenth-century "Ascent of Man" narrative. Many anthropologists and cognitivist thinkers of human origins have taken over a preformed view of religion, seen as a way of salving the tension that inevitably arose—and arose solely, so it is supposed, or at least, arose critically—only when hunter-gatherers settled down, became farmers, and developed large societies. These assumptions form a bottom line of conviction, resting on not a great deal more than ideological prevention, yet decisively inhibiting a sufficient curiosity about what is actually meant by religion, and what ritual enterprise it was that proceeded at Göbekli Tepe.

Girard is surely not among those disconfirmed in his basic presumptions by this new and strategically important archaeological find. On the contrary, he is shown to have been fundamentally correct when he speaks of the centrality of violence, and to have been highly prescient once more when he speaks of the priority and antecedence of the sacred as a generative matrix in the genesis of human culture.

Perhaps, then, we may now proceed to bring together the two terms thus validated and to enquire more directly what sense Girardian theory can make of archaeological data. Can this theory of "Violence and the Sacred" be said to point the way towards a cogent decipherment of the central enigma of Göbekli Tepe: the puzzle of what actually went on there?

We shall need here to take two new steps: the first interpreting the ritual activity of the site, insofar as this is inferable from its symbolic and mythical dimension; the second, reconstructing hypothetically what can no longer be observed, namely, the sacrificial functionality of this ritual design, with its sacred space and its highly characteristic layout in concentric circles. Each step will lead us in turn beyond the conclusions that the descriptive and empirical academic archaeologists, like Schmidt, have drawn from the—so far one-tenth excavated—22-acre site; and both steps, it is hoped, will tend to compose a holistic pattern of understanding that will integrate the extant data while remaining capable of being amended and refined as new data emerge.

Mythic Symbolism and Ritual

As we have seen, Schmidt is persuaded that Göbekli Tepe "was not a mundane settlement of the period, but a site belonging to the religious sphere, a sacred area." It seems, he thinks, to have been "a regional center where communities met to engage in complex rites" (2010, 240) But which rites? Schmidt's instinct, in pursuit of an answer, is to question the "extraordinarily rich symbolism that challenges our ability to interpret" (2010, 253). And firstly, he interrogates its animal symbolism.

Animals must be expected to be hugely present, both materially and symbolically, in the mental world of foragers who survived by hunting. The evidence of the filling debris is that of the food animals consumed at the site by builders and by "pilgrims" (red cattle, wild deer, gazelle, onager, wild pig, and wild caprovids were consumed) (Schmidt 2010, 242). Yet what, for their part, the reliefs adorning many of the monumental pillars depict is a wide range of different wild animals, such as predatory big cats, bulls, wild boar, foxes, ducks, cranes, wild asses, gazelles, snakes, spiders, and scorpions (figure 3), but also vultures and a hyena (figure 4). These—predominantly dangerous—wild beasts constitute an "iconographic repertoire" (246) that may have been progressively unveiled with the seasons (252).

If still baffled by the sense of this iconography, Schmidt is confident of the fact of its significance in the symbolic and mythological order:

> These reliefs open a view of a new and unique pictorial language not known before whose interpretation is a matter of important scientific debate. So far as can be seen, the mammals depicted are male. It remains a mystery whether the relief images were attributes of the pillars, or whether they were part of a mythological cycle. They may have had a protective aspect, serving as guards, or—perhaps more probably—are part of a horrific scenario somewhat like Dante's inferno. (Schmidt 2010, 248)

No images of hybrid beings (human-animal) have so far been found; these, Schmidt asserts, are creations of later cultures.[7] The same remark is applied to anthropomorphic beings with animal heads, a group he summarizes under the term "goat demon," known from Upper Paleolithic art (Schmidt 2001), "but so far not seen at Göbekli Tepe." And the same holds again for another image, the bird man, whose meaning, Schmidt says, "is unclear" (Schmidt 2010, 246). What these comments indicate most conspicuously is that Schmidt has in mind a sort of logic or grammar of ritual symbols (whether this is applicable locally or more universally); hence the expectation, here said to be disappointed—at least so far—of the appearance of these key images in this particular site.

Yet the assertions of absence and ambiguity are also themselves subject to interpretation. On the one hand, in an early account of his finding, he had listed animals "with human head," and a "bird on human head" (Schmidt 1998, 2). More interestingly still, the declaration that hybrid images are absent at Göbekli Tepe has to be qualified in the light of other statements. Schmidt tells us that a billy goat is one of the three animals adorning in

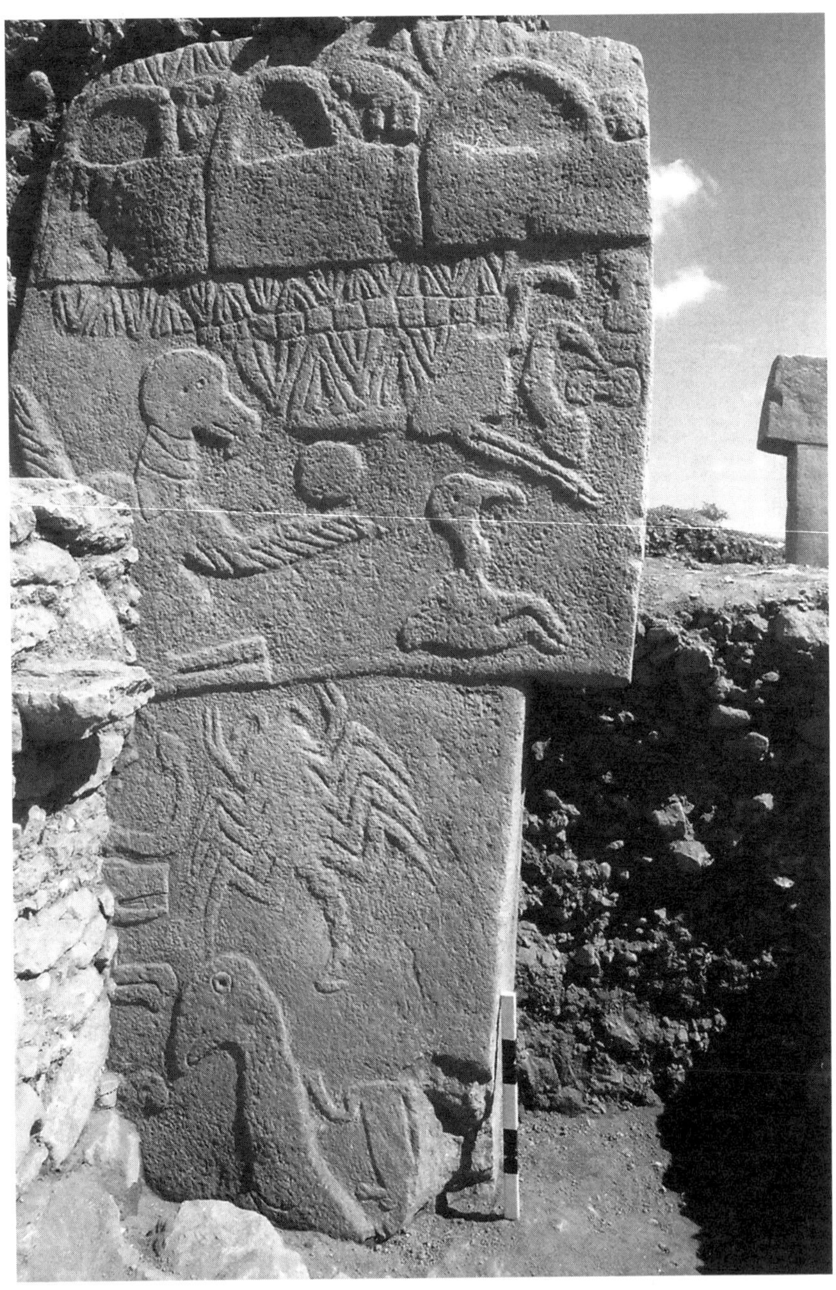

FIGURE 3. Pillar 43 in Enclosure D. © DAI, Orient Department.

FIGURE 4. **Fragment of a decorated pillar found in the debris of Enclosure D, north of pillar 18; photograph: K. Schmidt. © DAI, Orient Department.**

high relief the porthole stones discovered near the upright central T-shaped pillars, which are, by his own account, of anthropomorphic tenor (Schmidt 2010, 252). He suggests that these stones are close to, and very much like, the base or socket stones that can, in one enclosure, be seen to be holding the central T-shapes upright. So that the association of animal and human is in fact present virtually, anticipating implicitly the hybrid forms Schmidt declares to be missing.

This reminds us strongly of Girard's view that the victimary ritual starts in total unawareness of itself, and progresses towards an ever-inadequate awareness through the practice of representation and ritual organization. Iconography and its symbolic logic, that is, function like a dream in process of an ever-unfinished awakening. So that the pictures are always saying more than their creators can clearly grasp, or realize pictorially, or, of course, explain; yet the further advanced they are in the process of awakening, the more they represent and declare explicitly the logic that generates them.

This perspective opens up the possibility of a fully Girardian interpretation of Göbekli Tepe. The goat-demon, whose subterranean presence-absence at this site can in fact be discerned, sounds suspiciously like the Girardian scapegoat,[8] as perceived by the community at the point of victimary slaughter. More than that: it situates the range of fearsome animals specifically depicted in a relationship to the human subjects and actors of Göbekli Tepe that can be described as one of victimization-through-violence and of sacralization. The animals depicted are of course really frightening, in an immediate and concrete sense; but they are also demonized, i.e., held to be guilty of all the woes afflicting the community, including violence born of intra-community conflict, and the perceived violence suffered from acts of cosmic nature. It is in this sense that the goat is a goat-demon.

Schmidt's entire iconography is thereby placed under the sign of a dynamic of transformation implied by the victimary pharmacology that Girard has described: a polarity of life forces is here being reversed symbolically, from negative to positive, i.e., from death to life, from disorder to order, from violence to peace. On reflection, it will be seen that this dynamic explains the bird-man image, which Girardians will recognize from a striking analysis of a Tikarau myth in *Things Hidden* (Girard 1987, 106–7); in mythic imagination, the bird man literally flies away from the cliff (over which he is in sober fact pressurized to jump by group violence, thus falling to his death on the rocks below). His flight is, then, the mythically coded expression of a victimary guilt reversed, and resacralized as a form of benevolent provision towards the community. It is a sign of an ex-victim who, in the process of sacralization, has escaped his guilt and become divine. By extension, this same coded logic explains also a curious overlap between the two lists of Schmidt's animals: ducks and gazelles are to be found in each list, because both possess at once the mundane property of being comestible and the symbolic attribute of flying or leaping.

Schmidt's iconography of course looks towards the animals that threaten and terrorize: on this point, Schmidt's intuition of a Dantesque nightmare scenario is highly pertinent, at least to the dream or nightmare from which the symbolic-mythic ritual is attempting to awaken. Through ritual acts of counter-violence, including ritual baiting and sacrificial slaughter, what is felt to be the malefic potency of these animals is appropriated, their meaning for the community reversed. The demon becomes sacred by virtue of his function as emissary victim. And the conferred sacrality (which is also a stolen or appropriated potency) confers on the victimized animal a status as totem or guardian of the community. We may thus think of the bird man, symbolically speaking, as the scapegoat liberated: the true spirit of the sacralized animal.

Our preliminary conclusion must be that Girard's reading of Çatalhöyük would appear to provide a real hermeneutical key to the antecedent—and correspondingly more implicit—symbolic-mythic grammar of Göbekli Tepe; it helps us decipher its most notable—and carefully noted—ambiguities. Of course, this fact implies a new flexibility in Girardian theory itself (in relation to its first delivery, as a single structuralist scenario of *ab origine* human sacrifice). Girard himself now seems very happy to admit an interpenetration of hunting and ritual practice, such that the first may have preceded and even overlapped with the second (see his chapter in this volume). We can only reflect that such an interpenetration would be entirely natural in the mental world of hunter-gatherers, whose artifact weapons would be, indistinctly, at the disposal of both their material needs, on the one hand, and their symbolic desires and mythic imagination, on the other. Animal baiting may well have been a proto-form of human sacrifice—or an adjunct to it.

Can a Girardian understanding of the carved animal reliefs help us interpret the symbolism of the pillars themselves? For Schmidt, "The T-form of the pillars can easily be interpreted as anthropomorphic, as some of the pillars appear to have arms and legs: they are, in other words, stone statues of human-like beings" (Schmidt 2010, 244). In fact, it helps us to distinguish more sharply than Schmidt does between the smaller, supporting ring-stone pillars and the 18-foot-high twin pillars at the geometric center of the circle—these latter being set apart both by their greater height and their attitude, facing not so much inwards as (given that their polarity already stands at the center of the circle) towards each other. Both types are, in some sense, stylized representations—and/or representatives—of human beings. But in what sense, exactly?

Schmidt notes the excitement with which the central pillars (only) were first discovered to be subtly carved with what looks like a ritual stole and a loincloth (2010, 245). He seems disposed to conclude that this suggests priests at the center, with lesser acolytes attending and supporting from the intermediate wall-linked rings—and perhaps, if the earth banks outside the outer-walled ring turn out, as he supposes, to be spectator ramps, a vast congregation of ordinary pilgrims looking on or looking in from outside towards the sacred space.

It is possible—he says prudently—that only certain persons were permitted to wear the stole—the stole being an important element of a ritual robe (2010, 244). Perhaps the stone buttons, which occur in large numbers on the site, also contribute, he thinks, to this same scheme of self-representing ritual design.

Yet this is not quite what is suggested by his notably tentative, but perhaps more prescient, conclusion:

> The question of who is being represented by the highly stylised T-shaped pillars remains open, as we cannot say with certitude if concepts of god existed at this time. So the general function of the enclosures remains mysterious; but it is clear that the pillar statues in the centre of these enclosures represent very powerful beings. If gods existed in the minds of early Neolithic people, there is an overwhelming probability that the T-shape is a first known monumental depiction of gods. (Schmidt 2010, 254)

If we follow a Girardian logic, this very tentative supposition becomes more transparent and much firmer: the monumental T-stones at the center represent darkly—i.e., without clear consciousness of their function and sense—the process of sacralization itself. They are the poles between which this transforming communal electromagnetism of sacralization operates; and the supporting rings themselves express mythically the social force field thus generated. This sense is conveyed invincibly by the vertically plunging view of Enclosure C offered in photographic representation by figure 5.

Schmidt himself provides a series of supporting evidence in favor of this reading:

> An important role must also have been ascribed to the pairs of pillars at the centre of each space which tower over the other pillars. It seems probable that they depict twins, because twins, or at least pairs of brothers and sisters, are a common theme in mythology (Levi-Strauss 1991; Meixner 1995). (Schmidt 2010, 244)

If we care to read Girard in addition to Levi-Strauss and Meixner, however, we will know that the symbolic and mythic significance of twins is that they epitomize the dynamics of the mimetic crisis and its scapegoat resolution.

FIGURE 5. Enclosure C seen from above; photograph: K. Schmidt. © DAI, Orient Department.

They allude to threatening undifferentiation and to the violence born of a rivalry that both precedes and follows from this (Girard 1987, 28–29). Behind the twins is the phenomenon of conflict and crisis within the social group, which is resolved only by the killing of one twin by the other. In later developed mythologies (including Babylonian creation stories),[9] the slaughtered twin is often buried under the founding stone of the city—this differentiating sacrifice being synonymous with the act of foundation on which civilization itself is based. In his chapter of this present volume, William Durham, after Bruce Lincoln (1975, 1981), speaks at length of the presence of primordial twins in Indo-European foundational myths.

The *dédoublement* of the central pillars, if it is related to this symbolic logic of twins, could well have the sense of a saving and founding differentiation. This is something directly suggested by the differential ornamentation appearing in Enclosure D, where "the western pillar is wearing a necklace in the shape of a crescent, a disc and two antithetical elements whose meaning is not understood"; whereas the "eastern pillar also holds a fox in the crook of its elbow" (Schmidt 2010, 239). Each pillar attests, that is, to the ambiguity of cosmic forces (just as, for instance, Kali is, in Hindu mythology, the deity of creation and destruction, life and death); but a founding differentiation is introduced by the ritual itself, which is played out in the most sacred space between the stones, and which is such that, at the outcome of the ceremony, by way of signifying its action of transformation, the second pillar carries a tutelary and totemic wild animal.

This transformational and founding sense is reinforced if we consider that the pillars themselves are mounted in base-socket slabs that strongly resemble the "porthole stones" said by Schmidt to offer an access to the world of the dead. If so, we are perhaps in the presence of a first allusive hint at the sacrificial nature of the ritual action itself that is played out in the most sacred space between the pillars: the victim enters the world of the dead (metaphorically, "he climbs through the porthole"), and, in his place, a god arises to protect the community. This transformational account chimes well with the double porthole stone, which Schmidt instinctively considers to be of capital significance.

Is this transformation the founding difference of the twin T-shapes; the secret of the central "space in-between"; and the functional raison d'être of the Göbekli Tepe site? If so, we need not share Schmidt's inhibitions as decipherer, or follow him in wondering whether god is involved. The archaic gods, on this view, are sacralizations of collective human forces symbolically and mythopoetically activated; and Göbekli Tepe, as interpreted by the light of a Girardian template, shows us how this happened (without, of course, saying anything at all of metaphysical import).

Was Göbekli Tepe a Sacrificial Site?

The Girardian reading of the symbolic logic of the site's iconography and its monumental design takes us very convincingly into the mental world of the early humans who built and ran this extraordinary temple complex. But can we be sure that these meanings were duly enacted? Is it reasonable to think that this was a site devoted, in actual and sober fact, to a ritual of sacrifice?

Peters and Schmidt mention the possibility that "the pillars could have witnessed the performance of hunting rituals, initiation and passage rites, spiritual encounters or funeral practices" (Peters and Schmidt 2004, 179).

Schmidt also mentions the presence of "bones, which exist in huge amounts" (2010, 241):

> It should be mentioned that the bone material from the backfilling includes some human bones. Their appearance is similar to the animal bones—they have been broken into small pieces; several have cut marks; and it appears that they were treated in a similar way to the animal bones (2010, 243).

A recent, detailed scientific and forensic analysis of these human bones confirms their ritualistic manipulation, alongside a significant presence of skull fragments (Gresky 2011), which were part of the ritualistic practices of many archaic populations, as confirmed for instance by similar findings in Çatalhöyük (Hodder 2006, 23).[10] Schmidt mentions, only to relativize it—and probably rightly, since there is no evidence of carbonization—the possibility of cannibalism; and he suggests instead that the treatment of the human bones may relate to special rituals performed with the buried, but subsequently disinterred, dead. His reticence may, however, be the sign of the typical overcautiousness that archaeologists and anthropologists have shown in the past half-century in reference to prehistoric cannibalism. The evidence for cannibalism has been growing steadily; it may well be that recognition of the ritual violence of human sacrifice will emerge in its wake from a lingering post-Darwinian shadow zone (or "shudder zone") of misrecognition.[11]

Because of its abundantly evident cultic vocation, Göbekli Tepe in particular is a site that, like others in the region, asks to be considered and studied in this new light, given the amount of evidence it displays. Nerissa Russell, discussing similarly the occurrence of animal sacrifice in Çatalhöyük, particularly with reference to the hunting scenes (Russell 2012), which are discussed also in this volume by Girard, makes reference to archaeological evidence of human sacrifice at Pre-Pottery Neolithic B (PPNB) Çayönü in southeast Anatolia (Loy and Wood 1989), at PPNB Khirokitia on Cyprus (Dikaios 1953), and at Pottery Neolithic Ain el-Kerkh in Syria (Tsuneki 2002), while Sharon Moses has discussed the presence of child sacrifice in Çatalhöyük (Moses 2012).

The strongest evidence, however, probably lies in a simple and immediate deductive probability: if the Stone Age weaponry—knives, axes, arrowheads—is found in such extraordinary profusion at this ritual site, is it not most economically logical to think that they arrived there not just by chance, with the pilgrims, but because they were manufactured on the site for the ritual purposes of the site: namely, the sacrificial immolation of animal and/or human victims?

The iconographic images also suggest sacrifice, animal or human: "The representation of a headless human with erect penis is recognizable quite clearly. The state of the man could indicate a violent death, and his company of scorpions, snakes, and vultures strengthens this impression" (Schmidt 2006, 39). We note also other images consistent with this interpretation: a boar, splayed out upside down with its feet in the air (on the rim of one of the porthole stones); or the image of the vulture grasping in its claws two severed human heads. The design and layout of what Schmidt calls the circles or the enclosures of this temple complex are also highly revealing, particularly in light of Girard's theory. The circles separate the sacred and the profane spheres, both excluding the mass of the pilgrims, who are relegated to the role of spectators standing on the earthen ramps beyond the outer perimeter, yet at the same time engaging the participation of all, as suggested by the human-like T-stones facing inwards towards the center, perhaps representing ritual representatives (shamans or early priests) in whom the crowd find their own drama expressed and through whose actions it is played out—representatives who, perhaps in the order of ritual precedence, as marked by their iconographic insignia of animal images, advance into the third, second, or first ranked circle, leaving the innermost circle to the victim, who is both most intensely identified with and, at the same time, done to death sacrificially, both victim and god, as the two towering pillars suggest.[12]

It is thought that the innermost circle of this Dantesque structure was most generally without an entrance, and was accessed by the priest-sacrificers by means of ladders; though a temporary breach may well have been made to admit the animal or human victim. For this reason, no doubt, the multiple walls create a massively secure and deliberately concentrational structure—not only to exclude the profane but also to contain the potent pharmacology that proceeds ritually in the most sacred space in between the two tall T-stones. For these walled rings, supported by the community and representing it, are designed also to imprison the victims, as in many other ancient arenas.

If we look at the entrance, it is a funnel or tunnel reminiscent of the Roman gladiatorial arena; if we look at the circles or rings within, they often form a labyrinth, such as is familiar from mythic representation of the Minoan bull-leaping arena.[13] If we measure the vertical dimension of this space, we will realize that the arena is sunken, improving visibility for the banks of spectators just as in the amphitheaters where Greek tragedies were performed, so Girard suggests, as an aesthetic development, precisely, of the ritual of sacrifice (Girard 1977, 178).

There is a further element that points to a Girardian understanding of the ritual practices at Göbekli Tepe, consistent with Schmidt's findings: namely, the view that Göbekli Tepe was also a site where extensive feasting, with large consumption of alcoholic beverages, was held (Dietrich et al. 2012). As Girard claims, rituals would always try to reenact the primordial sacrificial event of a spontaneous, collective, violent frenzy ended by the unanimous convergence on a random victim whose killing brought order to a community plunged into a total mimetic disarray; such a ritualistic reenactment would include the repetition of the hallucinatory paroxysm of the mimetic crisis, achieved through trance techniques, or by the use of drugs or intoxicating food or drinks (for instance, during Dionysian Mysteries or Kaingáng rituals) as prelude to the ritual killing of human or animal victims (Girard 1977, 145, 134).[14]

A final and related argument is to be found in another simple deduction: whatever proceeded had to make a potent, life-transforming difference to the community. This much we know from the very fact that, when it failed to do so, the temple builders began again, in the hope that the next temple—and, no doubt, the next sacrifice—would do so.

Girard explains this riddle cogently. He points to the fallacy underlying ritual sacrifice: it is false and self-deceiving to think that the victim is genuinely responsible for the ills offloaded onto him by the community. Not addressing the real causes, such a pharmacology developed around the emissary victim cannot, in any genuine or permanent way, remedy the ills addressed, even if its assured failure is temporarily disguised by the pacifying, reordering, and generally therapeutic social effects of the sacrificial ritual. This same pharmacology will be tried again, therefore, as soon as its effects wear off, and as the ills of conflict and violence reassert themselves—producing, in time, the same evidence of failure. Misrecognition of process and agency and the failure to learn from ritual failure, plus the need for expedient remedies, equals vain repetition.

Göbekli Tepe illustrates this Girardian equation precisely, with this unexpected but entirely confirmatory harmonic that, if belief in the efficacy of the ritual wore down only slowly, this was because, for a long time, hope sprang anew in the vain expedient of reprising the same ritual formula in an infinitesimally displaced site. It is as though the favor of the gods would be won, or their disfavor removed, by more, newer, harder labor until hope and belief itself ran out.

◆ ◆ ◆

It is not, in the nature of the case, possible to claim that this preliminary Girardian reading stands validated beyond the possibility of either doubt or of correction. Yet it has the merit of integrating the data intelligibly, cogently, and economically; as a research hypothesis, it works where lesser framings of theory, and provisional overviews, visibly do not. And we are perceptibly close here to the point where empirical discovery and the deductive certainties of the theorist join hands.

We conclude that Girardian theory has a deserved place at the table of further research, indicated by Klaus Schmidt:

> But to understand the new finds, archaeologists need to work closely with specialists in comparative religion, architectural and art theory, cognitive and evolutionary psychology, sociologists using social network theory, and others; it is the complex story of the earliest large settled communities, their extensive networking, and their communal understanding of their world; perhaps even the first organised religions and their symbolic representations of the cosmos. (Schmidt 2010, 245)

Notes

1. As Ian Hodder writes, "Çatalhöyük is as much a cemetery as a settlement. It is as much a ritual centre of production. These various functions are integrated in the house" (Hodder 2006). "Some of the feasting seem associated with the foundation and abandonment of houses" (Hodder 2006, 172). The seventy-year cycle of habitation and reconstruction may indicate a ritualistic practice based on astronomical observations, and resonates also with early Jewish writing, in which there is a connection between temporal cycles based on the seven sequence and apocalypticism, i.e., destruction and ritual reconstruction of devotional building, as expressed for instance in Isaiah

23:15, Jeremiah 25:11–12, 29:10, Daniel 9:24–25, Levi literature, and in the Apocalypse of Weeks (1 Enoch 93:1–10, 91:11–17).

2. This hypothesis is mentioned by R. Hamerton-Kelly following Karl W. Luckert's book *Stone Age Religion at Göbekli Tepe: From Hunting to Domestication, Wayfaring and Civilization* (2013), which includes a foreword by Klaus Schmidt. See also our companion volume, *Can We Survive our Origins?*

3. Ofer Bar-Yosef, professor of prehistoric archaeology at Harvard, is more cautious: "They haven't found much habitation, but they will. . . . It's impossible to have such a large site without people to take care of it." Schmidt acknowledges there must have been a few residents—"personnel" he calls them—but insists the site was exclusively a ritual destination rather than a settlement, which would make it unique for this period (Curry 2008, 280).

4. "The economic motive is not sufficient to explain domestication, but sacrifice can result in economic practices that gradually become independent of their origin. . . . domestication is only a secondary effect, a sub-product of a ritual practice that is nearly identical in every case. The practice of sacrifice has been extended to extremely diverse species, including human beings, and only chance, the accident of selecting a certain species in combination with its given aptitude, has made for the success of domestication in some cases and its failure in others. In this sense sacrifice became a means for exploring the world" (Girard 1987, 70–71).

5. Writing in the 1920s and 1930s, well before the advent of radiocarbon dating and other methods of absolute chronology that are now standard in the field, Childe had no way of measuring the rate at which mobile populations of hunter-gatherers in diverse environments began to settle down into more permanent communities and adopt new subsistence practices involving the domestication of plants and animals.

6. Dating from as early as 13,000 BCE and ending as the Ice Age drew to a close, the Natufian villages—despite being sometimes considerable settlements—were peopled by foragers, not farmers; they hunted gazelles and gathered wild rye, barley, and wheat. The discovery of these proto-villages, without farming or animal domestication, was the first discovery to destabilize Childe's version of how complex societies began (Mann 2011, 56).

7. "The earliest known evidence, anywhere in the world, for large-scale distributions of composite figures is concentrated around the first centers of urbanization and state formation in the ancient Near East and Eastern Mediterranean regions, the composite beings that appear at the dawn of urban life, towards the end of the 4th millennium BC. . . . [However,] the issue here is not whether Palaeolithic and Neolithic societies created images of imaginary beings. It is beyond doubt that they did (cf. Nakamura and Meskell, 2009), although the number of convincing examples is smaller than might be imagined" (Wengrow 2011).

8. This concept is not to be understood in its modern or its Biblical senses, but simply, at this stage of cultural development, as an "emissary victim." For this consideration see Dawson (2013) and our introduction to this volume.

9. R. Hamerton-Kelly treats this theme in his chapter of our companion volume *Can We Survive Our Origins?*

10. The practice of artificially modifying the human skull has been a part of human culture as far back as 45,000 years BCE (Trinkaus 1982), and it has been shown to occur on every inhabited continent (Dingwall 1931; Ortner 2003).

11. "Cannibalism tends to invoke a strong emotional response, and for that reason the standards of proof for accepting archaeological evidence of cannibalism seem to be unfairly high" (Stoneking

2003; see also Diamond 2000). However, as Ann Gibbons has argued, "the skepticism with which archaeologists once regarded claims of cannibalism among human ancestors is dissipating, thanks to a set of rigorous new criteria for identifying its marks on human fossils." Now archaeologists are making a strong case that the practice may have occurred among our ancestors as early as eight hundred thousand years ago; among the Neanderthals; and more recently, among the Anasazi, the Aztec of Mexico, and the people of Fiji (Gibbons 1997). Moreover, a new study of molecular variation at the prion protein gene locus in human populations (Mead et al. 2003) seems to suggest that "once we were cannibals" (White 2001). The strong selection documented for the prion protein gene is consistent with the growing view (however disquieting it might be) from archaeological evidence, that cannibalism may have been widespread among prehistoric populations (see Fernandez-Jalvo et al 1999; Marlar et al 2000; White 2001).

12. Michel Serres, in *Les origines de la géométrie*, discusses the sacrificial origins of abstract forms of calculation and measurement, which were mapped onto the social structure, where social circles or strata were organized through mechanisms of progressive exclusion. In this originary social topography, everybody concentrically faced the *Kentron*, the center, which etymologically defines both a tool used to torture a victim and the victim herself (Serres 1995, 141).

13. Sacrificial rituals might have originally included the agonistic deadly fighting between animals and humans, as in the later Roman gladiatorial arenas.

14. Interestingly enough, there is also an ongoing discussion among archaeologists about the hypothesis that the discovery of fermentation and the use of beer in religious rituals have led to the domestication of early cereals, which were "better suited to making gruel or beer than bread because of the glume adhering to the grain" (Dietrich et al. 2012, 689)—thus confirming Girard's hypothesis that religious rituals brought about, as an accidental byproduct, the domestication of plants and animals (Girard, Antonello, and de Castro Rocha 2007).

Works Cited

Allaby, R. G., D. Q. Fuller, and T. A. Brown. 2008. "The Genetic Expectations of a Protracted Model for the Origins of Domesticated Crops." *Proceedings of the National Academy of Sciences of the United States of America* 105, no. 37: 13982–86.

Curry, A. 2008. "Seeking the Roots of Ritual." *Science* 319: 278–80.

Dawson, D. 2013. *Flesh Becomes Word: A Lexicography of the Scapegoat or, the History of an Idea*. East Lansing: Michigan State University Press.

Diamond, J. M. 2000. "Talk of Cannibalism." *Nature* 407: 25–26.

Dietrich, O., M. Heun, J. Notroff, K. Schmidt, and M. Zarnkow. 2012. "The Role of Cult and Feasting in the Emergence of Neolithic Communities: New Evidence from Göbekli Tepe, South-Eastern Turkey." *Antiquity* 86: 674–95.

Dikaios, P. 1953. *Khirokitia: Final Report on the Excavation of a Neolithic Settlement in Cyprus on Behalf of the Department of Antiquities, 1936–1946*. Monographs of the Department of Antiquities of the Government of Cyprus 1. London: Oxford University Press.

Dingwall, E. J. 1931. *Artificial Cranial Deformation: A Contribution to the Study of Ethnic Mutilations*. London: John Bale, Sons & Danielsson.

Fernandez-Jalvo, Y., J. Carlos Diez, I. Caceres, and J. Rosell. 1999. "Human Cannibalism in the Early Pleistocene of Europe (Gran Dolina, Sierra de Atapuerca, Burgos, Spain)." *Journal of Human Evolution* 37: 591–622.

Gibbons, A. 1997. "Archaeologists Rediscover Cannibals." *Science* 277, no. 5326: 635–37.

Girard, R. 1977. *Violence and the Sacred*. Baltimore: Johns Hopkins University Press.

———. 1987. *Things Hidden since the Foundation of the World*. Stanford, CA: Stanford University Press.

Girard, R., P. Antonello, and J. C. de Castro Rocha. 2007. *Evolution and Conversion: Dialogues on the Origins of Culture*. London: Continuum.

Gresky, J. 2011. "First Examinations on Neolithic Human Bones from Göbekli Tepe, Turkey." *American Journal of Physical Anthropology* 144, 150.

Hodder, I. 2006. *The Leopard's Tale: Revealing the Mysteries of Çatalhöyük*. London: Thames & Hudson.

Lévi-Strauss, C. 1991. *Histoire de Lynx*. Paris: Librairie Plon.

Lincoln, B. 1975. "The Indo-European Myth of Creation." *History of Religions* 15: 121–45.

———. 1981. *Priests, Warriors, and Cattle: A Study in the Ecology of Religions*. Berkeley: University of California Press.

———. 1986. *Myth, Cosmos, and Society: Indo-European Themes of Creation and Destruction*. Cambridge, MA: Harvard University Press.

Loy, T., and A. Wood. 1989. "Blood Residue Analysis at Cayönü Tepesi, Turkey." *Journal of Field Archaeology* 16, no. 4: 451–60.

Luckert, K. W. 2013. *Stone Age Religion at Göbekli Tepe: From Hunting to Domestication, Wayfaring and Civilization*. N.p.: Triplehood.

Mann, C. C. 2011. "The Birth of Religion." *National Geographic* (June): 39–59.

Marlar, R. A., B. L. Leonard, B. R. Billman, P. M. Lambert, and J. E. Marlar. 2000. "Biochemical Evidence of Cannibalism at a Prehistoric Puebloan Site in Southwestern Colorado." *Nature* 407: 74–78.

Mead, S., et al. 2003. "Balancing Selection at the Prion Protein Gene Consistent with Prehistoric Kurulike Epidemics." *Science* 300: 640–43.

Meixner, G. 1995. *Frauenpaare in kulturgeschichtlichen Zeugnissen*. Munich: Frauenoffensive.

Moses, S. 2012. "Sociopolitical Implications of Neolithic Foundation Deposits and the Possibility of Child Sacrifice: A Case Study at Çatalhöyük, Turkey." In *Sacred Killing: The Archaeology of Sacrifice in the Ancient Near East*, ed. A. M. Porter and G. M. Schwartz, 57–78. Winona Lake, IN: Eisenbrauns.

Nakamura, C., and L. Meskell. 2009. "Articulate Bodies: Forms and Figures at Çatalhöyük." *Journal of Archaeological Method Theory* 16: 205–30.

Ortner, D. J. 2003. *Identification of Pathological Conditions in Human Skeletal Remains*. 2nd ed. San Diego: Academic Press.

Peters J., and K. Schmidt. 2004. "Animals in the Symbolic World of Pre-Pottery Neolithic Göbekli Tepe, South-Eastern Turkey: A Preliminary Assessment." *Anthropozoologica* 39, no. 1: 179–218.

Russell, N. 2012. "Hunting Sacrifice at Neolithic Çatalhöyük." In *Sacred Killing: The Archaeology of Sacrifice in the Ancient Near East*, ed. A. M. Porter and G. M. Schwartz, 79-95. Winona Lake, IN: Eisenbrauns.

Schmidt, K. 1998. "Beyond Daily Bread: Evidence of Early Neolithic Ritual from Göbekli Tepe." *Neo-Lithics* 2: 1–5.

———. 2001. "Der 'Ziegendämon': Archäologie und Religionsgeschichte." In *Lux Orientis: Archäologie zwischen Asien und Europa. Festschrift für Harald Hauptmann zum 65*, ed. R. M. Boehmer and J. Maran, 381–88. Geburtstag: Rahden.

———. 2006. "Animals and a Headless Man at Göbekli Tepe." *Neo-Lithics* 2: 38–40.

———. 2010. "Göbekli Tepe—The Stone Age Sanctuaries: New Results of Ongoing Excavations with a Special Focus on Sculptures and High Reliefs." *Documenta Praehistorica* 37: 239–56.

Serres, M. 1995. *Les origines de la géométrie*. Paris: Flammarion.

Stoneking, M. 2003. "Widespread Prehistoric Human Cannibalism: Easier to Swallow?" *Trends in Ecology and Evolution* 18, no. 10: 489–90.

Symmes, P. 2010. "History in the Remaking." *Newsweek*, February 18.

Trinkaus, E. 1982. "Artificial Cranial Deformation in the Shanidar 1 and 5 Neandertals." *Current Anthropology* 23, no. 2: 198–99.

Tsuneki, A. 2002. "A Neolithic Foundation Deposit at Tell 'Ain el-Kerkh." In *Magic Practices and Ritual in the Near Eastern Neolithic: Proceedings of a Workshop Held at the 2nd ICAANE, Copenhagen University, May 2000*, ed. H. Gebel, B. Hermansen, and C. Hoffmann Jensen, 133–43. Berlin: Ex Oriente.

Watkins, T. 2010. "New Light on Neolithic Revolution in South-West Asia." *Antiquity* 84: 621–34.

Wengrow, D. 2011. "Cognition, Materiality and Monsters: The Cultural Transmission of Counter-intuitive Forms in Bronze Age Societies." *Journal of Material Culture* 16, no. 2: 131–49.

White, T. D. 2001. "Once We Were Cannibals." *Scientific American* 285: 58–65.

Willcox, G., S. Fornite, and L. Herveux. 2008. "Early Holocene Cultivation before Domestication in Northern Syria." *Vegetation History and Archaeobotany* 17, no. 3: 313–25.

PART FIVE

The Evolutionary Hermeneutics of *Homo religiosus*

Intrinsic or Situated Religiousness

A Girardian Solution

Warren S. Brown, James Van Slyke, and Scott Garrels

During the Enlightenment, human beings came to be designated *Homo sapiens* in reference to the human capacity for rationality. However, as perspectives on human nature have expanded, other designations have been proposed that emphasize other characteristics of human persons: *Homo faber* (toolmaker), *Homo socius* (social), *Homo oeconomicus* (economic), *Homo amans* (loving), and *Homo religiosus* (religious). In each case, the purpose of the term is to designate a characteristic unique to humankind. Given that the particular capacity designated is believed to be a universal attribute of human beings, it is often presumed that there must be an immediate evolutionary/genetic substrate, as in a brain system prewired for that particular characteristic. This essay will explore the presupposition that such unique and important characteristics of humankind must necessarily have been the direct product of biological evolution.

The Augustinian/Cartesian Residual

While the fields of psychology and neuroscience generally reject body/mind or body/soul dualism, current research on the most important, high-level, uniquely human capacities such as religiousness continue to be influenced by a residual of the Augustinian/Cartesian formulation of human nature. In Western thinking, St. Augustine established the idea of an inner soul or self based on the Neoplatonic suggestion that contemplation of the divine required an inward turn towards one's soul (Cary 2000). He described his own spiritual experiences in terms of a radical reflexivity (that is, looking inward for the source of spiritual life). In this formulation, that which is most truly the self, and therefore most thoroughly human, is an inner, nonmaterial part (mind or soul). The essence of the person was not considered to be the whole physical being engaged with an external world; rather, the real person was the soul or self that was a part residing somewhere inside the body. Philosopher René Descartes contributed a sharper distinction between body and soul (or body and mind). Unable to imagine how rationality could be manifest by a physical mechanism, and influenced by Augustine, Descartes argued that humans have a distinct nonmaterial, internal entity that constitutes the rational mind.

Most modern scientists, philosophers, and even theologians have discarded this Cartesian formulation by asserting a more physicalist (embodied) view of human nature. However, even within this modern understanding of persons, it is still hard for many to avoid the idea that the most unique and important attributes of humankind must reside inside the head. Many physicalist theories of human nature still view the mind as existing entirely inside in the form of brain functions that are distinct from the rest of the physical person and distant from the social environment. This is the view that Daniel Dennett has referred to as "Cartesian materialism" (Dennett 1991). Instead of a body and an inner soul (or mind), we have a body and inner brain functions (i.e., brain-body dualism). Along with this view comes the assumption that all that is important and unique about human nature must be identified with functions or properties that reside inside individual human brains. This view relegates interpersonal relations and social systems to a secondary status with respect to our understanding of the origins and development of critical aspects of human nature. Due to this Augustinian/Cartesian residual, it is presumed that everything that is important about humanity must be both inner and individual.

With respect to evolutionary discussions, this Augustinian/Cartesian residual of innerness and individuality engenders stories about the biological evolution of brain systems somehow directly related to the specific human characteristic currently in focus. Thus, the presumed background story is about genetic transmission and selective biological advantage, rather than a story about the evolution of human culture and its impact on the cognitive and social development (particularly early childhood development) of human beings. The dominant causal line extends from genetics to brain structures, to cognitive characteristics, to social and cultural forms, rather than from the social context to the formation of the cognitive and social capacities and characteristics of persons.[1]

Cognitive Science and Neuroscience of Religious Experience and Belief

With respect to the particular case of human religiousness, this essay argues for the necessity of avoiding the Augustinian/Cartesian residuals of inwardness and individuality, and incorporating modern understandings of the self-organization of mental systems and environmental scaffolding of most human higher mental capacities. This move would avoid the presupposition that because religiousness is universal in humankind, it must therefore be a genetically endowed evolutionary outcome involving physical brain systems specific to religion, or that religion came about as a byproduct of the cognitive tendencies of individual persons that evolved for other reasons. The Cartesian residuals in understanding human religiousness will be discussed with respect to the neuroscience of religious experience and belief, and what is called the cognitive science of religion.

Brain Activity and Religious Experience

A reasonable body of recent research and theory has been aimed at describing the neural substrates of religious behavior, belief, or experiences. There are empirical studies in cognitive and social neuroscience that attempt to map patterns of brain activity associated with religious experiences using functional brain imaging, or to elicit religious experiences via magnetic stimulation of specific brain regions, as well as reports in clinical neurology involving religious experiences in patients with epilepsy. In general, these studies presume that religiousness per se is a product of biological evolution, and, thus, there must exist brain systems that are specific to religious experiences that are in some way unique to humans. The following is a description of a few selected examples of these studies.

There is a longstanding literature in neurology that suggests that in some individuals with right temporal lobe epileptic seizures, intense religious states are experienced during the aura leading up to their seizures. In these persons, experiences of religious awe, ecstasy, or ominous presence appear to be a product of abnormal electrical activity in the right anterior temporal lobe. The subjective experience of this form of aura is illustrated in the following self-report from one patient: "Triple halos appeared around the sun. Suddenly the sunlight became intense. I experienced a revelation of God and of all creation glittering under the sun. The sun became bigger and engulfed me. My mind, my whole being was pervaded by a feeling of delight" (Naito and Matsui 1988).

Although somewhat rare, such clinical reports led neuroscientist V. S. Ramachandran to speculate on the existence of a "God module" in the brain., i.e., "dedicated neural machinery in the temporal lobes concerned with religion" (Ramachandran et al. 1997, 1316). Saver and Rubin suggested a less outrageous interpretation in their "limbic marker hypothesis," proposing that the limbic system tags certain encounters as "crucially important, harmonious, and/or joyous, prompting comprehension of these experiences within a religious framework" (Saver and Rabin 1997). Thus, it is not at all clear that such abnormal temporal lobe activity necessarily creates a specifically religious state, as opposed to a state that patients interpret as religious based on prior experiences, a priori beliefs, and/or cultural expectations.

Abnormal activity of the temporal lobes can be induced artificially in non-epileptic individuals using transcranial magnetic stimulation (TMS). Michael Persinger described experiments where TMS of the right temporal lobe resulted in the person reporting a "sense of presence" (Persinger and Makarec 1987). This "sense of presence" is sometimes experienced by the person as the presence of God or angels or other supernatural persons. This led Persinger to suggest that all persons who have religious experiences are having microseizures of the right temporal lobe. However, religiously interpreted experiences are not a consistent outcome of this form of TMS, and

Persinger's results have been difficult to replicate. It is likely that the experience associated with the stimulation only becomes religious based on attributions given to the experience by the participant based on prior experiences and contextually primed expectations.

Newberg, d'Aguili, and their collaborators are credited with some of the earliest work involving functional brain imaging during religious meditation (Newberg et al. 2001). They recorded regional brain activity (as indicated by single-photon emission computed tomography, or SPECT) in Buddhist monks and Catholic nuns during meditation. The results indicated that both groups showed increased bilateral frontal activation and decreased right parietal activity when they reached a state that they experienced as oneness. Decreased activity of the right parietal lobe was interpreted as a correlate of the absence of a sense of self experienced in such meditative states. In a replication of this research using functional magnetic resonance imaging (fMRI), Azari and colleagues found a different pattern of brain activation during meditation on a psalm (Azari et al. 2001), while Spezio and colleagues reported an even different pattern of brain activity during a meditation-like activity called "centering prayer" (Ly et al. 2008). Newberg et al. also used SPECT scanning to investigate patterns of neural activity during a more expressive form of religious experience called glossolalia (speaking in tongues) (Newberg et al. 2006). Here again, the patterns were quite different from those found during meditation or centering prayer.

Several conclusions can be drawn from this brief sampling of studies of brain activity associated with religious experiences: (1) Different structures and patterns of brain activity are identified in different studies. Thus, there does not seem to be a single structure or system that must be involved for the experience to be reported as religious. (2) There does not seem to be a brain structure or system that is uniquely involved in religious experiences. (3) The religious nature of the experiences in these various experiments and neurological disorders is most likely due to the participants' a priori beliefs and expectations, or to the social and semantic context within which the experience occurs. For example, abnormal activity of the temporal lobe is interpreted as religious out of a cultural matrix of prior assumptions about what a religious experience is like.

The Cognitive Science of Religion

The field referred to as the cognitive science of religion (CSR) considers cognitive mechanisms that seem to play an important role in the formation of religious belief. The field argues that basic cognitive capacities, formed during evolution to solve adaptive problems (Barkow, Cosmides, and Tooby 1992), produced universal cognitive features that foster the emergence of individual religious thought and behavior, and therefore help to explain the origin of religion. Thus, the basic architecture of human cognition is thought to make certain aspects of religious belief easy to learn and comprehend. CSR attempts to describe ways in which different cognitive processes play an important role in the formation of religion and religious beliefs.

For example, it is presumed that cognitive templates evolved that allow humans to easily identify different kinds of categories of objects (such as persons, animals, or artifacts) based on important features (Boyer and Barrett 2005). The counterintuitive hypothesis argues that the conceptual construction of religious beliefs contains features of an intuitive ontology based on these cognitive templates, and that religious beliefs maintain certain aspects of the cognitive templates while violating them in predictable ways (Boyer 2003). For example, the idea of a ghost uses the person template, which acts as a schema for certain features of ghosts (they can move, they have intentions, etc.), but other natural aspects of this schema are violated (ghosts can walk through walls and come back to life after being dead). Maximally counterintuitive beliefs (beliefs that violate too many features of the cognitive template) do not tend to spread because of the pressure they put on individual memorization, but the minimal violation of natural categories that occurs in many religious beliefs are presumed to increase their salience and make them more memorable (Boyer 2001).

The capacity for identifying agents is another cognitive mechanism thought by CSR to be particularly important in the formation of concepts of the supernatural (Guthrie1993; Barrett 2004). Many religions invoke supernatural agents to explain a variety of natural phenomena, such as inferring the intentions or interventions of gods as an explanation for natural events. Inference of agency is related to the idea of a "theory of mind," which is the ability to infer, in a reasonably accurate manner, the intentions and beliefs of another person. For example, studies demonstrated that persons tend to attribute mental phenomena (intentions and emotions) to animated geometrical shapes (simple triangles) moving and interacting on a video screen, seeing them to be chasing, coaxing, or hiding, or as manifesting emotions such as affection and fear (Heider and Simmel 1944). To be accurate, persons in these studies do not believe the animate shapes actually have these intentions and emotions, but rather they use these categories to narrate what they have seen. Similarly, six- to seven-year-old children tend to believe that someone, rather than something or a random process, created different sorts of natural phenomena such as mountain ranges and animals (Kelemen and Di Yanni 2005). Even if parents and teachers explicitly endorse an evolutionary framework, children under ten years of age tend to favor creationist accounts of the natural world rather than evolutionary accounts (Evans 2001). This evidence led Deborah Kelemen to remark that children are promiscuous in their teleological accounts of the natural world (Kelemen 1999).

This bias towards agentive and teleological explanations is presumed to explain why children readily use and understand concepts about supernatural agents such as a god. For example, children readily discriminate between the omniscient knowledge of God and the limited knowledge of mothers during a false belief task. Thus, even after the developmental milestone of recognizing the potential for a parent to believe something that is false, children still retain the belief that God would not be fooled by a box that usually contains crackers, but that actually contains pencils (Barrett, Richert, and Driesenga 2001). While observing a puppet show about a mouse that was eaten by an alligator, children very easily reasoned about different mental states the mouse might be experiencing, despite the fact that they explicitly understood that the mouse was dead (Bering and Bjorklund 2004).

Some have argued that religion is a misapplication or unintended outcome of cognitive capacities evolved for other reasons—often referred to as the "byproduct theory." It is presumed that without the misuse of certain cognitive capacities (such as a theory of mind), individual humans would not be religious, and human societies would not have developed religions. As one writer describes it:

> Recently psychologists doing research on the minds of infants have discovered two related facts that may account for this phenomenon. One: human

> beings come into the world with a predisposition to believe in supernatural phenomena. And two: this predisposition is an incidental by-product of cognitive functioning gone awry. (Bloom 2005, 2)

A major problem with this interpretation of CSR is that of causal reduction.[2] Can the causes of a highly social and cultural phenomenon that is as complex as human religion be reduced to the direct outcome of the misapplication of such basic cognitive tendencies? Would it be more probable to assume that the development of religion in humans was based on social and cultural processes that are, nevertheless, compatible with the capacities of the human mind?

Both the neuroscience of religious experience and the cognitive byproduct theories of human religiousness fit well within the Augustinian/Cartesian residual of presuming that everything that is characteristic and distinctive about humankind must be both inner and individual in its origins. If a phenomenon is commonly found in human groups, it must, in this view, be related to a genetic/biological trait that is inside individual persons, rather than due to a learned adaptation to commonly experienced social and environmental forces.

Self-Organizing Systems, Situated Cognition, and Externalism

Over the last several decades, alternatives to the focus on the inner and individual origins of human capacities have been proposed within cognitive science and philosophy of mind. In general, the proposal is that much of what is most sophisticated, high-level, and important about human nature is not innately resident inside individual persons, but rather emerges in engagement with social, cultural, and interpersonal structures and systems outside of persons. While it may take certain rudimentary, genetically endowed brain structures and processes to initially engage these cultural systems (such as the tendency of newborns to look at faces), the origin and existence of a large proportion of the capacities and attributes most characteristic of humankind are the outcome of interactions with the physical and social environment. The essence of this new movement in cognitive science is to see the individual as inescapably enmeshed in constant, ongoing feedback relationships with the environment of social systems and cultural artifacts, where thinking, cognitions, beliefs, and language emerge out of these bodily interactions, and where cognitive processes are always contextually situated (Clark 1997).

While space does not permit description of all of the nuances of this theory of human cognition, there are several principles that need to be mentioned. First is the idea that human neural systems are, at least to some degree, self-organizing such as described by theories of complex dynamical systems. While genetics provides basic guidelines, what develops as a person is a self-organizing response to the physical and social environment. A second important principle is that cognition is situated and embodied. These terms express the idea that human mind cannot be extracted from its engagement in specific physical, social, linguistic, and cultural contexts. Thus, what is available to think with offline are residuals and memories of embodied situational interactions. The processes of thought are rooted in emulations and simulations of bodily interactions with the world. Thus, knowledge is always situated in that it is elicited with respect to the contexts in which the organizational process occurred. Finally, the concept of "externalism" emphasizes the notion that if the mind exists in interactions with environmental context, then the mind is at least partially external to the person within the space where person and environment intersect. A great deal of our knowledge cannot be elicited independent of the specific social interactions or physical artifacts in which the knowledge was gained. Thus, any later realization of the intelligent cognitive process requires the presence (situationally, or at times within one's imagination) of the physical artifacts or social context.

As alternatives to the Augustinian/Cartesian residuals of inwardness and individuality, these new theories suggest that human cognition is constituted by bodily processes that self-organize in ways that allow persons to effectively engage the external physical and social world. Persons become increasingly intelligent and cognitively complex, as well as unique individuals, as they incorporate adaptive responses to the particulars of their intelligent external sociocultural environs. Over eons of time, humans built into society, culture, and language important conceptual tools, allowing persons who come later to have a much richer and culturally more sophisticated environment within which to develop. As philosopher of mind Andy Clark has said,

> We use intelligence to structure our environment so that we can succeed with less intelligence. Our brains make the world smart so that we can be dumb in peace! . . . It is the human brain *plus* these chunks of external scaffolding that finally constitutes the smart, rational inference engine we call mind. (Clark 1997, 180)

In many important cases, the social environment is prior to the human capacity and is the force that causes a person's neurocognitive systems to organize in a manner we understand as intelligent.

Thus, the alternative view that gains more distance from the Augustian/Cartesian residual is that, while humans have somewhat enhanced neural machinery with respect to other primates, what is most unique about humankind is the way the machinery progressively organizes itself to interact with the physical and social environment, which evolves in complexity and sophistication. When studying uniquely human capacities like religiousness, the critical questions are not about the machinery itself (that is, about evolutionarily acquired brain systems), but about how embeddedness in the social processes of human interactions cause new capacities to emerge through a process of self-organization—capacities that cannot be reduced to underlying brain systems or evolutionarily acquired cognitive mechanisms without substantial loss (Murphy and Brown 2007).

Mimetic Theory and the Origins of Religion

Mimetic theory provides a robust scenario regarding the origins of religion in which religion is not the outcome of neural or cognitive systems, nor a byproduct of human mental capacities gone awry. In this alternative theory, byproducts of human cognition such as promiscuous teleology or agency bias play little role at the origins of religion, although these may (or may not) play some secondary role in the various specific forms taken by religions.

For Girard, religion came into existence as an inter-individual, social solution to the problem of ubiquitous rivalry and violence in human groups. According to Girard, there is a fundamental tendency in humans for intense competition and rivalry based on our unique capacity for imitation—specifically, the imitation of desire (mimesis). Without social structures to constrain it, this rivalry inevitably leads to violence in human groups. Much of Girard's anthropological research is an attempt to understand how humanity has survived its own mimetic violence (Girard 1977). Because violence is one of the most imitative of all human behaviors, once initiated it has the potential of spreading quickly to those within its proximity through group contagion, upsetting existing bonds of community, and leading to cyclical acts of violence and revenge. Girard reasoned that without some natural way to limit mimetic violence and bring it to an end (such as dominance patterns found in other animal societies), the likely result would have been the eventual extinction of our species.

For Girard, the phenomenon that made social stability possible, and that ultimately led to cohesive human culture, was emergence of the process of displacement of violent tensions among members of the community onto an arbitrary or surrogate victim. Girard argues that those early human cultures that were able to survive their own violence did so by becoming progressively focused on a scapegoat. That is, the focus of violence was turned onto a particular individual who served as the scapegoat for the multiplicity of inter-individual rivalries. The eventual and inevitable killing of the scapegoat provided a powerful solution to the violence between individual persons and brought peace to the community. All had joined together in the hatred of the scapegoat, transcending in the process their personal rivalries. Because of the seemingly mysterious resolution of widespread interpersonal conflict, the scapegoat came to be understood as the guilty party causing the community discord, and the process of killing the scapegoat came to be viewed as a divine solution.

While complex and wide-ranging, Girard's anthropology asserts that archaic culture and religion had their origin in the same type of event: a mimetic crisis of undifferentiated rivalry and violence (all against all) that eventually polarized and self-organized into a collective murder (all against one). According to Girard, this event had the effect of creating an unprecedented sense of communal bonding that eliminated group tensions while at the same time establishing important social distinctions: that between a community and its antagonist. In the attempt to prevent further spontaneous episodes of uncontrollable violence, this scapegoat sacrifice and its resolution of discord was repeated and thus made available for imitation and cultural transmission on a ritual basis. This, for Girard, is the origin of ritual human sacrifice. According to Girard, religions worldwide have certain core similarities because, while diverse, the rites and prohibitions that constitute them are nonetheless a variation on the institutionalization of the same scapegoat mechanism.

Thus, Girard presents an origin of human religion that is not rooted in human neurobiology or cognition. Religion is neither an expression of ubiquitous childhood fantasy and promiscuous teleology, nor a byproduct of human cognition gone awry. Rather, religion is a cultural response that emerged in human society forced to organize in some way to mitigate violence and promote harmony.

Of course, it is not the case that human cognition and its characteristics play no role in the Girardian scenario. Certainly mimetic desire, at the origin of the rivalry and violence, is based on the tendency of humans to imitate one another, including the evolution of the uniquely human capacity for imitation of desire. In addition, once religion has begun to develop, tendencies to anthropomorphize and find humanlike agency in animals or inanimate objects may have played into its elaboration. But religion itself is the solution to a problem of human society—its predilection for violence. Even imitation and mimetic desire, as a root cognitive capacity in Girardian theory, are several steps removed from the origins of religions.

There is much more that Girard has written about mimetic theory and religion, but the main point for the purposes of this essay is the idea that the origins of religion are interpersonal and social (Girard 1977, 1982, 1987). Indeed, Girard speculates that the discovery of the scapegoat solution may have occurred at a time in human evolution that was prior to the development of many of the cognitive characteristics that are considered importantly human and are foundational to CSR. Thus, religion would not be a byproduct of the evolution of mental tools, but rather religion is an environmental (societal) force that causes further cognitive evolution to take a particular direction. If religion is in any way cognitively natural to children (as CSR suggests), it has become so because of the influences of religion reflects itself back on the evolution of human mental capacities and on the cultural world within which infants undergo cognitive self-organization.

Summary

Human religiousness is a product of situated and self-organizing processes compatible with Girard's mimetic theory. It is an error to look for the source of everything that is unique about human beings (including religion) inside individual persons. Two forms of current research and theory (the neuroscience and the cognitive science of religion) both presume that human religiousness is somehow directly engendered by neurocognitive processes. By way of contrast, recent theories in cognitive science view human higher mental and social capacities as largely self-organizing in interactions with the physical and social environment. As a consequence, cognition is largely situated in that mental capacities exist as enacted or imagined interactions between the person and the environment. Girard's proposal regarding the roots of human religiousness as a theory is consistent with embodied and self-organizing cognition. Religion is understood by Girard as a situated cultural solution to an inter-individual and societal problem in which the only specifically human evolutionary/genetic trait involved is mimetic desire and its tendency to engender violence, the opposite of intrinsic religiousness.

Notes

1. The section was taken in part from Brown 2006. This article is also found in Jeeves and Brown 2009.
2. An important review of the philosophical status of the cognitive science of religion is provided in Van Slyke 2010.

Works Cited

Azari, N. P., et al. 2001. "Neural Correlates of Religious Experience." *European Journal of Neuroscience* 18, no. 8: 649–52.

Barkow, J. H., L. Cosmides, and J. Tooby, eds. 1992. *The Adapted Mind: Evolutionary Psychology and the Generation of Culture*. New York: Oxford University Press.

Barrett, J. L. 2004. *Why Would Anyone Believe in God?* Walnut Creek, CA: AltaMira Press.

Barrett, J. L., R. A. Richert, and A. Driesenga. 2001. "God's Beliefs versus Mother's: The Development of Non-Human Agent Concepts." *Child Development* 71: 50–65.

Bering, J. M., and D. F. Bjorklund. 2004. "The Natural Emergence of Reasoning about the Afterlife as a Developmental Regularity." *Developmental Psychology* 40, no. 2: 217–33.

Bloom, P. 2005. "Is God an Accident?" *Atlantic Monthly*, December 2.

Boyer, P. 2001. *Religion Explained: The Evolutionary Origins of Religious Thought*. New York: Basic Books.

———. 2003. "Religious Thought and Behavior as By-Products of Brain Function." *Trends in Cognitive Sciences* 7, no. 3: 119–24.

Boyer, P., and C. Barrett. 2005. "Evolved Intuitive Ontology: Integrating Neural, Behavioral, and Developmental Aspects of Domain Specificity." In *Handbook of Evolutionary Psychology*, ed. D. Buss, 96–118. Hoboken, NJ: John Wiley & Sons, Inc.

Boyer, P., and C. Ramble. 2001. "Cognitive Templates for Religious Concepts: Cross-Cultural Evidence for Recall of Counter-Intuitive Representations." *Cognitive Science* 25: 535–64.

Brown, W. 2006. "The Brain, Religion, and Baseball: Comments on the Potential for a Neurology of Religion." In *Where God and Science Meet: How Brain and Evolutionary Studies Alter Our Understanding of Religion*, vol. 2, *The Neurology of Religious Experience*, ed. P. McNamara. Westport, CT: Greenwood Press.

Cary, P. 2000. *Augustine's Invention of the Inner Self: The Legacy of a Christian Platonist*. Oxford: Oxford University Press.

Clark, A. 1997. *Being There: Putting Brain, Body, and World Together Again*. Cambridge, MA: MIT Press.

Dennett, D. 1991. *Consciousness Explained*. Boston: Little, Brown and Co.

Evans, E. 2001. "Cognitive and Contextual Factors in the Emergence of Diverse Belief Systems: Creation versus Evolution." *Cognitive Psychology* 42, no. 3: 217–66.

Girard, R. 1977. *Violence and the Sacred*. Translated by P. Gregory. Baltimore: Johns Hopkins University Press.

———. 1982. *The Scapegoat*. Translated by Y. Freccero. Baltimore: Johns Hopkins University Press.

———. 1987. *Things Hidden since the Foundation of the World*. Translated by S. Bann and M. Meteer. Stanford, CA: Stanford University Press.

Guthrie, S. 1993. *Faces in the Clouds: A New Theory of Religion*. Oxford: Oxford University Press.

Heider, F., and M.-A. Simmel. 1944. "An Experimental Study of Apparent Behavior." *American Journal of Psychology* 57: 243–59.

Jeeves, M. A., and W. S. Brown. 2009. *Neuroscience, Psychology, and Religion: Illusions, Delusions, and Realities about Human Nature*. Radnor, PA: Templeton Press.

Kelemen, D. 1999. "Why Are Rocks Pointy? Children's Preference for Teleological Explanations of the Natural World." *Developmental Psychology* 35, no. 6: 1440–52.

Kelemen, D., and C. Di Yanni. 2005. "Intuitions about Origins: Purpose and Intelligent Design in Children." *Journal of Cognition and Development* 6: 3–31.

Ly, M., A. Tan, and M. L. Spezio. 2008. "The effect of meditation on neural systems implicated in social judgments." Paper presented at the Meeting of the Society for Neuroscience, Washington, D.C., November.

Murphy, N., and W. S. Brown. 2007. *Did My Neurons Make Me Do It? Philosophical and Neurobiological Perspectives on Moral Responsibility and Free Will*. Oxford: Oxford University Press.

Naito, H., and N. Matsui. 1988. "Temporal Lobe Epilepsy with Ictal Ecstatic State and Interictal Behavior of Hypergraphia." *Journal of Nervous and Mental Disease* 176, no. 2: 123–24.

Newberg, A., et al. 2006. "The Measurement of Regional Cerebral Blood Flow during Glossolalia: A Preliminary Study." *Psychiatry Research: Neuroimaging* 148, no. 1: 67–71.

Newberg, A., A. Alavi, M. Baime, M. Pourdehnad, J. Santanna, and E. d'Aquili. 2001. "The Measurement of Regional Cerebral Blood Flow during the Complex Cognitive Task of Meditation: A Preliminary SPECT Study." *Psychiatry Research* 2: 113–22.

Persinger, M. A., and K. Makarec. 1987. "Temporal Lobe Epileptic Signs and Correlative Behaviors Displayed by Normal Populations." *Journal of General Psychology* 1114: 179–95.

———. 1993. "Complex Partial Epileptic Signs as a Continuum from Normals to Epileptics: Normative Data and Clinical Populations." *Journal of Clinical Psychology* 49: 33–45.

Ramachandran, V. S., et al. 1997. "The Neural Basis of Religious Experiences." *1997 Society for Neuroscience Conference Abstracts* 1316.

Saver, J. L., and J. Rabin. 1997. "The Neural Substrates of Religious Experience." *Journal of Neuropsychiatry* 9: 498–510.

Van Slyke, J. 2010. "Challenging the By-Product Theory of Religion in the Cognitive Science of Religion." *Theology and Science* 8, no. 2: 163–80.

Homo religiosus in Mimetic Perspective

An Evolutionary Dialogue

Paul Gifford

Scott Atran puts his finger on what may be the trickiest and most fundamental of our "fundamental problems of evolutionary theory": Why religion? Why so much of it, in such bewildering variety, so persistently and so perennially? What is it, in the perspective of mimetic theory, with *Homo religiosus*?

"From the viewpoint of evolution, religion ought not to exist: it is costly in material sacrifices and in emotional expenditure; it imposes on us efforts to adhere to beliefs which defy common sense" (Atran 2009).[1] Some of us might feel inclined to question this particular formulation; or at least to enquire what sort of religion, and whose religion, we are really talking about. Since when was religion—since when was evolution itself—subject to the measure, the criterion, or the sanction of "common sense"? And can we specify more usefully why religion—however we understand it—is so puzzling when viewed in evolutionary terms?

Is it perhaps that it represents an anomalous byproduct of human cognitive development, a sort of archaic dream-thought that once had a certain adaptive or survival value but that we are now stuck with, so to speak, beyond its sell-by date—and to which the larger part of humankind nonetheless still clings with extraordinary tenacity; whereas, enlightened scientific reason sees only a regrettable infantile attachment to a shadowy otherworld of supernatural agency, more or less explicable functionally, insofar as, in one way or another, it makes good the deficiencies of our—still very imperfect—knowledge and mastery of this world?

That would seem to be Atran's basic take on the question, and the view of many Western intellectuals with him. That is the framing hypothesis projected by what we might call the cognitivist paradigm (i.e., the model of interpretation constructed by, for, and around the act itself of positive, rational, preferably scientific cognition). "Religion put to the test of evolution"—to cite the subtitle of Atran's book in its French-language version—will always, insofar as it follows the logic and the persuasion of that paradigm, tend to retrace that form of understanding, and to verify that hypothesis about the nature and status of religion.

Contrariwise, religion might appear to us enigmatic and paradoxical for just the opposite reason: because it transcends the closed system of natural causalities posited by scientific method in dealing with mundane realities; because it addresses and invokes the transcendent forces and energies man encounters beyond himself; and because it caters to an excess in desire, discovered within, that is the mark and the most authentic anthropological clue as to man's real destiny. This might provide an alternative hypothesis—or, just conceivably, a complementary one. We might perhaps agree to call this type of account the relationalist paradigm.

Our twenty-first-century science of evolution increasingly (I believe) beckons to the second hypothesis outlined above; and the fundamental anthropology developed by Girardian mimetic theory allows us to grasp, perhaps for the first time, how this alternative account might work, and why it indeed brings a vital complement of understanding.

The dialogue I envisage between these positions will engage, respectively, the first and second halves of Girard's œuvre—the two wings of the Girardian chateau. These point, successively but in concert, towards what French philosopher Henri Bergson was the first to call *The Two Sources of Morality and Religion* (1932).

Hominization: Accounting for both Continuities and Quantum Leap

It seems crucial, first of all, to register the fact that mimetic theory indeed offers us what the cognitivist paradigm markedly does not give: namely, a genetic and generative account of the evolutionary origins of religion, showing how religion is integral to the emergence of human culture as such, and so of humankind as such.

Of course, Atran acknowledges that *Homo sapiens* is, in some sense, "the religious animal." He can scarcely avoid doing so, since his research as a leading social anthropologist of religion causes him to study constantly the stupendously far-flung subsequent effects of this basic datum; he is professionally engaged in chasing them to all points of the compass. But he gives as little as possible of credit to that recognition, since the disciplinary and hermeneutical mindset he brings to this task persuades him that *Homo religiosus* is spooked or haunted and, cognitively speaking, "up a blind alley." Moreover, he does not consider himself bound to determine what generates that starburst of proliferating forms and enduring effects in the first place: he does not think back etiologically, that is, to the principle of these phenomena. Indeed, he firmly declines to do so. Religion, he says, is so ill-defined a phenomenon that it must be a waste of time even asking how it began (Atran 2002, 15 [2009, 27]). For Girard, by contrast, *Homo sapiens*, by virtue of the very process that carries him over the threshold of hominization, beyond animal antecedents, and forward from the hominids, is always and essentially *Homo religiosus*. Girard gives us a generative account, conforming to the nature itself of the process of evolution, which is, most fundamentally, a form of "coming-to-be." His is a genetic theory, not in the late and specialized sense of invoking genes (selfish or otherwise), but in the primary and perennial sense that it plots genesis, and because it offers a nodal and originary account of the role in that process of religion. This is crucial, hermeneutically speaking, if we believe (with Aristotle) that the act of knowing has to be adapted, appropriate, and adequate to its object.

What is it that makes Girard's theory presenting *Homo sapiens* as the emergent religious animal so illuminating and so cogent? We might answer briefly: because it meets, better than any other known theory, the two primary requirements resting upon any theory of emergence: it accounts for both the most significant continuities and the quantum leap involved in the passage from animal to human. More than that: it holds these two vast and complex imperatives of understanding together according to the simplest form of reciprocity. It is a beautiful theory in the sense that $E = mc^2$ is a beautiful theory.

Where are we to pick up the thread of emergence and coming-to-be that produces hominization? Girard teaches us to look for the thread of mimesis running through biological, animal, and human nature. The octopus imitates the colors and forms of the seabed refuge into which it subsides (squid and cuttlefish share something of this capacity for imitation and camouflage); the lyre bird mimics the call of any other bird in the forest; apes learn to copy, hence to understand and to emit, in turn, warning calls. They learn to use the most basic tools; they even reproduce a range of appropriate group behaviors; and the group intelligence thus acquired allows them to be social animals. In fact: all their proto-cultural characteristics are explained by a more advanced, complex, and enabling aptitude for imitation. And *Homo sapiens*, in one sense, just prolongs this development, save that he does so exponentially, his enhanced brain size permitting more and more complex applications and more and more advanced potentials of the aptitude for mimesis.

In the twenty-first century (as distinct from Darwin's own nineteenth century) we have greater difficulty in coming to terms with the quantum leap that separates us from our animal forebears. The basic phenomenon is of course visible enough when viewed retrospectively and historically; but retracing and accounting for it as an emergent reality without dissolving it into a gradualism that loses sight of the advent of the novelty we are observing, and which explains nothing, is a baffling hermeneutical challenge, rarely measured adequately or assumed as such by today's evolutionary scientists.

We say to our offspring when they mimic us: "You little monkey!" (i.e., our language actually picks up this continuity before we are consciously aware of it). Yet recent observational studies in this area inform us how little, comparatively speaking, the higher apes do, in fact, imitate, when set alongside their exponentially advanced and now quantum-leap separated human descendants. The same differential recognition occurs in behavioral comparisons of human and animal violence, a field where Paul Dumouchel detects a persuasion of method that seeks—and, inevitably then, also finds—only analogies and continuities, which it then fails to interpret adequately.[2]

This is perhaps because the thread of continuity linking animal and human is easily intuited and verified (once the initial shock of Darwinian descent has been assimilated), since it has the same etiological shape as Darwin's hypothesis. The discontinuities, however, are much more complex and elusive; and it is at this more challenging frontier that the breakthrough offered by Girardian theory intervenes.

Girard quotes with approval the Jacques Monod of *Chance and Necessity*:

> It is the powerful development and intensive use of the simulative function that, in my view, characterises the unique properties of man's brain. This is so at the deepest level of cognitive functioning, the level on which language depends, but which it reveals only in part. (Girard 1978, 132; [1987, 194])

He comments:

> There is reason to believe that the power and intensity of imitation increase with the volume of the brain throughout the whole line leading to *homo sapiens*. In the primates closer to man, the brain is bigger relative to all other animals. It must be this growing power of imitation that triggers the process of hominisation, and not the reverse. (1978, 132–33 [1987, 94–95])

Mimetic capacity, Girard also shows, is the great multiplier of purely animal conflicts, based on competing needs. Since humans represent and respond reactively to the inner life of conspecifics, their rivalries generate mimetically a runaway dynamic of desire turbocharged by rivalry and vengefulness—a dynamic that is incremental and contagious in character, and thus always potentially catastrophic for the social community.

As brain size increases, therefore, and mimetic capacity with it, there must come a point of critical phase change, rather like the one envisaged in René Thom's catastrophe theory, where a relatively minor incident, or series of them, can trigger incalculable consequences in the system of reference, disrupting group understanding, destabilizing the social community, and opening up an entirely new set of potentials and probabilities—which here means all the things making up what we commonly refer to as cultural development and civilizational advance.

These include symbolicity and language:

> You can't resolve the problem of violence by the means of emissary victimization without, at the same time developing a theory of the sign and of signification. . . .
>
> Before getting to the sign, we must, I think, see in the victimary mechanism, in its most elementary form, a prodigious machine for awakening mental attention of a new, non-instinctual kind. As the group frenzy moves beyond a certain intensity, there is a mimetic polarization on the single victim. Then, having discharged itself against the victim, violence is spent and suspended, and silence replaces mayhem. The stark contrast between the fierce clamor and the succeeding deathly silence, between extreme commotion and sudden pacification creates a context maximally favorable to this new form of attention. As the victim is everyone's victim, she is the focus in that instant of the gaze of the entire community. More powerful than the purely instinctual object, consequently, than the food-object, the sex-object or the dominant co-specific, is the corpse of the collective victim and it is the corpse that constitutes the first object of this new type of attention. . . .
>
> Slight as it may be, the "consciousness" that the participants [in the founding murder] have of the victim is structurally linked to the prodigious effects attending her passage from life to death, and the spectacular and liberating reversal occurring in that moment. The only meanings that can appear are those of a double transference, the meanings of the sacred, conferring on the victim the active responsibility for the whole affair. . . .
>
> It isn't necessary to postulate that the attention-awakening mechanism worked all at once. . . . There must have been blank and near-fruitless outcomes . . . but however slight, if there are cumulative effects, they already point the way towards human forms of culture. (Girard 1978, 139 [1987, 99–100])

What Girard has singularly and centrally grasped here is that the newly demanding tasks, dilemmas, and challenges that cause brain size to increase over time, permitting the emergence of recognizably human characteristics, are also, reciprocally and simultaneously, what brings groups of hominids and early men into the greatest possible danger: that of wiping themselves and each other off the map through the effects of intraspecific violence. Human progress and human peril, that is, have a single common origin in the auto-regulating advance of the capacity for mimesis.

This recognition leads him to interpret together, as reciprocal realities, dialectically, the seeming opposites of altruism and rivalry, group cooperation and group conflict. Girard sees that, in humans uniquely, the threat of intraspecific violence does not vary inversely to the potentials for social intelligence, altruism, and group cooperation, as it is commonly held to do; on the contrary, it varies in tandem with them, in a directly proportional way. The greater the degree of cooperative interactivity and group intelligence, the greater the risk and the peril of human violence. Human violence is turbocharged by our very superiority, which is what makes it always excessive, perpetually threatening to overflow all containment by animal (i.e., hardwired and instinctual) mechanisms of self- preservation (pecking orders, submission rituals, proto-cultural bonding, etc.).

Unlimited violence is, inescapably, the obverse of the selfsame potentials that make for human superiority. At the same time, the very intimacy of this connection is precisely the reason why it belongs also to a blind spot of human self-recognition—still and most singularly so in modern cognitivist accounts, where unsightedness is accentuated by an ideological prevention that leans always towards a moral optimism ever-implicit in narratives of evolutionary ascent and human progress. Rousseau could never, for this reason, have arrived at this peculiarly seminal Girardian insight; but it is equally foreign also to Jared Diamond, to Steven Pinker, and to Scott Atran. It is predictably missing from cognitivist theories of human and animal violence as such. Girard speaks here of "the invisibility of the founding murder" (1987, 105–38).

The vocation of mimetic theory, by contrast, is to recognize, explore, and interpret that crucial linkage specific to humankind between mimetic aptitude, conferring an expanding potential for higher functions and more complex interactivities, on the one hand, and escalating, contagious, unstoppable violence, on the other; and to show that, among the originating processes of hominization, violence was—as it remains to this day—the nodal and originary problem on which turns not just the threshold phenomenon of a new speciation (hominization), but the entire travail in historical culture-time of the humanization of *Homo sapiens*.

"Mimesis grafting itself onto biological mechanisms, and thereby super-activating them" (1978, 133): this, Girard claims, is the essential vector of the quantum leap of hominization. Intraspecific violence will go critical just when *Homo sapiens* becomes most at risk: from his prolonged infancy ("so much to learn"—but that makes him vulnerable); from his newly invented artifact weapons (he is clever, *habilis*, but his cleverness also multiplies the destructive power of teeth and claws); and from a series of environmental factors (such as climate change and competition for scarce resources). At which point, the hardwired defenses still serviceable in animal communities for restraining or containing intraspecific violence will be swamped and overcome.

A new Demand then exists, generating a quite indispensable new Response—and generating it, within the logic of selective adaptational advantage, necessarily, in the sense that it represents the only alternative to extinction, i.e., to violence so great and so grave that it simply puts an end to the evolutionary adventure of the hominid line as such. It is the condition of our survival.

> Mimetic rivalry, inevitable and unavoidable, means essentially, as we know, the disappearance of any objective stake to play for, and the switch into a mimesis of appropriation, which pits members of the community against each other, and thence into a mimesis of antagonism that ends up uniting them against one victim, thus reconciling them. Beyond a certain threshold of mimetic potency and charge, animal societies become impossible. This threshold corresponds to the threshold where the victimary mechanism appears: and that is the threshold of hominisation. (Girard 1978, 133 [1987, 95])

Does the cognitivist paradigm grasp anything of this hypothesis? Only "as in a glass, darkly." Although he sets out to sift and test religion by examining it in evolutionary perspective, Scott Atran never seriously addresses at any point the possibility that religion might have a survival value; nor that it might confer any selective advantage. He insists, both in beginning and in concluding his book, that "religions are not evolutionary adaptations and have no particular evolutionary function" (Atran 2002, 12 [2009, 24]).

He does, to be sure, concede that they may have a certain utility for communities and individuals in processing existential dilemmas. But then what of the nodal and originary dilemma faced by the species in the very process of its evolutionary emergence? How did we cross the threshold of hominization without, in this passage or transition, being wiped out by the very thing that was driving the hominid line across it: namely, better and better—but then also more and more destructive—mimesis?

Containing Violence, Bonding-and-Binding: The Survival Value of Religion

What mimetic theory points us to here is the all-important scapegoat mechanism, defusing the mimetic crisis and thereby generating the creation of the archaic sacred. Mimetic theory asserts that a single scenario, repeatable (of course) and (no doubt) various in its concrete expressions, can be specified, which, for the first time, harnesses the symbolic and sacralizing powers of human psychic potentials in a decisive cultural invention—that of archaic religion. This both restricts human violence in a quite new, and newly effective way, and, in the very act of so doing, kick-starts the invention of all the practices we know as cultural.

The scapegoat mechanism, is, on the one hand, a lightning conductor discharging the perilous electricity of mimetic rivalries and so also of contagiously proliferating and escalating collective rage. On the other, it involves a largely unconscious, but soon semi-duplicitous, moral manipulation, deflecting the blame for social disorder, and manipulating, as in a dream, the brutal resolution it finds in scapegoat murder. In short, the victim is divinized, and becomes the supposed sacred source of all the inventions developed by *Homo sapiens* against the recurrence of the mimetic crisis.

From this construct, the most basic matrix of religious belief, can be traced, in all logic—but also with much supporting experimental confirmation—the entire system of prohibitions, taboos, or interdicts, and of the moral codes that develop out of them: eventually, therefore, of laws and legal systems and institutions, too. Likewise, the ritual forms and practices, most especially sacrifice, which reenacts ritually and repeatably the founding murder. It does that, of course, through the bloody immolation of new scapegoat victims, thus celebrating the saving Life-principle of the community. The sacred action representing these foundational things is staged and replayed, as it were, to newly bonding, and newly salutary (or salvific), effect.

From the same religious matrix comes, lastly, myth: which is the telling, and later the writing, of the story that bonds and binds us—the religious story that confers identity, and with it, social coherence, authority, confidence.

The birth of culture is thus entirely continuous with the mimetic crisis and its scapegoat resolution. It implies, it derives from, and it is driven by this formidable first attempt made by proto-humans to manipulate symbolically, magically, the transcending life forces they experienced as so threatening, and to convert these transcending energies and forces from a negative to a positive valency, by means of the victimage mechanism—the vital end product of which is a sacralizing framework of supernatural agency (Girard 1987, 48–83).

Religio comes from *religere*, which means to bind together, to constrain or obligate. This is what constitutes source no. 1 of religion and morality. Now, thanks to Girard, traced to source—i.e., pinned down to a detailed, coherent, actually explicative, and in principle testable, scenario of genetic emergence.

Now, of course, this Girardian account of religion as the matrix of culture gives considerable comfort to the dimension of Scott Atran's analysis, stressing its functional utility as an instrument of social organization and control. This is the only take on religion that, from his viewpoint, really does make sense.

Religion, he is persuaded, is really about human social bonding-and-binding; it is about shaping this construct of the human social psyche, and naturalizing the control of it—thus establishing (for instance) the nonrational conditions of devotion and self-sacrifice, which allow individuals and societies to knit together and withstand the toughest of trials. It is about creating an organic solidarity, or cultural identity, just as Durkheim first suggested (1893).

Atran and Girard certainly agree on that. As a fellow Durkheimian, Atran does recognize that religion is the matrix out of which develops the entirety of human culture. Not only so; he acknowledges specifically that "sacrifice is at the heart of the religious system" (2002, 4 [2009, 14])—an insight in direct resonance with the core of Girard's theory. Yet Girard's theory alone elucidates and validates, with the precise, strategic intelligence required, this considerable and agreed evolutionary datum.

And it is Girard alone who then goes on to add a vital qualifier: at least, that is what *archaic-sacral* or *natural religion*, from the beginning, is all about. A series of new questions must at this point be thrown into relief. Is religion, then, ever anything more and other than the archaic sacred? Does religion itself evolve; and can it, in evolving, be revelatory? If so, what does this mean, in evolutionary terms, for *Homo religiosus*, whose descendants, it seems, we all are?

If cognitivist interlocutors are to follow and understand Girard adequately from this point on, a Bergsonian parenthesis is, at this point, required. Its function will be to illuminate the strides that Girard makes intuitively, with prodigious flair, like a hound on the scent; steps that, however, can leave many of his readers well behind, sometimes with the sense of one—or several—quantum leaps too many.

Understanding the Two Sources Model of Religion: A Bergsonian Parenthesis

I am not wishing to suggest that Girard himself is a crypto-Bergsonian; nor that the philosophic syntax of Bergson's thought is the only one that can make the second wing of the Girardian chateau accessible (i.e., intelligible, hospitably receivable, open to exploration, and rewarding in research terms) in the eyes of cognitivists and others whose normal first instinct when noting Girard's engagement with religious texts, or at least with Judeo-Christian ones, is suspicion, if not summary dismissal.

Girard himself, because of his hugely consequent flair for the continuity of his sacrificial theme, as it recurs with near-infinite variations in the vastly diverse contexts of cultural production, far-flung in both time and space, often circulates freely amid archaic religious forms, while invoking consistently, by way of counter-distinction, the canonical texts of major religious traditions (Judeo-Christian in particular, albeit with a significant look sideways, also, at the Vedic scriptures)[3]—pausing only rarely, meanwhile, to elucidate the wider hermeneutical problems raised by this diversity, and making no general or consolidated account of his vision of *Homo religiosus* as formed by evolutionary process.

To the unwary, this trail-led selectivity can appear suspect. It may remind us of the racing pigeon, who takes note of the vast landscape of teeming religious varieties, but only in order to verify the quickest way home towards a covertly preordained religious position. Many (including not a few of Jewish culture or religion) who otherwise follow the trail of Girardian insights ardently fall away at this point, sometimes wishing to pursue mimetic theory while detaching from it, selling off or rebuilding the other wing of the chateau.

Here, Bergson can supply us with the missing category distinctions, the classifications, the careful historical time frame, the causal connections, the hermeneutical syntax that are capable of opening up once more a discussion that is thus closed down. He has the merit of elucidating what is at stake, and of deepening our awareness of the evolutionary parameters, precisely, of the evolutionary dialogue we are pursuing.

This intermediary role is entirely appropriate. To cognitivists, Bergson offers very significant guarantees of affinity and understanding. He recognizes extensively their own view of the social uses and misuses of religion, anticipating their understanding of the role of cognitive templates misapplied to extramundane or transcendent objects, and conceding that natural religion is, to a vast extent, a matter of mythical fabulation, which is, on the one hand, proliferating and often wildly absurd in its referential claims and relational pretensions, while, on the other, remaining covertly indispensable in its social functioning. In dialogue with Levy-Bruhl,[4] he discusses the primitive thought world and its evolutionary survivals, overlaid by, but capable of resurfacing intact from, the mental corridors and cupboards of contemporary humankind.

On this basis, Bergson develops an impressive typology of religious forms, evincing an equally impressive generative poetics that reconstructs their variational coming-to-be in time and space: starting from animism, shamanism, totemism, and ancestor worship through belief in spirits, and thence to polytheisms ancient and modern and the emergence of the great world religions. He shows how different socioeconomic and cultural contexts, interacting with different types of organization and different degrees of individuation permitted within the body politic, produce a constantly evolving panoply of mythic invention—all such productions being describable as representational constructs making good human psychosocial deficiencies, particularly dysfunctions of group identification and solidarity; the entire heterogeneous set proliferating in time and space as contextually shaped adaptive variations (Bergson 1932, 236–66).

To Girardians, meanwhile, Bergson makes what seems initially to be a far slighter and more ambiguous signal of elective affinity: He recognizes in principle the central and near-universal role of ritual human sacrifice in ancient religions ("a habit found in most ancient religions, perhaps all of them if we go back far enough" [1932, 275]), while yet offering no account of its functioning in the emergence of religion: neither of the static religion of social conservation that he first distinguishes, nor yet of the second, dynamic, insightful, and socially progressive current of religious inspiration, which he opposes to the first as something irreducibly distinct in its nature and human significance, and as having a different source and origin.

Everything turns on this key distinction, which Bergson introduces as follows:

> I believe that to penetrate the essence of religion and to understand the history of humanity, we have to move now from static and external religion which has occupied us hitherto, to that dynamic and inward religion which is to occupy our coming chapter. The former was designed to ward off the dangers to which their intelligence made human beings subject; it was sub-intellectual. We may add that it was natural, since the human species marks a certain stage in the evolution of life; there, at a given moment, the forward movement came to a stop; humankind was set down within the whole process, along with its intelligence, along with the dangers intelligence brought with it, along with the fabulating function that was to keep these at bay; along with magic and elementary animism, too; all this emerging *en bloc*, all answering the needs of the individual and the society, each of these limited in their ambitions, that nature has wished to produce. (1932, 258)

But "creative evolution," as Bergson calls his descriptive-but-global phenomenology of evolutionary process, viewed in its incontestable dimension of emergence presents, observably, a new surge forward:

> Later, and by an effort that might not have happened, man wrenched himself out of his turning around on the spot; he re-inserted himself into the current of evolution. That was dynamic religion, no doubt associated with higher intelligence, but distinct from it. The first form of religion had been infra-intellectual; for reasons known to us [see *infra*]. The second, for reasons we shall indicate, was supra-intellectual. It is by setting these realities directly in opposition to each other that we can best understand them. For only these extreme religions are essential and pure. The intermediary forms which developed in ancient civilisations could only lead the philosophy of religion astray by generating the conviction that we got from one extreme to the other by means of a gradual improvement or progress; a natural error, explicable from the fact that static religion survived in part within dynamic religion. (1932, 259)

Most modern readers, seeking to grasp the implications of this key statement, may well experience a certain double take in adjusting to Bergson's project of a positive metaphysics—that is, a philosophic reflection operating in a space opened up by the human sciences (sociology, ethnology, and the history of religions) in relation to the natural sciences. This is not quite evolution as recognized by the life sciences. But Bergson would add here: as known to each of them, according to a disciplinary particularity, embedded in its own particular mapping, framing, and editing of reality—all of them practicing unconsciously the reductive and immobilizing fragmentation that intelligence itself cannot help effecting when it tries to lay hold of the aliveness of living things. This reality being, in his view, an Unknown, to be apprehended holistically, according to its own proper nature, which is essentially duration, transformation, and movement. The paradoxes of Zeno furnish Bergson with an emblematic illustration of the impotence of the rational mind, in its most characteristic—philosophic and scientific—modes, to apprehend "the living" ("*le vivant*": all phenomena in which life is present), save mechanically, in a deforming and impoverished transcription that enables humans to manipulate life for certain practical purposes, without a truly strategic understanding of it.

He sends the cognitivist, and *all practitioners of human intelligence*, back to the auto-centered loop set up by the intellect as it seeks to address life on its own terms—that is, by means of a formally closed equation resolvable in principle by procedures of intelligibility congenial to itself, but foreign to the reality they would objectify and grasp. This Bergsonian caveat, we may think, is salutary, and much required, in particular, by discussions of *Homo religiosus*. In the matter of the evolution of life itself, and most especially on this particular topic within that general field, we are all, ultimately but quite literally, in the position of not knowing what we are talking about.

What interests Bergson, by contrast, is a strategic, second order: understanding, attaining, insofar as may be, the inner reality and essence of things—evolutionary processes being here reviewed in their overall patterns of creative emergence, always in the attempt to apprehend something of the nature of that essential and mysterious life-current or life-thrust (*élan vital*), which Bergson sees as impelling holistically the entire self-organizing evolutionary process.

In this precise sense (a sense that Darwin himself might conceivably have accepted had his disciplinary horizons been explicitly confronted with it and challenged by it), Bergson modifies and corrects Darwin. His *Creative Evolution* argues, indeed, that if species evolve, it is under the agency of some unobserved, deeply intrinsic energy or impulse of transformation, much more profoundly and more truly than it is due to the action of environment—this latter constituting the inflecting material conditions (selective or adaptive) of change, rather than its true agential cause. Bergson always sees, in the disturbance of the myriad material factors that resist its action—like so many displaced and reordered metal filings through which, as we infer, an electromagnetic current must be passing—the invisible hand of the *élan vital*.

Intelligence and instinct, on this view, are two fundamental tendencies of the dynamics of the life-energy traversing and transforming matter from within—tendencies originally united within its thrust: indistinctly at first, but then emerging separately, and dividing along the two great evolutionary paths that they anticipate and trace out, each leading towards the common term that nature seeks or wants: namely, higher and more intense sociality. The first culminates in instinct-perfected communities such as ants and bees, the second arriving at human communities, ordered—more ambiguously and fatefully—by the endowment of intelligence; that is to say, by a capacity opposable to, detached from, and critical of, the carrying life-thrust that produced and nurtured them. Bergson invites us to recognize here a price paid for human intelligence, freedom, and creativity—and, in particular, the dangers referred to in the passage quoted above, as requiring the protection offered by the socially determined and static first form of religion.

As a strategy for achieving sociality, intelligence is a highly risky option in two senses (Bergson 1932, 277). Firstly, it makes individuals discrete centers of desire and independent goal seekers, which is a formula for dissension and anarchy (and, if we believe Girard, devastating intraspecific violence). This effect is entirely absent in instinct-driven insect communities (where the individual is instinctually preprogrammed to conform to the general will). Secondly, it introduces into human existence a consciousness of death as the fateful terminus of all existence as such. This evident and inevitable end point risks further detaching the individual from the community, turning him towards self-reflection and self-concern; it directly discourages in him the *élan vital*, and it threatens to dissolve community.

Human sociality, under these conditions, looks distinctly unstable: its prime motor is communicative and enabling intelligence; yet this is precisely what generates, simultaneously and contrariwise, a permanent threat to group survival, since, in addition to driving human advance, intelligence acts as both a brake on its dynamism, and a solvent of group cohesion (1932, 195–214).

Natural or manmade religion is the restabilizing answer to this intrinsic crisis involved in hominization. It is, for Bergson, a self-organizing adaptive adjustment, the advent of which is explained by the philosopher of the *élan vital* in terms of an action of residual supervision of intelligence by instinct. Bergson does not attempt to describe the modalities of this supervision; but it is clear that they could be explicated transparently in Girardian terms. He simply asserts that this effect is made possible by virtue of a residual solidarity of common origin within the life-thrust. Intellect, as it comes-to-be, arrives shot through with, or fringed by, a memory of solidarity with instinct (so that, for instance, primitive man is intuitively self-preserving, before and beyond any conscious rationality).

The principal value of this insight would seem to be that it suggests how cognitivist accounts of religion, for all their frequent pertinence, may not be well-framed in their founding assumptions. Natural religion, on this account, is not really about cognition (sound or unsound) at all. It is not, principally or primarily, any form of primitive metaphysics, philosophy, or science; nor is it overall a byproduct derived from these things, even if its development did eventually generate them—adjoining to itself at this point some of their elements and something of their character. In its first form, natural religion is a life-function; it is all about group survival.

More precisely, natural religion refers us to the dynamics of closed societies struggling to preserve their life amid the acutest perils from without and from within. It is the signature behavior of communities precariously bound together, intrinsically unstable, and requiring a potent pharmacology to reinforce their cohesion ritually (the point of social religion)—just as they require a severe morality to repress competition, conflict, and antisocial egoism (the role of social morality), and a potently formative identity narrative (the raison d'être of social myth-making).

Here lies the evolutionary point and purpose of natural religion, which is also the clue to its essentially conservative and potentially violent character, an evolutionary inheritance still very much in evidence in modern nation-states (particularly so in the view of Bergson, writing in the twentieth century, between Europe's two great wars), but also in contemporary fundamentalisms (as is painfully clear, in turn, to ourselves as denizens of the twenty-first century).

Any relational intention, any idea of wonder and of worship addressed to natural or transcending cosmic forces, let alone namable nature deities or a transcendent Creator, is, at least in its conceptual articulation, a late-developing potential, albeit a very genuine one, germinating out of that Bergsonian logic of "virtual instinct" or "intuitively fringed intelligence." Yet this very potential does, in Bergson's reading of the phenomenology of evolution, emerge and assert itself in the fullness of time, transformingly, from within the husk of social religion, which it causes to burst asunder. This is the emergentist plot line Bergson follows in distinguishing a dynamic and progressive religious inspiration, different in character and import from first-religion and derived from elsewhere.

He calls this second-order religion mysticism—understanding by this term an experience of contact or communion with a prior and constituting reality, an effective participation in the nature and action of the prime actor of creative evolution, namely, the *élan vital*. "In our eyes, the full development of mysticism is a contact established, and consequently a partial coincidence realized, with the creative effort which life manifests. This effort is of God, if it is not God himself" (Bergson 1932, 292).[5]

Bergson recognizes the rarity of mysticism in its pure form, and admits it often has to be discerned beneath a veil of incompletion and/or a confusing tangle of hybridizations. So it is, variously: in the pagan mystery religions (288–93); in Buddhism (296); in Hinduism (297); or in our own nationalistic European christianities of First World War vintage, designed to put "God on our side"—this latter hybrid form being, in Bergsonian perspective, an evolutionary resurgence of, or throwback to, first-order (static or social) religion.

Contact with the principle of nature is evidenced and authenticated by "a quite different figure of attachment to life, a transfigured confidence" (286). And this transfiguring effect extends, via the great religious figures who most powerfully embody, articulate, and transmit it, to a remodeling of first-form morality itself, of first-order religion itself, and of the entire outlook and action of the originally closed societies that bred both of these things. It thus inflects, in the end, the course of evolutionary world-process itself insofar as it is invested in or confided to humankind.

The most striking examples given of cultural reprogramming and societal transformation are the Hebrew prophets, who remodel the notion of justice, making it categorical and transcendent (Bergson 1932, 54); and the Christian gospels, which overturn the "parochial" altruism of the closed society, pointing in its stead to a genuinely open—positively loving and universal—altruism in the image of God (292).

Second-order religion, consequently, is dynamic. Not only in the sense that it is religion sourced in and resourced from the *élan vital* itself (rather than in and from the unstable, fragile, and deficit-ridden social psyche of emergent humanity), but also in the sense that its transfiguring action in history transforms closed societies operating under the evolutionary sign of parochial altruism. In both respects, the new religion is the novel sign of the *élan vital* itself as it emerges and expresses itself within evolved humanity. Love is, in Bergson, another name for the life-thrust in the higher reaches of its emergence, where it appears as "the essence of the creative effort" (171). Again, this figure of sense has powerful Girardian resonance.[6]

Fully formed mysticism, Bergson concludes, is that of the Christian mystics. "Just consider what a saint Paul, a saint Catherine of Siena, a saint Francis, a Joan of Arc and so many others achieved in the field of action" (1932, 299). Ecstasy is a moment only of the mystic's trajectory. "The love that consumes him is not simply the love of a man for God, it is the love of God for all men. Through God, enabled by God, he loves humanity with a divine love" (304). Action follows from ecstasy: "He would wish, with God's help, to finish the creation of the human species and make humanity what it would have been immediately, if it had been able to be constituted without the help of humankind itself" (305). Here again is a theme of vast and re-echoing Girardian resonance: that of an acceptance and return of love, imitating the effort of creation itself, in order the better to realize freely a divine filiation or likeness—a shared pattern that we might perhaps call "theologal mimesis."

In short, a phenomenology of religion-in-evolution shows something else to have passed through static or social religion, the human clay being comparable to the earth-matter already reworked into new patterns by the creative life-thrust, and which, passing, transforms human societies in its wake. Not completely, not purely or undeniably so, indeed; but still, already quite recognizably so.

Is religion, however, still the appropriate label for catching up conceptually with this distinctive-and-capital, but still highly elusive, novelty? Bergson asks this question explicitly (1932, 284). He concludes: "It is indeed a religion which confronts us, but a new religion" (287).

Bergson has, in fact, traced out the general form of what we began by calling the relationalist paradigm of understanding applied to *Homo religiosus*. He founds it, hermeneutically speaking, in a form of immanent transcendence: evolution-borne, yet effecting also in evolutionary time an action of revelation.

Where, unguardedly, we had presupposed and posited just one source of religion, Bergson points to what a consequent and strategic phenomenology of evolutionary emergence most conspicuously invites us to think: namely, that there may, in fact, be two.[7] As a public warning notice prominently displayed at French railroad crossings has it: "*Un train peut en cacher un autre*" (One train may be hiding another).

Girard and Dynamic Religion: The Payoff of the Two Sources Model

We are now in a position to see Girard's originality in relation to the other paradigm of understanding whose general form and potential legitimacy we have just allowed Bergson to outline for us.

According to the first (cognitivist) paradigm, when religious phenomena are put determinedly "to the test of evolution," what we are led to say about them is that there are innate or hard-wired structures of cognition, of emotional responsiveness or of the aptitude for social relationality that are preprogrammed in us biologically. These structures "tend to channel human thoughts and actions along paths of cultural development which tend also to be religious ones—which explains the long-lasting transcultural success of religion" (Atran 2002, 280 [2009, 354]).

Our psychic inheritance nudges our primary human emotions, individual and collective, inciting them to generate their own existential meta-representation of supernatural agency. So that the religious creativity of *Homo religiosus*—his narratives and his dreams, his altruistic love poems, his Other-addressing rituals and liturgical play-acting—is considered *en bloc*, until further notice, to be a direct offprint of that evolutionary inheritance as triggered by the dilemmas that arise when hominids, slowly and progressively, cross the threshold of intelligent awareness and self-awareness.

It appears, however, to be a major objection against the cognitivist paradigm that it is a backward and downward reading of *Homo religiosus*. The beliefs, behaviors, and practices studied under that name sit in an environing landscape made up of the evolutionary forces that, all invisibly, still configure our mental world. Atran rightly presents this landscape as a controlling metaphor of his book (2002, 10–11 [2009, 22]). *Homo religiosus* is always being considered as a function of the occult matrix of his own biological origins—and these origins are indefinitely rediscovered by the sociobiologist, and insistently projected by him as the real key to an understanding of believing humankind.

There are further difficulties in the hermeneutical order. We have seen that, if Bergson and Girard are right, the most archaic forms of religion, intentionally speaking (i.e., in terms of their motivating raison d'être), are only very secondarily about cognition, sound or unsound. They may indeed involve *méconnaissance* and generate myths; but, primarily and fundamentally, they are about group survival—responses to dire need in a world made threatening by internal and external perils.

Another problem is that—for want of any recognition of a second, more ultimate source of religion—*méconnaissance* (miscognition) becomes the only formula for interpreting religion generally, in its entire range of forms and types, throughout the whole of evolutionary space-time. This in turn means envisaging *Homo religiosus* in the mode of permanent Bergsonian fabulation, and, in the end, it means taking an atavistic compulsion to misapplied mental dribbling as the sole and sufficient clue to the nature of religion; which both strains plausibility, and leaves a permanent deficit in respect of the declared end goal of explaining its remarkably persistent and perennial character.

It also means collapsing evolutionary time in order to see evolutionary-residual forces and patterns at work structurally. But might religion itself not also evolve dynamically in evolutionary time, within and beyond that unchanging, biologically determined landscape? And even in such a way that we might come to detect in it, not just the ghost of Christmases past, but, so to speak, the prefiguration of Christmases still to be? Within cognitivist horizons, this imaginative opening is not easily entered into. Ockham's razor does not acknowledge added value. It has no cognizance of—and it is not equipped to cope with—the progressive complexification of systems in evolutionary time. It cannot recognize the evolutionary emergence or coming-to-be of *Homo religiosus* himself. It does not "do" ontogenesis.

Must we not conclude, then, that this ghost-haunted landscape is, therefore, reductionist in its hermeneutical form? If it is genuinely instructive to discover evolutionary shadow-structures uniting the most diverse manifestations of religion, we need a healthy skepticism when confronted with the implied conclusion that this variety is all "much of a muchness." Atran, visibly, is never happier than when, in a single section, chapter, paragraph, sentence, or turn of phrase, he manages to encompass animism and magic, the Bornean headhunter, a nice bit of medieval witchcraft, a modern cargo cult or two, Islamic fundamentalism, and some aspect of orthodox Christian belief. As he himself acknowledges cheerfully: that's "what he does" (2002, 8–9 [2009, 19–20]). Yet the shadow grasped is really always a shadow of static, first-order (archaic-sacral) religion; while the fact that religion itself evolves and itself changes the human landscape dynamically is destined, in this hermeneutical perspective, to remain forever a mysterious and suspect piece of poetic hearsay.

Girard, on the other side of the debate, is not concerned to theorize systematically his challenge to cognitivist Suspicion. But his understanding that humanity is born out of its religious dimension gives him a very strategic vantage point: firstly for questioning what we mean by "religion." (Archaic-sacral structures can, on this account, underlie the most avowedly secular and atheistic behavioral forms; so for instance—to quote one thought-provoking example—in the ideological mind that conceived and executed the Holocaust of European Jews). And then, equally, it is a platform for following the advance of that phylum of religious development that Bergson declares to be most alive, or transformatively dynamic.

At the same time, Bergson's strategic mapping of human religious development enables us to recognize the acute pertinence of Girard's narrowly focused searchlight, and the value of his powerfully following flair, as text-based reader of its dynamism. The Bergsonian mapping also highlights the originality of Girard's approach to *Homo religiosus*. It explains his fruitful ability, as an Irregular of brilliance, to highlight problems that more conventional academic journeymen, for all their specialist competence, fail to contextualize adequately in big-picture evolutionary terms.

We see at once, for instance, why Girard does not pause much to consider the almost infinite play and ramification of diverse forms of sacrality and/or of religiosity, generated out of the matrix of the archaic sacred (first-order religion): magic, superstition, witchcraft, cargo cults, gaming, etc.—and why he is only moderately concerned to branch out into the field of comparative religion. A derivation is indicated for some of these ramifying offshoots in *Violence and the Sacred* (see chap. 11) and, more sporadically, in *Things Hidden*. Yet the archaic undergrowth represents for him a sideshow in terms of evolutionary emergence—the equivalent, perhaps, of Bergson's stagnant pools developing at the fringes of static religion and the closed society, byproducts of the *élan vital* rather than expressions of its carrying current of emergence.

We also notice at once, in contrast to the abstract generalities of Bergson's strategic mapping of evolutionary emergence, the concrete and performative character of Girard's account of man as religious animal. We have already observed the way in which mimetic theory anticipates the finding of the world's earliest temple at Göbekli Tepe, enabling us to decipher its symbolism and probable sacrificial function. Where Bergson speaks of life-thrust and intuitively fringed intelligence, Girard—while no doubt illustrating these same realities in his own thinking!—grasps much more concretely the anthropological centrality of mimetic desire: a precise specificity of approach that enables him to present a sharply particularized and, in principle, testable scenario of origins. Where Bergson, speaking of hominization as a nodal and originary crisis in evolution, discusses this crisis only in airily abstract terms (the "contradiction of consciousness and life"), and identifies the existential perils it brings only as those of deviant individualism and the consciousness of death, Girard spots the number one peril of intraspecific violence, and deciphers cogently, at source, the hidden complicity of violence and the sacred. This decipherment is a major achievement: it is quite crucial to have a precise and adequate grammar of evolutionary foundations, not least when referring to modern fundamentalisms, and all forms of regression, primitive survivals, archaic resurgences—and their alleged opposites and antidotes.

Exactly the same precise, realistic, cognitively performing functionalism is to be observed when Girard, retracing independently Bergson's general figure of the advent of dynamic religion, undertakes to pin down this process also, in his reading of the Jewish and Christian scriptures. This is too vast a chapter to be examined here in detail, and the reader is referred to the section of our companion volume that does deal with it more adequately.[8] Some general points on the implications of this reading for his account of *Homo religiosus* are, however, called for here.

Elucidating this transition is a challenge hardly less daunting than conceiving hominization itself; and, once more, the difficulty is that of reconciling continuity and quantum leap. Girard's demonstration is framed in just these terms.

The containing husk of first-form social religion figures prominently in his reading. The beginnings of the Hebrew Scriptures (and the Christian Old Testament), he insists, confront us with a horizon of archaic-sacral practice entirely recognizable from other religions-and-mythologies. The environing world of the archaic sacred is hugely present also within Israel itself: sorcery, soothsayers, fertility cults, child sacrifice—the entire gamut of idolatrous and very violent sacralities unfolds here, as backdrop and, not infrequently, center stage.

Characteristics of first-religious culture persist: the alimentary prescriptions in Leviticus, or the ritual use of animal scapegoats, superseding human ones. Human sacrifice is not so far back that it cannot be recalled as a displaced and rejected form of piety, as in the story of Abraham and Isaac. And, similarly, institutions such as the priesthood, the sacral monarchy, and, later, the temple all refer back to archaic-sacral prototypes. There is the overarching presence of the binding-bonding tribal God, who is the massively constituting cornerstone of the cultural identity of the people of Israel.

Nor does this reading let us forget the profoundly significant context of ancient disorder and violent crisis, running through all the major stories of Genesis and Exodus, in the conquest narratives of the historical books, then on and on throughout the great episodes of national catastrophe, prophecy, and renewed exile. The founding murder re-echoes in these texts: fatefully committed by one warring brother against another (Cain and Abel); recalled in the equally founding victimization of Joseph by his brothers—and all this in the newly focusing context of a humano-divine struggle (Jacob and the Angel). As echolocated by all these multiple traces, the generative matrix of the archaic sacred is an entirely recognizable and conditioning context of emergence.

Far from being embarrassed by the residual presence in the Hebrew and Christian Scriptures of this shared matrix, and of mythological elements common to many religions worldwide, Girard goes out of his way to underline these things. Such common beginnings serve, precisely, to measure an original and far more remarkable pattern of textual and historical emergence, which, as he demonstrates with impressive rigor of exegesis, asserts itself increasingly as the scriptural story unfolds.

Elementarily, what we observe is that the editors of the first books of the Bible reshape their material, setting up a new perspective, a new pattern. Thus in the Edenic prologue of Temptation and Fall, for instance, we recognize the very formula of the mimetic triangle. But now it is rivalry with God that is being staged, and represented, and here presented explicitly as the fact and the fault of mimetically suggestible, blame-shifting humankind, obeying its older and deeper—should we perhaps say, its evolutionary—other voice, here superbly well-cast as the Serpent. Accursedness and exile are still presented here as divine initiatives (an echo of archaic-sacral logic); but they are also shown clearly enough to be self-inflicted human wounds, and, in direct challenge to archaic-sacral logic, they provide occasion for a new prohibition, placed this time on the greatest possible Object of sacralizing, rivalrous, and appropriative desire.

Could intelligent, free, created, and creative humanity be also the real Violator: the real generating agent of violence and the sacred? Does *Homo religiosus* exercise a real choice in respect of his sacralized Objects? What would it mean to envisage that object as Subject: as Creator and prime Interlocutor-Actor? Can it be that the god of other tribes—but then, surely, also of ours—is not yet quite God enough, and that the creative Source precedes and transcends social origin?

Cain, though he founds a culture, is not presented as justified in killing his brother—unlike Romulus, founder of Rome (and all other mythic founders). Where is his murdered brother, whose blood "cries out from the ground" to God? It cries not for vengeance, but for room to declare the truth of the founding murder, thus acknowledging explicitly what archaic ritual practice confesses covertly: that a limit must be set to the corrupting contagion of violence; such is the mark of Cain.

Here is a prohibition on violent reprisal pointing towards the development of the Law itself: first "an eye for an eye"; but then, a more radical commandment, "Thou shalt not kill." Cognitive question: how far and when, in comparable traditions, does the God of social religion cease to be perceived as a vengeful and bloody upholder of social order?

Such glimpses pre-trace the emerging pattern of demonstration: Girardian exegesis shows us the tangled threads of the archaic sacred being unraveled; responsibility for violence being tentatively laid at the right address; archaic sacrifices modified and ultimately abrogated as universal socio-symbolic expedients for patching up potentially violent religious, political, or socioeconomic crises.

From the beginning, in short, the biblical texts are engaged in demystifying the archaic sacred: deciphering its dubious credit transfer operations, discrediting its declared villains, vindicating its vilified victims, and even, little by little, contradicting and correcting its auto-generated and all-too-human theology of sacred violence. This process gathers pace throughout the Hebrew scriptures.

The Book of Job, to cite a single example explored in depth by Girard, gives voice to the Victim; while Job's so-called friends, with varying voices, and degrees of justification, express contrapuntally the standard archaic view that if you are touched with affliction, it must be God's hand visiting punishment upon you. The God denounced by Job belongs not just to a peculiar Hebrew tradition of retributive justice; he is the God of the archaic sacred (or primitive religion) as such, i.e., a monstrous Double, required, engendered, and projected by man's ancient, devious, and universal game of exorcising violently his own violent shadow.

Which fearsome deity, born of the social psyche, constitutes, in evolutionary terms, the inherited default setting of man "the religious animal"? This particular text stages, therefore, the entire ambivalence of the archaic sacred, and of its Hebraic verticalization. Ultimately, suggests Girard, Job wrests the deity out of the process of persecution to envision him instead as the God of the oppressed and the downtrodden. For the first time, the Victim can say: "I know that my redeemer [or: vindicator] liveth" (Job 16:19; 19:25). We might say: Job has learned out of bitter experience the difference between source no. 1 and source no. 2.

Jewish and Christian exegetes have sometimes spoken about "religion" (as anthropic construct and inheritance) being here purified, monotheized, desacralized, or verticalized. But in order to see that process vividly at work, and to comprehend what it most deeply entails, we have to be able to see what Girard shows us: namely, the buried, underlying, and superseded first-form of religion. We do need to know what the archaic sacred looks like and how it functions, since first-religion is the model and the measure of the differential process, a sign of its covenanted relational transformation. Without it, we cannot envisage adequately *Homo religiosus*: in his real multidimensionality, his evolutionary emergence and potential, his spiritual dynamism. Still less can we begin to envisage his God.

The ultimate performative value of Girard's reading is that it asks the right hermeneutical questions. Are we witnessing a "skyhook" tugging humanity upright and heavenwards (Daniel Dennett's picturesque, if theologically crude, image [Dennett 1995, 73–80])? Or is this a human rocket, immanently fueled and projected heavenwards from below, by a creative surge of Bergson's *élan vital*? Are these answers mutually exclusive or are they complementary? And how would we know the difference, or recognize the reconciliation, between them?

What, in fact, do we actually mean by "religion"? Girard, patiently faithful to his cobbler's last as text-based fundamental anthropologist, does not say. But like all demonstrations of extreme pertinence, his analysis raises powerfully, in relation to man-the-religious-animal, the questions that it declines to answer.

Girard's reading is performative in a second, hugely pertinent sense. It prepares us to understand that the immense place accorded to represented violence in the Judeo-Christian scriptures, in excess even of that accorded to it in Greek tragedy, is part of the unfolding pattern of originality and is a mark not so much of some special and deeply suspect affinity for violence, as cognitivist commentators eagerly assume, as of an acute anthropological awareness, and a singular honesty, about the intrinsic rootedness in humankind of sacred violence per se. This is a quite crucial demonstration: both for today's sworn adversaries of religion[9] and for people of religious faith.

The ultimate respect in which Girard's anthropological readings of religious texts can be said to be highly performing is in genuinely explaining the pivotal phenomenon identified by Bergson: the game-changing significance and vast subsequent resonance in human history of the Christian gospels.

They are seen to be addressed precisely, and as nothing else is, to the deep-laid foundational complicity between violence and the sacred, as delivered in evolutionary time by religion. They are addressed to the identification, remediation, and transformation of mankind's fearful and violent shadow, with its misshapen, self-harming sacrality. This implies, among other things, two figures of sense, more fully explored in *Can We Survive Our Origins?* Firstly, the opening up, in the Kingdom preaching of Jesus, of human social morality, based on parochial altruism; and secondly, the inversion and reversal of the founding murder in his sacrificial death.

Girard sees the Jesus of the gospels as understanding very precisely the inherited shadow of *Homo religiosus*. For the first time, the founding murder, with its process of emissary victimization, its constitutive logic of concealed untruth, and its irradiating consequences of renewed murder and cyclical, societal, and national crisis, is fully grasped and explicitly proclaimed by Jesus.

This perspective allows Girard to read the gospels in algebraic simplification. The more the world of the archaic sacred, challenged by Jesus, declares its secret and concealed principle of founding murder, the more violently it resists exposure; and the more it resists exposure, the more radically the truly divine counter-logic of Love is called forth and declared in reply. In particular, the apocalyptic warnings of Jesus are seen to link the preaching of the Kingdom on the one hand, and the Cross on the other, in one continuous weave.

In the end, the gospels as read by Girard show that the Love divine must itself suffer in full the most extreme worldly consequences of violence, in order that the lie at the heart of the archaic sacred be ultimately "nailed." Beyond a critical point, therefore, the Son of Man resolves to enter into the Founding Murder—as Victim. Only so can the very spring and principle of sacred violence in the human heart be reworked into a triumph of Love.

What appears very simply from this reading is that, short of the originary point fixed by evolution in the process of hominization, there is, on the "ancient road of unrighteous men,"[10] no adequate revelation, no strategic conversion point, and no pivotal point of leverage for further evolutionary emergence within world process.

The cognitive question posed here, therefore, is not simply: do other traditions also move away from ritual immolation of human victims and towards a message of love? It is: what gives this precise case its unique form of symmetrical inversion, and its unique dynamism in reworking the sacrificial motif?

Conclusion

Girard himself has never concealed the fact that, with the theologians of the New Testament, he detects here the action of the ultimate Source. He sees the new mimetic model proposed to human desire as re-creating the human subject and the human community as such, and as renewing the entire field of evolutionary emergence and potential as such.

At this crux, anthropology must either call to theology, or else rearm furiously against it. What difference does it make, Girard is asked, that God exists and reveals himself—and not that the man Jesus makes God up? He replies simply, without evasion or complication, but also inclusively, as one exemplar among others of *Homo religiosus*, relationally addressed by this refounding Event, and personally aligned with the figure of sense he discerns in it:

> What difference? It means that sacrificial history in its entirety, the moral and religious history of humanity before Christianity, is a holy history. . . . It means that the pagan religions were a first way towards God, and that the practice of sacrifices was a way of containing violence at some level, not the desired one, but one tolerated by God [in an evolving creation].
>
> The crucifixion shows that men reject the truth of God and that God, not wanting to triumph by force, which would have no sense for him, manages to manifest himself to us without violating human liberty. In order to do so, he consents to serve as our scapegoat, but without becoming divinised in this capacity, without becoming divine in the sense of paganism. It shows that the truth of God can't appear without being thrust away. To repent truly, as in the sense of Peter or Paul, is to understand one's personal participation in the expulsion of God. Instead of divinising human violence projected onto the scapegoat, Christianity divinises the one who, through a death freely accepted (not in the least like a suicide), escapes the circularity of falsehood and of man's god-generating violence. (Girard 1994, 167–68)

His personal response, of course, engages René Girard. The relationalist paradigm of interpretation, explored in its ultimate logic, requires this; just as, more covertly, the inverse—atheistic—response models and declares something of this same logic in the "Four Horsemen."

It is to be hoped, at all events, that our dialogue between paradigms of interpretation of *Homo religiosus* will have made available to all, whatever their faith-allegiance, a clear intelligence (at least) of the Girardian figure of sense.

Delivered in evolutionary process by source no. 1, *Homo religiosus* is henceforth laid open to the call and the action of re-creating source no. 2. The simplicity of this formula, together with its power of integration of vast and complex energy fields—each generating irradiating questions for further research—may indeed remind us of $E = mc^2$.

Notes

This essay, as originally conceived for presentation at Stanford University, was a dialogue with Scott Atran, Research Director in Social Anthropology at the French National Center for Scientific Research (CNRS), Paris. In practice, my designated interlocutor preferred to engage with Girardian theory from the side of religious violence and peacemaking in the contemporary world, the subject of his most recent—and most excellent—book *Talking to the Enemy* (Atran 2010). His contribution, for this reason, figures, appropriately, in the companion volume to this one, *Can We Survive Our Origins?* Meanwhile, my own contribution retains its original dialogic form, and, of course, it remains open to further live dialogue, a number of such viva voce exchanges having since intervened.

1. I quote from both the original 2002 English-language edition of this book and its French-language translation (2009), which has some interesting revisions.
2. Paul Dumouchel reviews in detail the empirical evidence and the arguments around it in his chapter "A Covenant among Beasts: Human and Chimpanzee Violence in Mimetic Perspective," in the companion volume, *Can We Survive Our Origins?* For a cogent demonstration of hermeneutical inadequacy on this point, see Dumouchel, loc. cit.
3. See Girard (2011). Bergson, interestingly, endorses Girard's sense of the importance of the sacrificial theme in Vedic writings (Bergson 1932, 293).
4. Lucien Levy-Bruhl is the author of philosophic works on "primitive mentality," using, but also contesting, the findings of the British pioneers of ethnology and anthropology. See notably *L'âme primitive* (1927) and *Le surnaturel et la nature dans la mentalité primitive* (1931). The other principal interlocutor is Emile Durkheim, whose key work *Les formes élémentaires de la vie religieuse* appeared in 1912. Bergson's religious typology invokes the history of religions as known at the Sorbonne in the early twentieth century.
5. This cautious and courteous formulation beckons at the same time to exegesis by evolutionary creationists (Jewish and Christian) and to Spinozan pantheists. It will explain why Bergson was found elusive in his time by many who insisted on hard-and-fast metaphysical certainties, and why he often incurred reproaches of "immanentism."
6. See, for instance, the passages from *Battling to the End* quoted in the introduction to *Can We Survive Our Origins?*
7. An analytical philosopher might well quibble with the word "source," as used here of first (static or social) religion, when what is actually meant is a contingent historical origin, i.e., point of emergence within time-bound evolutionary process. Bergson's insight, retained here, is that cognitivists do perforce treat it as an absolute or ultimate source. A similar complexity exists in the designation of "first" and "second" sources. The "first" in evolutionary (chronological) perspective may not be the truly first *ontologically*.
8. See section 2 of *Can We Survive Our Origins?*: "Rebooting Evolutionary Survival: Is Christianity Crucial?"
9. The author of this chapter once put this point to Christopher Hitchens at a public launch of his book *God Is Not Great: How Religion Poisons Everything*. He declared it interesting and promised to read Girard, but never subsequently, up until his untimely death from cancer in 2012, gave any signs of having done so.
10. This quotation is used by Girard as the title (in the original French version) of his study of the Book of Job (Girard 1985). I give here a direct English translation of the original French title of the work otherwise known to English-speakers as *Job: The Victim of His People*.

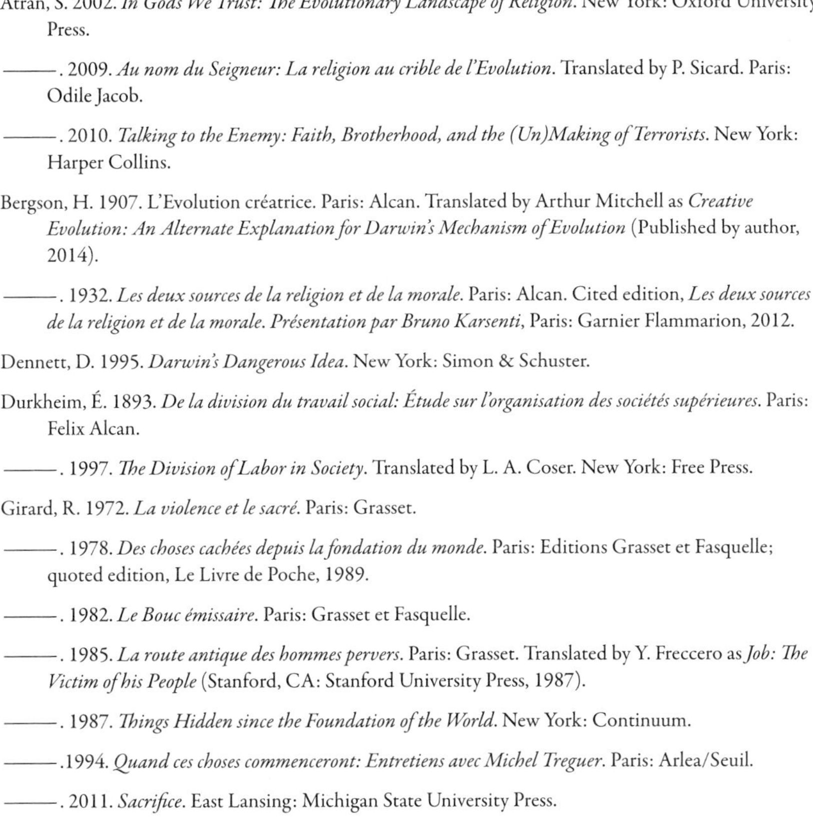

Works Cited

Atran, S. 2002. *In Gods We Trust: The Evolutionary Landscape of Religion*. New York: Oxford University Press.

———. 2009. *Au nom du Seigneur: La religion au crible de l'Evolution*. Translated by P. Sicard. Paris: Odile Jacob.

———. 2010. *Talking to the Enemy: Faith, Brotherhood, and the (Un)Making of Terrorists*. New York: Harper Collins.

Bergson, H. 1907. L'Evolution créatrice. Paris: Alcan. Translated by Arthur Mitchell as *Creative Evolution: An Alternate Explanation for Darwin's Mechanism of Evolution* (Published by author, 2014).

———. 1932. *Les deux sources de la religion et de la morale*. Paris: Alcan. Cited edition, *Les deux sources de la religion et de la morale. Présentation par Bruno Karsenti*, Paris: Garnier Flammarion, 2012.

Dennett, D. 1995. *Darwin's Dangerous Idea*. New York: Simon & Schuster.

Durkheim, É. 1893. *De la division du travail social: Étude sur l'organisation des sociétés supérieures*. Paris: Felix Alcan.

———. 1997. *The Division of Labor in Society*. Translated by L. A. Coser. New York: Free Press.

Girard, R. 1972. *La violence et le sacré*. Paris: Grasset.

———. 1978. *Des choses cachées depuis la fondation du monde*. Paris: Editions Grasset et Fasquelle; quoted edition, Le Livre de Poche, 1989.

———. 1982. *Le Bouc émissaire*. Paris: Grasset et Fasquelle.

———. 1985. *La route antique des hommes pervers*. Paris: Grasset. Translated by Y. Freccero as *Job: The Victim of his People* (Stanford, CA: Stanford University Press, 1987).

———. 1987. *Things Hidden since the Foundation of the World*. New York: Continuum.

———.1994. *Quand ces choses commenceront: Entretiens avec Michel Treguer*. Paris: Arlea/Seuil.

———. 2011. *Sacrifice*. East Lansing: Michigan State University Press.

Hitchens, C. 2007. *God Is Not Great: How Religion Poisons Everything*. New York: Warner Twelve.

About the Authors

Pierpaolo Antonello is Reader in Italian literature and culture at the University of Cambridge and Fellow of St John's College. His main area of research is the relationship between literature and science. He has also worked extensively on René Girard's mimetic theory. With Girard and João Cezar de Castro Rocha, he published a long dialogue translated into nine languages: *Evolution and Conversion: Dialogues on the Origins of Culture* (2007). He also edited several collections of essays and books by Girard, including *Miti d'origine: Persecuzioni e ordine culturale* (2005, with Giuseppe Fornari), and a series of dialogues between Girard and the Italian philosopher Gianni Vattimo: *Christianity, Truth, and Weakening Faith: A Dialogue* (2010). He is coeditor of the series "Italian Modernities" for Peter Lang, Oxford, and he is a member of the Research and Publications committees of Imitatio: Integrating the Human Sciences.

David P. Barash is an evolutionary biologist and Professor of psychology at the University of Washington, Seattle. He is a Fellow of the American Association for the Advancement of Science and the author of more than 250 research papers and thirty-three books, including *Buddhist Biology: Ancient Eastern Wisdom Meets Modern Western Science* (2013).

Warren S. Brown is Professor of psychology and Director of the Lee Travis Research Institute at the Fuller Graduate School of Psychology. He is a research neuropsychologist/neuroscientist, currently most interested in the cognitive and psychosocial impact of agenesis of the corpus callosum and childhood hemispherectomy in older children and adults. He has also studied callosal function in dyslexia, attention deficit hyperactivity disorder, multiple sclerosis, and Alzheimer's disease. He has also done research on brain wave changes associated with aging and dementia, language comprehension, dialysis treatment for kidney disease, and attention deficits in schizophrenia. Brown and colleagues from other institutions have been involved in research into the psychology and neuroscience of exemplars of the virtues of compassion and generosity. He is also the author or editor of four books on science and philosophy/religion: *Whatever Happened to the Soul?*, edited with Nancey Murphy and H. Newton Malony; *Did My Neurons Make Me Do It?*, with Nancey Murphy; *Neuroscience, Psychology and Religion*, with Malcolm Jeeves; and *The Physical Nature of Christian Life*, with Brad Strawn.

Paul Dumouchel is Professor of philosophy at the Graduate School of Core Ethics and Frontier Sciences, Ritsumeikan University, Kyoto, Japan. His books include *L'enfer des choses: René Girard et la logique de l'économie* (with J. P. Dupuy, 1979); *Émotions: Essai sur le corps et le social* (1993); *Against Injustice: The New Economics of Amartya Sen* (edited with Rieko Gotoh, 2009); *Le sacrifice inutile: Essai sur la violence politique* (2011); *Economia dell'invidia* (2011); and *The Ambivalence of Scarcity and Other Essays* (2014).

Jean-Pierre Dupuy is Professor of political science at Stanford University. He is a member of the French Academy of Technology; head of the ethics commission of the French High Authority on Nuclear Safety and Security; director of the research program of the Imitatio Foundation. His books include *On the Origins of Cognitive Science* (2010), *The Mark of the Sacred* (2013), and *Economy and the Future. A Crisis of Faith* (2014).

William H. Durham is Bing Professor in Human Biology at Stanford University and the Stanford Director of the Center on Ecotourism and Sustainable Development (CESD). A MacArthur Prize recipient, his research focuses on biological anthropology, ecological and evolutionary anthropology, cultural evolution, conservation and community development, resource management, environmental issues, as well as Central and South America. His main interests are ecology and evolution, the interactions of genetic and cultural change in human populations, and the challenges to conservation and community development in developing countries. He is the author of *Scarcity and Survival in Central America* (1995) and *Coevolution: Genes, Culture, and Human Diversity* (1991).

Giuseppe Fornari is Associate Professor of history of philosophy at the University of Bergamo (Italy). His research deals with the history of thought in the widest sense of the term, from an inquiry into the origin of culture to all aspects of human creativity (philosophy, religion, myth, art, and literature). He has written extensively on Greek tragedy, pre-Socratic philosophy, Leonardo da Vinci, Nietzsche, Bataille, and Girard. His books include *La bellezza e il nulla: L'antropologia cristiana di Leonardo da Vinci* (2005); *Da Dioniso a Cristo* (2006); *La conoscenza tragica in Euripide e in Sofocle* (2013); *Storicità radicale: Filosofia e morte di Dio* (2013); and *A God Torn to Pieces: The Nietzsche Case* (2013).

Scott Garrels is a licensed clinical psychologist in private practice and Adjunct Professor in the School of Psychology at Fuller Theological Seminary. He received the Travis Award for Integration in Psychology and Theology (2003) and was awarded a Templeton Advanced Research Program grant from the Metanexus Institute (2006). He is the editor of the volume *Mimesis and Science: Empirical Research on Imitation and the Mimetic Theory of Culture and Religion* (2011).

Paul Gifford is Buchanan Professor of French (Emeritus) at the University of St Andrews, where he directed the Institute of European Cultural Identity Studies. His publications in French literature cover topics in poetry, ideas, politics, love and desire, textual genetics, and cultural identity. His publications include *Reading Paul Valéry: Universe in Mind* (1999); the coedited *2000 Years and Beyond: Faith, Culture and Identity in the Common Era* (2002), which offers contributions by René Girard, Paul Ricœur, Jürgen Moltmann, and others; and *Love, Desire and Transcendence in French Literature: Deciphering Eros* (2006). He is a member of the Institut des Textes et Manuscrits Modernes of the Paris-based Centre National de la Recherche Scientifique (CNRS). He is one of the very few non-French academics to hold the most prestigious of France's many doctorates, the *Doctorat d'Etat ès Lettres*. He is a qualified and licensed Lay Reader of the Episcopal (Anglican) Church.

René Girard is Andrew B. Hammond Professor Emeritus at Stanford University and a member of the Académie française. He is the author of nearly thirty books translated in more than twenty languages, including *Violence and the Sacred* (1972), *Things Hidden since the Foundation of the World* (1978), and *The Scapegoat* (1982).

William B. Hurlbut is a physician and Consulting Professor in the Department of Neurobiology at Stanford University Medical Center. His primary areas of interest involve the ethical issues associated with advancing biomedical technology, the biological basis of moral awareness, and studies in the integration of theology and philosophy of biology. In addition to teaching at Stanford, he has worked with NASA on projects in astrobiology, and as a member of the Chemical and Biological Warfare working group at Stanford's Center for International Security and Cooperation. From 2002 to 2009, Hurlbut served on the President's Council on Bioethics. He is the author of "Altered Nuclear Transfer," a proposed technological solution to the moral controversy over embryonic stem cell research.

Melvin Konner is Samuel Candler Dobbs Professor of Anthropology at Emory University. His MD and PhD are from Harvard, where he also taught. He did field research for two years among !Kung San (Bushman) hunter-gatherers. His books include *The Tangled Wing: Biological Constraints on the Human Spirit*; *Unsettled: An Anthropology of the Jews*; and *The Evolution of Childhood*. He is a Fellow of the American Association for the Advancement of Science and has written for *Nature*, *Science*, the *New England Journal of Medicine*, the *New York Review of Books*, the *New York Times*, *Newsweek*, and many other publications.

Zoey Reeve is a PhD candidate at the School of Social and Political Science, University of Edinburgh, Scotland. She has degrees in psychology, terrorism and international relations, and politics. Her doctoral thesis examines the process of radicalization from an evolutionary and social psychological perspective.

James Van Slyke is Assistant Professor of psychology in the School of Humanities, Religion & Social Sciences at Fresno Pacific University. He is also a Research Assistant Professor in the Travis Research Institute at the Fuller Graduate School of Psychology and a Tobis Research Fellow at the Center for the Scientific Study of Ethics and Morality at the University of California, Irvine. His research is primarily in psychology of religion, moral psychology, and religion and science. His first book, *The Cognitive Science of Religion* (2011), was based on a grant from the Cognition, Religion, and Theology Project at the University of Oxford. He was also lead editor and contributor for the volume *Theology and the Science of Moral Action: Virtue Ethics, Exemplarity, and Cognitive Neuroscience* (2012), which was based on a grant from the Center for Theology and the Natural Sciences entitled "The Rationality of Ultimate Value: Emotion, Awareness, and Causality in Virtue Ethics and Decision Neuroscience."

Index